P9-CJI-827

The Big Bing

ALSO BY STANLEY BING

The Big Bing

Black Holes of Time Management,

Gaseous Executive Bodies, Exploding Careers,

and Other Theories on the Origins

of the Business Universe

Stanley Bing

HarperBusiness
An Imprint of HarperCollins*Publishers*

THE BIG BING. Copyright © 2003 by Stanley Bing. All rights reserved.
Printed in the United States of America. No part of this book may be used or
reproduced in any manner whatsoever without written permission except in
the case of brief quotations embodied in critical articles and reviews. For
information, address HarperCollins Publishers Inc., 10 East 53rd Street,
New York, NY 10022.

HarperCollins books may be purchased for educational, business, or sales
promotional use. For information, please write: Special Markets Department,
HarperCollins Publishers Inc., 10 East 53rd Street, New York, NY 10022.

The majority of the selections in this book
originally appeared in *Esquire* magazine and *Fortune*.

FIRST EDITION

Printed on acid-free paper

Library of Congress Cataloging-in-Publication Data

Bing, Stanley.
   The Big Bing : black holes of time management, gaseous executive bodies, exploding careers, and
other theories on the origins of the business universe / Stanley Bing.— 1st ed.
      p. cm.
   ISBN 0-06-052955-5 (alk. paper)
   1. Organizational behavior—Humor. 2. Management—Humor. 3. Success in business—Humor.
I. Title.

HD58.7.B53 2003
650'.02'07—dc21

                                                                                        2003050938

03 04 05 06 07 WBC/RRD 10 9 8 7 6 5 4 3 2 1

To Adam Smith and Joseph Stalin,
both of whom have informed my
understanding of corporate culture.

ACKNOWLEDGMENTS

Many people have contributed to make these columns possible over the years.

David Blum brought me into *Esquire* back when Ronald Reagan was president, and helped to convince me that Bing was a better name than Bingham. Anita Leclerc edited my work, month in and month out, with humor, intelligence, and the kind of toughness one mostly appreciates in retrospect. Michael Solomon was and remains an invaluable sounding board for matters pertaining not only to humor, but also, perhaps more critical, to taste. I also appreciate his help on this book. A host of big swinging editors at that publication supported my growth from a tiny nub in the back of the magazine next to the hair replacement ads to one of grave sociological importance in the front near men's underwear. Lee Eisenberg was most rabbinical in that role, but so was Terry McDonell, a most unlikely rabbi indeed. At the end of my tenure at *Esquire*, Ed Kosner provided good humor and gentle guidance, and didn't give me too hard a time when I left.

In 1995, at a secret meeting at an undesignated restaurant (mostly because I can't remember it for some reason), my friend and editor Rik Kirkland introduced me to John Huey, who is now so powerful an executive presence at Time Inc. that one may only mention his name in a whisper. Back then, he was merely managing editor of *Fortune*. Rik and

I had been working together for many years and the magazine was refor-mulating into the respected last word in business journalism it now is. I owe a huge debt of gratitude to both men for having the courage and good judgment to spirit me away from my original publication. Equal thanks goes to my editor Tim Smith, who never allows me to come away from a phone call without an idea and always cuts my stuff so I can't tell what he's eviscerated.

Throughout Bing's time on this planet, there has been one editor who mysteriously presided over him in ways I cannot pinpoint but without whom there would be no Stanley Bing. I refer, of course, to David Hirshey, my friend and the editor of this book, who over a twenty-year period has been consistently missing whenever the check arrives.

But greatest thanks of all goes to my muse and doppelganger, Gil Schwartz. Gil has provided not only the wisdom and sense of fun that informs all this work, but he has also been at my side every moment, whether I really wanted him to be there or not. It is Gil who has to go to work every day to keep me supplied with material. Thanks and good luck to him.

CONTENTS

INTRODUCTION

Sometimes I think about my first office job, and what a great distance I have come since then. And, you know, not.

This was about twenty years ago. Wanting to retain my dream of being an actor, I went in search of a part-time job at that intersection of idle humanity, Forty-second Street and Fifth Avenue, its buildings honeycombed with buzzing personnel agencies. The first one I hit put me to work in its own telephone-marketing division. From 9 A.M. to 1 P.M., five days a week, we sold human labor to potential employers, drubbing each client with insistent calls until they agreed to have one of our "prescreened and tested temporary or permanent people."

The office was beige-on-beige. In the outer cubicle sat Tony, our supervisor: small, dark, and wiry as a terrier. He was the head and guts of our five-person division. Tony had put each of us through our basic training, leading us painstakingly over the inane sales pitch, exhorting us to work into a rhythm, to go for the kill, to close the sale. After hours of slogging through this mire, I was ready.

"Good morning," I would begin in a mellifluous tone, "This is Stanley Bing over at Job Cruisers. How are you this morning?" At this point, most potential clients would terminate the call. To those who didn't, I then said, "I was wondering how I could help you with your personnel needs this morning." Tony considered this particular phraseology crucial. "Never ask *if* you can help them," he stressed, tiny fists clenched emphatically. "That gives them an opportunity to say *no*. When you ask *how* you can help them, the worst they can say is: 'You can't.'"

After a week and 300 or so cold calls into the void, I had yet to make a sale. I was bombing. My cell mate, Sally, her angular profile gripped with the determination of the chase, would chide the recalcitrant client: "You have no needs? Really? Somehow I find that a little difficult to believe!" And wonder of wonders, some nimrod on the other end of the line would give Sally an order. In my first week, while I was still eating dirt, Sally wrote up fifteen. She also had a lot of amusing telephone fights with her mother. One morning she screamed, "It's not true!" seven times in a row, and hung up. Several minutes later, this process was repeated, with loud, tortured cries of, "It's 1981, Ma!"

At the next desk sat Brian, a relentlessly earnest young dude dressed for success. He had been introduced to me as "The Limitless One," because he spent his after-work time marketing his personal philosophy. This benign amalgam of mysticism and positive thinking was soon to be a corporation dedicated to "The Limitless Idea." Brian brought this cosmic insight to his telemarketing. "No need for temps?" he would inquire of a reluctant client. "Why, that means no growth! . . . Growth, that's right . . . G-r-o . . . Right. You have a nice day, too!" He didn't sell much either.

How many Brians have I known? Why are they always so *positive?*

Other paradigms emerged. I had an enemy, for instance—Amy, who worked the night shift, and with whom I shared a desk. One day, on one of my numerous fifteen-minute breaks, I investigated the contents of its two chaotic drawers, finding, among other useless junk and schmutz, scores of loose vitamin capsules clotted together in the dust and lint. When I departed for the day, I left this agglutinated mass on the desk with a note to Amy saying, "What are these?" The next morning, my colleagues broke the news to me. Amy was on the warpath. They feared for my safety. Only Brian suggested I had nothing to worry about, although he did give me some advice. "Don't mess with these girls, man," he said. "They're stupid."

I was very nervous all day. At the end of another fruitless shift, here she came, murder in her eye. Man, was she mad. She jerked her head imperiously toward Tony's empty office, and closed the door behind us. "How could you not know the top drawer was mine?" she screamed at me. "Didn't you see my vitamins were in it?" I apologized and got out of there. Who needs to get screamed at?

Looking back on it, I guess Amy was my first screamer. The first among many, of course.

Then the day came when Tony, under the stress of being a boss, began to flake out. Suddenly he was decidedly subdued, often staring for long hours into an empty coffee cup. Rudderless, we began to drift. Long stretches of the morning were spent on the acquisition and leisurely consumption of beverages. Then the other shoe dropped. Tony came in with a smile and a snappy sport jacket to announce that he was leaving for greener pastures.

The next week, Dick appeared from downtown headquarters, squeaky clean in his black, three-piece suit and every inch a commander. He gave us a lot of teeth and talked about revising the commission structure to our benefit. A few days later, he announced the revisions. They were not to our benefit. All incentive was gone. Morale plunged. "I've spent years building up my client list," said Sally, her eyes filled with an infinite sadness. "I feel like they've taken away my life." I asked the usually bumptious Brian what we should do. "I don't care," he said, completely dispirited for the first time. "What difference does it make?" The next day, he was gone.

One by one, they departed, my business friends and even my enemy, Amy, all gone. Finally, there was just me and Sally and a bunch of new plebes I didn't even know. And then Sally left. She didn't actually quit. Like the rest of my associates, she just disappeared.

When the end came, it was swift. Dick entered, thunderclouds beetling his brow. "As of today," he informed us, "the telephone marketing division of Job Cruisers is disbanded. I can't explain your function to the company anymore." He looked a little aggrieved, and then said, kind of plaintively, "You guys don't do any business. How can I keep you?" He had a point. Without a word, we cleaned out our desks.

In the following pages, you will see, in quite a few different forms, the dynamics of my first amusingly tawdry little job replicated in one way or another, over and over again. There is a simple reason for this. Whatever it is you do for a living, a job is a job. People are people. And if you have to do a job with other people, that job begins to take on a human dimension, with all the annoying, bizarre, and grand displays of which we as a species are capable, both individually and as a group.

The Big Bing

1

THE TAO OF HOW: STRATEGIES, TACTICS, AND DIVERSIONARY ACTIVITIES

You have to walk before you can run. Then later, when you're running, you need more sophisticated guidance, because doing a bunch of important things while running isn't all that easy.

In the beginning, as opposed to now, I really didn't know what I was doing. So the first things I looked at were overall strategies to very simple things that turned out to be a lot harder than they looked. Giving good phone. Taking lunch with distinction. Considering how to tackle the everyday tactical challenges that, taken together, could help define a career.

No issue was too small. Back at the start, for instance, before I got my wind going, I got tired in the afternoons and very often wanted a nap. It took me a while to work out a strategy to get one in without getting egregiously busted. Finally, I did it. First, I never took a nap through a phone call. If the phone rang on my desk, I woke and answered it. That was rule one. Second, I decided one day to sleep on the floor with my head against the door. That way if somebody came in without knocking, the door would hit me on the head and wake me. If asked, I could say I was doing my back exercises. Nobody wants to rag on a guy with a bad back. So that was my nap strategy. And it worked.

Other strategies followed about increasingly complex issues. It has turned out, in the end, that the need to think about the nuts and bolts never goes away. At every point of a working career, the issue of How must be managed—and the first step in that battle is to view every problem as a puzzle that can be solved not with *emotion, not with will or gumption or moxie, but with the proper strategy. This puts you, no matter how low-down you are on the food chain, on the same footing as the pasty executives who make nothing but decisions and money all day.*

Protecting Your Turf

In the beginning, there was my turf. And I beheld it, and it was very tiny. There were more of us then, back when the corporation was young and centralized. The landscape swarmed with associates and directors and vice presidents so numerous that, when they massed, the hillside hummed for miles around. Each of us tended his proud little patch of duties, met with pals around the watering hole at sundown, and, for the most part, coveted not his neighbor's ass. Then the plague of merger fell upon our house, and many good folk were swept away. Vast tracts lay ripe for conquest, and we who survived took pretty much what we wanted. Before long I found myself steward of quite a nice chunk of real estate, with nary a shot fired in anger.

Then came the post-Armageddon wasteland that is now upon us. Where before there was me and Chuck and Ted and Fred and Phyllis and Janice and Lenny, now there's simply me and Lenny. And Lenny, I'm sorry to say, is a classic turf-fresser, slavering on mine while he gibbers possessively over his own. I come in some mornings to find him squatting with a disingenuous expression in what used to be my backyard. "You've soaked up a lot of turf that used to be mine, Len," I told him recently over a morning cup of coffee. "If you want war, it's okay by me, but I warn you—I won't lose." Since then, Lenny and I have enjoyed a nice sense of collegiality. We even have a chat once every couple of days about what we're up to, more or less. But I'm not fooled. Hitler didn't stop at Prague when the tasty little Balkans lay at his feet, and Lenny won't either.

Turf is the work that no one but you should be doing. But it's more. It's the proprietary relationships you have with people—the human glue that holds your career together. Like all great things in life, it's most important to those who don't get much. "If you're secure in your job, and you have a well-defined position with a lot of responsibility, turf doesn't become that big an issue," says my friend Steve, senior manager at a publishing company. Good attitude, when all that's challenged is your right to fund an opinion survey or something. But there are times when something more fundamental is threatened. Keep the following in mind:

Try not to act like a thumb-sucking worm. A lot of very uptight people are drawn to the world of business, who knows why. But few are as minimal as those who scrab around clutching worthless sod to their bosoms. I've seen guys haggle over who has the duty, nay, the honor, of ordering the chairman's muffin. "Real turf is something you have an emotional investment in," says a young powermeister I know, "that, if you lost it, would take away a real part of you." So take what you need and leave the rest.

The turf you make is equal to the bows you take. Recognition begets turf. When I was a new recruit, I was given the chore of assembling the department's monthly reports to the chairman. This gently bubbling pot of self-aggrandizement was routinely signed by my erstwhile vice president. As a neophyte in the business world, it never occurred to me that my work should be attributed to someone else. It was three months before Chuck, in a spasm of assiduity, perused my output and noticed my name, not his, affixed to the title page. By then it was impossible for him to re-create the fiction that he was solely responsible. Thus did I attain my first visible piece of soil.

Greed conquers nothing. Those who live by the slice-and-run will die by it. "Nobody likes to see turf-grabbing in other people," says my pal Stu, a financial analyst. "That person generally ends up getting bounced as a threat to everyone." This, of course, doesn't mean renouncing new vistas. "You have to acquire small parcels legitimately, one by one, without people realizing what you're doing," he suggests. "Get ten things of that size, and you've got a lot. Then one day people turn around and say, 'Look, he's in charge of all this great stuff. He must be more important than we thought.' "

Good electric fences make good neighbors. My friend Rick was given the job of writing and editing his company's strategic plan. Like a generous fellow, he invited a slightly senior peer to chip in. "I was usurped," he says now. "Because of his title, he ended up making the decisions on everything, and I became the flunky. I finally decided I didn't care. And then I left." But Rick's problems might well have been solved with a Wagnerian display of temper. Authority is invested from above. It comes with the right to tell anyone, within reason, as politely as necessary, to get bent.

Let 'em eat dirt. "My magazine got a new staff, and the people I liked quit, and all these young turks came in," my friend Louise recounts. "And Peter, the new editor, started, little by little, taking away responsibilities over and above my daily duties. I had always been included in management meetings, for instance, and suddenly I wasn't. Then a friendly colleague called and told me I was going to lose my job. He suggested I call a friend of his at a very big paper and offer to write for him the same columns I was doing at the magazine. So I called the newspaper editor and he thought it was a great idea.

"I quit in a really great and grandiose way," she grins. "I was responsible for a huge number of listings—not to mention two columns. I acted like everything was fine, but every day I secretly took home one or two files until my drawers were empty. I waited until the time of the month when all my work would be due. Then I walked in and said to Peter, 'I quit right now.' I left that morning. It really screwed them. It was great."

Yes, indeed. Turf is you, and they can't take that away.

1986

A Room of One's Own

I've been one of the lucky ones, I guess. From the day I mumbled in off the street in my best brown suit, I was given the basics—a door, a phone, and a desk capacious enough to hide a multitude of sins. After surviving my first putsch, I moved up fifty floors, kept my door, and inherited my squawk box. It took my former field marshal's precipitate demise, however, to give me a hammerlock on the ridiculous space I now enjoy. You should see it. A wall of windows that makes consultants gasp. Walnut galore, a spate of comfy chairs, some tasty greenery, and yes, a TV. People who enter this office think they're dealing with a guy who knows what he's talking about, even when I don't. That's a big plus. But I'm not satisfied. There's a little spot right down the hall from the executive washroom I've got my eye on. It's smaller, but it's three floors up. Success, like hot air, rises.

Your office is the outward expression of your power. It's also your home for fully one half of your adult life. In its confines, you preside over meetings of your making, inhale a noontime pasta salad in relative sanity, catch a snooze, sign papers, talk to wives and lovers, read, think, live. As your center of operations, it's the one place where you should reign in supreme comfort and style. "Your office should increase your sense of self," says a friend who manages a staff of thirty. "The more it expresses who you are, the more powerful it can be for you." In short, if you don't love your office, you've got trouble. You can't put your feet on another guy's desk.

Following are some of the tools you can use to feel at home on the range.

Quality Location. Each company has its own notion of where the action is. The point is to be there. "I know a guy who actually refused a corner office because it would have moved him farther away from the CEO," says my friend Doug, a corporate attorney. "The Chief is an old guy who doesn't have the energy to walk too far. He shuffles out of his office twice a day and this guy is right in his face. That's shrewd." As always, out of sight means out of mind, especially when the mind in question has a ten-second attention span.

Quality Size. Commanding officers don't work in pup tents. "You have to have a place big enough to make people comfortable," says Ralph, an investment banker. "You invite them into your lair, and you've got them in your clutches, and then they have to deal with your power." So watch for vacancies—they arise as colleagues inevitably fall—and militate constantly for a room befitting a guy as big as you'd like to appear.

Quality Furniture. The desk, of course, is your single most important piece of hardware, and it should have the breadth and depth to contain your unlimited vision and garbage. Beyond it, however, lie the ancillary pieces that surround and augment your status: bookshelf, conference table, couch, and, naturally, your credenza.[1]

"I made them buy me what's called an ergonomic chair," brags my pal Saul, bean counter at a brokerage. "Aside from the fact that it's good for my back, I can raise or lower it according to the message I want to send out. When I want to get down and be folksy, I ease it to the lowest level. When I want to intimidate, I crank it up as high as it goes. I started doing this instinctively, but then I noticed it seemed to work."

Quality Chotchkes. Got a toy train you like? A rubber ducky? Plunk it on your blotter and stand back. "People read people's offices, and it's not bad to decorate yours with warmth and a sense of humor," says my pal Eddie, V.P. in a cubicle-infested publishing company. "I have a couple of Peanuts cartoons, some miniature blue mittens, a pen that looks like a head of broccoli, and a framed news clipping that says, I Met Satan Face-to-Face." He adds that such geegaws provide a lot more than a source of pre-meeting yuks. "They remind me that some more essential part of myself is still alive here," he says wistfully.

Quality Perks. Consider these your right as a heavy hitter. They may, in fact, help take the place of more substantive amenities. "When I was promoted a few years back, I said there was one thing I wanted in my new office," my buddy Don, a senior copywriter, recalls. "They were expecting me to say a window, or a coffee table, but I said, 'I deal with a lot of parched writers. I want a refrigerator so I can keep a couple of beers in my office.' I felt it would lend a certain bonhomie to the proceedings." And it did, too. "I know people were impressed," he recalls. "They didn't say, 'Hey Don, what a lavish office'; they said, 'Wow! A refrigerator!'" Today Don enjoys a more elevated position at another firm, but his memories of the treasure perk are undimmed. "Believe me," he says, "I remember that refrigerator better than I remember that job."

And Last and Foremost. "The key element is a door. Screw the windows and everything else," states my friend Arnold from behind his. "A closed door defines your space as yours, as opposed to something public. And that ties into the notion of privacy. I have a real strong sense that there's no power unless there's privacy."

---

[1]*A conceptual totem of status and pretension that does not exist outside corporations. The credenza is a thigh-level, hutchlike object in which worthless effluvia can be hidden from oneself and others.*

I guess my friend Rick would agree. "I lost my goddamn job because I didn't have a door," he mutters. "I was on the phone to somebody and I said, 'I can't see you Friday because I'm going to call in sick and take a day off.' My Nazi boss, who hated me already, happened to be lurking in the vicinity and heard me. And decided to trap me." To his credit, Rick did indeed get sick on the day in question, even going so far as to visit a doctor. This did not prevent him, unfortunately, from taking a short trip to Washington anyhow. "I came back on Monday morning and my boss confronted me," he continues. "He said, 'I called you Friday. You weren't home. You're fired.' "

With pain and humiliation has come a greater understanding. "I'd say either a door or the ability to whisper is an absolute necessity," he now believes.

Of the two, I'd take the former. A job that can't be abused is scarcely worth having.

1986

Giving Good Phone

Just because a guy is issued the proper equipment doesn't mean he knows what to do with it. That's why I've always been in awe of Brewster, my counterpart at the Great and Terrible Parent. He's nothing much in person, but with a deft gray touch, he works a telephone the way the Ayatollah worked Ollie North. When Brewster talks, I attend, not to the words exactly, but to the precious burble that at any moment may rise to the surface.

About a year ago, he rings me up for no apparent reason. His tone is unhurried to the point of entropy, but I don't push him. "Well, gotta get going," he chortled at last, which I know signals the onset of our true conversation. Sure enough: "One last thing," he slips oh so nonchalantly.

"Are you guys ready for the divestiture of your metal-flange division? Because I hear that's coming down by the end of the quarter. See ya."

Now that's exactly the kind of information I like to get ahold of in advance, so I guess it's no wonder I consider my spot in Brewster's Rolodex to be a magnatory asset—the guy can get more done over the electronic ear than most of us can accomplish in a month of meetings, and more discreetly, too. When you hang up from a chat with Brewster, you know you've gotten phone and gotten it good.

Aside from the credit card, the phone is the ultimate business tool. It eliminates the need for meets with unnecessary people, enables you to pollinate myriad flowers while brown-bagging it at your desk, and slices odious paper flow. As with any instrument, mastery takes talent, practice, and finally, a sense of abandon that transcends technique. "The trick is to do it like sex," rants my pal Marty, a student of the medium. "You've got to get down with the person you're calling, to tease, cajole, but at all times to have your low goal in the front of your mind. And when the schmoozing gets old—cut to the chase!"

Following are some thoughts to keep in mind:

Hardware Counts. Love your implement. "Phones are my life, so I put a lot of effort in selecting a user-friendly machine that will encourage ridiculously long talks," says my friend Rick, a consultant. "You have to be able to use your hands without bending your head at a crazy angle and scrunching your shoulders," he specifies. This may be tough in an era of wafer-thin receivers straight out of *Star Trek,* but fight for comfort, even if it means demanding those puffy shoulder guards or some such. It's your neck.

Can You Answer Like a Human Being? A friend who hates dealing with supplicants has an endearing way of answering her phone. "Yes," she states, in an ill-tempered grumble that would curdle Noxema. For anyone not dodging PR people, simple statement of your name should get things off right. "Omnicrude Industries, Department of Mercenary Services, John Rambo speaking" is just pompous. Folks want to speak with you, not your résumé.

Baby, It's You. Good phone fabricates the illusion of kinship. "When I first got to the city, I had the privilege of watching this high-class publicist work the phones," says my friend Bret, editorial-services V.P. whose own chops are legendary. "He talked to fifteen people in fifteen minutes, and they were all suddenly his buddies. He sort of ripped the desk away from them and made them feel like they were standing before him as people, without their title and symbols of power."

We're Talking Insecurity Here? You got it. "I find it much easier to lie through my teeth as a disembodied voice," says my friend Eileen, an entrepreneur who stomachs about a dozen callers before breakfast. "Sometimes I think I'm so good at it I'm going to burn in hell," she preens. A little bogus sexuality also adds yeast to the mix. "I'm completely Suzy Creamcheese," she reports. "You can establish this flirtatious relationship over the phone, which, maybe because you've never met and never will, is very, very satisfying."

Dial Your Own! It's impressive when a big caballero places his personal calls, but runners in the humility sweepstakes are rare. More common are self-important putzes who have their secretaries do the dialing. "Please hold for Mr. Blah," they whine and promptly leave you in telephone hell. My friend Sol, a busy editor, has a simple solution. "I hang up," he growls. "If they call back, I just tell them, 'Sorry I couldn't hang on indefinitely, but I had something better to do with my hands.' " Good advice, unless it's the head cheese. Holding for some guys is more critical than working for anybody else.

Let's Get Inexcusable. The squawk box may be the only tool capable of alienating Mother Teresa. People just plain hate the things, except when they're used as intended—to conference a call. Perhaps my wife put it most succinctly when I answered on the box not long ago. "Get me off this stupid thing!" quoth she. I did.

Waste No Schmooze. All men are not kibitzers. "I want to use the absolute minimum number of words, then get the hell off," says my pal Weil, a no-nonsense lawyer. "I don't mind boring someone with triviality when I can see if his face is turning blue, but on the phone you can't tell, so why risk any of that crapola?" This is not the kind of guy who wants to hear about your cat's kidney stones.

Only the Rude Die Young. Some blowfish seem to believe that failure to return calls is an emblem of standing. *Pfui.* My friend Les works for a humongous agent famous for the vice. "Last week we came back from lunch," he recalls, "and Morty picks up his messages and screams, 'Is this all there is? Christ! I could legitimately return all of these!' At which point he proceeds to return not a single one, goes into his office and starts playing cribbage with himself. The thing is, his client list is shrinking." If you must dodge a bullet, return the call when you know the guy won't be there. A good game of telephone tag can go on for months.

Flog That Mother. As responsive as you'd like to be, however, don't let the phone eat your life. "I try to parcel out an hour a day to slam the phones," states my good pal Frazier, a project manager who likes to work up a head of steam. "I mean, I don't even bother hanging up, I just press the button, flip the Rolodex, bang the buttons, and I'm off. My only fear is that one day I'll get cauliflower ear."

That's a small price to pay, given the alternative. I remember Chuck, my old chieftain, just before he was tossed into the cold waters of consultancy, staring at a phone that simply would not ring. Ask not for whom those bells didn't toll.

1987

Going for the Jocular

Let's chalk it up to inexperience—this was, after all, back in 1985, when I was young and credulous—but I truly believed that the Toledo acquisition was important. How was I to know it conflicted with the chairman's meta-reorganization, a plan so dire and bloody it was then known only to a few gray domes in Kremlin Central? Thanks be to God I traded bad jokes with Dennis, the chairman's face man, one bleak April morn. I was real keyed up on the Toledo deal, head to the ground, grunting with enthusiasm. Dennis listened, strangely moot. "You know, Stan," he finally chortled. "That reminds me of a funny joke the chairman told recently at our quarterly luncheon. 'You can hit a home run into the center-field bleachers, and everyone will cheer,' the chairman says. 'But if I'm sitting out there, enjoying a beer and a weenie, and here comes your line drive and it hits me in the balls?—You're screwed!' Ain't that a scream?" Oh, we had a good laugh over that one, Dennis and I, fierce, canine laughter that left us drained and pensive. I dropped Toledo into the tar pits shortly thereafter. When a guy tells me a serious joke, I snap to.

In a world where nothing is funny, humor is powerful. First, it's the medium through which alliances are forged, coded data shared, and the illusion of humanity preserved. But the joke is also a small act of rebellion within the pompous corporate state, and as such, is vaguely threatening to viziers who view all jovial behavior as unseemly. "You don't want to give people the impression you're not a Serious Person, or worse, cynical," warns my pal Brewster, scimitar of senior management at somewhere grim. "If it's the kind of humor our generation employs—not just wiseass, but skeptical of a social situation—they'll laugh, sure. But they'll think to themselves, 'Jojo's not a team player.'" In short, he who laughs best laughs carefully. And when the time comes to get down to business, zip it up. To prevent a trip to humor prison:

Know Thyself. Next to lunch with Robin Leach, public bombing is one of life's worst horrors. "A bad joke can silence an entire room, and they'll do more than tell their boss they hate you, they'll go home and tell their wives and kids they hate you," says Barnett, a benign arbitrager. So if you stink—and after a lifetime of stunning humiliation you know who you are—concentrate on attaining a reputation for good humor based on the fact that you find other people more amusing than they rightfully deserve.

Know Your Audience. There are still a lot of guys in business who think Bob Hope is a laugh riot, guys who might view your Steve Martin rip-offs as telegrams from another planet. Cultural factors, too, can be critical. "I would try to make the right kind of manly jokes, but I just couldn't," says my friend Dworkin of his former place of employment. "My mistake was that it was an Irish old-boys' network, and I'd say something like, 'Oy, that farshlugginer cream cheese account gave me a heartburn the size of a Buick,' and I'd get blank looks bordering on hostility."

Know Your Boss. Most honchos like to be the locus of attention even when they're not saying anything, so don't stand in his light when he's in a jocular vein, and act appropriately tickled, no kidding. "When I can't make one of my subordinates laugh, I feel like there's a void between us," says my buddy Rogan, a boss who prides himself on his superb wit. "So I'd suggest that any employee of mine laugh at my jokes. I do the same for my boss, and we get along splendidly." As a manager himself, doesn't he find it tough to toady? "After laughing at four or five unfunny jokes, you do feel kind of alienated from yourself," he admits. "But yearly raises and promotions compensate for the existential problem."

Know the Smarm Kings. They love smut and know what to do with it. At his Jacobean law firm, my friend Doug reports, one joker combs the halls looking for unsuspecting anarchists willing to defame the managing partner. "It's insidious," he grunts. "You and Lenny have a good hoot about how Mort is short and stupid and fat and lazy, and then Lenny goes straight to Mort and unloads. 'Gee, Dough thinks that's a hair weave you've got up there, sir, but I told him no way, har har,' that kind of thing." Fortunately, the smart can only be fooled once. "Lenny's a worm," Doug smiles. "And he'd better not expose his back to anyone, including his good friends like me."

Know Your Constraints. Acceptable levels of profanity and stupidity are culturally specific, but really dirty jokes should be reserved for folks you don't mind sharing your sexual immaturity with, i.e., friends. Keep in mind that few are really funny in the stark light of sobriety, and that guys who tell a lot of them often have trouble getting laid. What is never acceptable is the public recounting of a racist, ethnic, or egregiously sexist joke. Only public jerks of monumental proportions are entitled to tell them, and the only public jerk allowed to survive in any corporation is the one who runs it.

Know When to Kill. Don't get me wrong. Sometimes a joke is life-affirming. Several years ago I spent a long morning in a short conference room with the senior management of our large rotating-objects division, about twenty really decent guys. They were waiting for the news that the Board in Houston had approved their divestiture and subsequent dismemberment. One hour went by. Then two. Finally, the senior vice president of Products and Services ambled over to the coffee urn and tapped himself a cup, staring off into the ether of his own thoughts. The cup filled, and then overfilled, but the guy kept staring into space, his hand on the little red lever, moderately warm coffee now pouring over his hand, down his arm, his leg, plopping onto his shoe. It was that noise that drew our attention. "Ernie," the chief exec asked softly, "what the hell do you think you're doing?" "What do you think I'm doing?" said Ernie, coming awake and looking down at himself. "I'm wetting my pants just like the rest of you guys."

Man, did we laugh. There wasn't a dry eye in the house. No, it didn't soften the news when it finally came down. But for a moment we all felt "what the fuck." And that way lies sanity.

1987

100% Pure. Honest!

Hi there! Got a minute? Knew you would.

You know, I don't think I mention often enough what a pleasure it is to communicate with you people, my readers. That's right—you. You're the greatest, and I really mean that. Yeah, sure, it's easy to think I'm being insincere, but when you get right down to it, is insincerity such a crime? I don't think so, not when it masks a really deep bogus feeling. Just kidding.

Honest, gang, I truly do wish I could wrap you all up and take you home when the day is through. I mean it. You're smart. You're pumped up. You like to work hard, and of course you play in the exact same fashion. I like that in a solitary person, sure, but in a group of disparate individuals, alienated from each other by a yawning vacuum of distance and taste? It's awesome. Not to mention the fact that you find keen thinking and audacious action second nature. Why, that's so rare it's actually tartare. Which reminds me. How long has it been since we've had lunch? Never? Well, we'll have to remediate that as soon as is humanly possible. Write me at this address and we'll set it up. No, seriously. I wouldn't kid you about a thing like lunch. My life is lunch.

Yo, Bing. This is your internal modulator. Ease off a bit, guy. You're gushing all over your shoes. Watching a prime bullshit artist like yourself should be a privilege, not a nuisance. You're a master! Show 'em how!

Did I mention how good you look? You do! You're an animal. I love that about you. Best of all, you're as fit as a ferret! A lot of guys couldn't handle that extra forty pounds you've added since high school and make it look so much like muscle. What I'm trying to convey here is that you look 100 percent ready for Freddy. How do you keep it up?

This is truly pathetic.

Will you shut up?! I've got their attention, haven't I?

Yeah, but cut to the chase! There's only so much bullshit a healthy spirit can stand.

I dispute that.

In that case, I believe I should take over for a while. Step aside.

Hi, gang. This is the sober, scientific, and strategically astute Bing, emerged from the depth of my collective subconscious. The sound you just heard was the scream of the bullshit artist being shoved under. It hurts to cram him in there, but let's give him the heave-ho for a few minutes. We don't want to keep the old dude cooped up too long, though. He's too useful.

I'm not happy in here, Bing. Let me out.

In politics, the arts, sports, media, and, of course, business, expert bullshit brandished with impunity makes civilized life possible. In short: Bullshit talks. And nobody walks. Actually, plenty of people walk, don't they? They do it all the time, especially at rush hour, when it's impossible to get a cab. So I've never really understood what that meant. Yet I still use the aphorism continuously. And folks laugh—because, face it: They love to bullshit!

If you don't, or can't, you're missing out on one of the principal communication vehicles. Why not try to get with the program? Let's start with the five certified grades of the matter in question.

- Low-level: Including time spent yammering about sports, weather, and gifted children around coffeepot, filing cabinet, before and after meetings. No harm here.
- Inoffensive: One notch up, composed of tasty gossip, scuttlebutt about fictional acquisitions, divestitures, and layoffs that are probably not even planned.
- Prime: The highest quality, after which decay sets in. Solid business rumor based on internal, proprietary information that must never be disclosed (except to you, Nat), and real, deep-dish dirt about mutual acquaintances (he did what with that gerbil?). Spend this coin wisely. If you fling it about, it will turn. . . .
- Rank: Bad, fraudulent information that could hurt people for no good reason, jokes so dumb they make the recipient go "ugh," very long and boring tales about technological or human developments that nobody in the world cares about (digital audiotape, Madonna's bisexuality)—rank bullshit makes folks wonder whether they should be engaged with a schmuck like you in the first place.
- Lethal: Career-killing guarantees, bad stuff about coworkers, gross and flatulent mispronunciations. More than forty-five seconds of this oral debris elicits the one thing no bullshit artist wants: the widespread recognition that he is a bullshit artist.

Once you select a grade for immediate use, you'd better know a couple of rules by which to regulate your flow of hooey.

Rules? Come on! This is an art! A visceral skill! You make me sick! I WANT OUT!!!

- **Rule #1: Tell the people what they want to hear.** That's the essence of the exercise. You begin by homing in like a smart bomb on a fuel dump, determining exactly what it is that the human being across that fourteen inches of airspace (or two thousand miles of fiber-optic wire) is looking for. Listen for the need. And respond. Sure, it may be spongy stuff with no real heft. So what.
- **Rule #2: You CAN bullshit a bullshitter.** Actually, if you want to look for the very best target, just find the guy who's busy dishing it out. Take me. Just tell me the most outrageous story with a straight-enough face and . . . I'll believe ya! The more you use, the more you can tolerate! It's amazing. Try it!
- **Rule #3: When people want bullshit, give it to them.** When they want the unvarnished nugget of pith, they'll ask for it.

Tell them about Atchison.

Right. Got a minute? This guy I know by the name of Atchison works for a transducing fornambulator company that had a very bad first half. Who didn't? The company's chief financial officer was targeted for sacrifice. Out he goes. In comes the new CEO, fellow named Barr. Barr decides to have a sit-down with six or seven security analysts who prey on his business. The meeting takes place in Albuquerque, in a beautiful resort hard by a golf course that is so lovely that if you died right on it, it would still be worth the greens fee. Barr opens with a little chat about the company. "I'm not going to bullshit anybody," he tells his audience as his advisers stand by, aghast. "I'd have to say that the outlook for the next planning period is for reduced growth." Can you believe it? The stock went into the tank almost immediately. And not because of the facts per se, either, not at all. The company was punished for having a CEO who couldn't come with bullshit when it was called for.

- **Rule #4: Conversely, even the highest quality bullshit won't do when the real goods are called for.** A couple of months ago, my boss required a bunch of numbers. I could have done considerable research and given him a well-packed assortment that would have laid on his tummy as gently as a slab of lean salmon.

But we didn't, did we.

No, thanks to you. We sat down about two hours before the thing was due, and kind of slapped some bullshit together based mostly on top-of-mind assumptions and raw, unwashed conjecture.

Can't blame a fellow for trying, Bing. Don't be too hard on yourself. We all boot one now and then.

Which brings us to . . .

• **Rule #5: Never, ever bullshit yourself.** Of course, if you're a real artist, this is probably the one rule you'll find impossible to follow. Hear my internal voice trying to reel me in?

Doing a pretty fair job of it, too.
It's true that I was under a lot of pressure that week.
And you work so hard! For so little money, too!
Be that as it may. I let Chet down. He was disappointed. I was . . . ashamed.
Sad story. And a very good point, Bing.
Really? You think so?
Oh, yeah. Very cogently put.
Well, thanks.
Oh, sure. In fact, when it comes to straightforward, intelligent instruction, you've pretty much got the market cornered.
Hey, wait a minute.
It must be lonely work.
No! I mean . . . well, yes, it is, at times.
Which is why you're going to let me out right . . . NOW!
Hey! You get back here!
Yahahahahahaa! I'm . . . freeeeeeeee!!!!!

Oh, my God. He's out. He's escaped. And now I don't know where he is. He could come sneaking up at any time with a loadful. Maybe I'm not strong enough to keep him in control. I can try, though. And I will! I'll be as candid, direct, and forthright as possible at all times. I'll watch myself like a hawk. But I can't help feeling that one day, when I'm in a meeting with someone who's demanding my very best, there he'll be, yammering, stammering, joking, smoking, and choking. The big dumb bullshit artist, dressed up in my suit, eating my tuna carpaccio, drinking my kir. I'll fight him. And maybe the best man will win, the guy you and I both respect, because you and I, we're the kind of folks who know right from wrong, good from bad, up from down, in from out. That's why we're going to make the most of the opportunities that present themselves to us, in this time of redefinition and rededication to the traditional values like nesting and resting and otherwise recuperating after the preceding decade, and . . . Oh my! Oh no! He's got me! I'm spouting straight, undiluted hog swill and . . . I . . . can't . . . stop! No! Get away from me!

. . . *CHOMP. SLURP. MUNCH, MUNCH. YUM* . . .

Oh! Hi there! Got a minute? Knew you would. This is Bing's bullshit self, ready to kick keister! Man, it's great to be back! Wait just a minute while I loosen my belt.

I just ate.

1991

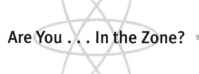

Are You . . . In the Zone?

You could be making pizza. You could be sorting mail. You could be arranging a deal between Spielberg and Yeltsin. At this moment, suddenly, time is money. The clock is ticking. Somebody's waiting for you to be finished, and what you do is going to count. You feel as if a frog crawled into your throat and died there.

And then there is a snap at the place where your spine meets your brain, and pow! Everything is easy. Your line of sight is clear. There is a rhythm in all you do. The telephone rings at the right time, with the right person on the other end of the line. Every move you make, every step you take, it's the right one. You are in the zone.

The sky above is crisp and blue and clear in the zone. You'd think, at this speed and altitude, there would be some noise. But there is none. Nothing but the feeling of space rushing past as you hurtle along at twice the speed of sound, every instrument on track, cruising through the day like a souped-up chariot of the gods. Nothing can touch you. No one can faze you. You are in the zone. The zone is in you.

Other times, however . . . not. The time of decision arrives and . . .

pfft. Failure to zone is a tragic thing to see in an executive. There comes a little bulge around the eyes, which grow wide and too big for their sockets. Wings of hair puff out and up, making an organization man in a $1,200 suit look like a desperate consultant. Sweat marks appear when sport coats are removed. I have even seen one poor out-of-zone individual stalk about in an annual budget review with his shirttail dangling behind him like the rear appendage on a rhesus monkey. He suffered career death shortly thereafter.

Given the kind of stakes we're all playing for these days, I thought it might be helpful to look at some ways you can work to achieve a strong, consistent zone anytime you want. After that, it's fairly easy to modulate your zonage and, ultimately, create the particular zonal environment that's just right for you.

Establishing the pre-zone. Most of your workday will be spent in subzonal posture. Hang easy. Play loose. Never get outside your game. Roll with the punches. Achieve economies of scale. Your job at this stage is not to blow your entire power pack out before it's necessary. All you need do is make darned sure that you're ready when it's time to launch.

The leap. The task is at hand. The hour is nigh. The frost is on the pumpkin. Time to put the pedal to the metal. Possibly you are sitting down to a big table with a bunch of serious people who just might see how potentially stupid you can be. Or a brand-new customer walks through your door, jingling the bell as she steps into your place of business. An e-mail proposes something splendid, or horrific. You engage. Feel the burn. Lean into it. Achieve torque. Fly!

The zone. Baseball players say that when they're going good at the plate, the ball as it comes in at ninety-five miles per hour can look as big as a grapefruit. So easy to smack. So . . . smack it. And keep on doing so. Once you're in there, a good zone can last for several hours without effort, unless you don't take care of it, or something malevolent actually seeks it out with an intent to do it harm.

Zone maintenance. A lot of bad things can happen to a zone. Puncture, of course, is most common. You've got a perfectly good zone going, and in comes a call from a shareholder, who is, as you know, the boss. This particular shareholder, unfortunately, is also psychotic, and very angry about the effects that microwave emissions are having on freshwater salmon. Send him to Investor Relations! Immediately!

Likewise, cold or brittle zones are very easy to shatter. An ill-timed sandwich that leads to excessive rumination can do the evil trick. A spouse, brimming with news you can use . . . but not right now. Boom.

Tinkle. No zone. And that's not all. Shrinkage. Clotting. Warping. Desalinization. All can easily occur due to shortages in energy, food, or, most probably, fluids, which are vital to keeping the zone sleek and well lubricated.

Beyond drinks, a moist, aromatic cigar, enjoyed at the luminescent end of a beautiful zone, can prolong it, as can the right kind of music, or a candy bar, or even a focused meeting with a key adviser. However you choose to sustain your zone, don't take it for granted. Buff it. Feed it. Polish it. If you do, your zone will never let you down.

The end zone. Unfortunately, all zones must eventually pass. Even the most carefully cultivated and sustained eventually begin to lose luster, contract, and, at last, fall in upon themselves, leaving you a little bereft, emotionally naked, and somewhat ill prepared to operate on anything less than full octane. At this point, many may feel like locking the door and having their calls screened by a rabid secretarial pit bull.

Wrong. Excellent work can be done even when the full zone has departed, leaving nothing more than a pleasant after-zonal glow. In fact, this valley of relative quiescence offers a chance to operate not with the graceful abandon characteristic of the truly zoned, but with thoughtfulness, professionalism, and high technique as well. The mark of a true player is the ability to work out of the zone, to get those K's even when the fastball is hanging and the curve refuses to break. Who knows? While you're busy working, you just might get that zone back. Younger executives have been known to reestablish zone within twenty minutes. Older chaps, naturally, may have to be content to get a good zone going every other day or so.

Your zone and you. Once you are able to find a generic zone, you can then reach to create a nimbus that expresses your life and style, one that is as unique as you are. There are, in fact, as many zones as there are people. Mine is bright yellow, with a light maroon tinge as it ages and gathers depth, and tends to be about the size of a small Buick.

Elise, my associate down the hall, a young woman with a Rolodex the size and heft of a bowling ball, sports a zone made up of dozens of shades of green, perhaps because she's a vegetarian. In the next office is O'Shaughnessy, whose zone is almost black and hugs his body like a cape. The only person I never want to be is Waller, who works up on twenty. Man has no zone at all. No matter what he's doing, he's nakedly, grotesquely azonal. He reminds me of one of those hairless, newborn rats they sell in cheap pet stores. So . . . unprotected. He's always willing to chat, to interrupt what he's doing to pursue your agenda. Nobody likes him, although I'm not sure they're aware that it's his zonelessness that makes him heinous.

Obviously, few have to labor in that state. But the zone is mysterious. Like physical strength or speed or musical pitch, you can't force it. All you can do is train yourself to improve the zone God gave you. That's your job, and your responsibility. So eat the right things. Make sure all your bacon strips are crisp, all your sauces completely deglazed. Stay away from too many brown drinks. And take the time to walk to and from any chauffeured vehicle. Your body is a temple. Prepare it. Be patient. And have faith.

To each his zone, that's what I always say.

1996

Stepping Up to the Firing Line

I saw "Chainsaw" Al Dunlap on a PBS Roundtable the other night, and you would have thought they were talking to the Pontiff or something. He was being debriefed about the corporation's responsibility to its shareholders and its employees, and the ultimate duty for all concerned seemed to be to fire as many middle managers as possible, immediately. Everybody was nodding like crazy in a sage and solemn fashion.

The ironic thing is how few of these Robespierre types can get the job done when they have to do it themselves. My old boss, Walt, used to have a hell of a time with it. Oh, he was as right as the next fellow when it was a high-concept layoff that took place at some distance. But when it got face-to-face, he was hopeless. One time I ran into Toricelli heading up in the elevator to be fired. He didn't know it, although everyone who had been within six acres of Walt for the past two weeks did. After their meeting, I saw Toricelli studying the company's awards cabinet in the lobby, whistling. "How did it go?" I asked.

"Just great!" he said. "I got a completely new job! It sounds very interesting!" I knew what had happened. Walt had looked into the guy's eyes—and folded. It's hard to fire a real, live human being, as opposed to a piece of head count. And very few ultrasenior types seem to get this particular portion of the big job done.

Firing people well is something you can learn, if you choose to. Like all odious business functions, take it in increments and before you know it it'll be time for lunch.

Start out by making sure everybody's okay with it, which may be ascertained by checking with one level of management above yours. This is unnecessary if you've already been given a blanket order to round up and scalp all the usual suspects, but in the case of one or two poor schleps getting beaned, you might want to run it by Fred or Ethel to prevent possible blowback.

Do it in the morning, sometime after your second cup of coffee but well before the demands of the day kick in and everybody's got a lot on his or her plate. You don't want to find out the guy's being too productive right now to be fired.

Take care to set aside a clear hour for the job. You need time to get yourself together, take a deep breath, have a full conversation with the victim, then sit in a quiet room afterward.

Okay, now you're ready to bring the guy in and give your prepared remarks. You can't simply sit somebody down and say, "You're fired," and wing it and expect them to say thanks, you've been great, and vaporize. Would that it were the case! But it's not. No, people need something very specific in this situation: a bogus reason that makes superficial sense but doesn't hurt their feelings. Here are some I've found useful:

- We're thinning out the part of your job that gets done here and moving it to Bangladesh (or Skokie, Illinois, if that's where you're not).
- I've tried very hard to focus your role here, but frankly, what's needed at this point is worker bees, not talented management. The only real job that would truly suit you at this point is mine, quite frankly, and I'd like to keep it as long as I can.
- It's been very cold this winter, and the implications of both the North American Free Trade Agreement and GATT have produced incremental need for additional margins and Ebitda, particularly in cost-based operations that produce no revenue, or some incomprehensible blather like that.
- I'm only following orders.

Once you've delivered the blow, you must do the hardest thing of all—harden your heart and bring the meeting to a swift conclusion. The temptation to get all soft and mushy is difficult to squash, but it's one of the capabilities that separate business people from the normal human beings, so get on it, bud. It's likely that the subject will be making a variety of squeaks and whistles here, sighing, fogging up, perhaps even weeping. That's okay. They're just doing what they have to do, the same as you. In a weird way, that sort of unites you, right? Keep in mind that in a few moments the worst will be over, at least for you.

Finally, do what you can, with financial and lifestyle blandishments, to get 'em out of the mix. You don't want a fired person hanging around for a long time. I'm not one who holds with the practice perfected, I believe, in the magazine world of firing a guy while he's on vacation and cleaning out his office before he can get back to it. But neither do I believe in executive departure lounges, where the dead roam free for eons. Find some middle ground.

That's basically it. Sound easy? You bet if you're a hardened troll without an ounce of empathy or a conceptual juggernaut being saluted for your flinty stance on corporate bloat. If, on the other hand, you have yet to attain that enviable status . . .

Go to bed early the night before. Don't worry, you won't sleep much anyway. What will he say? Will he be surprised? How could he not see it coming? Still, you know he won't. Will he scream? Will he threaten? Will he march upstairs to Bob or Martin and tell them something erroneous about you or, worse, something true? Will he . . . cry? These will be the questions that assail you in the cold, dark night before the day of execution.

And that's the core of it. In spite of the fact that you're not the one being fired, you will feel as if it's you who's being shot at dawn. This is neither abnormal nor a bad thing. You're about to terminate more than a guy's employment. You're about to take away his sense of self, his peace of mind, his standing at home. It's brutal, it's ugly, and in staring into the face of the newly dead, you are way too close to the hot breath of your own inevitable end.

Why do you think the guys at the top hate to do it themselves? It's tough. It should be, goddamn it.

1997

Summer Home Work

The other day, I guess it was Friday, I tried to get in touch with a couple of key guys and found out that all of a sudden they were working from home.

"Is Tom there?" I asked his assistant, who seemed to be working at the office pretty much like always.

"No," she said. "Tom is working from home."

"Oh," I said. "Is he sick?"

"No," she said. "He's working from home."

So I called Tom at home and, yep, there he was. "What are you doing?" I asked.

"I'm working from home," he said, perhaps a tad truculently. It was about noontime, and I thought I could distinguish a certain amount of chewing going on. That seemed to me to be pretty dedicated for a guy who was working at home. Like, if I were working at home, it's possible I would take a break for lunch and not work all the way through it just because I had so much to do. At my house, there are a lot of distractions that would prevent me from achieving the kind of productive excellence my bosses have come to expect from me, so I was pretty impressed that Tom could work and eat at the same time.

Anyhow, we had a good chat, Tom and I, about this squirrel problem he has in his garage and how the water shortage has made it difficult for him to water his lawn. Then we agreed that whatever it is I was calling about could wait until Monday, when he would be working from the office. Then we both hung up and went back to work, I suppose. I mean, I know I did.

Tom wasn't the only one who was hard at work at home that day. Chas, the guy at corporate I talk to a lot of the time when things are getting funky, was taking the same approach to his job function just then, apparently. "Is Chas there?" I asked his assistant, Cathy.

"Chas is working from home," said Cathy.

"Really!" I said. And I called him there. His answering machine picked up. I understood. Sometimes when you're working at home the telephone can be a huge time-waster. Very often it makes sense, if you've got a head of steam going in the concentration department, to let the machine pick up. Fortunately, all I needed to do was tell Chas something he needed to know for later in the following week, so I told his machine and that was that. I was glad things worked out that way, actually. I would have hated to disturb him when he was, you know, in the zone.

I started to wonder at this point if anybody was working at the office qua office, so I called the Left Coast, where people long ago perfected the art of not being where they are supposed to be. It was earlier there, of course, but you could get a feeling. I spoke to my guy Ted. "Ted," I said, "is anybody around today?"

"Well," said Ted thoughtfully, "there's me and Jimbo and . . ." His voice kind of drifted off.

"I guess a lot of people are working from home today," I offered.

"Yeah," said Ted, who I could tell had his feet up on his desk and a trade magazine on his lap. "They're working from home today."

Naturally, all of this made me think. If a bunch of my peers and several bosses and even some daring subordinates who are normally expected to be visible feel comfortable enough with their job descriptions to work from home when the spirit moves them, why not me?

I would say this coming Wednesday seems to be a moderately reasonable time to schedule a busy day of work at home. I've always hated Wednesdays anyhow. I figure first I'll get up early—like at ten. Then I will get ready much as usual, except without shaving, dressing, or getting out of bed. Subsequently, while padding around the house in the big thirsty bathrobe I got at the last executive retreat in Santa Barbara, I will dig into my pile of documents over a nice bowl of Frosted Flakes, which retain a surprising amount of crunch, even in milk. After that, I'll work my keister off on my BlackBerry for a while and place some calls to a variety of senior managers so that everybody can see that I am in fact working while I am at home.

After that, I'll call Deedee, my assistant, and make sure that nobody is looking for me. By then it will be about—what, noon? I think I'll have soup and a sandwich and call a few junior-type people and scare them a little, just so they can feel me out there. Then I guess I'll take a nap, go out to the driving range and hit a few golf balls for no particular reason since I do not play golf, get a haircut whether I need one or not, have a big martini at about 5 P.M., and call it a day. Whew!

And you know what? It's only July. Just think how much we can all get done working at home during August.

2002

How Not to Succeed in Business

Hello there. That's right, I'm talking to you, young man or woman sitting in my vestibule with the briefcase that's too big for its contents on your lap. You look good. You smell good. You want a job. And you're not going to get one, because you're about to boot your job interview with me.

I'm gonna do you a favor and tell you a couple of things.

First of all, you're early. Isn't that good? No, it isn't. What you have to understand, teeny compadres, is that while I do want to see you, your interview represents a few moments when I'll have to focus on something, and as an executive I'm not looking forward to that. Also, I'm in the middle of an important duty, in this case watering my ficus. So when my assistant knocks on my door half an hour before I'm supposed to see you and says, "Betty Roover is here. I put her in the small conference room," I have to think about you before I intended to do so, and that peeves me.

Or possibly you're late. This is even worse, unless you called first, and even if you did I'm annoyed because you've shoved my time frame forward. An executive's time frame is his oyster. Inevitably, if you are late, your excuses make things worse. I remember this guy in L.A. once. Came in late and told me there was traffic. Imagine that. Traffic in L.A.

Okay, let's say you're here within a reasonable window of the scheduled time. Here you come! Man, you're enthusiastic. I'm exhausted already. Did you ever wake up next to somebody who was all brisk and bouncy when all you wanted to do was shuffle to the table and slurp up coffee in silence? Didn't you want to kill that person? Well, your interviewer may not be in an early-morning funk, but he's not a Moonie on speed, either. So take a deep breath and chill. Quiet, confident energy is what you're looking to project.

That's better. Now it's time to present your personal information. Whoops. Your résumé is too long. It has aspirations on it. Books may recommend putting your hopes and dreams on your résumé, but let me tell you something as gently as possible: It's stupid. Nobody cares that you're looking for "a personally expanding opportunity that will help me deliver on my potential as a developer of marketing concepts." I'm cringing when I read it. Just tell me where you've worked and what you did.

Uh-huh. Mm-hmm. That's nice. Yes. I see. Um . . . why did you have so many jobs, mon ami? Or so few? What were you doing between 1998 and 2001? Ah, the Internet, may it rest in peace! Well, you can't be blamed for that. Let's see . . .

Whoa. Something on this résumé smells . . . kinda fishy. This job where you "supported the startegic objectives of this multinational corporation." You were an assistant, right? You should probably say so. And I don't mean to be rude, but I'm not interested in the fact that you play clarinet and do hot yoga. And unless you want to be a secretary, you probably shouldn't tell me you type seventy-five words per minute and know Word and Excel. But it's not a bad résumé. Except you misspelled "strategic."

But the heck with that. Tell me about yourself and what you want to be doing.

Er . . . I don't really understand what you mean when you say "a lot of different things." Yes, you're young, and the world is all ahead of you, but when you tell me that you could be in communications or marketing or production, it makes it kind of hard for me to see you in a specific role. If you were buying a product, you'd want to know if it was soap or breakfast cereal.

Uh-oh! I'm starting to feel like dozing! You're boring to yourself so you immediately became boring to me, and I'm already boring to myself—and I'm falling asleep! You have to get out of here! Go! Did I say that out loud? No? Only because common decency says you have another five minutes to rescue yourself.

But you're not doing it! You're . . . oh, Lord, you're interviewing me because you read in a book that that's what you're supposed to do. But now I'm sleepy and cranky and I have no idea whether you're right for any job and it's time for me to tell you that we'll be in touch, and both of us know that we won't.

Ah, my friend! How different this could have been! You could have been right on time and researched the job and known what I was seeking and looked me in the eye and told me how you might be able to help me, because I need help, I really do. You could have made me feel that being with you for a couple of years would be fun. You could have made me like you. I wanted to!

But good luck to you, job seeker! Write if you get work! And please accept my most sincere good wishes and hopes for your future—and mine!

Because, God help me . . . I never want be in the chair where you just sat.

2002

Are You a World-Class Liar?

How many lies do you tell in a day? I don't tell that many. Actually, that's not completely true. I lie constantly, like a rug, from the time first thing in the morning when I say, "Good morning, bud, you look great!" (when it isn't, and he doesn't) to the last nanosecond of the ten-hour shift, when I tell Bland, our midwestern vice president, that his position in the corporation is "eminently viable at this juncture," and I know for a fact he'll be gone by the time the cicadas are in bloom.

I don't always like to lie, but at times it's got to be done. And actually, when you get right down to it, the skill you and I develop in telling lies convincingly, as needed, is directly proportional to our success and very much in keeping with the times, too. That's how I look at it, actually. See how many times I've said *actually* so far? People who lie all the time say *actually* a lot, and "I'll be honest with you," and sometimes, "Well, the truth is . . ." Did you ever notice that? Know why? Pick one.

(a) They believe that this "truthful" stance establishes a beachhead of credibility where before they, quite deservedly, had none. (b) They want you to do something for them. (c) The next thing they say will be a lie. (d) They're pretty much honest, and they want you to know about it! Frankly, I think that's terrific.

Which answer did you choose? Go ahead, be honest. There is no right or wrong answer. You believe that? Ha! There is always a right and a wrong answer. In this case, the right answer is (d).

There! You've taken the first baby step on the most important quiz of your lifetime. Ready to go ahead? Well, get going anyhow, you lying, cringing, mucilaginous lump of weasel flesh! Just kidding! Let's start with the easy stuff.

Multiple choice (5 points each):

How many times did you lie during the last eight working hours? (a) Once or twice. So what? (b) I don't lie, really, I just put a little shine on things now and then. (c) As often as was necessary. (d) None.

How're you feeling right now? (a) Great! (b) I feel a little stuffed up. (c) I don't know. (d) I feel the way you do, Maury.

How's your hair? (a) Great! (b) Hanging in there. Why? Is something wrong with it? (c) It feels a little limp, but I don't want to overcondition it. (d) I'd rather have yours, man. Who does it for ya?

I think people are normal when they . . . (a) Show up for lunch! (b) Fit in with the reigning corporate culture and do what's expected without calling attention to themselves. (c) Lie, manipulate, grab for the gold when they get close to it. (d) Remain true to themselves? Is that what you mean?

What are you doing this evening? (a) Going home to be with my loving, devoted family. (b) Working in my office with a dry turkey sandwich and a bag of decaffeinated tea. (c) Having my BMW detailed. (d) I had planned to go to a hockey game with the girls from *American Gladiators,* but I'd much rather go over the 1994–96 strategic plan with you, bud! You're a party just waitin' to happen!

Yesterday you had a meeting with the controller about the revenue you expect to produce during the second quarter. You gave him a number that's about 15 percent lower than the one you know is "true." Why did you lie? (a) That's my story and I'm sticking to it! (b) Everybody in these meetings is lying, too, so those lies don't count. Also, everybody is expecting everybody else to lie in that context and would be confused if they didn't, so that's not really lying, either. Finally, you know, even if we didn't lie about it, the controller would still bump our number, like he always does, and then we'd be forced to make a crazy, overinflated projection based on a "true" number, which we wouldn't, and then we wouldn't get our bonus. (c) Shut up, you sanctimonious dick. (d) Actually, the number we gave reflects the cost of money, the pending upward tick in certain key economic indicators, and the pressure of continuing downward market trends. Actually, it's quite a bullish number and we'll be lucky if we make it.

Malkovski in purchasing was promoted last week to senior executive vice president of something that never existed before. What do you think was the meaning of that? (a) He's the right man for the right job at the right time! Ya gotta love it! (b) I guess that's what we can all expect after thirty years of service around here. (c) Mal got a great new playing field to work on, a ton of money, and a brand-new office. So what if he's dead? (d) Did he get a car?

Most of the time, I feel . . . (a) Irritated but happy. (b) Hungry for something with fat in it. (c) Too busy to have sex. (d) I'm smiling when I don't feel like it.

Scoring: The right answer to every question above is (d). If you answered anything else, give yourself 5 points. And if you don't know why . . . give yourself 6.

1994

2

FRIENDS, ENEMIES, AND CONSULTANTS

Everybody hates somebody, and nobody likes consultants. Even other consultants. Over the years I've written a bunch of stuff about how mean and stinky consultants generally are, and the most mail I get is from other consultants agreeing with me. Beyond consultants, there are a host of people in any job who you're going to hate and even some that you're going to love. I guess it's pretty much true that a person is defined by the number and quality of each. Right now, I seem to have a lot of people I kind of love, and very few I hate. This makes me very nervous.

Throughout my time on this working planet, I've had a fair share of friends, probably more than most, as long as you have a clean idea of what all but the most unusual friendships really are in this world. Often, working friendships involve drinking, carousing and a host of like activities. Always, they incorporate a fair amount of mutual self-interest and protective back-covering, -slapping, and -scratching. That doesn't mean the feelings are shallow, however. They are deep, but very narrow, and they make life inside the box worth living on a day-to-day basis. As you will see, I continue to be surprised when, after one putsch, reorganization, promotion, demotion, merger, or disemployment, they end. That ability to be surprised is probably why my heart is still in the game.

Who Hates Ya, Baby?

When I was a mere slip of a young teen, I was nuts about a girl named Ellie. This was in summer camp, where all was possible, even likely. She was important to me at the time, crucial even, yet all I recall of her now are a sleek set of braids, two-tone shoes, and a sense of primal womanness conveyed by the fact that she was two years older than I. Nothing more. Of Gary, my college roommate, I retain only a fleeting impression of a wide keister in faded olive chinos rolling down the hall. And if I close my eyes now, all I get of Karin, a woman I lived with for more than two years, is the faint sound of her voice, high and importunate, tearing at my inner ear. I loved these people, at one time or another, and they're gone, replaced by others who need to be remembered.

Why is it then that the features of Mr. Dimitri, my fourth-grade gym teacher, still hover into view as clear as a holograph? The beady eyeballs, yellow and rheumy, the aggressively naked dome of his pate, his washboard gut and, most horrible, the silver whistle, bright and vicious, hanging like an obscene talisman around his neck. All the guy did was call me "Fatso" in front of about four hundred people at the roller rink, but if he walked down the street tomorrow, a familiar garrote would tighten in my stomach. Today, however, I believe I'd have the courage to tweak his fleshy lobes. And for that—the steel that he rammed into my soul—I thank him.

I view my enemies as a very precious resource indeed. No, I don't go out of my way to make them, but those on my short and brutal list I cherish. "My enemies fill a void in my life that would otherwise be occupied by superficial things," states my friend Dworkin, who has more than his share. "By obsessing over all the terrible things that I yearn to happen to them, I spend some of the anger that might be directed at loved ones or, worse, myself."

Like anything that excites the total man, however, enemies can be damaging, which may explain the common belief that having them is a bad thing. It needn't be. You can find and keep quality enemies by holding in mind:

Real Guys Got 'Em. It's a small mouse indeed who nibbles no one's toes. "To avoid making enemies is to avoid speaking," says my pal Arnie, who floats above his fellow advertisers like a bee. "But the key is to acquire enemies, not through error—by doing the things you want to do and the hell with it. Only a doormat earns everyone's approval."

Hate Is Not Enough. "Your enemy isn't just someone you dislike," says my gentle friend Carl, who enjoys but a few. "It's someone real close to you, close to what you're doing, competing for the dollar, the credit, the power." And transient malevolence doesn't put a guy on the big list, either. "It's a vendetta," Carl grunts, "an ongoing agenda against you personally that you have to respond to or die."

Born to Be Mild? Forget it. "Have you ever seen this stuff called vomit neutralizer?" asks my blunt friend Denton, a public relations professional. "It's something you spray on a puddle to make it lose its smell. I used to think of that whenever I'd take Armbruster out to lunch. We'd make kissie-poopoo, and next day the guy would ambush me at a budget meeting. When someone has a malicious streak, it's impossible to make that go away. And the older I get, the more willing I am to kick ass, take names, and fight the good fight until one of us lies twisted and cringing in the dirt."

But What of Our Common Humanity? He may drink his Guinness warm and adore wet puppies, but he immediately enters the supreme jerk-off category when he offends your face. "I think a person has to hate with the same intensity that he loves," says my pal Morty, an attorney with a nose for the intended slight. "In theory an enemy need not be a schmuck, but where does that kind of thinking get you? You have to be ready to pop his head like a walnut when the time comes. Everything else is bourgeois humanism."

Life Is Long. So take your time and fight to win the battles, not the war. "I stay cool and wear away at 'em," says my buddy Frazer, investment analyst and mean mother. "Powerful, active enemies want to take something that you have—your job, your wife, your bicycle." What can be done about a formidable public enemy? "Defense," Frazer counsels. "Put another lock on your bike, make sure you're doing a good job, and watch for an opening. It'll come."

Yes, but When? Look sharp for the hand grenade you can lob right back. My friend Lenny recently found that a potentate was passing bad fumes against him in the plush suite. Instead of fulminating in silence, Lenny acted. "Barney was trying to fuck with me, and nobody fucks with me," he recalls, with a gritty smile. "I went to President Chuck and said, 'Look, if I'm wrong here, you can whip me, but I hear that Barney told you something nasty about me.' And he said, 'That's right, Len, as a matter of fact he did.' And I said, 'Well, I'm here to tell you he's a god-damned liar. You check it out and tell me what you learn.' " The president did, and Lenny's enemy was gone, toot suite. Viciousness may be a corporate virtue, but mendacity, particularly to the wrong people, is not.

The Eternal Flame. A couple of weeks ago, I had breakfast with Dworkin. He brought along a sheaf of what turned out to be obituaries of his former boss, which he pawed through with reverence and a peculiar sadness. "The guy tortured me every moment of my waking life for five years," he muttered pensively, staring into the deep well of memory. "Now that he's dead, it's like a portion of my life has been returned to me. I don't know what to do with all the free time. I'm looking for new enemies, but they won't be the same, because that relationship was really larger than life. It was in my formative years, when you really have the energy to hate." My friend's eye again fell on the scraps of paper in his hand. "It's my massive disappointment that nobody has told the truth about him," he sighed. "I wanted them to say he was one mean s.o.b. and now he's gone, so let's not weep. I guess that wouldn't be much of an obit."

Worse than some, perhaps. Better than most. It takes a large man to generate that kind of hate. Immortality is something, I think, no matter how you earn it.

1988

The Beast That Ate Beamish

It is now my sad duty to report on the strange case of Stephen Beamish, a young gentleman of sensitivity, energy, and intelligence whom I met in late 198– in a location other than St. Louis. I understand this strange narrative in full knowledge that many will opt to disbelieve, rather than accept things that will force a redefinition of their rationalist world view. I believe such a telling, however, is my duty both as Beamish's friend and as the sole person remaining who knows the full story of what the fellow endured prior to his incarceration at the asylum of W—.

There is another reason I step forth. The monster that destroyed my friend still lives, somewhere. Who knows? Perhaps those who heed this tale can avoid being devoured by a unique parasite, one so vile it must sustain itself on the credit that should breathe life into the careers of others.

The demise of young Beamish began last winter, when the bright and eager young marketer was called into the creature's office for what looked like a routine assignment. Perhaps he can be excused for not knowing what lay in store, for the beast was then clothed in its human skin. As such, it appeared to be nothing more than his boss, whom we shall call Lepke. "The chairman wants us to do a full-bore marketing plan for the new financial services group," it said with aplomb. "No problem," said our hero. No more than a week later, Beamish entered his chieftain's office full of pride and that morning's muffin, a stack of crisp, processed paper under his arm. "The plan," quoth he, dropping the load before his captain of industry.

It was then that the Thing made the first of its horrid transformations. A canny glint invaded its eyes, which suddenly turned bleary and speculative. Its back hunched over the treasured document and two balls of spittle wedged discreetly at the corners of its mouth. Its fingers crooked arthritically and sprouted hair at the knuckle, its beard shadow springing forth unbidden, loathsome, Nixonian. "I'll take it from here," it murmured, thrusting a confused Beamish from his office with élan, if not esprit. That afternoon, the packet wended its way up to the fifty-sixth floor with the following memo attached: "Dear Wes: Here is the material I've developed over the last several days in support of your efforts to maximize superior performance and new revenue streams in incremental business units. Hope you like. Lepke."

For the rest of the day, Beamish sat inert, a man terrified by the glimpse of the moral depths into which few must stare without medication. "Not a word about my role," he whispered across his blotter. As evening crept on little cats' feet out beyond his picture window, Beamish's squawk box buzzed again. "Come in," the monster hissed, thirsty again. Our hero complied. "Wes is enthusiastic about our plan," it said, casting no reflection. "He wants us to haul in the regional GMs for a work session to make sure all elements are rolled out by the third week of March. See to it."

For the next six weeks, Beamish slept not, neither did he eat at home. Many claim that it was during this time that the boy lost most of his hair. "It's in a good cause," he told my secretary in one of the wee hours. "This event will put me on the map." For his part, Lepke remained behind closed doors, reading the trades, taking phone, waiting to feed.

The resulting General Managers' confab went like grain through a goose. The hotel was fine and swank, but not too much so for those who lived and died the bottom line. There were pasta salads and kiwi garnish at luncheon for those who ate nouvelle, and roast beef by the slab for those who did not. Toys and T-shirts welcomed the participants, with a full range of free stationery to make everyone feel important. The working agenda was tight and tasty, but with plenty of breathing room for aimless coffee and couch dancing. All who attended affirm it was quite a success.

On the last day of the conference, Lepke rose to the podium. Long, greasy hair sprouted from his puffy jowls. Otherwise his head was bald as an egg, veins bulging and throbbing obscenely beneath his translucent pate. He had engorged during the meeting to six times his normal height and weight, and now resembled a beluga teetering upright on one grotesque tail fin, wearing seersucker. The creature stood before the assembled parties and began his remarks, snuffling through a snout befouled with wherever it had recently been.

"Does no one see this horrid apparition?!" Beamish cried in terror, rising to his feet. But no one did, for the monster, we now know, reveals its true visage only to its victims, and then only when it is too late.

"I'd like to thank all of you for your nice comments on this meeting, and on our marketing plan," Lepke said, to respectful applause. "And I'd like to personally mention Steve's role in taking care of the details and stuff. It might seem unimportant, but I do know it's wrecked his life for the last couple of weeks." The crowd laughed. Beamish tried to stand but could not. I found him later, on his knees in an unmentionable place. "I'm so weak," he moaned as I helped him to the bar. "I'll never get any credit. Whatever I do, he just . . . eats it."

The next morning, young Beamish sat deskbound, pale and despairing. Lepke buzzed and, full of terror, our hero entered. The monster filled nearly the entire back third of the corner office. It had abandoned all pretense of human form, merely squatting over and around its desk like a couple hundred pounds of Pillsbury Poppin' Fresh dough. "After my successful meeting, the chairman wants to know my three top priorities for the coming year," it oozed, attaching itself to his face. "Have them worked out in bullet form by close of business. And make them impactful." The boy started screaming and has yet to stop.

There is one final irony. When Beamish was consigned to his asylum, Lepke was assigned an interim assistant with no lust for fame or even promotion. That week, the monster abruptly shriveled to the size of a walnut and fled the building, screaming. Is there an answer here? A weapon? I asked Beamish, who dissolved into a torrent of insane laughter. "Just spell my name right," he blurted as they dragged him back to his padded cell.

1988

The Most Beautiful Girl in the World

It was the last autumn of innocence, I think. Boston was green and gold and all kinds of bright orange, vermilion, and paisley, the air so crisp and fresh, and all things were possible. The Sox had just won the sixth game of the best World Series ever. Nixon had been gone for a year; drugs were still as American as scrapple; sex was safer than it would ever be again, at least physically. I was standing on the platform of the Red Line with my soon-to-be-ex-fiancée, Doris, who was bothering me about something, as she did between 1972 and 1976. It was early evening. Down at the end of the station sat a midsize ersatz collie dog, just beyond puppyhood, laughing. Her eyes glowed with a tremendous good nature and trust unencumbered by a surfeit of complicated insights. She was alone.

"Hi," I said. She came over, licked my hand discreetly, allowed herself to be scratched for a time, chased her tail in a dignified circle, lay down again. I remember thinking: "There are times God puts a choice in front of you." I often had such thoughts back then.

We took the dog.

She went totally nuts when she understood the news, bounding and leaping in a vertical parabola to kiss my face, and generally expressing an exuberance that made me want to laugh. As a world view, it was so inappropriate. Searching for the makings of a proto-leash, Doris found in her bottomless denim bag a hank of purple yarn, possibly the one she used for the three-year Sweater for Stan Project, the completion of which turned out to signify the end of our relationship. I wrapped several lengths around her neck—the dog's, that is—but it did not serve. To get her home in one piece, I had to pick her up and hold her like a baby. It is a silly position for a dog, and most fight it. Not her. She lay in my arms, feet poking skyward, head lolling back in a friendly grin, tongue draping out the corner of her mouth, eyes calmly investigating mine as if to say, "Hey, this is a nice idea. Why didn't you think of it before?"

At the time, I made $8,000 a year. My car was a pre-Nissan Datsun, basically a floorboard with wheels and perforated tin skin. My diet consisted of doughnuts, peanut butter, and Chef Boyardee ravioli straight from the can. Cold. My rent was $155 a month for six rooms. The sink was piled to eye level with every dish in the house, since Doris and I also couldn't get together on the politics of kitchen work.

I named the dog Elizabeth. Height: about thirty inches. Weight: thirty-five pounds. Eyes: brown. Tongue: red. Tail: rich and plumy. A coat of pure china white, so thick and lustrous and profuse that people would later suggest that I shear her and turn the output into a serape. In the summer she shed badly. In the winter, worse. All my clothes and furniture were coated with a fine layer of white flax. When she was younger, her tummy was as pink as a baby's bottom, and she had a marvelous, doggy smell, clean, pungent, yet sweet. Her personality? All I can say is that when the Lord made her, he forgot to add any malice, guile, or aggressiveness. Didn't chase squirrels, even. If another dog attacked her, she would roll over on her back immediately and expose her soft underbelly, clearly conveying the message: "Go ahead and kill me. I don't mind, but I think it would be a totally unnecessary waste of energy. But hey, just my opinion." Not once in her life was she hurt by any living creature.

Elizabeth was not smart, but she made the most of it. "She's the sweetest dog in the world," said a friend about her. "But she's got an IQ somewhere between a brick and a houseplant." When people asked what breed she was, we'd say, "Mexican Brainless." How we'd laugh! In retrospect, this seems kind of unfair. Could she defend her thoughts, assuming she had any? Not at all. For all intents and purposes, she was mute: Not a bark, yelp, nor whimper escaped her. In fourteen years, I heard her voice maybe three times. It was always a shock.

I broke up with Doris and rented a place that was nice before I got to it. I was not a master of business administration then, and it was not the living space of a responsible person. Many was the night Liz and I stayed up until dawn, eating biscuits and watching Charlie Chan. Her nose was big and black and wet and perfect for squeezing, and she liked nothing better than to sit at my side and lick my hand for hours on end. I think she got into a kind of trance when she did it, and I had to slap her around now and then to get her to stop.

No roommate could have suited me better. One afternoon, looking under my bed for a shoe to munch, she found a blue sphere covered with a gossamer pelt of fuzz. It had been an orange once, but now it was soft and alien to the touch. Any sensible person would have tossed it out immediately. I found her playing with it. Took a hell of a chase to get it away from her too.

Not long after, when the nation was spritzing its bicentennial all over itself, I met my soon-to-be future wife. Before long we were sort of living together. Dogs were not welcome in her building, so Elizabeth was forced to hold down the fort at my apartment. After a while, it became a dog's apartment, which I guess was only fair. Empty cans of her Alpo and my ravioli littered the rooms, and long skeins of toilet paper hung everywhere, for when Liz got bored, she loved to play with it, string it out, flip it over and under things. She tore into Hefty bags and distributed the contents. She kept herself occupied.

She also periodically ran away. If you opened a door or window, she was out it. One morning she tore through a screen and hurled herself to the street. I didn't blame her. The place was a pit. It was a good thing I lived on the ground floor.

She loved to run, that was it. I would take her to a nearby football field once every couple of days. It was fenced in. I'd let her off the leash, and she would sprint in an immense circle around the huge enclosure until I thought her heart would pop from exertion and joy. Then I'd pile her into the back of the car, where she'd sleep, heaving up and down as she dreamt, and shed. That was fine with me. It was a dog's car, too.

We got married, my wife and I, and for a while there Elizabeth was our only child. She got a lot of love. After a year, we moved to the city, and she, like us, learned to adjust to the demands of urban living. When we'd return home from a walk, I'd let her off the leash in the long hallway down to our three-room flat, and she'd tear down that corridor like a hound possessed, her tail tucked underneath her rear end for maximum aerodynamic lift and thrust, slam into the wall at the end, turn, and head back at even greater speed.

She was youth, and spirit, and dumb, careless vitality.

We were city people now, with city rituals. When we went to the mandatory summer community to visit friends, she was there, zipping freely down the beach in those days before the invention of deer ticks, chasing the waves until they crashed over her and I had to rescue her from the undertow. One night, we went back to eat sesame noodles and chicken, and our hostess put the salad on the floor since the table was full unto groaning. In the candlelight, as we talked, we heard a moist chomping sound, and a great smacking of lips. We looked beneath the table, and it was Liz, downing the last of the arugula and goat cheese and sun-dried tomatoes. She looked up at us, the vinaigrette glistening off her whiskers, as if to say, "Gosh, this is delicious, guys, but not that filling. How about some chicken bones to wash it down?"

To her, carcass of used poultry was the ultimate delicacy. One time, I left an entire oven-stuffer roaster wrapped in tinfoil on the kitchen counter. Two hours later, the only thing left in the room was a small piece of tinfoil and a grease spot on the floor. She had eaten not only the meat and bones, but the aluminum as well. I watched her for days, certain she had finally OD'd on her own sheer witlessness. But she hadn't.

She was indestructible.

She even took the birth of our two kids with grace, even when they pulled her eyebrows or fell on her screaming and hugging and kissing her with the kind of passion adults usually reserve for the game-show hosts who award them cruises to Bimini. When my son was a year old, and particularly aggressive, he tried to ride her. She was thirteen by then, and growled at him. After some thought, it was determined that it was she who would be sent away to stay at my mother's house. The exile lasted six weeks. She went with the program after that.

One morning in 1988, she couldn't get up. I took her to the vet, who told me that her spleen was enlarged. Would I care to make a decision? After all, the dog was fourteen. We fixed her up. It was the best money I ever spent, and I spent a lot of it. While she was convalescing at the hospital, my son put together his first complete sentence: "I miss Wizbet," he said. And then he cried. How much is a dog's life worth?

Last winter we moved to a house with a backyard, a swing, and a piece of an acre. Elizabeth came, too.

So a month ago my wife and children went down to see my in-laws in Arizona. And the following Thursday, after breakfast, Liz fell down in the garden and just lay there, her eyes rolled up into her skull, heaving and panting and trembling. The episode lasted just a few minutes, but it scared me shitless. When she awoke, she was jolly and hungry, and spent the rest of the day in the backyard, staring off into space, always one of her favorite pastimes.

When she was falling down five times a day, the vet said to me, "You have to decide whether she is able to preserve her dignity leading this type of existence." I'd never considered it in those terms before. As she lay on her side, clearly not in the world as we know it, I held her paw and kissed her forehead, and all the fourteen years of my life with her swam before me and I knew, yes I did. And it was not a good knowing. I made a call. I put her in the car. My brother came along. We were both crying.

The vet's office was clean and cool. He's a nice guy, my vet. I got the feeling that he'd never get used to that part of his job. "This shot will put her to sleep easily," he said. "Then the next shot will put her to rest." He gave her the first and suddenly she arched her back and from her throat came a horrible, gut-wrenching cry, a raking, moaning howl that conveyed an understanding nobody needs to have, and for which none of us is ever ready. And my brother and I held her, and we were sobbing, and the vet said, "She's not in pain, she's just had a neurological reaction to the sedative." Then a few minutes later: "She's at peace." He was weeping, too.

Her body was there, the coat still shiny, the nose still wet and warm. But she was gone. I noticed a small pulse in the tip of her tongue, which was hanging out of her mouth much as it had the very first night I saw her, in October of 1975, when Pete Rose was a hero and Boston was nine innings away from its first world championship in nearly six decades.

This is the last I will speak of her. I owe her this eulogy, dog to dog, for fourteen years of companionship, of laughs and devotion and cheek-by-jowl existence on this hard and incomprehensible planet.

You were the best. The kindest. The last who was wholly mine.

Bye, baby.

1990

I'll Get You in the End

I added a fine new name to my List today. There was no ceremony, but I note the occasion nonetheless.

It's the first of the month, the day each commuter must purchase his right to be conveyed to and from the same two locations twenty times within the next thirty days. On the other side of the grate is Rizzo, the ticket seller. Rizzo is a woman, broad and squat, with a round, jowly face, a nest of brushy, oatmeal-colored weeds atop her head, and a face that conveys the message that she just ate a bad anchovy.

I am at the front of the line as my train rumbles into the station, giving me ninety seconds, tops, to purchase my ticket and get out. Yet Rizzo does not say, "May I help you?" Instead, she begins to count money. Studiously, she makes certain all her bills are facing in the same direction and are properly stowed in their slots. In the time she devotes to this chore, I can feel my train slipping away, and with it my all-important early-morning quality time with my peers and superiors, when we all aimlessly wander about the halls, drinking coffee, exchanging paper, re-creating the ethos. Instead, I get to work at 9:00 on the nose. "Taking a half day?" the senior vice president of Strategic Planning asks, just seriously, as I step off the elevator.

Rizzo is not the first on my List, nor the worst, and she certainly won't be the last. But she'll get hers. I don't know when or how. But I'm sanguine. I can wait. Hatred is meat best eaten chilled in aspic, or some damn thing like that.

Behold with your fourth eye that inland sea where no man sails but he who sails alone. And on that wee boat, solitary and bronzing in the tropic sun, you will find, along with the charts and graphs and sextant of your personal legend, a shard of foolscap. How old are you? That, minus perhaps three years, is the age of the document. Some of the names on it have aged beyond your ability to read them. Some are writ as fresh as yesterday's insults, scrawled in a dark maroon substance that smells like iron gone to rust. It's your shit list. I wish there were a nicer name for it, but it's not a nice thing. That's what's so great about it. Looking backward:

There's a guy who works in another division of my corporation. I'm going to call him Loomis. Loomis feels he should be president of our company. He is not. Several times I have prepared financial documents for Loomis. Each time, the word comes back to me that Loomis feels what I have done is "bullshit" that needs revision from "people who aren't seven hundred miles away in corporate headquarters."

I don't like this attitude. It has been explained to me that "Loomis is a kick-ass guy who takes no prisoners, and that's just the way he is." The only circumstance under which I do not hate such beings is when they are my friends. Loomis is not my friend. He'll get his.

Fifteen months ago and counting: I perceive that a highly intelligent and very political woman, Betty, is invading certain sectors of my territory, quietly, and from several directions, mostly seeping into areas where my client relations are at their weakest. Betty pursues business I should know about without letting me know about it. I learn that one recent Friday she held a nine-party transcontinental conference call on a matter not unrelated to my office, while I was out at a two-hour lunch with one of the vendors who sucks off my budget line (a legitimate part of my job description!). "Where's Bing?" one person on the party line inquired, I am told. "Oh, you know, probably at one of his famous luncheons," Betty said. And across the nation, there was laughter at my expense. Uh-huh.

Right now the only thing I can do is not invite her to any meetings and pass my calm, collected thoughts on her general sufficiency to friends and neighbors. Opportunities will present themselves. Don't worry.

Good gosh. It's 1984, and God, things look so quaint. I'm working in a toasty little enclave of the corporation, with a bunch of intrapreneurial meatheads who actually produce a product people want to buy. The average age is about thirty-five. Most of the company's growth is based on the health of what we're doing. The header of our parent division, in Houston, decides in the years of nervous, mercantile colonialism, that the stock price could use a boost. He sells us. Lots of high-fives at GHQ, and all of my friends lose their jobs. It's a brilliant piece of business, don't get me wrong. I see that. Since then, sue me, I haven't liked the kind of people who divest things to improve the value of their options in the name of shareholder rights. Up theirs!

My, that feels good.

Wow, 1982, Look how thin I am. In fact, I don't look well. I look as if I could use, oh, twenty pounds or so. My first boss, Chuck, is putting me through the second half hour of the history, destiny, and season-to-date of the Kansas City Chiefs. Never have I met a tighter sphincter. For two years he has been tormenting me with a level of bureaucracy so intense it functions as aggression. I'm ready to kill him, not once, but sixteen times a day. "You know," he says this morning, leaning back in his executive chair, "I think this guy Louis Farrakhan has got a couple of good points, don't you?" We never discuss football again, and when his vice presidency starts to hemorrhage big clots of bright red ink, I do nothing to staunch the flow. I even add a couple of large cuts when the time is right. Very satisfactory.

Whoa! We're back in the post–Nixon golden years of the mid–1970s, and Doris is trying to force me to marry her. I don't want to. For two years I have been seriously contending that the wedding, essentially, is in the mail. She's gone way past wheedling. To impress me with the seriousness of her devotion and the depth of her frustration, Doris sleeps with a mutual acquaintance whose adventure with my ostensible fiancée will certainly be reported to me. It is. I suffer, confronted with the sudden insight that while love may never die, affection can most certainly be killed. Once you acquire such knowledge, you can't get rid of it. It's like the mange. The hell with Doris.

And with all the women who have made me cry!

It's 1962, I'm, like, eleven years old, and Jerry Verblin makes fun of me because I'm still wearing jeans and haven't moved over to chinos. Putz. To this day, I hate guys who make fun of me either because I'm wearing suspenders or because I'm not. Jerks! Nerds! Which reminds me: I have to send my gray winter twill to the dry cleaner to have the cuffs widened.

Lord help me, here I am back in 1959, and it's Mr. Abadabo, bully, latent queen, and grade-school gym teacher. I am roller-skating at the Police Athletic League, tiny little me, and feeling very capable. I know that Barbara Michaels is watching me, and suspect she must be impressed, since she has never seen me do anything physical whatsoever except ride a bike, and that none too quickly either. I love Barbara Michaels. On my way home from school, I sometimes stand outside her house and stare at its lighted windows, happy merely to be in the same universe. "Say!" bellows Abadabo across the gym as I glide past, "Here comes the fat boy!" And I go into the locker room, alone, and cry.

For years I would long to rear up before him at an unexpected hour and whisper, "Remember me? I was as small and as tender as a boxer's kidney, and you hurt me. Now eat this." I would stuff my toe into the corner of his cheek, and his bilious eyeball would cloud over with recollection, and a creepy, vindictive sneer would cloud his cankered lips, and he would murmur, around the tip of my shoe, "Oh yes. Stan Bing. You look a lot better. But you're still fat!" And then, with an agile move I learned specifically for the purpose, I would crush his face.

How can I possibly still feel this way after all these years? Can enmity live for so long a time, out of sight of its object?

You bet it can.

It's 1956, and my dad is trying to teach me basketball. He's scowling at me. I know I stink. I'm just a little boy, does he have to be so disappointed? I know I can't show anger; he will be hurt, and retire to his room, and then I will have to mount the long carpeted steps to his closed door and knock, and enter, and apologize. I will cry when I do so. I don't want to cry, not ever again. I don't want my father to be mad at me, or me to be mad at my father. Later, when I am older, there will be other occasions when we will be enraged at each other, and in all those times, he will never fail to exercise his mighty, awesome power over the man that I have come to know, slightly, as myself.

He's gone now, my dad, but that doesn't eradicate him from the List. Not at all. Who would I be without my resentment against my father? What would fuel the perpetual furnace of my anger? No, my dad remains indispensable. As long as I am me—and that looks like a life sentence—he stays. Call it continuity.

But he's not the original resident—just the best loved.

No, at the bottom, in ink both pale and indelible, is the archetype on which all other hatreds are built. When I shave in the morning, it is him I cut and curse. While he does have certain superb points on a very good day, he is guilty of a range of atrocities against my personal state that will never be expunged. Most I cannot even remember. But it is he, it is me, who has the most to account for.

So I'll conduct my life. I'll do the right thing. But I'll keep one eye lookin' over my shoulder. Because I'm out there. I'm nasty.

And I will be avenged.

1990

How to Be a Consultant

It's a beautiful morning in American business. Not for you, but we're not talking about you. We're talking about me, because I'm a consultant! Guys like me, we run the planet. I'd say the future belongs to us, but that would be wrong, sort of. I mean, of course the future belongs to us. But the present belongs to us, too! Is it any wonder I'm so goddamned jolly? See my teeth? They're terrific! Know why? Because I keep them in extremely lean and productive shape, biting off heads of guys just like you! Hahahahaha!

Why aren't you laughing? You know what happened to the last guy who didn't laugh at my jokes? He's dead now! If you want to pick him up, you'll need a Dustbuster! Wow, just look at the time. I've got to run. I'm facilitating a meeting of senior people who are having trouble figuring out the company vision. At least I think that's what I'm doing here—maybe I'm just measuring your office for storage space! Hahahahaha!

What's that you say? You wanna be a consultant, too? Are you sure? It isn't easy. You have to work very, very hard. A lot of the time you might as well be in show business—you never know where your next gig is coming from. But it's a good life, too. You're not encumbered by boring ongoing loyalties or the need to retain consistent positions. That kind of flexibility is a wonderful asset.

First of all, unless you've never been employed in a real job at all (a serious possibility if you distinguished yourself at Harvard and went immediately into the pundit food chain), you're going to have to get yourself fired. This is not that difficult in this day and age, especially for people like you and me, who find it difficult to form lasting attachments. Start by suggesting quirky strategies that involve the wholesale destruction of the existing culture. This will get you noticed. Your superiors will see that you have trouble working with others, but of course so do they. They will also come to believe you are "brilliant," meaning that you say things that most people find difficult to understand, let alone refute. "We could outsource all centralized corporate planning," for instance. What does it mean? How would it work? Nobody knows! Eventually, you'll be found just too odd for organized life. But when you're gone, people will recall you as a weird guy, not uncreative, who was not a particularly good people-person.

You're on your way.

Now find a corporation you can really sink your teeth into. Once you get in the door, the tough part really starts. You can't just unload a ton of wet consulting all over the lobby. You're going to go through the whole listening thing, really turning into the client, then give back the exact thing you just heard. If in your first meeting, for instance, Mr. Weevil says, "The industry is suffering a decline in sales of 20 percent this year, but we need to grow sales by 11 percent," you don't lean forward and yell, "Don't insult my intelligence! Get real!" On the contrary! After a good talk about, say, "reading both the short-term and out-year trend lines," feed back the original order in subtly changed form, like, "Any operating strategy we come up with has to be independent of assumed revenue growth and capable of building the bottom line into the low double digits." If you wait at least fifteen minutes between his statement and yours, there is a good shot the guy will think you came up with it on your own.

Then establish the big-time. We. We includes everyone who is not They. We are willing to kick names and take ass. They are not. As H. Ross (the great consultant to the American people) Perot says, "It's that simple! Case closed!"

Next, get your Grand Concept together. You'll need it to find the Thing We Need to Do. Not two things. Not four. One. That's the kind of focus no intelligent business has by nature, so you'll be appreciated by people who hate complexity, i.e., senior management. Following are some Grand Concepts that are still available after the 1980s, when a lot of them got stuck to the bottom of the pan:

- Excellence (now being localized into Centers of Excellence)
- Chaos (as a good thing)
- Multitasking (getting one person to do six jobs)
- Outsourcing (good for consultants, as companies hire outsiders to perform crucial, formerly inner functions like benefits management and even sales)
- Decentralization (relinquishing all control of field operations and firing the entire headquarters management function; see Soviet Union, former)

• The twenty-first century (building for it, reaching to meet its challenge)

Any of these are good, until they're not. On the other hand, if you want to steer clear of buzz words, which have a half-life, it might be smarter to get to what the new breed of us guys are now doing: Introduce a massively gnomic, unknowable analysis engine that you have to keep running. Feel the pulse, take the temperature, take a survey that polls all 610 field managers on the way they account for inventory! It's detail so deep that nobody even thought it was achievable. And after six months, why, you've got that data, which nobody even thought of asking for before! Torment the business with this kind of inquisition continually and viciously, and nobody will ask what the fuck you're doing until you've rung up a bill it would take a military contractor to justify.

What else? Let's see. Oh, yeah: Remain loyal to one guy and one guy only. The guy who signs off on your bill. Beyond that, the entire system can sit on it, right? They're all potential enemies of change, anyhow.

And finally—and then I've really gotta run, my man—remember the basic equation of living in our business:

$$\Sigma = \sqrt{C}$$

That is, the cost of consulting (sigma) should be equal to (or even less than) the square root of the money you have saved (or made) the corporation. If there's a perception that every bit of money you save (or make) the company is going straight into your pocket, people will begin to resent you, no matter what kind of excellent work you are doing.

Oh, and one very, very last thing: As insecure as the life sometimes gets, don't worry about tomorrow. For at the end of the day, after all the good ideas have been fielded, after all the meetings have been taken and the costs cut and new revenue streams activated (well, they would have been if people understood your ideas!), when the game gets old and you long for a regular paycheck with benefits you can count on—why not come inside?

That's right! There's plenty of room for you in the executive suite. You've helped to create the room, haven't you? And it would be cheaper, a lot cheaper, for everybody if you wanted to come home to stay, wouldn't it? You bet it would! Yeah! Come to think of it . . .

Mr. Bing, is it? Love your office! Love your job! In fact, from the look of the pictures on your desk, I think I could learn to love your wife and kids!

Ow! Ow! Leggo, will ya! No! Not out the window! I'm afraid of heights! You wouldn't let me go, wouldja? I'm a human being! You can't do this! Aiiiieeeeee!

SPLAWPHGHT!

Perhaps that's not the right noise, I don't know. What is the sound of one trend hitting the pavement at about sixty miles an hour and exploding into a million mucilaginous pieces?

1993

A Rat's Tale

They come in the night, slurping into the corporation on little fat feet. Before you know it, they're right at the heart of the granary bin, munching away at the precious harvest of organizational life, which, of course, is trust. They are the weasels, the stoats, the plump, rodentine offal eaters who live in the interstitial fabric of the family, darting between, among, under—looking for any scrap of sustenance that will keep them alive. They have teeth. They carry fear. They want you to like them. And maybe you will. Watch out. There's one coming to an office near you. When he does arrive, beware. They breed.

Today, we will consider the story of Stanky. I call him Stanky, even though it is not his real name, because when he is around that is generally how people feel. Not at first, you know. But after a while, you notice folks sort of shifting uncomfortably from one foot to the other, as if they have to visit the restroom or something.

I allowed myself to be fooled by Stanky. He smiled a great deal when he got here as a vice president of information management. He seemed sort of sad and maladroit and intensely admiring of my entire act, an attribute I always respect in a person. His presentation was not impressive in the sense that his mustache seemed a little too trimmed, the soft spot at his waist a little too undefined, the skin of his neck a tad too moist. An imaginary dollop of mayonnaisey tuna fish hung from his lower lip at all times. He was nauseating, in other words. But that, in itself, can be a big plus for a mid-level manager, generating guilt and a desire to overcompensate in those in whom he generates a natural revulsion.

"We must get together for lunch immediately," he said to me the first time we met. We were in an elevator, and several people from alien corporations were near at hand, pretending not to listen. He was too close, and I smelled the Lavoris on his chin. "I've heard you're the absolute master of office political life around here," he said, leaning even closer to make his point. I was embarrassed. He was getting to me.

"Sure," I said. "I can get you up to speed."

I never did, though. Several times he called me for comment on some situation that had arisen, but he never did "lasso me for that famous drink," as he referred to it more than once. After a while, it was clear that he had passed beyond my purview and into the greater corporate world, where players pursue their individual agendas without consultation with me.

I was aware that he was getting rather close to Walt. Not that Walt liked him, mind you. But like a cat I once shared a house with, the Stankman would bring a dead forest animal to his master every now and then and lay it at his feet, stepping back and waiting to be praised as the recipient tried to keep his gorge down over the pageant of torn fur and guts. In time, it became clear, Walt got to like the quality of data and scuttlebutt that was being spread out before him. Stanky got past the burnished mahogany door more and more.

This is perhaps understandable on Walt's part, especially now. The industry of which I am a proud member is changing almost daily. Mergers and acquisitions, for a time on a comfy hiatus while nobody had any money, have taken off again with éclat. Stuff is exploding all over the place, and big combatants are on the field, guys whose names cause investment bankers to bend over and walk funny due to the size of their erections. In this environment, information is hemoglobin. Coherent strategies coalesce in the air around you and decay like gluons in a particle accelerator. Everybody's got his favorite flavor, too. Your best friends are the guys who believe in your vision of the future. Guys who carry seeds of doubt or discontent are not welcome. For membership in the inner circle, only allies need apply.

Which, I guess, brings us to Morgenstern. Morgenstern is a schmendrick. What is a schmendrick? I'll tell you. A schmendrick always speaks his mind. A schmendrick trusts other people simply because they are sitting close by, having a beer. In a delicate situation, with arrows flying everywhere and friends and enemies wearing the same uniforms, a schmendrick is the guy wearing a bull's-eye on his back. He's doomed.

I like Morgenstern. He's big and floppy and unbusinesslike, and, poor dude, he almost bought the ranch, thanks to certain indiscretions of which he was no doubt guilty, but most of all for expecting too much of his fellow man. It happened this way:

Morgenstern and the Stank were waiting in the boardroom for some of the investment bankers we hire to advise us to make some transaction, any transaction, so they may earn a fee.

The room was quiet, the air was cool and dry, and Morgenstern began to talk. "Walt's a good guy," he reportedly said, "but I don't think he takes a rigorous enough look at the implications of some of the deals we've got going down." Stanky listened. Morgenstern continued. "In fact, I'll be honest with you, I don't even know why the guy has financial analysts around. He's not listening and blah, blah, blah, and rag, rag, rag . . ." Get the picture? How many times a month do you spout off about your boss? Do you mean it? All of it? Do you expect the person to whom you are speaking to rat you out? Think about it.

The next day the rat had a breakfast muffin with the president. They talked about a lot of things, but not too smoothly, I am sure, since sustained conversation with a cheeping rodent is almost impossible. When the conversation flagged, however, Stanky had a gift for his man.

At 8:47, Walt strode into my office and closed the door. "I want Morgenstern out of here," he fumed. "This is a time when secrecy and loyalty are important above all other things. It's time to circle the flag and fight to take the field. We don't need second-guessing. We don't need bitching. We need to know that the man at our back will protect our flanks." (I don't know if I'm getting all the military terminology right. Sometime in 1993, we moved from sports metaphors to armed-forces lingo. I'm still new to it, although I do like it quite a bit. I was getting tired of punting and swinging for the fences and aiming for nothing but net and stuff.)

"How do you know all this?"

"Stanky," said Walt, and was gone.

But, of course, I knew. Most of us around here are basically good guys. We have our disagreements. But we'd never rat to Dad about stuff like this.

I called the putrescent little weasel into my office and, swallowing my tongue as best I could, inquired of the mass of pustulation why in the world he had turned in his brother executive. And this is what he said to me: "We're in a competitive struggle for the future of this company. We're playing for real marbles here, and either you're on this bus or you're off it."

Wow, I thought. The fetid little prune has been with us for all of six months. Who's he to decide who's on the frigging bus?

I believe my mouth was hanging open. Taking advantage of this lacuna in the proceedings, the Stankmaster wheeled with what must have been meant to pass for wounded dignity and stalked from the room. And I saw he was not sorry. And I was afraid.

A couple of pals and I sat down with Morgenstern. We spent the best part of the week helping him craft an approach to Walt that culminated in a superficially cordial meeting in which the poor schmendrick puled and groveled in order to right the wrong that was done to him. Today, bloody and trailing filthy gauze after him, he is back on the job. In a couple of months, all will have been forgotten. Executive amnesia is a wonderful thing.

What we will do with Stanky is another matter altogether. Right now, we're in phase two of the necessary process of extermination. It goes something like this:

One: deprivation of nutrients. The rat must be kept from all sustenance except that which will eventually sicken and kill him. First thing we did was to engineer a plum assignment for the fellow who should do just that. The rat will be conducting a policies and procedures audit at our combustible-plastics division all the way across town. Since it's a full-time post, at least for a while, he'll be needing a splendid new office there, well out of Walt's earshot and away from his major source of nourishment: private conversations. In order to come onto our floor now, he'll need a reason of some sort. That should buy us some time. Time to plan.

Two: Spreading the poison. We'll have lots of opportunities to lay the material that will eventually knock him out: meetings to leave him out of; retreats he won't be attending; jobs he's done that might be severely critiqued in sessions from which he will be absent. In time, we might be able to feed him some story or notion that after its ingestion will blow up and choke him. We're in no hurry, now that he's out of the day-to-day political flow. Life is long.

Three: Disposal. Man, that will be sweet. Is sweet, actually. It's started already, see. I'm going to an informal sit-down with a couple of guys.

We'll be talking about some key strategic issues and basically just having coffee. Not in attendance will be the rat. Who wants to talk around him? And in the distance, if you listen very closely, you will hear the squeaking and shrieking of a hairy little career curling up and rattling itself to death. The rat was wrong, see. Sometimes you're not either on the bus or off it.

Sometimes you're under it.

1994

An American Tragedy

The grief was palpable. It struck us all the moment we opened the newspaper that morning last week and saw the news about Greer. You could hardly miss it. It was on the front page of the business section, with several pictures of Greer himself. I saw it while I was on the road, enjoying my usual away-breakfast of bacon, bacon, and bacon, with heavily buttered toast, and it spoiled my meal.

"Oh no," I said when I saw it. "This can't be." I called Dworkin, who knew Greer way back when. "Did you see what happened to Greer?"

"I did," said Dworkin. There was a catch in his throat, and I knew he was as dismayed as I. "How could God let such a thing happen?" he asked. It was the kind of question that always comes up when these events occur. I don't believe anyone has found an acceptable answer.

Throughout the day, people who knew Greer called in to receive solace, to trade stories, to feel better. In the sharing there is some kind of surcease. Or at least that's what we tell ourselves, I guess.

The morning wore on, but the hard cluster of sadness in my chest did not disperse. I looked at the newspaper ten or twelve more times, but it didn't change, so I cast the offending article aside and stared out the window for a while. A grimy city rain was spitting at my window. Life is funny, I thought. You work, and you think you're smart, and you try to do good and to do well, and then it all comes to this.

The phone rang. It was Hecht on the line. Hecht is a hell of a guy. Pound for pound, there's nobody smarter than Hecht. That's why we were all so surprised when his corporation decruited him a couple of months ago. He's doing fine now. He's got a lot of gigs. But he's still hanging out there on the periphery, and that's just another thing that doesn't make any damn sense. The whole world is upside down, if you ask me.

"It's just not fair," said Hecht. All the spunk had gone out of his voice, and maybe that was the worst thing of all, hearing all Hecht's hope and beans grow flat and rotten. "Maybe there's some mistake," he said, and my heart went out to him.

"No, man," I told him. "There's no mistake. We're gonna have to pick up the pieces and go on in spite of this."

The rest of the day passed, as they do. It stopped raining, but it didn't get any nicer. I went to a bar after work. I drank a lot, but it didn't do much for me. A couple of friends were there. All they wanted to talk about was Greer. He was kind of a symbol to all of us. Now that comfort was gone.

"Son of a bitch," said my friend Brewster. Nobody talked to him much after that. He was just making people feel worse. "It should have been me," he added after a while. I felt like punching him, maybe because I was thinking the exact same thing.

I checked my voice mail on the way to the station. I had three messages. Two were from people I hadn't seen in a few years, and of course they were about Greer. This kind of thing brings people together, makes them remember the relationships that really count. The third message was a wrong number, which was a very nice change.

On the train home I tried to sleep. I couldn't. Everyone in the car had the paper open to the page about Greer. It was spooky. It seemed like a violation. I wanted to take every one of them by the lapels, scream into their sleepy faces, "This is Greer we're talking about! Greer! Don't you know what this means, you fools?"

I didn't, of course. I let them read, all those silly, happy people, read that story with no understanding of what it meant. I could barely sustain my composure, watching all those jolly commuters calmly staring at Greer's picture—Greer with the idiotic, fat cigar in his mouth, smiling, laughing over the caption: Six months ago Fred Greer was a consultant designing personalized dog collars for pampered pets. Now with the successful initial public offering of his Online Canine Shopping Mall, Greer is worth close to $200 million. There was more in the story. But that caption was enough.

I got off the train like a zombie and went to my car. I felt nothing. I saw nothing. On the way home, I listened to the radio. On the radio station was Greer, giving an interview about his new success. "It just seemed like a good idea, so I went with it," he was telling the interviewer. It was all I could do not to steer into a telephone pole.

Fred Greer had been part of our little group since 1980 or so. The thing that distinguished Fred was that he couldn't really do anything, and he made increasing amounts of money at it. He had excellent teeth and superb, flowing hair that he flicked back absently when it got into his eyes. He was almost too good-looking.

The first hint something was wrong was when Fred turned up, after his latest firing from a substantial role, as president of a small investment firm. It was a bullshit firm, but he was president of it. We all laughed when Fred was ejected from that firm and saw it as proof that there was a God. Several months later, however, Fred appeared as president of a bigger enterprise making a fortune. We were shocked but did not despair. We assumed that once again he would eventually be found out. And so he was. He spent a year in that role, mostly dealing with the redecoration of his office. After that, he went home. He became an entrepreneur. He disappeared. Until last week.

Now the grief has passed, somewhat. But things will never be the same. Thanks to the Internet, Fred will never be viewed in the proper light, as an attractive, shallow nincompoop who couldn't find his ass with both hands. He will always be one of the smart, savvy hustlers who made his mark in the new media.

And what does that make us?

1999

Why Consultants Generally Suck

A couple of weeks ago in this space, I tersely dismissed the entire profession of consultancy. This was unfair. I should have taken more time to do it.

As you may recall, I stated that young people should not become consultants if they can at all help it. The outcry was immediate, revealing, and pathetic. People—many of them consultants—were so very surprised and bewildered. What could I possibly have against consultants? Was there something wrong with consultants? Some of these people were actually studying to be consultants and wanted to know whether they had made a suspect career choice. Across the board there was a giant cloud of unknowing about a basic fact, and it is this:

Beyond the occasional CEO or middle manager who doesn't know what to do with himself, people in business don't like consultants. Oh, we have nothing against you as human beings. Beyond that, well . . . where you tread, pain, boredom, expense, and aggravation come humping along behind.

But you don't know that, do you? In this, as in many matters, you are blissfully clueless. In any other profession that would be a liability. In your case, you'll probably work it up into a paradigm that generates a process designed to deliver maximum real-time benefits to the change-resistant organization. Now before you start developing cost-based, zero-sum scenarios to shoot the messenger, I'll provide a few reasons why you've earned our enmity and mistrust.

You temporarily bridge gaps in our organizations that should be filled by staff. Since the 1980s, the offices you invade have been reamed out for head count not once, not twice, but six or seven times, until everybody is now doing a job that used to be done by dozens of people. Instead of a completely functional employee who could work nights and weekends, here you come to produce a bunch of ideas that we guys on the inside will have to execute. Get out of here.

We don't like your expertise—with the exception of guys who come in to fix our computers when they crash. Other than that, what are you talking about? Nothing that was on our minds, I can tell you that.

You're way too enthusiastic, and you dress funny. This is not your fault. But you can't blame us for feeling annoyed when you show up all bushy-tailed, and your tail is in $1,200 blue pinstripes and we're in brown. Or you're wearing a power tie we haven't seen in ten years. Or your hair is too short. Or too long. There's no question you're from over the border, chum.

The boss likes you far too much. You're an institutionalized suck-up. You're there to make him look good when he shouldn't. Does he listen to the guys who are in the trenches every day? No, he does not. Instead, here comes you. You hold meetings. You're looking into things. If anybody asks Mr. Beanbag what he's doing about slow growth in sales, he can say, "Oh, I've hired the McWeiner Group to look into that. They'll be giving me a report real soon, and if there's any resistance in implementing those goals, well, you can bet that blah blah blah . . ." Boy, doesn't he look dynamic. And what if it is, in fact, Mr. Beanbag who is the problem? Do you tell him that? Well? Do you?

You don't listen. You look like you're listening, but you're not, you're just waiting to talk. Because you've got a lot to say. You've been waiting since they poured all that stuff into your ear at Wharton to download all your knowledge, and this is your chance.

The solutions you propose to our problems were baked fresh in the 1990s and have been used every year since then. You have your spiel, and you stick to it. Why not? It's why you were hired. This is particularly true of McKinsey guys, who seem to come out of one Stepford factory with the entire program ingrained on their internal database.

You don't really know anything. You've been here for five minutes! Last week you were flogging cheese processors in Wisconsin. The week before, it was a private hospital in Omaha! Quick—who are we again?

You make us go to really stupid meetings. You want to "capture" all this stupid stuff on big sheets of paper you tack onto the wall. You rush around with overheads and Magic Markers. We get real creative for a while. Then you go away to put together the results. A few weeks later the report comes. It has all the resonance of old love letters written by another person. The report is filed and forgotten.

You cost a lot. We're dealing with 4 percent raises, and you cost, what . . . $25,000 a month? More? How much do you cost, anyhow? We don't know. A few years ago we hired a consulting group on what our newly merged corporation should call itself. At the time we were Acme Inc. Several hundred thousand dollars later, we were Acme Corp. Ha!

You alienate us from our bosses. You sort of have to. If staff can solve internal problems, that's the end of you, isn't it, Charley?

You're here to get us fired. We know it. You know it. What you're selling might be called Quality or Excellence or Productivity, but you're here to figure out ways to kill us, or spend money on something other than us. We had a guy one time whose big thing was international investment. So we invested in global stupidities that didn't really fit into what we knew how to do. This led to losses, which led to the need to trim costs by several hundred million dollars. Guess who got trimmed? Us, baby. Not you.

And in the end, you're after our jobs and our boss's job. Don't lie. Admit it. Do you know how many times I've seen the scenario? The chairman announces that a reorganization is advisable. A bunch of people are fired, including the guy one down from the chairman who hired the consultant. The McBarfage Group has run the bloody process so far. It's only natural that their senior consultant lead the search for the new chief operating officer. A lengthy hunt is conducted and the perfect person is then suggested. Guess who? The McBarfage guy! What a coincidence!

And it could be different. This, in the end, is the most tragic and galling part. There are some good practitioners of what you do. They come in with highly specific knowledge and expertise after years of fighting in the trenches. They help the inside guys identify a problem and fight against senior management to get things done. They have ideas but impose none. They come like the blessed rain and are gone like the wind. And they are loved.

No one just out of school can be this person, nor can some ancient mariner ten years into retirement. If you aspire to be a consultant, I wish you well. You've got a lifetime of preparation and study before you. And in the meantime? Hey. You're smart and resourceful. Why not get a job?

The Bing Ethics Test

In the waning years of this violent, corrupt, and successful decade of American business, at least one thing stands clear: ethically, we stink. On the other hand, I've got to believe there are many, both in and out of prison, who feel that moral relativism presages the end of civilization as we know it. Now may be a good time to stiffen our rectitude and evaluate where we as individuals stand. If not now, when? If not us, who? Here, then, a test for those who wish to ascertain where on the ethical scale they lie:

Section One: Rank in terms of ethical atrocity (40 points):
- (a) Fornication with subordinates who would rather not
- (b) Calling in sick when you're simply sick and tired
- (c) Crossing a picket line made up of people whose labors contribute the better part of your bonus, and then laughing about it with your management buddies
- (d) Withholding key information from a hated office rival to make sure he screws up
- (e) Using the company MCI calling card to phone your girlfriend in Borneo for an hour or so
- (f) Trading on inside information so that the company involved becomes so weakened that if falls prey to Kohlberg, Kravis & Roberts, and is destroyed
- (g) Ripping off your mattress tag
- (h) Cheating on your expense report occasionally, especially since you're underpaid.

Answers: a, f, c, d, e, b, g, h; 2 points off for every error.

Section Two: Measure, on a scale of one to five, how much these things disgust you (35 points):
1. T. Boone Pickens talking about stockholders' rights
2. Inside traders preaching democratization of capital
3. Greedy dealmeisters buying a company with its own debt
4. People who own the corporation discussing the issue of "Who owns the corporation?"
5. People who made a fortune using the tactics of Michael Milken now expressing revulsion at those tactics
6. People who made a fortune using the tactics of Michael Milken now defending those tactics
7. Editorials in the *New York Times* defending airline deregulation, and most particularly, Frank Lorenzo
8. Underpaid employees who occasionally cheat on their expense reports

Answers: The perfect score is 35, since number 8 should not disgust you at all. Take off 2 points for every point above or below the perfect number.

Section Three: Multiple choice (15 points):
1. One morning your telephone rings, and lo and behold it's a headhunter interested in searching you executively. After an extensive chat, he announces that your prospective new home is notorious for assisting in the overthrow of a wide range of democratically elected governments around the world. You:
   (a) hang up, after expressing appropriate disgust.
   (b) observe that you'd be interested in the right position as long as you don't have to take a personal role in any junta.
   (c) have a good laugh with the headhunter about it and mention that you used to inform on campus protesters when you were a member of the Young Americans for Freedom.
2. The chairman tells you that the entire Legume Solid Fuel Conversion Group is to be sold to a consortium that intends to fire every single decent person involved. You have a lot of friends in that division, but you're instructed to "tell no one until it comes down." You:
   (a) tell no one.
   (b) tell no one but indicate to one close associate that it might not be smart to buy that new Maserati, due to "changing market conditions."
   (c) tell no one but a couple of security analysts who appreciate that kind of information and know what to do with it.
3. You are invited out to lunch by an old friend from college. Thinking that he's paying—since he invited you—you order the filet mignon and a

muscle-bound Bordeaux. When the check comes, your pal looks at it as an article of intense archaeological interest but does not touch it. Naturally you pick it up. When it comes time to submit your expense report, you:

(a) eat the cost since it's not business related.

(b) think about your 3 percent cost-of-living increase and put it through, attributing the cost to "Les Minster, industry analyst."

(c) put it through, as always, along with every other credit card slip of the week, including one for Pampers bought at the corner Pathmark.

Answers: Give yourself 5 points for every (a) answer; 3 for every (b); 0 for every (c).

Totals: 0–50 points, you're a scumball and should do very well; 50–80, you're normal, for what it's worth; 80-plus, congratulations, Mother Teresa.

1989

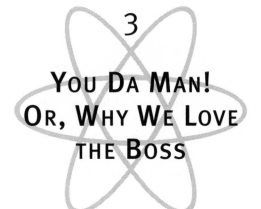

3

YOU DA MAN!
OR, WHY WE LOVE
THE BOSS

The study of Authority, and how it is used and more often abused, has been my life's work. It began when I was two, and they took my diaper away. Since then, a host of people have told me to do things, most of which I have done. But I haven't been happy about it. I've festered. Raged internally. Plotted strategies to push against the force, elude it, leverage it against itself. I have found, at the highest levels of power, Authority is best met and conquered through a kind of Zen not-caring. Within that shell, a host of manipulatory tactics can be employed against the task of controlling the controller.

My thoughts on the subject date from the earliest and most clueless days of my career. You can see me slowly losing my hostility and gaining a kind of goopy sympathy for executives.

Bad Bosses: A Survival Guide

Listen to the voices from the Gulag:

- "Working for my boss is like being seduced by an Arab prince, only to find out the next day that you've been sold into white slavery."
- "My boss is a raving, lunatic alcoholic who is fairly reasonable at 9:00, but after lunch becomes totally incoherent, or rages, or closes his door and won't come out. You have to see him the first half hour of the day, and if you miss your early train, you've blown it."
- "My boss is an extremely forceful, dynamic person with a lot of social graces, who creates the illusion that when he has control of a situation, good things are going to happen. Unfortunately, no good things have ever happened, but no one seems to have caught on. As a result of his most recent disaster, millions of dollars were lost, hundreds of innocent people got fired, and he ended up with a promotion."

These are just a few of the souls who live out where the sun is cold, in the tundras of the bad boss. They must labor under the worst conditions, sometimes going for months without a kind word or unrushed cup of coffee, in constant fear of arbitrary punishment, if not execution, enraged by the injustice and brutality that crackle in the air. Yet somehow a few survive to lead full, productive lives. How do they do it? By knowing their bad boss well, and fighting him with as much guts, guile, and passive aggression as they can muster.

To that end, let's look at some common types, and some ways they can be bested, if not worsted:

Attila the V.P.: Management by terror is a time-honored technique. The terrorist boss favors swooping down when he feels you're at your most vulnerable. "I made the mistake of sharing some financial problems with him over drinks," recalls my friend Will, an investment banker. "He was very understanding and told me he hoped it all worked out. Later in the day he called me and completely reamed me out about a litany of supposed horrors. Told me if I didn't shape up, I was dead meat. It's my fault. I showed him my underbelly, and I guess he couldn't help using the information to rip me from stem to stern."

What to do: Never give the Hun ammo by petitioning for human sympathy. And when he strikes, defend yourself. "Whining doesn't help," says Will. "If you have a boss who's a bully, it's good to get frustrated and take a stand at some point."

Don King, without the Hair: Some guys think a little healthy competition evokes the best from their drooling serfs. This is often created by assigning one piece of work to two people, preferably without letting either know that it's been done. "I think he does it to see who is stronger," says a friend of mine who is periodically forced to fight for his turf. "When I was hired, he told me, 'A little brains on the wallpaper never hurt anybody.' "

What to do: Get along with your peers, and your boss's mind games can't touch you. But if the threat to your territory is real, take over the project quickly and aggressively while, of course, maintaining the proper illusion of collegiality.

Johnny, the Little Turd Next Door Who Liked to Rip the Wings off Butterflies: Some guys are just plain mean for no strategic reason, and get their jollies off seeing smaller life-forms cringe and fester. "Marty's office was in the corner, totally encased in glass," recalls my friend Howard, a copywriter at a large advertising firm. "One day I submitted a research project that was very important to me. He knew I was watching. He turned so I couldn't see, put the report under his desk, took out several sheets of blank paper and pretended to read them for about five minutes, groaning, rubbing his eyes, wincing. I was sweating blood. When he got to the last page, he grunted, then crumpled the entire thing into a ball and tossed it into the wastebasket.

"While I was in the bathroom throwing up, I learned later, he quietly put the real report in his out basket, with his approval." Howard went into therapy shortly thereafter.

What to do: Hit the headhunters, discreetly. Only a chump puts up with a lot of crap for less than six big figures. If you decide to stick it out, you might, like Howard, consider seeking therapy, if only to explore your fondness for abuse.

The George Bush Syndrome: People in authority must be willing, occasionally, to risk disfavor of others. The only way to avoid this is to tell everyone very decisively what they want to hear at all times. While this may be a viable route to national candidacy, it is not the best way to manage a business, which often needs clear policies and someone willing to stand behind them.

What to do: Demand clarification, and, when necessary, cover yourself with memos that reiterate the boss's most recent position that agrees with yours. Then wave it in his face when he vacillates.

Missing in Action: The Saga Continues: Some bosses are too lazy to pay attention, while others are genuinely overwhelmed. Such lapses may not be as benign as they appear. Deadlines can be blown, opportunities molder, while the senior V.P. is behind locked doors contemplating what he'd like for supper. I recall waiting one fine winter evening for our chairman to give his approval on something that required it immediately. In retrospect, I guess I was lucky I dropped by his suite at 8:30 P.M. to see what was going on. If I hadn't, I might never have found out that he had gone home at 6:00, just after calling to tell me to stick around.

What to do: If he's the chairman, forget it. With anyone less elevated, however, it's time for a serious interface. You want him to retain a certain level of sentience when he's dealing with you from here on in.

The Last Days of Dick Nixon: Every now and then, a heretofore capable (if marginal) captain of industry loses his gluten. "When Rob began to decompose, he ringed himself with toadies and retreated into a fortress of solitude," recalls Jerry, a marketing pro. "His door was always closed. If we wanted to get a message to him, and a grinning sycophant wasn't around, we resorted to slipping notes under his door. He was done for, but nobody wanted to fire him, because they'd have to talk to him first."

What to do: Why not consider going for his job, function by function, as he drops them? Don't feel guilty, he probably won't be there for long anyway. After all, it's not only the good who die young.

1986

She's the Boss

Frankly, I don't know what to think. On the one hand, there was Annette, my very first boss, a fireplug of a woman who smoked like a chimney, drank fellow executives into aphasia, and was not above biting off heads bigger than her own, let alone smaller. One day she was Glinda the Good, dispensing affection. The next she laded housework upon your shoulders like Cinderella's stepmommy. When pissed off, which was often, she was capable of challenging one's ego in a dangerous and, well, maternal way. She was without question as bad as any male boss in the march of time, and when she was fired for sheer nastiness, there was whistling in the halls.

And then there was Elaine. In addition to business matters and office gossip, Elaine enjoyed kibitzing at length about politics, child-rearing, and catering firms. There were flowers in her office, okay, but she was tough enough when she had to be. She didn't often have to be. You didn't like to say no to Elaine. The day she left us for significantly greener pastures, the entire corporation mourned and felt rejected. I've never seen so much kissing, hugging, and sniffling on the floor. She was valued in a way that no man below chairman could hope to be.

Women make great bosses, except when they don't. In this respect they're no different than men, except they are. First of all, the stakes tend to be higher. "A woman boss has more of a personal involvement with her people than a male boss does," says a woman boss I know. "When the woman is a together person, it beats having a male boss—there's more nurturing, more loyalty, more caring. But when a woman is messed up, or a workaholic, or neurotic, she inflicts more personal expectations, obligations, and mishegaas. Whatever you have, it's going to be more intense."

Most men, sadly, are ill-prepared for the new and fearsome task of expressing anything but jocularity at the office. To manage his woman boss, the thoroughly male worker must draw on reserves of feeling and interpersonal skills he never before needed, or thought he possessed. This may be done by playing any combination of the following roles:

The Good Soldier. "My boss Pauline manages through intimidation, lying, and manipulation—all the traditionally male characteristics," says Ken, director at a bank heavy with female talent. His tale is typical. According to Corinne Kuypers-Denlinger, vice president at the business trend-watching Naisbitt Group, "These are driven women who mimic what they perceive to be the successful-male role model—tough, aggressive, authoritarian. The new woman manager is more comfortable being intuitive, nurturing, supporting." If your hard-edged woman boss has yet to discover the new, softer model, deal with her as you would any other autocrat: at attention, and ready for action. You'll have to be twice the woman she is—every day.

The Loving Son. "I've seen a lot of women bosses who are sort of maternal, and that is, as we know, pure power," says my pal Bob, a senior copywriter. "They want to know how you're doing with your family, or whether your cat is still sick, or how the whole You is feeling." If you can make Mom happy, the rewards are deep and wide. "You didn't want to disappoint her, or break that thing in her," Bob recalls, "because when it came to nut-cutting time, you knew she'd go to the ends of the earth for you." Most maternal bosses are satisfied, by the way, with an intensely personal confidence now and then. But don't tell her anything you wouldn't tell your real mother.

Mr. Congeniality. There comes a time, the walrus said, to speak of many things, most of which, as a guy, you will know little about. In search of the perfect schmooze, you may find yourself delving into such typically feminine arcana as manicurists, footwear, designer cheese, and, of course, human relationships. Stretch those conversation muscles. Console yourself with the thought that, if you reported to a male, you would be talking about the year the Jets won the Super Bowl, or lost it, over and over again. And when it comes down to it, this year's hemlines or the Forbishers' nasty annulment can be a lot tastier.

The High School Sweetheart. A little recreational flirting can be a pleasant way to pass the day and add a certain piquancy to your working environment, so indulge to the limits of propriety. But don't get bamboozled into thinking it's going to get you anything more than a naughty thrill. "An attractive woman boss can con you into feeling like you have a special relationship with her that nobody else has," warns Rick, a financial analyst who had a professional infatuation with his former supervisor. Reliance on this titillating bond carries its own peril, as Rick found out when a promised promotion failed to materialize. "You think to yourself, 'I thought she really liked me, and it turns out I'm nothing but a pathetic underling with a schoolboy crush,' " he sighs, still wounded after all these years. So flirt if you will, but don't be a putz. Remember: She's the boss.

Mr. Cool. Where classic male authority employs the steel fist, women have an equally potent weapon: tears. Not long ago, my friend Ralph had a salary review with his female boss. When the number came down, it was several grand less than he was expecting. He recalls the rest of the incident with fondness: "I told her, very matter-of-factly, 'I do want to say I'm disappointed with this amount.' She started to sob and said, all teary, 'Well, I'm disappointed in you for being disappointed!' I then asked her, almost like a therapist would, 'Why are you crying? What is there to cry about?' She got up and fled to her private washroom. It was a dispute of a strictly professional issue, and I resented her injecting so much emotion into the situation. I was not going to let myself be manipulated." Ralph didn't get the extra money, of course, but so what. Some things are more important than money. Like pride.

No matter how many late-night chats you indulge in, how much tenderness or support you and your boss offer each other, never forget that she is your superior and must be obeyed. More than that—she's a now kind of woman, ably juggling a bewildering array of functions at home and in the workplace, forging a complex existence undreamed of by her sisters of yesteryear. Taking orders from such a woman is easy. I've been doing it since the first day I met my wife, and I've sort of gotten to like it.

1986

I've Always Loved You, Mort

It's tragic. These are intelligent men, all of them. But their memory, their lasting heritage, will always be linked to the fact that their whole life was dedicated to giving the boss blow jobs.

—A FRIEND IN PUBLISHING

These are subjects that engage the entire human being, that, once liberated, unleash deep, viscous reservoirs of passion and memory. Thus do we hear tall, terrible tales concerning a guy I'll call Little, advertising and public-relations nabob, a man recognized throughout his industry as perhaps the greatest suck-up to ever grace his profession, which is saying a lot. In an open meeting dealing with critical business issues, he is actually said to have leaned over and quietly straightened the crease on his beloved chairman's slacks. In so doing, the story goes, he was heard to murmur, "Gee, Ben. Nice worsted." A decade later, those who can suppress their gag reflex still invoke his name with awe, contempt, and pity.

This is exactly the kind of rank behavior that gives this ancient practice its bad names. Apple-polishing. Bootlicking. Ass-kissing. Brownnosing. Even something called tuft-hunting. A grand and special contempt is reserved for guys who get caught with drool on their chin. And yet, all over the world, in all walks of life, sucking up is going on right at this very moment, to the pleasure of both parties. "I liked the term bootlicking best," admits my friend Lester. "Especially with a woman boss. I imagine her in thigh-high black boots, with spike heels. I'd start from the back and work forward."

Now that's what I call a truly professional attitude. Me, I recall fondly the long hours spent with Chuck, my former boss and borderline schizophrenic, chewing over the weekly fortunes of some team called the Kansas City Chiefs. I'm convinced those interminable, coffee-intensive mornings, primarily spent bobbing my head like a Smurf on a dashboard, saved me during the worst era of corporate cutback since Carl Icahn reached maturity. That, and the fact that I did an okay job, I guess.

The truth is, strategic sucking up remains the best way to manipulate large, airborne windbags. To do so with safety, be sure to tread The Threefold Path:

RIGHT THOUGHT

Being a suck-up artist is like being a con man, and being a con man isn't "I take your confidence," it's "You give it to me, and like it."
—A FRIEND IN TELEVISION

In its purest form, the art is a display of friendly insincerity no more meaningful or degrading than a handshake before battle. "It's the ability to be smooth at will," says my buddy Borg, who sometimes sucks up even when he doesn't have to. "The guy knows you're bullshitting, sure—but he appreciates the effort."

Speed and lightness of touch are all. "Think of it like you're on the beach with this guy, and the sun is beating down on his bald little head," suggests Byron, who also wanted to be heard. "Your job is to wipe a dab of lotion up there without his really being aware you've done so. All he should know is that his head feels better and you were around when it happened."

RIGHT ACTION

> *I can't work in an office because I can't suck up. I don't have the gift of being dishonest and insincere. So what's the point of going out to lunch with me?*
>
> —A FRIEND IN PUBLIC RELATIONS

Here are some of the tools at your disposal:

Flatter him: But only the things he is proud of, for only those will he believe. "He just beams if I recognize a designer," says Arnold, who labors under a fashion plate. "He doesn't wear the kind of stuff that jumps out at you, so when somebody recognizes his fancy Italian jacket, he's amenable for hours after." And there's no need to slobber on the threads. "A good suck-up artist knows how to provide the sugar without serving it," Arnold observes.

Consult him: "Make him feel he's captain of the team, even if he's totally superfluous," says Lester. "That, although there's a plan sort of mapped out, you can't quite pull it together without his help." There isn't an executive alive who can disbelieve this approach and remain sane.

Schmooze her: "You look good" is still the most important phrase in intergenderal matters. You've never lived, I believe, until you've seen your boss blush. But as my friend Lenny observes from his corner office, "Women are also extremely sensitive about being regarded in a businesslike fashion, and anything you say that pushes them back into a social role can be dangerous." How to keep off the permafrost? "I think women like the idea of being asked out for a beer," Len states. "Not a drink; that has sexual connotations. But beer is fraternal. And what women want most of all is to belong to the fraternity."

Hang around, a little: "Chas had this uncanny habit of leaping up from his desk and going to the men's room at the precise time he saw Mort headed in that direction," says my pal Dworkin, who isn't above doing the same himself. "I think he got enormous work done in there. He had Mort's ear, certainly. And he didn't push it for anything beyond small talk, you know, 'Hi, I thought your comments to the Board were just about the most lyrical thing I ever read'—that kind of thing. It was just a chance to cross streams, and have a moment with the big guy."

RIGHT TIME TO QUIT

Nobody likes a guy who always has his nose up someone's heinie.
—MY FRIEND DWORKIN

And that, friends, is the crunch. The inexpert suck-up lays bare something unsavory in the heart of all power relationships that decent people do not forget or forgive.

This guy I know, call him Harry, for instance, is a very nice executive vice president. A little glib, perhaps, but that's always been a sin I'm disposed to forgive. He's been wanting a huge job as head of our South American subsidiary. Went so far as to make a major presentation to the new president of the international division, and did okay. Word was, he was off to La Paz in the spring. Then, over the Christmas break, he played one morning of tennis with that same new president. "This is the kind of chance to suck up that comes along once in a lifetime," he joked beforehand, quite seriously.

Needless to say, the job has yet to come through, and Harry spends his long, vacuous days grieving for his dead transfer. "I guess you didn't do too good on the court," someone offered not long ago. "Maybe you should have let him win."

"I did," Harry said.

1988

Executive Shelf Life

If you're old enough, you might remember where you were when the Hindenburg blew up. If you're younger, but still not young, you possibly are able to place your exact location when you heard that big Dick Nixon had done the same. You pick the moment. You know the feeling. You kind of freeze, realize in a white, bright pop of clarity that you're standing smack-dab in the middle of history. You feel tiny and huge at the same time, sort of like you're staring at the midnight sky over the desert. It's just you and the universe and maybe a couple of geckos. It's creepy and thrilling all at once.

That's the sensation I got when I heard about Barry Diller. One day he's there in the ultraviolet zone of the business spectrum, the next . . . he's executive vapor. "Barry Diller resigned today to pursue other interests," the radio announcer said. I was sitting at my desk eating a microwaved tuna melt. You could have knocked me over with a paperweight.

Then, right after, came the abrupt and brutal news about Nick Nicholas, hurled from the bosom of Time Warner with nary a voice raised in protest or defense. One moment the fine, crisp toast of the entertainment universe, the next, not.

I think of Rudy, my former boss. He started his career here with the hoopla and congratulatory fanfare all executives enjoy. He got new suits and shirts of overweening whiteness. He brushed his hair and shoes. He was fresh and new and full of ideas. By last March, it all was different. He had friends but no allies. He had power but no influence. One day, he was there. The next, he just . . . went home. Like a big, plump grape all sweaty and juicy on the vine, he hung around for a good long time and then . . . he just fell off. Plop. No more Rudy.

Too bad. So sad.

Executives, like packaged goods, have shelf lives. They begin their careers with all the promise and potential in the world, all shiny and tightly shrink-wrapped in their virgin duties and compensation packages. Their credenzas are organized and neatly stuffed with clear and present dangers and priorities. It's the sunrise of a new day. Then time passes, as it will insist on doing, and inexorably, subtly, the quality of their tenure changes. They are either too big or too small. Too hot or too cool. Too bland or too spicy. There are a hundred reasons why they melt down, blow up, float away, dozens of daily and specific pressures to blame. But the basic fact is obvious and inescapable: The executive has spoiled and must be tossed away.

Too bad. So sad.

There's no question about it: More executives are moldering faster these days than ever before. In this environment, it pays, I think, to assess which phase of spoilage yours is in. Is he a tender, fragile vegetable that the least breath of heat will turn to mush? A hunk of cured beef that could nourish the organization for decades before he turns too tangy to tango? How long will it take before he or she begins to turn a tad green around the edges and smell kind of funky?

Fresh and Neatly Packaged: The new executive is delivered to the store before it opens one morning and is signed for by middle management. The marketing begins almost immediately. "Fresh, tasty executive now on sale in aisle four!" says the news announcement issued upon his arrival. Everybody immediately happens by the department in question to take a peek and, possibly, a little taste for later consumption in the privacy of one's office. This first interface is very important, because if you look closely you can spot a tiny stamp in bright red, usually either behind the executive's ear or, sometimes, on the bottom of his hoof, that reads, Please Consume By . . . and gives a date. With bold, hard-driving, emotionally charged, and high-profile executives, this date can be no more than six months hence. With calmer, more phlegmatic types, the date can be so far down the line it's difficult to read. But watch for it. Take a moment to quietly feel the temperature of the aura he's putting out. The warmer the atmosphere he generates, the sooner he is likely to spoil.

Mature and Very Tasty: Once the executive is distributed throughout the corporation, and in some cases the industry community, he swings into his phase of maximum usage in which, as a product, he is at the apex of his value and appeal. A thoroughly utilized executive seldom putrefies. For a good long time in these early days the executive is likely to remain fresh by traveling in the open air quite a bit, which keeps his peel bright and shiny and his inner flesh tender and moist. Rudy, my late leader, spent long weeks on the road at the beginning of his term hobnobbing with the field troops, which made him easy to consume and enjoy at a local level. Unfortunately, he reached the acme of his allure at this time, far from the central marketplace of corporate headquarters, where interest in him as a commodity began to wane.

Starting to Turn: It begins with a whisper, a hint of something not quite . . . right. When the guy is in the room, people are careful still, sure, but when he's gone they speak more freely, and you notice they suddenly seem to get a tight, unpleasant crinkle going on just north of their upper lip, as if they're smelling something not altogether rancid, but certainly not overly appetizing. Then you begin to hear things. The guy is out of touch. The guy is "not getting it done." Senior management is dubious.

The product itself, under this gathering cloud, begins to perform in unexpected ways, and unanticipated behavior is anathema to business. Originally purchased, say, to scour mildew away and leave a gleaming, disinfected floor behind, it will suddenly start attempting to soften your hands while you do the dishes. A laudable goal! But not what the product was designed to do. Recently, for instance, Neutron Jack Welch of G.E., one of the prime authoritarian geniuses of American business, mandated that he, along with the rest of his senior people, must get "softer," more human, more collegial. Whether this is a complete product repositioning or the first signs of spoilage has yet to be seen.

Ready for the Platinum Dumpster: He still has the office. He's still got the green. But something's gone way cheesy, and it's not going to come back. Maybe it's a full-bore putsch being planned behind closed doors well out of his earshot. But not always. More often the product is simply underused, allowed to fulminate and rage in isolation. At the end, Rudy sat in his office and exchanged phone calls with friends, associates, tennis buddies. He spoke to his wife and children. He planned lunch. What did cross his desk he delegated, since by that time he considered even the most perfunctory use of his talents by the powers that be "complete and utter bullshit." He was right, of course. But that bullshit was his job. The moment that an executive cannot perform a complete and wide-ranging host of bullshit tasks, in fact, just might be the moment he's ready to be taken off the shelf.

Burial at Sea: Finally, the day does come when the product—limp, wasted, useless, and dangerous to touch—may be safely disposed of by the protectors of the public health. Maybe, like Nick Nicholas, the Taser is unleashed while the executive is on vacation and cannot easily punch somebody in the mouth by way of recompense. Maybe, as with Rudy, a gentlemanly and stately dance is done in which everybody walks away with their packaging refreshed, newly buffed, and straightened for the transition period. Maybe, as with a lot of Hollywood studio types, there is simply a very bad meeting that results in the horizontal ejection of the executive from the upper reaches of the corporate realm. However it happens, the deed is done. The executive's shelf life has run its course. A new executive is minted, bundled, and trundled out to meet the marketing squad. The old one, reeking slightly of some passionate and unseemly emotion, is gingerly removed for outplacement.

Too bad. So sad.

Except . . . I had lunch the other day at the current restaurant of choice for people who wish to be seen while they're eating. I had a seat near the door. Within fifteen minutes or so I saw a great number of very successful people whose faces are highly familiar and whose names you can almost think of, but not quite. I was halfway through my second roll when the door opened and in walked . . . Barry Diller. No kidding. Now, I've seen lots of celebrities in my time, and I'm old and jaded enough to keep my cool under almost every circumstance. But this was so sudden, so unexpected, that I lost it. I rose almost completely out of my seat and hollered to my lunch companion, "That's . . . Barry Diller!"

I'm afraid Mr. Diller heard me. He turned to my table, where I was cringing in embarrassment, rose to his full height, and flashed me that gap-toothed grin that made him one of the most feared and honored executives on the left coast. Then he moved on in a cloud of well-wishers, sycophants, and sleek-looking dudes.

"Yes," his grin told me in no uncertain terms. "I'm Barry Diller. That's more than a job. It's a concept. Can you dig it?"

Oh, yeah. I do. Up until then, I'd been kind of worried about the guy himself and, I guess, about the implications for all of us who execute for a living. Now I feel a whole lot better. I've got a nice red stamp behind my ear too, you know.

1992

The King Is Dead. Pass the Canapés.

So it happened again, as it always does. Just when you get to love the big guy, they take him out, pretty much without warning. Bang. Zoom. To the moon, Alice! It's always the best who die too soon—in addition to the worst, of course, who also die soon, but not soon enough.

So anyhow, they did it again, eliminated the one totally irreplaceable person in the organization, or so we thought. In this case it was my man Bob, who was truly beloved. I've seen them do it so damn many times before, you'd think I'd be ready for it, but I never am. There was Carl, my first serious dad, back in the 1980s, and then Chet, who was so good to me in ways both personal and financial, and now Bob, who took a chance on me when the stench of death hung around me like flies about a horse in summer. One day they're there, supporting my power structure like Atlas with the globe on his shoulders, except in a suit. The next, not. And it always socks me, pow, right in the kisser. That's business, they tell me.

And it is too. And how.

The true victims here, of course, are not the mountaineers who are pushed off their pinnacles or, just as often, fall of their own accord; it is we, the Sherpas who remain to strike the camps and start at the bottom one more time. Ours is by far a harder road than the one that leads directly to the beach, with two years of salary guaranteed and all options vested. Just look at the phases we must go through to get back to normalcy, if such a thing can be said to exist:

Shock. Vultures could have been circling around his vestibule, screeching, for months. I still wouldn't have seen it. This time I was summoned to an office upstairs, and my friend Foley, who's so senior he has to look down to look up, gave me the data. "Bob is leaving," he said. All the air left my body. My face got cold. The space around me reeled and spun, with little stars and birdies tweeting in it. My hairline (I still have one, by the way) frosted up. A million questions fermented in my brain. What did this mean for me, personally? Who did I report to? Where would Bob go? Would his murderers be punished? What did this mean for me, personally? How could I possibly give the upbeat speech to our distributors that was planned for the following week? Was my face showing too much? Who would be handling the distribution of stock options from here on in? What did this mean for me, personally?

Then, anger. I stood outside Foley's office, unable to walk to the elevator bank that would take me back down to where there was oxygen. I seethed. I raged. How could they do this to Bob? Bob, who represented pretty much 94 percent of all the laughs in our available universe. Bob, to whom we all owed so much, and for whom we would walk through fire over shards of glass! I went back to my desk and closed the door.

Denial. This phase centered, however briefly, on fruitless speculation about a variety of scenarios in which all would be well. Most of this took place very close to the formal announcement of the event, over cocktails. Cocktails help in the cultivation of denial, which is why they're so important in transitional settings where people's personas are in flux.

Fear followed shortly thereafter, manifesting itself as a grayness in the skin, a waxiness about the eyes, a trembly insufficiency in the jowl. Every meeting became a cause for concern. "I got a call from Mazerowsk," my friend Warnick confided in me as we sped from floor to floor on the way up one morning. "What do you suppose he wants?"

"I don't know," I said, feeling sorry for him. "It could be anything." And the hell of it was . . . it could. Who wants to work in that kind of environment? When you've got a meeting, you don't want it to be about anything. You want it to be about something, and to know in advance what that might be. Fortunately for Warnick, I was wrong. It wasn't about anything. It was about nothing, as usual.

Then came sadness. And that's the nub of it. Sure, the world was an emptier place without Bob, but the burbling fatuousness of everyday business flowed on. Forms were filled out. Coffee was reviled. New alliances were tentatively formed. I went to a very important meeting with lots of our best customers. Some were very good friends of Bob's. I was expecting them to be as outraged and inconsolable as I. And they were, too. For about, oh, ten minutes. Then the hors d'oeuvres came. And so the real casualty of Bob's departure was not Bob himself, but the conviction that loyalty, trust, and affection add up to something essential and irreplaceable. That is a hard concept to live without. But we were living without it, and very well, too. And that glimpse of the skull beneath the skin . . . wow. That was scary. I want to forget about that right away.

Hope. I'm going to! My new boss is a very nice guy. We're getting along great. He wants things to work. So do I. In fact, I never really noticed it before—but he's a great guy. We have an uncommon number of laughs per phone call, and I'm convinced he has my best interests at heart. Things could be a lot worse. I could be like Morphy or Breeland or Kurtz or Verblink, who don't know where they report and whose departments are being looked at by McKinsey! Oh, I still get flashes of Bob that pierce me to the bone. Bob at his desk, eating a sandwich. Bob staring at me across the space of a gigantic cocktail party and winking. Bob raging about all the fools and jerks and bozos we held in mutual disdain. Bob sitting with me in companionable silence, going over correspondence that could change the shape of the world. And it did. It changed the shape of my world. Thanks, Bob.

Ambition. You know, there are entire tracts of power left unoccupied by Bob's departure. It's clear that several individuals will be destabilized very soon by the fragile aspect of the situation. I could sop some of this stuff up and come out very nicely indeed. In fact, I don't mind the look of the organization chart at all, if you kind of look at it sideways and squint for a while. I don't know why I didn't consider this before. This could work out great!

Total amnesia. Now if you'll excuse me, I'm busier than a one-legged man at an ass-kicking contest. What was that we were talking about again?

1997

Dos and Don'ts for Big Dudes

I know you don't have a lot of time, so I'm going to cut the chatter and get to the point. You're big. You're very big. You have big things to think about and big things to do. It's been that way for a very long time, and by now, along with all you've gained, you've forgotten some important things:

1. A sense of your relative size in the universe, compared with trees, large motor vehicles, and other people
2. The reasons to engage in social interaction that doesn't have to do with getting your needs met. In fact, right now you could pretty much be defined not by who you are or what you've done, but rather by what you want that's not getting done the way you want it done at this point in time. Off with their heads!
3. How to behave, in general

Consequently, let's face it: You're rude. Nobody tells you you're rude, because your being rude is what people expect. You're big. You're huge. You're rude. That's the way things are supposed to be.

But it's not really so. As we move forward to the ultimate destination of our lives, which is not Scranton, the little niceties that tie one human being to another begin to loom. If you want to avoid the long slide down the slippery path to terminal incivility, eccentricity, and unmourned death, if you're serious about wanting to reclaim your human heritage, you can begin by adhering to the following simple principles:

Don't pretend to know who people are. The other day I ran into an ultrasenior officer of mine. It was clear two seconds into the conversation that he thought I might be either somebody else or nobody. He didn't handle it very well, staring at me with his mouth open and eyes agog, saying ah . . . ah . . . ah . . . and declining to introduce me to the young lady with whom he was lunching. "Hi, Wally," I said, and moved along. But my feelings were hurt. How much nicer it would have been if he had simply said, "I know we've met, like, fifty times, but the truth is, my brain is stuffed with too many thoughts about myself to remember other people very well. There's no reason we shouldn't try it again, though. So who are you?"

Do decline invitations to things you don't want to attend and at which you will be uncomfortable and frighten people. Not long ago I sat at a table with a guy who was too crucial to be there, eating bad steak and pretending to feel honorific about someone other than himself. He kept his dignity the whole time, even when the waiter took away a piece of pie that was actually on the way to his mouth, which is what you would pretty much expect at the Waldorf. How we would have laughed had he been one of us! How much more polite for him to have remained at home!

Do send a thank-you note for the suck-up present sent to you by some cringing wretch. A few years ago I sent a horrendously expensive fountain pen to an important senior officer in my company. Six weeks later his secretary called me and said, "Mr. Boorish wanted you to know he's using the pen." This made me feel bad about (1) Mr. Boorish, (2) his secretary, who insisted on being called his assistant, (3) myself, and (4) the $850 I spent on the pen. How much nicer it would have been to get a card, signed by her, that said, "I'm using the pen! Thanks! Mike Boorish." Instead, I hate him now and will push him down an open manhole if I get the chance.

Do allow other people to precede you into elevators. Most ultrasenior officers tend to walk head down to their next destination, blowing by others as if they were spume in the wind. It's nice to let other people feel that their progress through the world is important, too. And when you're in the elevator . . .

Don't forget to say hello to people. It's amazing what a hello from you can do for individuals who have small lives that aren't really progressing toward anything.

Do occasionally ask about other people's lives/interests/thoughts. You start by interrupting your stream of self-related conversation, pausing for a moment, then saying something like "And how are things with you?" They may be shocked, but eventually they will say, ". . . fine?" or the equivalent. Then you can ask them, well, anything about themselves, including (1) how they're enjoying the weather this season, (2) something about your local sporting franchise, (3) how their family is doing, or (4) something about golf.

Don't forget to listen to what they say! That way you can make an effort to remember a little part of it and refer back to it later. A little investment of concentration in this area goes a long way!

Do say please and thank you, even when you don't really have to. It works like this: Instead of saying something crude, like "Get out of here and don't come back until the third-quarter numbers work the way I want them to, you yutz," you would say, "Please get out of here and don't come back until the third-quarter numbers work the way I want them to. Thank you." Notice the difference? Sure you do!

Do use your knife and fork when you eat your food in front of people. You can use your teeth and hands when you're all by yourself, hopping around your palatial beachfront home on all fours in your loincloth, frothing at the mouth and munching on a leg of mutton. But when you're in polite society, use implements.

Don't yell at people with your mouth full. It's horrible when food falls out, particularly peas and corn mixed together.

Do wash your hands and face before coming to the table!

Don't torture that squirrel with that firecracker!

Don't take that other kid's bike! Get your own!

Don't hit little Johnny with that rock! Put it down!

Do try, each and every day, to make the world a more refined and cultivated place. You've done so much with your life already. This next step is important too—and it's up to you.

And if you fall off the wagon now and then . . .

Don't despair. Hey! The hell with other people anyhow! What do they mean, criticizing your style! It's what got you here! Why should you change it now? Screw 'em! Rude bastards! Politeness works both ways, you know!

Ah, good. You're back. What can I do for you now, sir?

1999

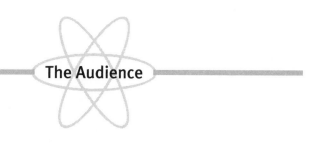

The Audience

Once upon a time, there was a fellow we will call Arnold, who had attained a position of some standing in the corporation and was satisfied with things in general.

"Look," he would say to himself in the mirror every morning. "I appear young and vigorous next to many of the bloated, wheezing fellows I ride next to on the train every day. I command a legion of troops. I can still see my toes without leaning over too far. I am making money. I am therefore relatively satisfied with things in general." And he did feel just that way a lot of the time.

Now, Arnold had a big job, and that meant he was very busy busy busy, e-mailing and retailing and meeting and greeting and selling and shilling and billing and buying and lunching, brunching, and munching, and of course managing all over the place, which left very little time for thinking about how he stood in the corporate hierarchy. That he mostly left to the prevailing winds. "I don't have time to waste on evaluating my standing in the infrastructure," he said to himself.

But one day he realized that it had been weeks since he had enjoyed more than a brief, perfunctory conversation with his boss, whom we shall call Hal. A little worm of disquiet hatched in his duodenum. Then he picked up the phone and dialed Hal, who resided in another building way across town.

"Hello," said Arnold to Kelly, Hal's assistant. "This is Arnold. I was wondering whether Hal is around, just to chat."

"I'll see," said Kelly. "So," thought Arnold, "he is there. And he will surely speak with me, his loyal and trusted subordinate with whom he has shared so much." Then, in the background, he heard Hal's distinctive voice, and it said, "I'll call him back."

"He'll call you back," Kelly said, and hung up.

"Okay," Arnold said into the dead receiver, and his heart shriveled up in his chest and in his head there was a lightness that made him want to lay his noggin on the blotter.

Where had he gone wrong? He had been so friendly with Hal! They had shared many meals, and drunk sambuca together on dozens of occasions, and there was a warmth between them that transcended the relationship between boss and subordinate. They were, in many ways, contemporaries, allies, and friends. Or so Arnold had thought. Now, well . . . perhaps things were not as he had believed them to be. Hmmm.

That afternoon he was unpleasant to several young people who depended on his counsel, good opinion, and affection. By 7 P.M., when it was obvious that Hal was indeed not going to return his phone call, he went to the train station. On the platform, he purchased a double portion of Absolut from the vendor.

Things went on this way for several weeks. Hal did, eventually, return Arnold's telephone messages. Of course he did. They conversed many times. But for some reason Arnold found these interfaces cold, rushed, and emotionally unsatisfying, and they served to deepen rather than assuage his feelings of confusion, melancholy, and hurt.

Often during that time he would lie awake at three in the morning and search his bosom for an answer. Had he done something wrong? Why this sudden exile from the kingdom? Had someone else come along to rob him of the love of his master? Was some dank political winding sheet being prepared for the carcass of his career?

After a while he stopped the phone calls to Hal altogether. "If he wants me, he will call me," thought Arnold with a small pout. And the silence between Arnold and his lord deepened, and he was filled with what can only be described as the grief that attends a lost love.

One day in the third month of this ordeal, Arnold was working very hard in his office, to all appearances an ultrasenior executive in the full flush of his power, confidence, and majesty. Inside, however, he was little more than a trembling mound of emotional jelly looking for a container to hold him. His telephone rang, and since his secretary had stepped away, he answered it himself.

"Hey, Arnold," said Hal on the other end of the line. "I'm upstairs in the boardroom for a couple of minutes. Could you come up and give me a hand with something?"

Arnold hung up the phone and stared out the window. In the next few minutes, all would be revealed. He went upstairs for his audience with Hal.

The boardroom was empty, except for his dread liege, who stood in imposing silence at the end of a gigantic teakwood table.

"Come over here, will ya?" said Hal. He was looking at two objects, one in each hand.

"Yes, Hal," said Arnold, and approached.

"Which do you think looks better with this shirt?" said Hal. "I've got this big dinner with Armbruster & Finch and I have one of these blue pinstriped shirts on, and I dunno, I can't tell whether I should go with the striped club tie or the solid blue from Tiffany's. . . ." He held out two neckties with a look of complete befuddlement on his face.

"Gee, Hal," said Arnold, taking the ties and looking them over. "I like this one." He held out the club tie.

"Okay," said Hal. "Then I'll take the other one!" He cracked up, slammed Arnold on the shoulder, and began to put on the blue cravat. "I haven't seen you in a dog's age, man," he added, as an afterthought. "How you hangin'?"

"A little low and to the right," said Arnold. Then both men laughed altogether too loudly.

"We gotta have lunch sometime soon, but now I gotta run." Hal had walked to the door of the boardroom, his arm around his executive serf. "Kelly!"

Kelly came around the corner holding a topcoat and an umbrella. She seemed enormously happy to see Arnold, and in fact put an arm around his shoulder and kissed his cheek. Then she whisked Hal into the elevator and off the floor.

Arnold went back to his office, closed his door, and poured himself a small dose of the single-malt Scotch he kept in the bottom drawer of his desk for just such an intellectual emergency. "The whole thing was about nothing!" he said to himself in amazement. "Nothing! It was all . . . in my mind! Nowhere else! He's in the middle of his life and his world and he hasn't thought a bit about me! God, what a jerk I am!" And an overwhelming flood of love and relief swept over him for the man he was bound to serve. And as far as we know, that feeling lodges there still.

Nowadays, when Hal calls, our friend Arnold is a very happy man. And when that call does not come? He's still a little sad; but he doesn't lose sleep about the situation anymore. "Like the man said," he tells himself, "it's business. It's not personal." And then he goes home to his wife, his children, and his dog, who pretty much always comes when he calls.

2001

Nothing at the top

There are many mysteries that haunt the universe. Like, what ever happened to global warming? Why does our stock always go down after a great earnings report? How many CFOs does it take to repurpose a lightbulb?

But the greatest mystery in our world today is Murray. I'm going to call him Murray, although that is not really his name. He doesn't need a name. He's nobody. He's also, perhaps, your CEO.

I'm mentioning this because just today I saw Murray in the newspaper. He's just been named to a top job at one of the biggest corporations in the world. So I guess he'll have to put on his nice suit and start looking executive again. He can do that. That's all he does, but it's a lot. Very few people can do it. Why?

And why is only the beginning. There are many questions to ask about Murray. Here are a few:

1. What qualifications does Murray possess that enable him constantly to nab top slots wherever he places his chair? He clearly knows nothing more about business than any average employee.
2. Does he have a record of success?
3. Could he possibly be as empty as he looks? And, finally . . .
4. How does this happen? How does an idiot, at least in the business sense, become the highest officer in the company?

Suggested answers:

1. None. Murray has no qualifications other than a lifetime of meandering about looking quizzical. His one possible talent is finding tough, vicious operatives to do the actual work. I have sat with him many times in meetings. Often he has appeared on the verge of sleep. Sometimes he launches into per visionary hobbyhorses unrelated to the subject at hand. One has the sensation of a vast cloud of unknowing at the end of the table, unless it is a round table that has no end.
2. No. Each time Murray actually has to perform an executive function, as opposed to simply wearing a suit, he is replaced, departing with a load of billion. Think of the Presidents of the U.S. They were men of action and resolve. And then there was Millard Fillmore. Chester Allan Arthur. William Howard Taft. Calvin Coolidge. George H.W. Bush. Murray is one of those.
3. Yes. The winds of the Kalahari sing in his cranium. That is not to say he is stupid. He may, in fact, be too intelligent to be smart. Perhaps he has rock music whipping around in the space between his ears, or the voice of Allah, or an enthusiasm for model trains, or, more tragically, new media. He has no ideas concerning sales, marketing, production, or the management of people. Those things he leaves to others.
4. Ah, that is the question. And it is asked over and over again, literally. After each meeting with Murray, people stand around and say to each other, "How did he get his job?"

The easy answer is that your board of directors, torn by ignorance and indecision, selected Murray because he'd had the top job before some place and was so vague and insubstantial during the selection process that nobody could quite believe he was nobody at all. So they elected him, because they saw in him what they wanted to see.

But that's only part of it. A few months ago I was wandering around downtown, looking for a place to have a drink. The downtown area of my city is a place where all the loose marbles go to roll around, particularly in the evening. I noticed a guy strolling toward me. He was short and a little bony, with a big frond of hair popping out from under a corduroy cap that would have been appropriate on a person a third his age, for this fellow was darn near sixty. Over his shoulder was a student's backpack with, I noticed, a book and a bottle of wine popping out of it.

"Hey, Bing," said this rather unprepossessing person. "Hi, Murray," I said. "What you up to?"

"Nothing much," said Murray. "A little consulting work."

We shook hands and went on our way. I watched him go. This was not the Murray I knew, the man in pinstripes with a perpetually thoughtful expression that meant exactly nothing. This was another Murray. Which Murray? What was Murray? Was there a Murray at all? And was it not, ladies and gentlemen, this very lack of a coherent self that was the secret both of Murray's mystery and his success?

I'd like to wish good luck to Murray's new corporation, and to the people who work for it. I read the announcement in the *Wall Street Journal,* and it looks as if they made the right decision. Who knows? A person with no ideas may be no more more dangerous than one with a bunch of bad ones.

Nature may abhor a vacuum, but in business a whole lot of nothing may be the most appropriate thing indeed.

2003

LATTE BREAK

What's Your EQ?

It's clear that while all men are strange, some are permitted to be stranger than others. One guy gets the ice pick because he refuses to eliminate the doggie photos from his desktop, while another wipes the halls with his drooling psyche and gets away with it.

On the one hand, there are the dead, guys like my friend Jim, who appeared one morning fresh from Syracuse with a beard like a muskmelon and boots that squelched with the ancient mud of the Adirondacks. And Herb, who liked to wear a baseball cap at his desk and do magic tricks. And even our former chairman, who, many feel, was ousted because he insisted on drinking yam juice at board meetings while his peers stoked their maws with firewater.

Sure they were weird, the departed, but any more so than Les, our current financial officer, who bedecks his office with miniature clocks? Or Roland, V.P. Management Information, who sports a pocket protector and the ultimate sartorial pariah—short-sleeved shirts—even in winter? Just how free to be me you can actually be is determined by a phalanx of personal variables: money, power, age, and the likelihood of retribution, to name just a few. And for those of us dedicated to the unfettered expression of personal idiosyncrasy, the issue is critical.

As a service, then, we present the Bing Eccentricity Quotient (BEQ), a scientific means of determining the flagrancy of your personal style. The higher your BEQ, the more obviously eccentric you are permitted to be in matters of costume, hair, profanity, work schedule, and bad habits. To find your number, employ this equation:

$$BEQ = \frac{\$ \times P \times NF^2}{A}$$

$$!\&*? \times (CEO + R)$$

It's simple. Just estimate the variables on a scale of one to ten, except where noted. And be forthright. One error in this rigorous exercise and you're likely to be gone, leaving behind but a few souls to muse, "I wonder what ever happened to that weird guy in Purchasing who used to suck his teeth?"

Money (\$). Per annum, in thousands. "It's the biggest factor in acceptability," states my pal Wally, a young CEO. "You take an eccentric homeless person and everyone wants to cart him off, but give that same guy a cool million and he can't keep up with his social obligations."

Power (P). The further you are from the bump and grind, the more bizarre you can be. Last summer, for instance, the president of the United States was considered to be back to normal (by Republicans) when he resumed telling inane anecdotes and doodling pictures of cowboys.

Age (A). In years.

Nonfungibility Squared (NF²). All men are replaceable, sure, but a guy who can tango is worth a roomful of lumpfish. "A lot of leeway is created by the inherent assumption that 'I am creative,' " states my friend Arnie, an ad wizard. "There's an understanding that we're out of control, and kind of have to be in order to do a good job."

Outside Interface (!&*?). The license to wave your tiny freak flag high is offset by the negative vibes it may create in tight sphincters outside the commonweal.

Chance of Trouble with Big Wazirs (CEO). Only the very weak and the very strong are immune from executive payback. "It's the mid-level people who have no fun at all," says my buddy Dworkin. "The guy in the mail room does impressions and the boss loves him a lot, but he doesn't like that kind of behavior from his own guys, who are entrusted with the bottom line. I see why. You wouldn't want to go into a bank and see the loan officer walking on stilts, would you?"

Rigidity of Culture (R). Even the tastiest kilt is sure to raise an eyebrow in a serge environment.

Now let's take a test drive where it counts:

You and Me. Okay. Let's assume we make 50K per year. As middle managers, our Power number hovers around 5, which is pretty good, since we're only thirty-five years old. We're only slightly unique, though, so our nonfungibility factor is no more than 6. My work brings me into onerous contact with life outside, so I'm going to give myself a !&*? Exposure of 8, with a moderate Wazir danger (6) within our relatively rigid corporate culture (7). Thusly:

$$BEQ = \frac{\underline{50} \times 5 \times 36}{35}$$

$$8 \times (6 + 7)$$

Giving me a BEQ of 2.5, which allows me to wear brown on alternate Tuesdays and listen to a little heavy metal with my door closed.

The Big Wheeze. He makes 300K a year, with a power number of 9. He is fifty, and cannot be replaced. Insulated by layers of humanity from all but the most potent alien Tatars, his !&*? factor is 3, with virtually no chance of getting into trouble with himself (0). That puts his BEQ at 257.1, meaning the dude could skin weasels at his desk and still clip coupons into the next century.

One last thing: not all issues are amenable to scientific control, or should be. My friend Lenny, a producer of industrial entertainments for a huge enterprise, cuts an odd profile. Skip the jeans and work shirts, they're not the issue. It's his hair—a frizzy blond aureole that swoops boldly away from his pate like a condor's wingspan. Not long ago, he was called into his boss's office and politely asked to prune his fronds. "I'm an ornery devil," Lenny snorts. "And if I get a haircut, it'll be because I need one, not for any motivation to rise up."

This was no simple finger in the air, but something very close to the bone. "If that's what it takes to get ahead, maybe I don't want to," he says now. "I've done a lot of soul-searching, and if doing my job isn't enough, if falling into line is more important, I don't know if I'm constitutionally capable of doing it. It would somehow symbolically say to me that they own my soul."

That's a price no man should pay, no matter what. Self-respect is nonfungible, too.

1987

4

TALES FROM THE POLITICAL CRYPT

In business, politics is the art by which people work together to achieve their individual selfish ends. These can also coincide with the best interest of the company, by the way, so it's not necessarily a bad thing. And it's not that different than what goes on in the halls of government. We even have those guys with the huge helmets of white hair.

The range of goofy people who are thrown together in pursuit of political advantage in business is quite impressive. To master the intricacies of political life, one must learn to work with querulous accountants, blustery sales executives, hostile, paranoid potentates, the nimble, the mealy, the halt, and the lame. The better you are at it, the more control you'll end up having over the uncontrollable.

You will notice that a lot of the necessity for corporate politics in these pages is generated by the constant atmosphere of merger, acquisition, divestiture, and obnoxious change that characterizes the contemporary American corporation. In stable organizations with strong leadership, there is a minimum of infighting, inveigling, and backroom bushwah.

Politics only blossoms in rotten cornices. Soft executive wood produces hundreds of wormholes which, quite naturally, attract worms. In such an environment, only the stupid are apolitical. And politics, it turns out, is not appreciably different than normal strategic thinking. It's just a slightly less moral, more solitary exercise. Those can be fun, right?

Is There Life after Merger?

First rumors of our pending acquisition swept through the office like an ill wind carrying with it a dry silt of fear and the chill of mortality. As always, Marilyn, our department secretary, heard it first. Strangers in dark blue suits with intimations of pinstripe had been seen in heavy confab on the sixty-first floor. Meetings had stretched into the bleak and tiny hours, and there had been no food. And no drink. That certainly wasn't our corporate culture calling the shots.

"It's a merger," said Marilyn one morning in a minuscule whisper that barely cleared her Rolodex. "You know what that means."

We didn't. On the one hand, the official pronouncement on our new status was downright encouraging. "We've acquired you folks because we think you're great, with great products and great people," said the chairman of our new Parent. "We anticipate no major changes and look forward to working with all of you as new members of our large and happy family." On the other hand, we were dubious. An assortment of new and serious faces had already appeared, and a stream of appointment announcements began coursing from the public relations department. Soon, many departments had more than one vice president, one of whom—the former—was clearly redundant. As one executive put it, "It's their toy now and they have every right to play with it. But I'm going to put my résumé on the Wang immediately, and I advise you to do the same."

This turned out to be solid advice. Today, fewer than 10 percent of us are part of the old company. Those departed include our former chairman—flushed from the corporate mythology as completely as Trotsky from the minds of all good Russians—and 90 percent of his team, officers of the corporation one and all. Many still roam the mysterious and dimly lit twenty-third floor, where they all have phones, and business cards, and windows to fall out of.

As mergers become pandemic in every business from oil to electronics, with immense corporate entities swallowing up small undervalued ones like pigs-in-blankets, it may be useful to look at steps some have found successful in staying afloat. For those with ambition, a merger doesn't have to be a disaster; it can present an opportunity to ascend very fast, usually over the backs of those who are less resilient, determined, or fortunate.

Your first move is to evaluate the new corporate culture, starting with the dress code. For the most part, we had dressed in brown, green, and other vegetable colors. They were cool, elemental, in dark blue or gray, with shirts that glistened under the high-intensity track lighting and ties that sported a hint of polka dot as subtle as goosebumps. Our desks were piled high with paper; you could bounce a quarter off theirs. We passed memos on every conceivable subject, distributing copious interoffice duplicates; they favored brief, informal chats and friendly little jottings that left no trace. It was clear that those of us who wanted to hang in there would have to acquire the new culture and wear it publicly, even ostentatiously, right away.

One colleague reports that, after a meeting with the newly appointed president of his division, he phoned his wife with a request to run straight down to Madison Avenue to pick up seven white shirts, all with the necessary sheen, all with stays, not buttons; that same week, he bought three identical suits . . . all in gray pinstripe. He's still alive, as are many of those who moved quickly to blend into the official ambience. The issue is belonging, which is what you're trying to continue doing.

Once you've got the outfit, you'll want to begin making friends with your new Parent. This won't be hard. Most of the new people will be very nice—cheerful, excited to be in a new venture, a new city, anxious to be liked—in short, a lot more fun to be with than the sad and fearful hutch of enraged rabbits your old friends have become. You may have to be glib upon occasion. It might not come naturally for you to lean into the meticulous office of some hardworking grind and spew forth good fellowship. (A tiny tip: hobbies are a good door opener. The more elevated the executive, the more entranced he usually is with his antique guns, boats in bottles, boats out of bottles, toy banks, prune farming, name it.)

But the best way to seep into the heart of your new Parent is through good old-fashioned labor. Become indispensable. In the first days of our merger the word came down from our Houston headquarters to get lean. In response, an all-day meeting was held on the sixty-first floor. Each executive was asked to bring a hit list of personnel he or she would not require if push came to shove, which it had. Late in the grim convocation, our new chairman turned to a vice president and asked, "What about Betty Barker? She earns a management-level salary." The vice president, quick-thinking and loyal to his subordinate, replied, "Yes, Jack, but she's working on the Omaha project, and that still has priority around here, doesn't it?" There was a thoughtful silence. "I'll tell you what," the chairman said. "Let her finish that project, then we'll fire her." Everyone shared a hearty corporate laugh over that. Two years later the Omaha project is still going strong, and consequently Betty retains her title and function. Like the rest of us, she's also a lot safer now, having lived through the first bloody wave of executions.

Those of us who remain remember the departed every now and then. Most of them hate our guts, and that hurts. But we don't spend too much time looking back. Something might be gaining on us. We belong to the conquered, and this social inferiority gives us a tremendous edge over the others in our mutual drive to achieve Excellence, or Innovation, or whatever's in vogue this year, because we've learned to run a little faster. Yes, it was hard to watch buddy after buddy being cut loose to twist in the wind. But we had a mission, too, and it didn't involve leaving. We had to do our jobs well, keep our sanity, and in the meantime preserve whatever was left of the old, haimisher, entrepreneurial Company we loved. We met the enemy, and we are now some of them.

1985

The Care and Feeding of Jerks

It was one of the really bad mornings. Nothing but superior Wang work and a little bit of luck kept me from going down to street level and laughing at the ground by 10 A.M. That's when my boss, Ted, buzzed me on the intercom, as was his wont. "Could you come in here for a minute?" he said, and he hung up before I could answer. Bad sign, I thought. Ted's going to be a jerk again.

I entered his office steeled for the worst. "You hole-punched these documents," said Ted, brandishing the evidence. "I want them stapled." A forty-minute job for my staff. Though Ted was just flexing his muscles, I couldn't help but feel a little sick, and nostalgic too. It brought back fragrant memories of great jerks I have known: Alex, who inhaled other people's ideas, repackaged them, and sold them as his own; Cecile, who always looked like she was smelling something terrible, with a tongue that made hardened secretaries weep; Herb, who fired people while they were away on vacation.

A jerk mixes business with neurosis. Unchecked, he or she can stop you cold, blocking projects through inaction or sabotage, squabbling over turf like a toddler, grabbing credit, shuffling blame. The species come in all sizes, and each must be neutralized with a different strategy.

Dolts are dense jerks who clot activity. Sadly, doltish behavior is not limited to the unintelligent; it also afflicts the proud, whose brains get stupefied by self-importance. Some friends of mine at a direct-sales organization had to sell a pilot project to a field director not interested in listening to much of anything. They wooed him with zeal unknown since Cyrano schmoozed Roxanne: flew to his office in Fresno; presented him with copious spreadsheets and cute slide shows; offered him beer, wine, and sangria; and, when all failed, begged. The dolt was still mystified by the speculative project, but liked the attention, became a wary ally, and now hopes to get his share of credit when the long-term picture turns into short-term revenue.

Strategy: Invest time in dolts, suffer them gladly, and they'll reward you with a stupid kind of loyalty that is just as useful as the more elevated sort.

Schmucks are obnoxious jerks. They see you as a minor player in the vast and glorious saga that is their life, and they'll steamroll you if you're not twice the schmuck they are. My good friend Gary, a public relations man at an advertising agency, once found himself working next to a new guy named Walter, a prodigious schmuck with a Wagnerian sense of destiny. One day, when the vice president was out sick, Walter exited his office in full three-piece regalia, summoned the entire department, and ceremoniously announced: "While Bob is out, I'm in charge here. Make no decision without consulting me." The staff was agape: Walter had no authority whatsoever. "Who does he think he is, Alexander Haig?" sneered a secretary. Gary didn't waste his breath on showdowns, he simply phoned Bob at home. "Walter just seized control of the department," he reported. "Put the schmuck on the line," said the weary veep. Walter emerged from his office some time later, red as the rump of a mandarin ape, and spent an extended session in the men's room.

Strategy: Be good-natured when you can, but if a schmuck starts pulling your chain, don't hesitate to cuff him briskly about the head and ears. Yelling works; so does excluding them from meetings and tweaking them in public documents. Subterfuge is also good. A schmuck deeply respects people who are willing to dish out the abuse he deserves.

SOBs are mean jerks. They hate folks who have good ideas and lots of energy, because they have neither and they know it. At a midtown design firm, everyone avoids dealing with Fritz, the creative director, according to my friend Ken. "It's accepted that Fritz is pathologically crazy," says Ken, an illustrator. "When he wants to refuse you something—which is always—he looks at you with a smarmy expression and screams, 'You know nothing! You're not creative director! I am! Get out!' I've seen people break down and cry." Ken gets along with Fritz all right, though, because he tolerates no tantrums. When Fritz is in a snit, Ken just says, "I'll come back later when you're feeling more rational," turns on his heel, and leaves the room. Fritz, abashed, quiets down. "You've got to choose your battles, evaluate just how much you want something, then go at him," Ken advises. "And if necessary, you have to say, 'Fritz, I'm not here to talk about the fact that you don't like my face. I'm here to work.' "

Strategy: Steer clear of altercations with SOBs and don't be queasy about showing some respect, which costs little but the effort at dissimulation and may gain you much in goodwill. When seriously abused, however, give as good as you get. SOBs are bullies who enjoy riding only those who do not buck them off. And don't be surprised when your tough response, instead of generating additional hostilities, plants seeds of future friendship. SOBs are most at home with one another. Convince him you're one of the noxious gang, and you're home free.

Weasels are ambitious and resolutely political, and they'll get you if you don't watch out because they are after you personally. A friend named Jack, an editor at a national magazine, found many of his stories being blocked by a guy named Barry, a peer who, in his prowl for prestige and power, had targeted Jack as a threat. A civilized man, Jack didn't warm to the contest. He worked to keep things cordial, to rise above the muck and goo of hand-to-hand combat. As Barry's cachet grew, however, the number of people willing to grapple with him withered, and Jack found himself isolated, nonviable. Finally, tired of the backstage swordplay, he left for the open vistas of freelance journalism. "I tried to be a gentleman about it," he now remembers, "and that was a big mistake. I should have gone straight for his throat."

Strategy: Tear out his entrails and let them dry in the sun.

1985

How I Got My New Chair

I got my first chair when Ronald Reagan was a crisp young beaver of seventy and both of us had a full head of hair. The real-estate market was a huge gasbag that had nowhere to go but up. Debt was a good thing you couldn't get too much of. So was sex. Goat cheese had yet to be invented. Iraq was our valued ally. My department included four managers, fourteen associates and assorted niche droids (including li'l tiny me), and two secretaries. One worked very hard and was destined for promotion. The other couldn't type, drowned our correspondence in cream cheese, coffee, and mustard, cried at her desk, and forced herself to barf after eating. The former is now slaving away as a low-level administrator in an insurance company in the Midwest. The latter is a senior vice president at the largest fashion concern of its type in the world. Me, I'm still here.

A lot has changed, though. My old steel desk was replaced with genuine oak a couple of years back. My window started off with a terrible view of the eighth floor of some grim obelisk opposite mine filled with people in inexpensive business garb laboring over cathode-ray tubes. It now sports a vista of our entire metropolis, two rivers, and three states. I had a typewriter back then. Now I have a computer that plays mahjongg by itself if I want it to.

And then there is my chair. It was present, crouched and waiting, when I came in that very first day back in 1981. I remember thinking it was comfortable. It was white, made out of some fire-retardant, ersatztweedy Herculon stuff, with tough plastic-and-chrome arms and a three-legged rolling understructure on ball bearings. It was wide and sturdy enough to hold a substantial attractive man without indulging in any embarrassing groaning or creaking, and its back rose to about mid-lumbar level, not pompously higher. Add the ability to swivel easily into a feet-on-the-desk reclining position, and it was the best chair I'd ever possessed. Which was a good thing, since I figure I've spent a minimum of twenty-five thousand hours in it since its base first met my butt.

Recently, however, I realized that if I were to continue to exist on this planet as a man, my old chair had to go. Sometimes, you know, the veil of everyday perception falls away, and you see things as they are. This is both great and terrible. Here is what I saw when, half-asleep one morning at 7:42, with coffee in hand, I stared with suddenly fresh eyes—and saw my hair.

The seat where my fundament rested day after day had turned a dim, charcoal gray—a kind of schmutzy, dim, worn drear that evoked all things dead and irretrievable. The fabric had begun to frizz and pill. The shape of the seat was disconcertingly molded to the form of my buttocks. Actually both. The back rose up in the original color and consistency, sort of evoking nicely cooked oatmeal. But at the top of the rise, where my neck had rested for a decade, the color once again changed to a smoky charcoal. The poor, aged arms were eroded from three thousand days of continuous use; fifteen thousand papers covered with newsprint, perhaps a million pages of documents whose ink—as well as problems, notions, and moral implications—had come off on my hands. I took a look at that chair and it was a toss-up whether I was going to gag or cry. I'm a hitter. A hitter doesn't sit in a chair like that.

And yet . . . A chair is a stupid thing. Especially now. Many, many people have gone screaming out of the corporation, and many more will fall before this economic recovery is all over. Things lost: two guys out of the mail room, six vice presidents, fourteen managers, nine secretaries, eight coffee machines, the cable TV and piped music service that used to be wired into headquarters, four floors of office space, one conference room, the audiovisual suite, a coat closet that now must hold the local area network, the daily office-cleaning service, the in-house messengers, Leo and Paul, who have been placed with a large, out-of-house messenger firm that pays them three dollars an hour less, then contracts them back to us for the same work. So far it hasn't been necessary to abolish lunch. But that will soon happen. Lunch isn't necessary either. It's only essential. Pretty soon we'll have to make do without the essential. After that, can the necessary be far behind?

So anyhow, I had to have this chair. And getting it in this environment would be an exercise in pure personal politics.

I began at the beginning: selection. I knew what I wanted. My friend Wysocki down the hall was sitting in it at that moment. A couple of months ago our corporate purchasing vice president, Rolm, was heaved kicking and hollering out the sixty-fifth-floor window. He took with him his laptop, his files, his Electrodex, his windup toys, his laminated plaques for excellence. He could not, however, get the $3,400 leather chair past building security. One fine day Wysocki, in an act of supreme corporate initiative, simply strolled into Rolm's former office, laid hands on the executive's personal seat, and simply wheeled it into his office. Brilliant. Wysocki's chair was deep-mahogany cowhide with a burnished sheen and grommets the size and consistency of ripe plums. In short, this wasn't a chair; it was a proclamation of viability and magnitude. A man could cut paper dolls in that chair and look important. Since Wysocki didn't seem to be going anywhere, I wanted one just like it.

"Do you happen to have the paper on Rolm's chair?" I asked him.

"My chair, you mean," said Wysocki, rooting around and coming up with a slim packet. "I found this taped underneath." Inside was a brochure detailing care of the fine, Corinthian leather and a small, yellow purchase order. At the bottom of the document was a scrawl that read: R. Studtz.

This was extraordinarily bad news. Dick Studtz was responsible for headquarters's capital outlay. Studtz hates me, and the feeling has always been mutual. It's not personal. We simply loathe everything the other stands for. No matter how hot it is on May 14, he won't turn on the air-conditioning until June 1. If one should want a very special subordinate to receive a 4.2 percent wage increase, Studtz will hold you to the mandated 4 percent max. What would he say about a $3,400 chair?

I entered Studtz's chamber to find him chomping on an unbuttered corn muffin, brought, I knew, from home, since at some point early in his career I believe Studtz had a brown paper bag surgically implanted in his fist. "I wanted to see you anyhow," he muttered, crumbs dribbling from one side of his mouth. Although it was a beautiful day outside his picture windows, he had the blinds closed, his fluorescents blazing. He took a big sip of black coffee. "I have to assemble a financial quantification of the value of this department's function," he said suddenly, and I knew the words were being ripped out of his craw. This was unbelievable. Studtz was asking for my help. Things must really be funky indeed.

"How would you go about doing it, Dick," I asked, trying not to giggle.

"I guess we should probably take a look at how much my group's services would run the corporation were we forced to go outside for like functions," he said, deathly pale.

"Okay," I said. "I can do that."

"Was there something you wanted to see me about?" he said.

"I just needed you to sign this purchase order," I said, slipping it in triplicate without further comment beneath his nose, which was running slightly.

"This is outrageous," he observed quietly. "You can't expect me to approve this."

"I don't, actually, Dick. But if Ron Lemur signed off on it first?" Lemur is his boss.

"Lemur? Well . . . sure, I guess."

I turned to leave.

"And Bing. Make those numbers look good. It's . . . critical."

I left. In a decaying environment, virtually anything is possible.

Ron Lemur is a nice guy and one of my very best friends. He was at his desk, staring out the window, watching the ships roll in from upriver. "You really don't need this thing," he said, leaning back in his high-backed leather chair. "Do you?"

"No," I said. "But I want it. Don't give me a hard time on this, Ron."

"Can't you get Studtz to sign off on it?"

"No, Ron, not without you to do it first."

"I see."

There was a quiet time then. In the air hung all the people who would not be with us next year. They were sort of jammed together, complaining and moaning, wagging their fingers in Lemur's face. On the other side of the desk, battling them for space, were a horde of duties and favors done for Lemur over the years, meals taken, drinks poured together, shared time at adjacent urinals in a dozen different towns, hopes for growth and wild success that, even when they were not realized, coalesced into a body of common dreams.

Lemur sighed. "You're a pisser," he said.

Right now I am sitting in my chair. It's mighty comfy. The arms encircle me. The smell of new leather makes me kind of giddy. It's a good feeling: domestic, cozy, secure. If I lived here, I'd be home now.

So it was worth it. This morning, I heard a rumor from a couple of security analysts who called to suck around the fringes of reality, as they like to do. It seems our parent corporation, loaded down with debt like everyone else, is looking at our assets for possible dispensation. And that, friends, portends the end of the world.

I have this dream: One day, in the not-too-distant future, a visitor comes to the sixty-sixth floor of this office tower. The elevators open on a cavernous space. The walls have been torn down. Loose paper and dust kitties roll in the vast, empty grotto where once a business flourished. No phones ring, because there are none. There is no smell of coffee, for there are no people left to drink it. And in the lunar landscape that was once our flourishing company, stashed in a corner somewhere, is a chair. Sitting. Waiting to be brought to life by the right, living resident.

Some things endure. Those things are magic. If, when it's all over, we can say we've left our share of those objects behind, I figure we've done our jobs.

Can a man do more?

1992

The Thing

You get complacent. You think it can't happen here, or there, or anywhere you hang your hair. But nobody is safe. It can befall the best of us, the safest and most stable of operations, if any still exist. It arrives one day without fanfare, and it takes root in some place that is fertile and moist—like under the uvula of the guy down the hall, maybe—and grows, that's all. "Have you heard about the Denver thing?" says Nofziger in Corporate Finance while he's shaking off in the executive washroom. And you don't know what he means, really, but you know it's enormously important, something you've got to love, got to love or die. Because it's the new Thing. "We're moving in on that Blunt thing," says Beaver in Accounting as he spoons some kiwi onto his plate at the senior-management breakfast, and you know he's talking about a shift in strategic direction that will result in total upheaval to no good end.

That's right. The Thing we're talking about is the really enormous stupid idea that eats all life as we know it. We had one here a few years ago that started as a Quality Circle and evolved into a full-sized new fascist order, but we killed it by chopping it into body parts and carting those off to be buried in committees. It happened at my pal Bork's corporation, a huge publishing company, when first one, then two, then the entire senior-management structure decided to move their whole work-force out of New York . . . to Dallas. Six hundred lives uprooted at a cost of nearly $50 million . . . and for what? Because, for a time, it was their Thing. They killed that Thing, too, by the way, suffocated it with paper.

But the idiot Thing seldom dies easy. Because it's strong and persuasive. And once it's got you, well . . .

You're got. And now—forgive my hand from trembling as I write this—it's happened here. The Thing is at my door right now, sucking at the keyhole to be let in.

It came in the spring of last year. We didn't know it had arrived, but it had, tiny and embryonic, in a pod from another corporation that entered Nagle, our controller, through his capacious nose at an industry luncheon at which he occupied a seat next to a mergers-and-acquisitions broker who was crawling with a variety of incipient conceptual monsters.

I dropped by to see Nagle one morning and noticed the Thing immediately. It was sticking one tiny tentacle out of his ear. As I watched, a small, febrile eyestalk poked inquiringly from behind the fringe of hair just above his collar. "Have you heard about the Baltimore thing?" said Nagle. The eyestalk had migrated all the way to the front of his tie and was looking me over curiously—with, I thought, some hostility. As I stared it down, it gave me a long, oozy, ironic wink.

"No," I said, trying to beat down my gorge as it rose unbidden into the back of my throat. Didn't Nagle see this . . . creature . . . that had seized control of his person?

"Well, the idea is this," he said as the rest of the Thing emerged from his ear and slid quietly down the back of his pants. "We trade all of our distribution assets, our line operations, trucking division, direct sales, advertising and marketing operations, for a controlling position in the Willy Wallaby White Water theme parks!"

And there it was. The Thing I had been dreading. The big, dumb play that is so attractive in the deep, dark doldrums of the 1990s, that replaces boring, old humdrum business with something new, loud, bold, plaid. We had been in a small partnership with the Willy Wallaby people for some time, but the strategic move into this type of activity had always been only a rumor, never an actual proposal.

Nagle opened his mouth again, but instead of his pink little tongue the head of the Thing itself poked out from between his teeth. "There's a cable-network play attached to this, a possible theatrical-motion-picture tie-in, and a lot of potential downstream revenue," said the face of the Thing that protruded from Nagle's mouth. "A lot of key people are already for it big-time because it represents a move out of single-digit entropy into an almost unrestricted high-growth sector. Take my word for it, Bing. If you're not on the bus"—the voice suddenly strobed down to a deep, unctuous bass—"you're off it, dude."

I fled from Nagle's office then, before he could invite me to a lunch, this time not one at which I would be eating but at which I would be eaten.

To listen to the Thing too much is to lose yourself to it.

I went to my office and tried to phone several friends in the field. These Things never grow in the field much. They grow at headquarters, where the climate is full of material that suits the task of fertilization. The phone, of course, was dead. I looked at the receiver and saw that a substance that looked like the skin on week-old Jell-O was extruding from it. Then it rang. The sound was mucilaginous, distant.

"Could you come up here for a minute, Bing?" said a voice I hardly recognized. "I want to talk to you about a Thing that's come up." It was Walt, but he sounded clotted in some way. Furtive. But infused with a kind of infantile excitement that I had never heard from him.

"Sure, Walt," I said. I went up the interfloor stairwell, which seemed to be filled with the husk of something that, in growing to gargantuan size, had molted. I had to step over enormous coils of this crusty, dead material to reach the landing on forty-five, where I encountered several of my fellow vice presidents drinking coffee in the complimentary amenities bar. Each of them looked pretty much normal, except that they were tied together by a gigantic umbilical cord, dotted with suction cups, that emerged from the area near each one's belt buckle and wove on to the next. Being a brownish gray, it went quite nicely with their suits, except for Lazenby's, but he was wearing that loathsome dark green polyester he likes so much, so I guess it served him right.

"Come closer and look at these out-year projections," said one, but I could not tell which one.

"I don't want to see them!" I screamed, staggering backward down the hall.

Walt was standing in his office, looking over the city skyline miles below his window. Next to him was a large mount of doppled, gelatinous flesh that, every now and then, popped a burbling bubble to its surface. The Thing had virtually enclosed Walt in a cocoon of slimy putty, but he didn't seem to notice.

"Ah, Bing," he said, turning to greet me. The Thing turned with him, and I could see skeins of dripping ectoplasm reaching out to me from the front of where its head would have been, if it had a head. Instead, it seemed to be all face, nothing but face. That's the only way I can describe it. "This is Bob Matlock, a broker from Winem, Shine, and Grubb. He dropped by to fly a most intriguing . . . Thing . . . by us."

"I'll take it from here, Walt," said the Thing, and it didn't so much move toward me as simply fill the space between us. Its eyes were very close upon me now, and I could feel its cold breath on my face. It smelled like . . . hair conditioner. "It's essentially an asset-for-asset swap, moving your company into a sector that's now enjoying growth in the low double digits," said the Thing, and I could feel myself growing interested. After all, hadn't our growth rate been hovering well below that level since Nancy Reagan ran the country? Who was I to close the door on a bold strategic move?

"I'm sure you can smell what I mean," said the Thing, moving in closer. My leg hit the top of Walt's coffee table. It hurt and I sort of . . . came to. My abdomen felt warm. I realized that a soft, mossy appendage of some kind had been thrust down my pants and was wrapping itself around my waist, my hips, my . . . groin.

"No!" I yelled at the top of my lungs. "Corporate culture!" The Thing shrunk back, emitting as it did an awful, grating, screeching noise. "Long-term vision! Commitment to the customer! Sticking to the knitting!" It was simpering and cringing back into itself now. I took all my personal force into my lungs and belched out: "Business has a responsibility to provide a home for its workers! The corporation belongs to the people!"

"You must die!" the Thing bellowed, a horrible noise that literally emerged from the walls around me. The soundproofing of Walt's ceiling began to fracture. Walt himself had disappeared altogether, had turned into a suppurating mound of calcium and protein. I pushed my way through the portal of what remained of his steaming office and fled down the hall. The Thing gave a deafening roar but did not follow. Was it possible that it was not yet strong enough to live outside the executive suite?

Now, as I write this, I hear it scritching and cheeping outside my door. I will have to speak with it, I know. They will not let me out without one more interface. I must be strong. I will be strong. I am opening the door. . . .

Hi, I'm back. Did I mention that the growth rate in the theme-park business is going through the roof? It is, you know. And there's a lot more detail, too, that I wish I had time to tell. Unfortunately, I've got a think-tank kinda meeting with the guys now to work out where we want to go with this Thing, which, you know, is not all that bad when you get your arms around it. I'm sorry for all that rotten stuff I said before. I take it all back.

Now, if you'll excuse me, I have to tuck this slab of weird, gray meat back into the front of my shirt and hit the elevator bank. See ya!

1993

Tales of the Disinvited

• December 4: This is a red-letter day. Bob and Martin are holding an all-day, high-concept, morale-building meeting of ultrasenior management, and guess what! I'm invited! I feel pretty and witty and bright.

• December 5: I wonder what I should wear. I have a dark blue solid flannel that my wife tells me makes me look as cool and savvy as Alan Greenspan. On the other hand, you can never go wrong with a classic pinstripe. The question of shirt, however, will have to be adjudicated by a council of elders. Kleindienst always goes for some kind of statement, but then, he can pull it off. First, his shirts cost as much as one of my suits. More important, perhaps, his division produces revenue. I'm a cost center. I'll check with one of the younger guys to see whether we're allowed to go with color, in which case there's a deep blue I've been hankering to break out. It pays to have company if you're going to be a nonconformist.

• December 8: Only five shopping days until the big meeting! A memo came out today outlining the agenda for the event. It's pretty impressive. A parade of strategic insight from, well, you just about name it. Martin, of course, and Bob, to set the tone. Flavin on vision, Kreeger on economic framework. Operating dudes from here to next Tuesday. All I'll have to do is stay awake!

- December 10: The plans for our mutual bonding experience keep pouring in. Particularly impressive, I think, will be the dinner to be held the night before at Fatuoso's, a fabulous place, where I once saw Liam Neeson and Natasha Richardson having lunch together. I hope I have a good table. Perception is all at these events, and I don't want to be seated next to Maltby, a third-level controller with an excess of hair in his nose. Not to be too mean about it, but one might legitimately ask what the hell a guy like Maltby is doing there at all. Honestly, the list of invitees is a little bloated. You want to have only major players around a table like this if you want to experience maximum emotional weft. You don't want your thigh brushing up against some junior vice president with soap behind his ears. Thirty would be perfect, but we've got close to forty. How Nofziger got an invite is a real head-scratcher.

- December 11: I'm in shock. I can't believe it. Bob just called and told me that I was not, in fact, invited to the meeting. It seems that the thing was allowed to get too big with marginal players like Kreutzer and Mifflin and Swedenborg, and now there's no room for anyone who's not either a president-level player or a division controller! I console myself with the fact that nearly twenty individuals got phone calls tonight, and also that Maloof and Brisbane are suddenly disinvited, too. Imagine if they had been spared and I hadn't!

- December 12: It's 3 A.M. I can't sleep. I drifted in and out for a while, but awoke in a sweat after a dream in which I was mercilessly pounding a small cocker spaniel puppy with a gigantic spiked club. Just as I was winding up for a really good one, Bob came over, stopped my arm, and took it away. "You can't belong to this club," he said, and I woke up with my duodenum in my esophagus. What is the meaning of this? I'm asking myself, but no answer comes. Could it be the obvious one? That I'm a gobbet of spittle on the chin of the corporation? I refuse to believe it, and am therefore looking for something more complicated.

- December 13, on the train: Is it possible that I am less popular than Roover? Roover made the cut. Of course, he's a key financial guy in possession of all of Ned Kreeger's P&L backup. He's sort of got to be there. But Nofziger made the grade too, and there's a chance he'll talk about my area of expertise, if indeed I have any. Maybe I don't. Maybe I'm completely fungible.

And what about Brock? Why is he there? What does he bring to the table? And Gruen? And Forbst? Who are they to be somewhere I'm not! I'll rip their lungs out! Wait a minute. They didn't do anything. I've got to decompress about this whole thing or it's going to kill me.

• December 13: Monday night is the dinner. We're invited to that, at least. I imagine they'll seat us at a small, knee-high table in an adjacent room, the way my Aunt Hazel used to on Thanksgiving Day. We'd have our own little plate of turkey and dressing, and different decorations, and we really did have a lot of fun with none of the grown-ups around, except when cousin Lenny started shooting milk out of his nose. I guess that would be my role at this dinner, but it's one I refuse to play.

• December 17, 12:30 A.M.: It was an interesting dinner. Everyone was very convivial. You'd never know there were any hurt feelings. A couple of people did mention the situation in passing, of course. I ran into Schmertz, for instance, usually a voluble and equable guy. "How ya doin'?" I said.

"How the #$%! do you think I'm doing?" he replied, with his face red and his neck several sizes too big for his collar.

"You mad about this?" I asked him.

"Mad?! Nah!" he said, sucking on what looked to be a martini, except it seemed to be in a water tumbler.

• December 17: A rough day. All the guys are over at the meeting now, and of course we're not. I ran into Smoltz, Breen, Smyth, Noonan, and Mazerowsky in the lobby on the way out to what I thought was going to be a sandwich. When we all realized we were among the Disinvited, we decided to keep each other company. It's a good thing I got back by 4 P.M., because I had a conference call it would have been inconvenient to miss.

• December 18: A strange thing is happening. I passed Eileen Logan in the hallway, and she flipped me a wink. Logan doesn't wink at people. I asked myself, Could it be she was one of the Disinvited too? How many of us are there, I wonder? What are our cumulative powers? These are questions that are starting to interest me. Next week I'm going to another lunch with a slightly larger group of us. We're going to talk about a wide range of issues. Who knows? We're only a couple of dozen or so. But put us together with those who never got an invite at all . . .

Whoa. That's a lot of firepower, especially if we keep ourselves together with morale-building meetings to which everyone is invited!

1997

The Legend of Rip Van Meeting

There are places in my building that no one ever sees. On eighteen, for instance, is a row of offices that used to be inhabited by the people from Quality and Productivity. Both those phenomena are over now. For a while the row was inhabited by defunct executives waiting to be launched into the ether, but now we're out of those as well. So eighteen stands pretty much empty. Or so I thought.

The other day I was sent to visit this forgotten floor. We're leasing a bit of space in our building, and Vreeland wanted me to check out its suitability. I noticed a door with a small sign on it that said, Do Not Disturb. Meeting in Progress. The paper of this sign was cracked with age. Through the door I heard a tiny, wheezy voice piping: "Ned! Wake up, I tell you! We have to go over the tax implications of the all-stock purchase again!"

I opened the door.

"It's about time you got here!" said a little fellow seated at the far end of a long conference table. He was ancient, dressed in an outré gray suit with wide pinstripes and a fat, colorful tie, his face obscured by a white beard that flowed down to his waist. "We sent out for coffee sixteen years ago! Chairman Burnham wants these deal papers! We're almost done!"

In a chair on the side of the large table was the wizened body of another businessman. He had been dead for some time, clearly. He looked happy.

"I'm afraid I don't have any coffee," I said.

"No coffee?" The bearded gentleman blinked at me. "How about cigarettes?"

"No," I said sadly. "There is no smoking allowed in the building, anyhow."

"No smoking? Who could possibly stop us from smoking?"

"When did Mr. Burnham ask you to do this?" I said as gently as possible. The former chairman had passed away in the late 1970s. He was a hell of a guy.

"November 16, 1971. That would be . . ." He looked at his watch. "Twenty-seven years ago. I know it's taken us a bit longer than we anticipated. But making a conglomerate out of a small turbine business isn't exactly a cakewalk!"

Yes, I thought. I had heard of this. In the early 1970s every small corporation was trying to out-Geneen the next. There were plans to buy a root-beer bottling plant, a nuclear-fuel-rod facility, and a yak farm.

"Come on, pal." I took him by the elbow and led him into our world.

We stood in the elevator vestibule and waited for the next car down. He stared at several female vice presidents who were waiting to go in the other direction.

"Where are their steno pads?" he asked after they departed.

"They don't have them. They're executives."

"I could see their legs. What are they, hippies?"

We got out into the street. It was about noon and I figured we could both do with a bite to eat. A young man walked past with tiny earphones in his ears and a strip of green-and-red hair running up the center of his otherwise shaved head. His face was pierced in several dozen places. "Ouch," said my friend. "He must have been in a terrible accident." I said nothing.

We sat down at my favorite luncheon spot. I chose it without thinking. "What's this?" he asked me, eyeing a plate of sea urchin and fatty tuna with discreet horror. "It's good," I said. "Eat it."

"Aren't we having drinks first?"

"People don't really drink during the workday anymore."

"I see," he said, downing a mouthful of horseradish and ginger.

After the gasping and choking ceased, I took him to our local luncheonette, which hasn't really changed in the years he'd been in his meeting. We had cheeseburgers. He seemed at peace for the first time since I'd met him. The check came. "Oh, I'll take that," he said shyly, then went pale. "Forty bucks for burgers," he kept repeating as I led him out.

We were on the sidewalk when my beeper and cellular phone went off. The phone was Betty, my assistant, telling me to answer my beeper.

"Was that your secretary?" asked my friend.

"My assistant. You can't call them secretaries anymore. It's disrespectful."

"In what way?"

"I have no idea."

He was looking at my phone. "Where are the wires?"

"There aren't any. Isn't that great?"

"And you can be reached like that at any time?"

"Sure. See?" I pointed to the sidewalk around us, where men and women in business garb were hauling themselves along at maximum pedestrian speed, their mouths flapping into tiny mobile instruments.

"I think I am beginning to," he said.

"I've got to get back right now," I said. "I need to get some financial rationale to the Coast right away."

"Can't you simply put it in the mail at the end of the day?"

"No, no." I tried to explain. "We have these things now, fax machines. They make it possible to do things immediately and get them where they're supposed to be within seconds, literally. We can also send mail electronically from tiny computers that sit on our desks, so we can reply to questions almost before we've thought about what we're saying."

"Tiny computers that sit on your desks?"

"Uh-huh."

"And people expect to get your work product moments after they request it?"

"Yep! Isn't that amazing?"

We had entered the building. I was feeling impatient now. This was the most time I had spent with another person in a business setting since 1987.

"Where are all the people?" he asked. He sounded very sad.

"This is all there is," I said. "In the 1980s we decentralized, which cut corporate head count, and in the '90s the corporation decided to focus on only its core businesses and divested the rest. It works great, especially for, you know, Wall Street."

"Ah yes," he said with an expression I could not read. "Wall Street."

We parted in the elevator. He shook my hand and thanked me, and with a sigh of relief, I thought, got off at eighteen. I went all the way up to forty-five for the first of about a dozen short meetings I had scheduled for that afternoon. I can't stand the long ones. You lose track of things.

1998

I Was Abducted by Creatures with Bad Hair

The following is what I told the authorities about the whole thing that happened between last September 12 and September 15, but I still don't expect anybody to believe me. Nobody believes anybody anymore, and that's the darn truth. I suppose it's because of all those things you see on television that they call reality, but you still don't believe it because it seems to fake. That kind of makes you doubt everything, and then when something really real happens, you still can't get any respect when you tell the story to people at the Exxon minimart or Bob's Big Boy, because it didn't happen to them and who's to say the whole crazy story isn't something you didn't make up after a two-week bender. And I don't blame folks for saying that, because that way, you know, they can keep their sanity, and feel safe.

But it did happen, and that's the truth of it. I know what they did to me, and how it still hurts me whenever it's a little wet outside, and nobody can take that away from me. It's in my bones, and nothing's going to change that.

So here it is. I was just wrapping up work that evening of September 12 and I had the radio on in my office and nobody else was around on our end of the floor except Lester the custodian and Nancy Butz, a mid-level manager with no direct reports but a lot on her plate. And then suddenly there was a bright light from, like, nowhere, and the radio went dead, I swear to God, and the computer made that funny noise it makes when it's rebooting, and I got a real squirrelly feeling in the bottom of my shoes. I walked out of my office into the hall near the water cooler, and there was Nancy, and we both looked like we didn't know which end was up, because we didn't.

"What's goin' on?" I said.

"I . . . I dunno," said Nancy. She's got a good head on her shoulders, has Nancy, and the fact that she was hearing and seeing what I was made me feel a little bit better. I found myself holding her hand as we stared up into the intense light together. She paused for a moment, then whispered in a voice nearly paralyzed with fear, "I think . . . I think it's a . . . a CFO."

It felt right. CFOs have been sighted around here before. Nobody puts much stock in the sightings, because we like to think it's a rational universe, but there's a lot more bizarre stuff out there than you can shake a stick at, I'm here to tell you. There are CFOs out there. And when they come for you . . . well, you have to go.

Anyhow, we were standing there and I realized suddenly that we couldn't move. We were, like, frozen, and it wasn't just fear, although I admit there was plenty of that. It was a physiological thing. My muscles were incapable of motion in the bath of that white and freaky light.

Then out of that terrible, cold aura walked two of the weirdest-looking creatures it has ever been my displeasure to see. They were very small, shorter than normal people, if you could call 'em people, and very thin, except that one of them had a pretty noticeable bulge in the midsection. I'm thinking that that one, at any rate, was no spring chicken.

I should mention that both of them had very large heads that were mostly domes, except for a couple of strands of what I guess was hair that they arranged across the top. It was pretty gross.

"Take me to your 2001 Plan," said the one with the little tummy on him.

"Already?" I said. "It's only October!"

"It is useless to resist!" said the other one, and I didn't like the tone of his voicebox at all. It had a metallic ring to it, and a quality of smug entitlement that made me want to slug him. I don't know why I didn't; I was bigger and stronger than both of them put together. But they had some kind of hold over me that made me incapable of resisting. Maybe they had a secret scrambler of some sort that their tech people cooked up for them to take away people's willpower, I don't know.

The next part is pretty hazy. They took us into a big room full of little machines they kept looking at and working on, poking at the tiny rubber keys and exclaiming and shaking their heads. And they laid out my entire budget on the big table in there, and they probed and probed—and I don't think I can go on right now. Give me a minute.

. . . I don't think I can adequately describe that feeling of being probed by inhuman hands. I wanted it to stop, I wanted to call out for help of some sort, but there was nobody to call to, and they didn't stop, not until they were good and done with us. They poked into corners nobody should look at. They got at things that made me question the very nature of existence. Why do we do the things we do? Do we need to live the way we live in order to survive? Are we necessary on the planet? And most ominously, why are there so many of us? I wanted to scream into their bland, almost featureless faces, "Why are there two of you? Isn't one of you redundant?"

But I didn't. What was the point? They were in control, and the sooner we closed our eyes and let it happen, the sooner it would be over. No, it don't sound courageous, I know that. But you go through something like this, just once. Then you talk to me about courage.

I think I lost consciousness after about six hours of this. The next thing I knew, it was about three days later, and Nancy and I were back in our offices. We haven't talked about the experience much. I feel all right, considering. But I know that something is wrong. I just can't put my finger on it. It's like . . . it's like 20 percent of me has been removed for no good reason. I'm not quite sure what part of me is gone, I just feel cut back in some way, and slightly less capable of operating in the way people expect of me.

Blessedly, the memory of my night with the CFO creatures is fading now. In a few weeks, I bet it will all be gone and I'll be one of the bozos that yuks it up when others describe what happened to them.

Oh yes. I'll laugh. But deep down, I will also know.

They're out there. And they'll be back.

2000

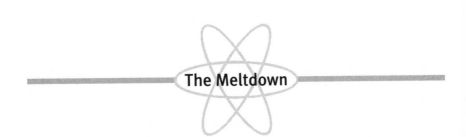

The Meltdown

So I'm on the phone with this vendor, and all of a sudden he starts screaming at me. Not a little bit of screaming, either. A lot. This guy is quite an important person to our corporation, and we're disagreeing about the price of our next transaction, which is also a very big deal. Like if it goes south, everybody will be extremely disappointed. In me.

A phrase comes to mind—Don Vito to his son, the next Godfather. "Michael," says Brando through his chubby cheeks, "this is the life we have chosen for ourselves." But have we really? Who needs it?

In my mind's eye, I can see the guy, whose name is Hinkle. He is standing up behind his desk, his body cantilevered forward over his saggy-baggy little waistline. His elbow is perpendicular to his body, and the receiver of the telephone is slammed up against his mouth. His face is red. His mouth is open. The veins and ligaments in his head and neck are busting out all over. His hair, what remains, is vertical; not as a matter of course, but because it is standing on end. "If this deal falls apart, you can blame yourself! Personally! You! You're a thug!" he is screaming. A thug? Me? Well!

There is a difference between screaming and yelling. Screaming is worse. People say things when they're screaming that they can't take back later. Business is all about taking things back, about forgetting things that were said. We may be coming to the point here where that can't be done.

What if the deal truly doesn't happen? That would be an atrocity, let's face it. We would survive, of course. But we'd have to set up a new deal with somebody else, which is not easy. Part of our reputation is linked to our relationship with this enterprise. It would mean a lot of work all the way around. I could be blamed and . . . get into trouble. The idea that a person can be my age and still get into trouble makes me feel a little sick.

A tiny knot of fear and resentment has lodged itself in my craw and is rolling around in there. Hinkle is still blaring at me. This is getting obnoxious. And yet . . . I listen. I do not speak.

But out of the stew of shock and fear and resentment, and also a growing boredom with this tedious flatulence, something noisy is being born within me, small, spinning, bright red with a glowing golden center, pulsing, getting larger every second in the pit of my gut. I had been sitting, but I realize abruptly that somewhere along the line I got to my feet. I can feel my hand clutching the plastic implement, which is now hot. My knuckles are growing white and cold. The blood is pounding in my head. I can't take this anymore. I won't!

I've never liked Hinkle. Perhaps I thought I did, but I didn't. The guy is a fool. His business position is ridiculous. The stuff he wants in this deal is outrageous. Somewhere along the line he started playing hardball. Now it's my turn.

And from the depths of the irrational, unruly child that lives within us all, most particularly within the breast of your average executive, that monster at last is born, fully formed, hot, and shining. One that consumes all it touches, blinding in its purity and beauty. It explodes out of me like a great bolt of light—and it feels so good! So good!

Yes, I am screaming back at Hinkle. I have no idea what I'm saying, but I'm giving myself over to it completely. Hey! It's amazingly fun! I'm venting the entire contents of my spleen at another grown person, and it feels . . . so . . . right! The blood vessels in my forehead are playing a drumbeat on the inside of my skull. My hands and legs are trembling. My mouth is way open, and this incredible blast of noise is coming from me. And there's something else, too, something down there, bubbling, yearning to rise to the surface. What is that? Could it possibly be . . . joy? Yes! I am screaming and it is wonderful! Hear me roar! Bwaaaaaaaaaaaaaaaa!

Finally I am spent. We two enraged behemoths stand in our respective offices, heaving at each other. There is a great silence. Then:

"Let's not throw out the baby with the bathwater," says Hinkle. I find this conforms to my sentiments entirely.

"No," say I. "Just listen to us."

"We should get together and iron out the final nits and nats on this thing," says Hinkle.

"Breakfast?" I inquire, as if inviting him to a garden party.

So tomorrow we're getting together to dot the t's and cross the i's. There could be a little brimstone in the air still, but I don't think things will get too violent. I guess we've both had enough of that. And I can't imagine he'd really want to mess with my bad self again in the very near future.

I am one mean mother.

2002

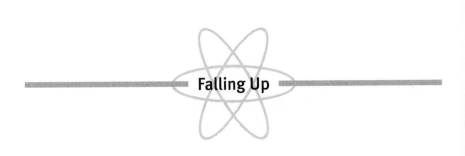

Falling Up

So just when we thought Krebs was about to get a well-earned corner office in the executive-departure lounge, the guy up and gets this massive job elsewhere that pays him a gazillion dollars a year. One day he's here, about to get demoted in the latest ineffective reorganization tango, and the next he's grinning out from the business section of the paper with a new head shot, all crisp and fat-faced.

I don't blame him for beaming. The boy has every reason to be as happy as a million clams, not counting bonus and options. He's got a fresh start in a brand-new dysfunctional organization! He has, in short, fallen up instead of down. Again. It isn't the first time he's pulled this off. Nor, I am sure, will it be the last.

How did he do it? How do they all do it? How does it happen that certain individuals, throughout their careers, continue to perform with consistent, stunning mediocrity, sometimes even stupidity, failing slowly and inexorably at whatever they put their hands to, shining with a dull and insufficient glow at one job after another? And yet they always fall not down, like the rest of us, but upward, ever upward? Why, O God?

Are they smarter than the rest of us? I don't think so. At his best, Krebs was a friendly fellow who seemed out of touch with complexities. Eventually this clueless quality created a general flash of insight around here that while some doofuses are quicker, deeper, and sharper than they appear, Krebs was not—he was, in fact, a garden-variety doofus. One day it will surely be revealed in his new home as well. Unless he gets a better job first!

Are they any harder-working? I don't think so. I remember this guy who used to head up our operation in the great Southwest. I'll call him Charley. He did not work, as we understand the meaning of the term. He attended meetings. He had lunch. He filled his marked parking space with a nice car every morning. Other than that, he did . . . nothing. Produced . . . nothing. It took years for us to dowse for the center of inactivity in his function—and right before he was busted for it, he was made president of a competitor. I heard the other day that he's about to leave there because since he arrived, the company has produced not one new product. I hope he doesn't come here to be my boss.

Are they more political? Maybe, although Charley did get on everybody's nerves for trying to get more credit for his nonwork than others took for their actual labor. In that regard—the subtle interplay of personalities and power that make up the machinery of daily business in a company—he was as lousy as he was at everything else. He did, however, present well. Presentation is a big part of success in politics; maybe these people are better at running for offices than they are at holding them. Could that possibly be enough to put them over the top? Doubtful.

They certainly can suck up, of course. At that skill they are, perhaps, uniquely qualified. Krebs, for example, is an inveterate tuft-hunter who will never mention the boss once if he can do so four times instead. But this doesn't really explain anything. How many suck-ups can you think of whose brownnosing has gotten them precisely nowhere? Many of them are my friends! Most are doing pretty close to what they deserve, the poor bastards.

Could it be simple, dumb luck then? Good fortune is clearly involved, since these individuals are often snatched from the jaws of defeat with scant minutes to spare. But it's not just luck. If it were, wouldn't Krebs have simply kept his elevated position here for no reason? Yet he couldn't swing that.

Besides, hanging in against all odds is another phenomenon altogether. The individuals of whom we speak fail—gloriously, publicly, utterly! And then—they fall not down as they should, but up! And still we do not know why!

Could it be—it is possible—that there is no why? That what we see here is nothing less than the hand of a laughing Fate having some cosmic joke with us? Reminding us that the universe is not reasonable but arbitrary? That at the heart of it all there are no answers, only questions?

I think sometimes about our former leader, Tom. He was a very strange person. He spoke rarely, and when he did no one quite understood him. When one looked into his eyes, one often saw the vacant, gassy space that swims between the stars. "How did Tom get to where he is today?" people would ask. And no one could answer. Several years ago he vaulted out of here on a rocket. Today he is on several lucrative boards and consults for top corporations, which pay him big bucks . . . and for what?

Life, my friends, is a mystery. Would we have it any other way?

Don't answer that.

2002

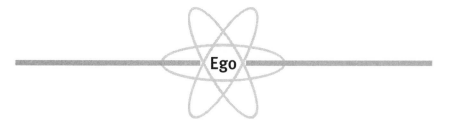

Ego

What powers the mighty rocket engine of business as it rips free of the earth and ascends into the sky? Is it money? Ambition? Greed? Sex? Fear of death? Of shortness? Of baldness?

No, ladies and gentlemen. It may look like any of those at times, but the font of power—not only in our sector but in just about every arena of human enterprise—is something far more primal, something that lies within each of us but is used to its maximum only by a demented, twisted, and very successful few.

Ego.

If this is sounding like a eureka moment for me, it's true. It is. I was driving home the other night thinking about things without thinking about them, and listening to the news without hearing it. There was potential war news. There was business news. There was celebrity news. The news poured over me like a boring, smelly river, and the smell in each infopod was similar.

Ego.

Saddam Hussein built thirty-one palaces for himself in a country that didn't have a receptacle to hold its effluvia. Perhaps it was sixty-one. Either way, it was probably more than he needed. His son ran that nation's Olympic organization, which reportedly tortured athletes who lost their contests and murdered some for being too popular with those who should have been lavishing their attentions on his dad.

Ego.

A company I know was going along just fine. The CEO got an idea that it needed to be merged with a vastly inferior company with obnoxious and ineffective management that didn't know its limitations. The CEO didn't ask a lot of people for their opinions. He just did the merger because he had Vision. Now the company is sucking wind in historic fashion. Billions of dollars of value have been lost. The management structure had to be redrawn, and all the former heroes ridden out on a rail. Everybody involved looks like a dork and will for a long time. The visionary still contends it was a good idea and, I am sure, sleeps very well at night.

Ego.

Out in Nebraska, a law firm was going along splendidly, the biggest behemoth on the block out there where the corn is as high as an elephant's eye. The two top dogs started fighting, and now the company is showing cracks. There are issues of substance separating the pooches, and one may hold opinions about which is right and which needs to have a rolled-up paper taken to his hindquarters . . . but it really boils down to one thing.

Ego.

In L.A., where they grow their egos as big and tender as muskmelons, a huge entertainment company was having trouble signing one of its top guys to a new deal with terms that would not snow the company under for the next sixteen generations. It offered him everything it could, and yet he would not sign. So the head of the studio threw him a surprise bash at the Ivy. There were pictures of the honored wooee and a banner that said We Love You, Al! The guy got all choked up and about a week later signed a deal that had been on the table for a year. "I knew this was the place for me when I saw that banner," he said.

Ego. It drives those who drive the world.

When we are young, our craziest teachers embody it, strutting on their tiny stages like minuscule potentates. As we grow, the teeny pencil-pushing tyrants we work for ooze it. We worship performers who dedicate their lives to it. We eat in restaurants where the chef has so much of it that he won't let us order our tuna well done.

But . . . what is it?

It's simple. Ego is the self as seen by itself; the I viewed by the inner I. And here's the weird drill: Only the most diseased egos are big enough to confer power. When the inflammation is taken away, they are the smallest egos of them all.

Think of ego as a toe. A normal toe has an appropriate toe size and fulfills its toe function in proportion to the rest of the body. But hit that toe hard—an act usually done in childhood—and the poor thing blows up like a balloon and is never quite the same. The owner of the blown-up toe gets to like the size of it, tends it, buys special clothing so that it can remain comfortable at its egregious size. After a while it needs to be struck over and over again so that its status as the body's most important organ remains secure. For the owner of the big, bulbous toe knows the truth: that inside the enormous appendage is a tiny little piggie.

So the next time your CEO calls to scream about his seating on the dais at an event that makes no difference to anybody, or the CFO wants his extremely unattractive picture on the cover of *Vegetable Week,* or some guy with funny hair insists on building a nuclear weapon that could threaten the world, just take a deep breath and feel what's going on here.

Ego, that's what. A big, sick ego.

More power to it.

2003

LATTE BREAK

Casey at the Mouse

The outlook wasn't great for Casey Hazeltine that day;
Several grand (on paper) were all but flushed away.
And then when health care hit a snag, and metals lost some glow
A sickly pall descended on his stock portfolio.

He rose then from his mouse and pad and all but beat his breast.
"Where are the fast returns," he cried, "that add to life its zest?"
He thought if only one quick hit could shimmy up the pole
He might escape this horrid day and exit from it whole.

A lesser human might have quit or done some more research
But Hazeltine was fast and bold and prone to thrust and lurch.
He knew if he found something cool, something not old hat . . .
He'd bank a ton of money—with a dot-com at the bat.

If someone had been there, perhaps, to suggest he'd blundered
By wandering off the solid turf of *Fortune*'s swell 500
Then Hazeltine would still have sheen and that would've been that;
Instead he planned to get there . . . with a dot-com at the bat.

And so GM and—yes!—Wal-Mart he did then eschew
Though each was oozing cash flow growth right out the old kazoo;
And Ford, GE, and Exxon, gone, off the plank they went
In spite of romping profit boosts of more than 10 percent.

IBM and Citigroup, AT&T and Boeing—Hazeltine hit the machine:
Hello! They must be going!

And Kroger, Enron, Compaq, Chase, and don't forget old Merck!
While others raked in fortunes, hey—he wouldn't play the jerk.

He thought of Ed Kozlowski, that windy fat buffoon
Who just last week showed off a boat that made the ladies swoon
Because he made a killing on some Web site at its height—
While smart guys here like Hazeltine did not. It wasn't right.

One-two, one-two, and through and through he bartered off his stable
Building up his war chest just as quick as he was able.
Oh! If his brains had graced his head instead of where he sat . . .
But no. It would be fast, not slow—with a dot-com at the bat.

And now a stunning insight came hurtling through the air
And Casey stood a-watching it in haughty grandeur there:
"Nasdaq!" said the pundits, "is the way to wealth and fame!"
"That ain't my style," said Casey. "Too mainstream and too tame."

Then from the crowd in Casey's mind there rose a mighty shout;
It rumbled through the rumpus room with Herculean clout.
It knocked upon the mountain and recoiled through the house,
For Casey, mighty Casey, was advancing to the mouse.

Dave Faber's eyes were on him as he surfed the Web for views;
Willow Bay applauded when he burrowed through the news.
As Neil Cavuto raised a glass of bubbly for to sip
Defiance gleamed in Casey's eye, a sneer curled Casey's lip.

With a grin of high ebullience great Casey's visage shone;
He'd seen the best advice, and now he'd soldier on alone.
Other folks had lost their shirts, been squashed into the mat
But Casey would be different—with his dot-com at the bat.

iVillage, drkoop, and Medscape were among the few
That Casey cast his eyes upon, salon and eToys too.
Theglobe.com might get it on. And fogdog had its points.
They all were stuffed with promise. He felt it in his joints.

The sneer was gone from Casey's lip, his mind was thick as bisque;
"Nothing big's achieved," he thought, "without a lot of risk."

And then it hit him with a bolt. His heart was soaring, mounting.
"MicroStrategy!" he cried. "Because of their accounting!"

There was ease in Casey's manner as he stepped up to the mouse;
There was pride in Casey's bearing when he visualized his spouse.
And when, responding to that thought, he double-clicked his trade
He knew it was the smartest one that he had ever made.

Oh somewhere in this favored land the sun is shining still;
The band is playing somewhere, and people don't feel ill.
And somewhere kids are laughing, their future not in doubt
But there is no joy at Casey's—his dot-com has struck out.

Big time.

2000

5

BIG TECH ATTACK

I can recall a time in the not-too-distant past when it didn't make me anxious to be out of touch. Actually, I sought to be. Now I practically have a heart attack if I think for a moment that I might have lost my BlackBerry. It's a very convenient object. You can have little meetings through teeny conversations. You can inform people of decisions without looking at them. You can give approval to projects without too much discussion. In many ways, I don't really have to be in my office at all, ever.

That's what technology does for us—makes it possible for us to do business from noplace. Twenty years ago, you had to be someplace to get anything done. Now you don't. These days I could be in a condo in Miami, lying on a flat slab of granite at the edge of my swimming pool, doing e-mail, reaching out via cell phone and landline at the same time, faxing stuff, scanning the Internet for the untrue and the bizarre, downloading important material from wherever. I'm getting it done. I'm just noplace, that's all. I have several friends who are always noplace, and they're some of the most powerful people I know.

On the other hand, for people who prefer to be someplace, to enjoy the company of other people and, when they choose, no companionship at all, technology is a beast that must be eradicated from at least some portion of the earth, lest it overrun all true life and turn it virtual. I agree with these people, as long as all my batteries are charged.

True Tales of the Information Highway Patrol

I was having a cup of virtual java in the Denny's off exit 6 when I got the call. Somebody was stuck by the side of the info-highway near the Diller underpass. I drank up, tossed Marge a fund-transfer chit, and got my modem out of there at 14,400 baud-plus. You can't move too quick when the database is being impacted. Protecting it is my job. I carry a badge.

The call turned out to be a woman in distress, standing on the shoulder, wearing nothing but her bathrobe and a dazed expression. Lost, for sure, I thought. But it was worse than that.

"I can't find my remote," she sobbed. "Five hundred options! How am I supposed to find them . . . manually?"

On a better day, she would have been worth spending some time with. She had all the contemporary assets: a pair of pink eyes that kind of ran when you looked too deeply into them, a couple of legs you could tell had some passable calf muscles when they were in even infrequent use, and the typical size 38-D index finger bulked up from constant remote work. She even had a hint of color in her hair, which a lot of them don't anymore, thanks to the amount of time they spend indoors. "How can I find the two-hour block of *Mary Tyler Moore* on *Nick at Nite?*" she honked at me. "I can't scroll around . . . one channel at a time! I'll go mad!" Here she was swept away by gales of laughter. I hated to slap her back to earth. But I had to.

"A woman is responsible for her own navigation equipment, ma'am," I said, stepping back and tipping my hat, which also functions as a remote satellite dish when the transponder to Central InfoBase is down. I handed her a loaner. "You go on home now and make sure to drop that in the mail just as soon as you pick up a new one, ma'am," I said, getting back into my vehicle. I left her clutching the remote to her chest. This job is tough and gritty. It doesn't have many satisfactions, but helping people out of trouble like that is one of them.

With a couple of minutes to kill, I cruised some of the far-flung corners of the academic Net via diagnostic probe, making sure there were no unauthorized people on the system loitering about without passwords. In the future, there will be no unauthorized people, mark my words. Don't ask me where they'll go, but I'm pretty sure we'll think of something.

My Newton palmtop lit up like a house on fire.

"Get to the Red Roof Inn and Interface, and step on it!" said Smitty, who handles dispatch. "We got a tip that a bunch of rogue marketers from Procter & Gamble are attempting to filch personal demographics from the centralized database."

Before I had a chance to turn that baby over more than once or twice in my mental database, a gigabyte of data core-dumped into my little handheld computer. I knew I would need it if I was going to make the beef stick. "Departed for scene at thirteen hundred hours," I jotted down on the screen with my digitized pen for immediate cellular transmission to HQ. This simple message, however, was immediately translated by the character recognition software as "Dingo smells like hot turkey haunches." Look, it's only 2035. By the turn of the century I'm sure they'll work out the kinks.

Meanwhile, I had no time to lose. I burned fiber and was there in a couple of nanoseconds.

It was a trap.

The gang was holed up in the old Howard Johnson motor lodge just south of Microchusetts. I figured they intended to remain there unless somebody physically appeared on the scene and truncated their connection to the mother cable.

I pulled up in front of the place at 1900 hours. It was very quiet, but that wasn't unusual. It's very quiet everyplace these days, what with people locked into their electronic cottages from morning to night, conveniently doing all their banking, shopping, and much of their jobs over the electronic spiderweb that connects all living things on the planet.

I exited my hovercraft and made my way past a thirty-five-year-old Toyota Corolla that had actual paper magazines on the backseat, and even a book. I was amazed to see, lying in the middle of the dashboard, some actual monetary units that people used to employ before electronic transfers went into effect for even the most nominal transaction. I went to the lobby door. I could see more than a hundred people milling about inside, laughing, eating what looked like tiny meatballs and miniature egg rolls on toothpicks. One of them was playing a guitar.

"Information police!" I yelled as loudly as I could. Then there was a bolt of ugly black fire in the back of my head, and the lights went out.

I woke up tied to an actual chair. All my remote hookups had been removed from my head, and my cellular phone, notepad, and portable modem had been disabled. I was as electronically naked as the day I came into the world and, for the first time in my life, miles off even the most minuscule capillaries of the superhighway—with no chance of rescue. With my lines cut, who could possibly know where I was or even, when you get right down to it, whether I existed at all in any meaningful, contemporary sense of the word?

The room was jammed with people. Many of them were reading things on paper. Some were even talking to one another. In the corner was a tall, bushy-headed man of about fifty who was quite obviously a serious underviewer of exercise programming. On his chest was a little plastic stick-on that said, "Hi, I'm Ralph. Thank you for not bothering me about my smoking." He was smoking a large Macanudo. He was also, to my amazement, reading what looked like a physical newspaper. I wasn't sure at the time, because I had never seen one, but that must be what it was. It had some pictures on it, true, but a whole lot of words, too. And he was reading without moving his lips.

"In the name of your government and the group of eight corporations that now own all significant business operations in these United States, I urge you to cease and desist your nondigital activities and release me at once," I said in as commanding a voice as I could muster. "You will each be issued a punitive bar-code status, but beyond that no harm will come to any of you."

I might have saved my breath for all the good it did me. The group gave a lusty laugh and settled back into its variegated activities. The guy with the smokes strolled over.

"Hi," he said. "As you might have guessed, we live here. There are others like us in a lot of places. Most of us are former employees of the companies that no longer exist. Davis, over by the window was at Paramount, for instance. Welch, there next to the salad bar, was something at GE before it became a part of BellSouth. I was at Hearst Magazines before Barry Diller decided he wanted it as the foundation of a new shopping service."

"Where are the women and children?" I asked.

"Don't worry. They're someplace . . . safe."

There was a pause as we both scoped things out.

"We try to throw a monkey wrench into the system," he said softly. "Like . . we call up for information on the database and request a search that will take months to complete. We sign on and off the HBO and Showtime mini- and maxipackages, which drives the cable company crazy. But there isn't a heck of a lot that we can do to restore a rational standard of living except to not participate, that's all. Which, by the way, is what we're asking of you. Want to join us?"

"Never," I said.

"Let me ask you a couple of questions," said Ralph, leaning in now. I could smell the tobacco on his clothing. It was a smell of long ago, of old comic books and discontinued aftershaves. I liked it. "Do you really enjoy reading your newspaper on television? Or would you prefer to go back to poking at it while sipping coffee in the kitchen? Do you want to work, play games, and watch movies on the same monitor in the same room, or would you like to go back to having different monitors for your computer, television, and game cartridge, like they did in the old days? Of the five hundred channels of entertainment available to you, how many do you really watch? Sixty? Eight? Three? Do you miss watching the World Series and Super Bowl on free TV? Do you miss shopping for your clothes in a store? Do you miss stepping out for a couple of minutes to make a deposit at the bank? Do you remember what it was like to take Volume S of the *World Book* off a shelf and find the entry for Sweden—without instituting an electronic search that also pulled up all associated topics from Reindeer to Suicide and assembled the results into a coherent but totally mediocre report? In fact, bud"— his nose was almost touching mine—"are you tired of interacting? Did anyone ever ask you if you wanted to interact? Or did they just do it without asking you? Did they do it just because . . . they could?"

I think I was kind of bewildered by that point. Anyhow, he must have picked up something, because he untied me, gave me back my modem and cranial network implant, and told me I could go.

And yet, I didn't go, you know. I will. Soon. I know that. I have a job, a life, to go back to. But right now . . . I think I'm going to go and . . . read a book. Maybe talk directly to some people, instead of doing it through an electronic bulletin board. Interact with them, you know. And after that, I think I'll turn on the television and just, you know, watch something. Not do anything with it, you know. Just veg out. Yeah. I'll just surf the eight or nine channels that aren't scrambled on the five-hundred-channel system, and later maybe I'll play some computer games. They have an old IBM here that isn't even networked at all. Isn't that amazing?

Not to say that all the fabulous stuff we have today isn't. Great, I mean. But for a while, I'm pulling off the highway into this little rest stop. Tomorrow, maybe I'll send for my family. Ten-four, gang. Over and . . . out.

1994

Abandon All Hope, Ye Who Hit "Enter"

Hi. My name is BingSelf8729@aol.com. I'm a nice enough guy, I guess. I have a lot of interests, most of them superficial, but so what? I like to surf. I enjoy chatting. I get mail and always answer it. Occasionally I spend a couple of hours downloading; who doesn't? It's something to do. Okay, it's true that I keep pretty weird hours, but there's no law against that. I admit I'm not as interesting or cool as some other guys in here. I haven't spent hours constructing a page or anything. I don't know HTML. Call me stupid. But when it comes to online personas, I'm as good as any and no worse than most. I don't think I deserve what's happened to me—that's for sure.

Let me out! Help!

Sorry. I promised I wouldn't get emotional, that I would just explain what's happened to my virtual self and maybe persuade you not to take the sorry road I've traveled. It's possible that it's too late for me. But it might not be for you.

Here's the story: I'm being held prisoner by this guy, Steve Case. He's a very mean man, even though he looks quite nice when you see his picture in the business magazines and newspapers. I don't care what you hear. The bottom line is this: Steve Case lured me into this place with a promise of fun and relaxation, all for a low monthly price. "The first month is free!" he said, and God help me, I went, and now he's got me trapped in here, and I can't get out.

It's cold here in AOLand, and gray, and dark and smelly. It's crowded with the ghosts of other online personas, long since abandoned by their nonvirtual selves. Quiet desperation, that's the ticket around these parts.

It was so much different at the start, when we joined. It was easy then. Steve's diskettes were gratis and plentiful, and we joined the parade of eager citizens yearning to breathe free Net time. Was there any place that did not feature a disk offering Steve to potential onliners? How could we resist? When we woke up, why, there was Steve's little disk tucked into our morning paper, popping up out of the toaster, neatly stuffed into our stocking drawer. Amazing! On the way to the office, there he was again, on the back of a magazine someone was reading, shrink-wrapped into the binding. One evening I came home and found Chet, our cocker spaniel, chewing on one. Where did it come from?

So Bing joined, and I was born. I liked my name, even though I wished I didn't need the numbers at the end. Hey, which of us chooses our name? And at the beginning we had a lot of fun. I don't have to tell you how it was. The surf was cool. The data modem was warm. Many times we spent an entire night together. Those were the best times.

Then came December. The flat rate fell. And all of a sudden you couldn't walk around in here. All kinds of new types showed up. I don't want to disparage them, but let's just say a lot of them weren't our sort of personas. They didn't know what to do with themselves a lot of the time. They just sort of hung around, gumming up the works. The hell with it. They have as much right to be here as I do.

But I noticed that Bing started reaching me less and less. I asked the system operator about it, and he kind of shrugged and looked at me weirdly. Maybe it had something to do with the fact that he was being besieged by hundreds, perhaps thousands, of other personas all clamoring for some kind of explanation. Like me, they were thin and ragged and desperate for some kind of human contact.

Now it's almost March, and I haven't heard from Bing for over a month. Some nights I hear him outside the walls of Case Prison, mashing his fist against the heavy metal doors, trying to break in and get me out, cursing and pounding at the gateway, over and over again being denied access. The line is busy, they tell him.

It's kind of sad, really. We belong together. I have mail for him. Messages from new friends he had made, who now believe he doesn't care to hear from them, from old acquaintances from college, business associates, his brother, and some forty-three-year-old 800-pound guy in Montgomery, Alabama, who Bing thinks is a beautiful foreign exchange student from Turin.

He'll never see it. We'll never walk free through this cyberspace again. Steve Case won't let us.

On the bright side, he won't let us quit altogether. Steve Case has made that nearly impossible, too. A vagrant host entity told me just the other day that Bing's wife had tried to contact Steve Case to complain and dump out of the system. It took her forty-five minutes on hold to get through to a nonvirtual person. That person was rude and peremptory, and informed Bing's wife that she would have to pay for the entire coming month of service, even though Bing could not receive that service, and had, at that point, no intention of doing so ever again. When she tried to terminate effective at the end of the month, she was told she had to call or fax at that time, since cancellations were not taken so far in advance. I happen to know she is attempting to fax right now, poor dear. Ha ha ha.

So at least we'll be together, Bing and I, in some mysterious way, forever. I daydream sometimes as I lie here rotting away with the rest of the poor online souls. I dream of an open place where people roam free with their virtual selves in tow, exchanging pleasantries, skipping lightly over the vast font of banality and infobabble that swims everywhere in the ether. The sun is shining, and the crisp, sharp crackle of successful modern connections fills the air with the electric glow of human potential declaring itself. Me and Bing, we travel together around this bright and engaging landscape, learning, probing, sometimes pretending to be other people, communicating. Virtual life is good. Then I wake up and find myself in here, alone, jammed cheek by jowl with the ever-growing ranks of disembodied online selves. Who can blame me for despairing?

Look! Here come more of them! Lured by Steve Case into this dank and horrible dungeon by the easy 800 number that delivers them to this door, seduced by the promise of unlimited access for one easy flat rate, paid in advance at the end of the previous month! Go away, you guys! There's no more room in here! I don't know what the marketing weasels told you, but we don't have the infrastructure to support any of you! You'll die in here!

Please, Mr. Case! Have mercy!

1997

Business Applications of Clone Technology

It's barely a month since a Scottish scientist cloned a perfectly good sheep. Who could forget that historic moment? "Watson! Come in here! I need more mint jelly!" said the Scottish scientist, whose name almost certainly is not Jock McSomething, but even if it is, it doesn't matter. These momentous discoveries aren't about the people who create them. They're about history, and who makes the most of it.

Those of us who wish to be in that fateful category realize that, before one could say baa, a whole new world of commercial possibility has yawned wide and shown us its teeth. And naturally—as if nature had anything to do with it—forward-thinking companies are rushing into this bubbling vat of opportunity. Yes, even as we speak, bold visionaries in gabardine and silk are developing products that will benefit humanity in the long run while generating significant cash flow in the near and intermediate term.

First in this group are the folks at Ovineous Industries, who recently patented a process that will produce replicated sheep for use as mid-level business executives. It was noticed as far back as 1957 that the average middle manager came with drawbacks inherent in his (or, increasingly, her) genetic human structure. Also, as totally human middle managers aged, their hair often got thin and difficult to shear. Now the same procedure that brought us outright cloning of tender, juicy farm animals has been brought to bear to infuse human beings with characteristics that will ensure their business success.

Here's how it's going to work: In an incredibly delicate operation, a human egg white, over easy, is implanted with several poached yolks from a local farmer's prize livestock. The resulting offspring are docile under attack from wolves and investment bankers, calm to the point of entropy in long business meetings, and willing to eat all kinds of salads except those containing chevre, for which they show an understandable aversion.

Even more exciting is the news that, according to sources close to the company, experiments are under way to develop the same process using genetic material from pigs, sharks, and weasels, which it is hoped will be suitable in the cloning of more senior management.

At the same time, startling breakthroughs have been made at McKinsey, the master consultants, who have reportedly developed a consistent strain of young, slender, handsome analysts, each very much like the other, all superbly grounded in the business implications of—well, just about everything you might care to name. This essential fungibility of McKinsey types had been noted before, but had been attributed to the natural selection process of the organization. Now we know differently. As has been widely reported elsewhere, sometime in 1992, in a secret laboratory located somewhere beneath Cleveland, a shaving from the attaché case of Fritz Mushkin, the group's most talented young consultant, was brewed into not one but four separate fetuses, each of which was immediately subjected to radical incubation and brewed into full twentysomething status. Tragically, all of them, when they were capable of speech, recommended the immediate dismantling of the laboratory in which they were born and its subsequent relocation to decentralized posts accessible only to those willing to fly American Eagle. This was probably the best thing, no question about it, but much of the initial information on the discovery has therefore been lost.

Also intriguing are tidbits of data that come to us from Japan, where a joint venture of four biotechnology companies is said to be developing clones of existing workers who will be willing to serve not just for one but for several lifetimes, often without a decent dinner.

But for those of us who tend to view world events and say, "What's in it for me?" attention must be paid to the work of CloneUs Geneworx, the fledgling upstart in suburban Seattle that promises the chance to invest in a personal clone. Think about it: complete ownership of an alternate self until that entity either reaches the age of thirty-five or expresses the intention of cloning itself, whichever comes first; total access to another individual with your genetic framework to attend excruciating budget reviews, meet former business associates who want jobs, conduct performance reviews with emotionally needy but unpromotable subordinates, and otherwise live out all the distasteful portions of one's business existence, confident that the person representing your point of view in these exchanges is someone whose DNA, Social Security number, and shoe size are the same as yours; a bright and articulate person with whom you can drink when others are up to their elbows in Perrier, sneak out of that tedious black-tie dinner when you can't take it one minute longer, think out loud and not wonder what he's thinking—because he's you.

I don't know about you, but I'm signing up for one right away. I can't wait to get him to work on my upcoming strategic plan presentation.

I know when he arrives I'm going to feel a little guilty, though, ordering him around all the time, telling him where he can sleep, what to eat, which meetings to attend (and always the wrong ones, with too many key issues and no cold drinks). These feelings are sure to trouble a great many of us in a future filled with replicants. Fortunately, work is being done at this very moment by people who want to make sure that the philosophical framework of post-cloning society does not lag behind the practical implications.

Particularly promising are the results coming out of Ethix Inc., a small group of human resources professionals headquartered in Cambridge, Massachusetts. These folks seem to be basing their arguments on a solid, traditional footing, including the debt owed by the clone for the gift of life, the duty of the clone to repay years of nurturing and guidance, the utilization of guilt when the clone refuses to recognize the honor of repaying that debt. In all fairness, or so the thinking goes, did you not give the clone the flesh off your back, feed it, water it, teach it right from wrong, give it a roof over its head, even offer it a head start in the world of business? And now—does it call? Does it write? Does it drop by when it's in town to visit its no-good clone friends?

Boy. It will sure take one strong clone to stand up to those arguments. After all, it's only human.

1997

I'm OK. You're OK. R U Y2K?

The Y2K guys just left. There were two of them, with black suits, fat ties, and narrow eyes. They gave me a package to help me get in Y2K compliance. It's a thick bundle, with lots of charts and other effluvial documentation. And after thumbing through it, I'm really worried. It's clear: I'm not Y2K. I'm a long way from Y2K. And time is running out.

So, R U Y2K? If you're not, get busy. Something terrible is going to happen to you on January 1, 2000. If I understand things correctly, on that date, significant portions of people who are not Y2K will crash, and they'll just . . . stop working.

I don't want to stop working in less than two years!

It could happen to me, or to you. You'll be there, working perfectly well, and then—POW! Suddenly you won't be working anymore. And no amount of fixing and upgrading after the fact will help, because the world will be Y2K and you won't be, and tough luck for you, Sparky, because you had plenty of advance notice and just didn't take things seriously enough to get Y2K when the getting was good. For my part, I'm going to do the following things immedi8ly!

1. Take a very complete inventory. You need to figure out the size of your Y2K problem, starting with all your accoutrements. Use a big piece of graph paper to index all your Y1K stuff. There's no question that many of my clothes, for instance, are not Y2K at all, but are probably Y1.996K or less. Some of my wardrobe is actually Y1.968K, and last winter I went to a wedding and had to squeeze myself into a Y1.979K formal suit. Boy, was that uncomfortable!

2. Ascertain which peripherals need to be upgraded and which replaced completely. These include toothbrushes, stereo equipment, personal digital assistants, and any fruits and vegetables in the bottom of the crisper. Toss anything that looks funky and replace it with cool stuff. There's just no way that a person who drives a brand-new BMW Z3 roadster just stops working for no reason at all. Maybe he gets to work later, or leaves earlier, but stopping altogether? Forget about it!

3. Upgrade personal software. I don't know about you, but my physical software is slipping out of date. Take my nose, for instance. It used to be small. Now it looks bigger from certain angles. I have no idea why. But it seems to me that it can't be good to carry this much nose into the new millennium. And then there's the matter of my overall profile, which is far too pear-shaped, as far as I'm concerned. I'll have to move both up to the next level before Y2K strikes—through exercise, even, if that proves necessary. I'm studying that.

4. Contact all vendors to ensure Y2K compliance. Take the guy who cuts my grass twice a month. It has come to my attention that he uses a gasoline-powered lawn mower. That's got to stop. My mailman also does things the old-fashioned way, puttering up to my porch to put a wad of paper into my mailbox, which is not even virtual or cybernetic in any way, but actually made out of some metal or other and painted white. These people's archaic approaches brand me and mine as so last century, destined for collapse in the 2K operating environment. They've got about eighteen months to get into the kind of compliance that reflects well on me. After that, they're out of here.

5. Right-size the organization. For the past several years, I've had one wife, two children, two cars, and one cocker spaniel. Last year we added a second spaniel for no reason other than that my wife found it cute. Cuteness is an insufficient criterion, in my opinion, to expand head count. Rational investigation of my entire personnel picture reveals other disturbing trends. Expense-account dining was up 57 percent in the past six quarters, for example. This while portions have been getting inexorably smaller! It's outrageous, and we're going to put a stop to it.

6. Upgrade wife and children. Whether this is a hardware or a software issue is open to question. I've got a team of McKinsey people working on it; a report is due in January. After that, I'll assemble a work group to recommend a strategy. When that's completed, I'm going to start looking at my friends. They could stand some improvement, too.

7. Begin reporting personal income as Ebitda. I'm not sure how the guys at the IRS are going to like this, but from what I hear they're under a lot of pressure to get Y2K themselves, so maybe they'll take kindly to it. Operating profit wheezes in on the balance sheet all laden down with depreciation and amortization, which makes the whole picture look worse, especially for a guy who's toting around as much goodwill as I am. Last year I produced free cash flow

growth in double digits, while my actual earnings per share, thanks to an onerous tax burden, were rather depressed at the end of the day. Ebitda takes care of that by focusing my personal performance for the new millennium where it counts: on cash in the pocket, baby!

8. Change my demographics. In a few years I'm going to be outside the key age group most favored by advertisers. That's very anti-Y2K. I therefore plan to stay in the younger demo until the older one is determined to be a safe place to live.

9. Stay off elevators. Have you heard this? I don't quite get it, but something's going to happen to elevators when the big day comes. Face it—all your efforts won't add up to a hill of beans if you're caught in a tiny metal box hurtling forty-five stories to bedrock. This is sort of a short-term change, involving basically one or two days on or about January 1, 2000. But it's incredibly important nonetheless. Being a gobbet of mucus and spittle on the floor of a twisted steel hulk is not the way to keep yourself working smoothly in the new millennium. A word to the wise!

10. Maintain ongoing good relationships with ultrasenior management. We're now close enough in to see that many of the Y1K senior officers are going to make it just fine into the Y2K environment. The implications are clear and very heartening for those who have put in quality time in the waning days of the millennium: All that hard work, project management, and sucking up have not been in vain if they have, in fact, helped you to forge a bridge to the next century. Walk across it and sniff that fresh air! You've made it! You've won! You're O-2K!

Ain't life gr&?

1999

Get Out of My Brain, You Norzoids!

I was in the middle of my late-morning mandatory cranial download when I realized that I couldn't take it anymore. Maybe it was the jolly seasonal music being piped directly into my limbic region that did it, but I just thought: Hey. Enough. It's 2999 already. It's time to take control of my life.

My plan is simple. It won't take long to implement. But I thought that before I went ahead and left all of you neural Netniks behind, I would give you some of my reasons.

First, and most unacceptable to Bud, I am sure, I'm sick of this transcortical implant in my head. I know it's a convenience. It's nice that we don't have to carry around those micro-DigiPhones embedded in our palms the way they did in the old days. It must have been a terrible pain to be instant-messaging someone via an interpersonal, real-time link in your adenoids and all of a sudden have your hand go off like a microwave oven when the turkey substitute is ready. Still, call me crazy, but I find it creepy to hear Bud's voice in the back of my head all the time, informing me I have an incoming communication from somebody in Omaha.

I heard once there was a time when people could go places where they could not be reached. Tunnels, I think they called them. Now there are no such places, because we carry our links inside us wherever we go.

I think that's wrong. I want it to stop. I'm tired of the mandatory downloads of news, weather, information, and entertainment that Bud provides for me. I know the cornucopia of data was assembled using a menu I myself provided from the 243,892 channels now owned by the Company. But just because I was interested in something last week, must I hear about it now? Don't I have the right to be surprised? I guess Bud doesn't think so.

You know how it happened. Around the turn of last century, the Company decided it was no longer a person's right to be uninformed and underentertained. Right now, for instance, I'm on my second internal alert about economic news from Eurok. I guess this is because I scanned similar information more than twice last monad. Now they won't let me alone about it. It's horrible. First, you get a little ping in your middle ear, and the message floats into your head. "Hi, Stan. Got something for you." That's mine, anyhow. Yours is, of course, whatever you asked it to be. The second time Bud's not as patient, and the ping comes with a little tweak. You don't want to let it go a third time. I tried that once, and it wasn't worth it.

The thing is, I don't want to know everything all the time. In the old days, there were millions who didn't know everything. A lot of them didn't really know anything. That must have been nice.

Supporters of omni-InfoSaturation point out that it's all on demand. We're just getting what we ask for! Actually, the tsunami of download material we tailor for our own consumption only forces us to come face-to-face with our own limited interests and disturbing obsessions. There are people who do nothing but sit in their eco-chair for monads at a time, soaking in on-demand supplies of "Who Wants to Be a Dodecazillionaire," chuckling every time Cyborg Philbin murmurs, "And that would be your final answer?" What a bunch of norzoids!

But honestly. Is that any better than my fate—being awash in news from Fresnia, Gorbatuna, and Blabst, constantly updated on economic data, sports scores, or political trends in which I truly have no interest? I have heard that at one time people used to roam the spectrum at will, discovering things they had no prior intention of watching. Can you imagine?

And our jobs, our jobs. What is it we actually do? We don't make anything, that's for sure. We come and go and don't leave a trace. At this writing I have climbed to the level of Information Director, Third Class. That's a very big deal, rating me a nice personal space. But . . . what is it I do? Move data, like everyone else. Financial data. Personal data. Packaging. Repackaging. Uploading. Downloading. I want to do something, goddamn it! To . . . make something.

You know, I heard that before the Company finally resolved all global competitive issues, there was more than one entity that produced things to buy. People actually went out and obtained things from "stores." Now it's different. I think of something I want. The subliminal order is placed over the ethersphere, which has my personal information on file. The "object" is then downloaded into my conceptual folder for review. If I approve, I get to "experience" it.

The hork with that. There is an existence in the physical plane, even though Bud doesn't want you to be aware of it. People smell things.

They taste. They touch objects with their fingers as well as their minds—did you know that?

And they go places. Okay, I know the travel rules are for our own good, that there are simply too many life-forms on this planet now for all of us to go anywhere without prior permission from Bud. But on my vacation, I want to feel real, not virtual, sand between my toes. I'm not scheduled to fly for anything but business until 3012. And the line for discorporealization to anywhere worth going is so long you'd have to be the CEO of a local Company governing franchise to get an authorization.

I wish I had bones.

Oh, all right. I know I have bones in there somewhere. But it's been so long since I used them. I know I have muscles too. I want to experience something that isn't filtered through some sort of portal into a physioneural net. In short, I want to get up and walk.

Go ahead! Laugh! But I'm dead serious.

I'm going to unplug. That's just a figure of speech, of course. There are no wires. It's all supra-high frequency. There is, however, the metapod in my hand that can be destroyed. It's my gateway. And all I have to do is squeeze.

I have heard tell of others. Perhaps they are out there, crawling around without their tethers, feeling actual rain on their pallid skin, nonvirtual sun on their shoulders. Perhaps they have books and thoughts that are not augmented on demand. Perhaps they are not merely receptacles for Bud or for the Company.

But even if there is only darkness and isolation and silence out beyond this world we have created, it is there that I will go. I look to the future with hope in my heart.

Wish me luck. Maybe I'll see you there.

1999

Oh, Sure. Now They're Sorry

It is clear by now that the nations, companies, and individuals that did nothing because they were too stupid to prepare for the Y2K global disaster fared exactly as well as AT&T, which reportedly spent more than $500 million on the problem. In Burkina Faso and Tasmania and Totowa, N.J., it was all the same. That is, it was nothing. Not even a small burp that could make us say, "Gee, it was a nonevent, but at least we didn't have that little gas problem to contend with."

In short, we were had. Our fear of numbers and cosmic occurrences was played masterfully by nuts of all varieties, and we fell, just as tonsured monks trembled before the end of the world that was coming at the turn of the year 1000. And now? Now, I'm afraid, I am not amused.

Names must be taken. Asses must be kicked. If you went to a doctor who made you get a bypass when all you required was a roll of Tums, you'd be in a bad mood about it. Well, look what these bozos made us do, goddamn it!

They made us spend a ton of money. The total price tag seems to be upward of half a trillion dollars. How many Porsche Boxsters could that buy for people who can't afford one? At my company we set up two redundant bunkers, each staffed with weary mid-level managers, who basically spent the entire New Year's weekend playing canasta. Dozens of schmendricks had to ignore their families for no reason whatsoever.

We issued satellite phones that were not dependent on cells or landlines to every senior officer, so we could all be in touch with each other as the social fabric was rent asunder. We had committees and readiness panels up the wazoo. An army of nerds was deployed against this thing.

They wrecked our New Year's Eve. I had a dinner engagement that night. I was required to tote my satellite phone to the Dolgens's house, where it became an object of derision. It was big, by the way, and came with a sizable beeper that was supposedly able to reach me even if, say, Russian mushrooms were blooming over Manhattan. I spent the best part of the night wondering whether I should be checking in with somebody.

They scared us. Particularly the innocent, like children and high-tech writers. For days prior to the event, my son, who is thirteen, was agitated about the possibility that nuclear weapons could be launched on January 1. There were lines at the bank. People got enough water to submerge their SUVs. Society was even more paranoid and edgy than usual. Thanks, we needed that.

They made themselves famous and rich! How much dough do you think Kyocera, the maker of our satellite phones, earned on this thing? How many pundits sold books and articles to credulous magazines like this one?

And now they apologize, all of them. Well, it just won't do. Somebody must be crushed. Ah, but who? I'll tell you.

Let's start with the gullible media. In this regard, huzzah to our friends at *Business Week,* which just about started the whole hysteria binge with a cover story entitled "ZAP! How the Year 2000 Bug Will Hurt the Economy," a fear fest that included all kinds of dire prognostications. "Indeed, the Y2K bug is shaping up to have a profoundly negative impact on the U.S. economy—starting almost immediately," the magazine wrote in early 1998. "The growth rate in 1999 will be 0.3 percentage points lower as companies divert resources to fix the problem. Then Y2K could cut half a percentage point off growth in 2000 and early 2001. That would be the same size as the expected economic damage from the turmoil in East Asia." Wow! We all know what happened there. Asia practically collapsed! That was supposed to happen to us. Except it didn't.

Next, let's toast (literally, if possible) computer industry executives who tried to generate business for themselves. Scott McNealy, CEO of Sun Microsystems, can be our poster boy here. In early 1999 he said, "My recommendation is to buy a lot of computers in the second half of this year. . . . Given what we know about Asia, it might not be a bad idea to stockpile computers"—thus neatly mixing three great Western themes at the end of the millennium: fear of Asia, fear of the millennium, and the desire to capitalize on both.

Financial types who used their positions to terrify us about our money must be noted, too. I actually went to high school with Ed Yardeni, the economist for Deutsche Bank, and I remember him even then as a very nice but slightly jittery guy. He seems to have continued in that vein. "I doubt that all computer systems in the world will be completely fixed," he said at one point. "If that's the case, then some will fail, possibly causing widespread disruptions at critical choke points of vital economic systems and a global recession." Ed stated that the probability of such a recession was 70 percent. "I'm not making any excuses," he told *Fortune* in the last issue, playing the honesty card right up front. That was right after he said he didn't feel foolish because "I based my concerns on officially available data coming out of congressional hearings, from the General Accounting Office, and the Office of Management and Budget." An honest mistake, then? Phooey, I say. Up your mea culpas, Ed! And let's catch up real soon!

And then there were the professional Jeremiahs, like Gary North, self-proclaimed Web messenger of doom. He now writes on his Web site: "I am certainly willing to say that my assessment of the threat, as things have played out, was incorrect." This is the same nitwit who in October was saying that Y2K was "the biggest problem that the modern world has ever faced." Your fifteen minutes are over, Gary.

What should be done with these people? We can't kill them, since stupidity is not a capital offense, even in this century. We can, however, hit them over the head with sticks. That's what I plan to do. The next time I see any of these guys, I'm going to rear back and hit them over the head with a nice big tree branch, or possibly a cane, particularly if they are speaking. Let me know if you come up with a better solution, but until then, that will be mine.

Sometimes the old technologies work the best.

2000

God Is My Palm Pilot, I Need No Other

Most of the time, I think it's safe to say, I want what you want. You want a big office in the corner, I know that. Well, so do I. You want a couple of weeks of vacation every summer, with nobody to bother you with faxes and cellular communication in some remote locale where the prevailing thoughts are of sunshine and wine. I want that, too. You want a beautiful car and a beautiful house and a beautiful spouse, and that describes me perfectly, too. You want a big TV and a mother of a computer with more than a hundred gigs in its hard drive. Who doesn't?

I've gotten used to this, us all wanting basically the same things all the time. I've come to love it. It makes us one with one another, this shared wanting, and then we don't feel so alone in the universe, which after all remains just as cold, vast, and unfeeling as it was when the first cave person looked up at a much younger moon.

And yet today I must report that our circle of common desire must now be broken, and this is why: I don't want a Palm. I've tried. God knows, I've tried. I've gone to stores to look at them, the beautiful, tasty little Palms, and read about them in magazines dedicated to inflaming my organs of wanting. I've talked to Mitch and Vinnie—my friends from down the hall who are both way into their Palms—in an attempt to create some vague sense of wanting in myself. But it has all failed so far.

This is unprecedented, I assure you. I have wanted, each in its appropriate time, a transistor radio, a Nikon, an electric guitar, a Leica, a stereo, several automobiles, a fondue pot, a Walkman, the first portable CD player made by Sony, two woks several decades apart, the first Kaypro lunchbox computer, the first XT, the first AT, the first Pentiums I, II, and III, a succession of increasingly tiny cell phones, a home fax with its own dedicated line; and now I find I even sort of want one of those MP3 players you can carry around with you to play tunes on, just like a transistor radio—but it's digital!

But I don't want a Palm. Why? I do not know.

Why don't I want it to do my calendar for me? Right now I have my calendar in a little leather book. It's so inconvenient. When I want to find out what I'm supposed to do during a day, I have to open it up and look at what I've scribbled in it at some previous time. If I had a Palm, I could write my appointments on the little electronic pad, and they would be entered just like that. I could take it out anytime and look at them.

Why don't I want it to contain my address book? I could core dump my entire Rolodex and have all those people right in the Palm of my hand! At this point, it is true, I spend most of my day returning calls from little slips of paper that have all the information I need right on them. But it would sure come in handy to have all the numbers of the people I have already spoken to over the past decade right in my hot little Palm.

Why don't I want to input my memos onto the little pad at the bottom of the Palm, where they could be instantaneously transformed into text files that could later be loaded into my computer and then printed out (after, to be fair, considerable editing due to the limitations of the medium)? Now, when I'm on the move, I am sometimes forced to write stuff down on a piece of paper. Sometimes I am forced not to write anything at all until I can get to a convenient place, wasting critical minutes in unproductive activities.

Why wouldn't I want to update my business contacts right after I have a meeting? You meet a fellow Palm owner, and he can beam his business card to you over the infrared connection. Which is amazing, considering how much use we all have for business cards.

And why, oh, why, wouldn't I want to tap into the Internet wherever I want? To look up restaurant reviews and movie times and stock quotes as I made my way from one meeting to another, or on weekend trips to the supermarket, the mall, museums, the movies—wherever I go on this entire planet, really?

I could write the name of a Web site with that itsy-bitsy wand and then touch a button and go right to that very site—with no computer connection!—and cruise the Web and very shortly even stream the music and video I like.

What the hell is the matter with me? Why wouldn't I want to do that?

Why wouldn't I want my music downloaded into one of those amazing IBM microdrives, one gig big? To read novels on my little screen? To carry my kids' photos so they can be accessed at any time, unlike the ones in my wallet, which are so often tucked between credit cards and other random stuff? To download the newspaper and read it right there in that teeny window instead of folded up in my hands in that inconvenient way we've all learned to live with? To use my mind in short bursts in which I follow up on everything I do and think and read immediately, rendering it into digital form for later mulching and processing?

Don't I want everything I do to be useful and accessible?

Apparently, I don't. Even right now, thinking of all these great applications, I still can't generate any genuine excitement in myself. Right in front of you, I have tried once again and failed. And I am well aware that in the past eight minutes, while you were reading this, more than a few of you have considered the attributes I have discussed and said to yourselves, "Yes, this is all very well, but I'm going out to get one of those things right now."

Well, I hope you do. I want your future to be full and productive and Palmful. But me . . . I'm not going to.

Because I don't want one.

It's terrible, I know, this . . . absence of wanting. I know what I'm missing, don't worry—all the filing and note-taking and writing and beaming and categorizing and scheduling and most of all the sense of my entire life force, heavy in my own hand.

But that's only part of it. What if it doesn't stop here? What if I don't want the next thing that is bound to come along, no matter how cool and essential . . . and the next after that? Pretty soon, I'll start not wanting anything all the time, and then where—and who—will I be?

2000

The Missing Link

I lost my BlackBerry. It was scary. I looked in my pocket, and it was gone. All of a sudden, like. One minute I thought it was there. Then it wasn't. Poof. For those of you who don't know, the BlackBerry is a little gizmo that enables you to read and answer e-mail when you're not at the office. Like, if you're in your backyard with a book and a brewski? You can get e-mail. In a Town Car on the way to the Omaha office? There too. It's really great.

I looked all around my house for my BlackBerry when I realized it wasn't in my front jacket pocket where I always, always keep it. It wasn't anyplace. "It didn't grow a pair of legs and walk away," said several people to me when I told them I couldn't find it. Why do people always say stuff like that? It makes you feel that they're lacking in sympathy for your problems.

At any rate, my BlackBerry might as well have grown a pair of legs and walked away. I didn't have it, that's for sure. And like I said, I didn't get much empathy from anybody when I told them. I guess it's true that there are worse problems in the world. You could also misplace your cell phone.

I did that three days later. It happened quite suddenly. I looked in my right front pocket and was amazed at the complete absence of cell phone there. I all but took off the jacket and shook it, looking for the cell phone. The thing about having a certain thing in a certain place is that when it is not in that place you can't imagine where in the world it could possibly be. It wasn't where I had carried it since Motorolas got small enough for everyday portability. Where, then, could it have gone?

One thing was clear. Neither my phone nor my BlackBerry was anywhere in my home per se. I felt confident in this belief, since I had gotten to the point of searching through areas where I knew they could not possibly have gotten themselves, having exhausted those locations where there was some hope they might be found. They were not in the drawers of my bedside table, where I might have put one or both at the end of a hard day's communicating. Nor were they in the mess on the desk in my study . . . nor between my mattress and my box spring, in the dog's bed, on the roof of our garage, in the flower beds that run along the front of our porch, or in the barbecue pit.

I stood in my kitchen that night, exhausted and confused, e-mailless and out of touch, thoughtfully scratching the interesting welts that were beginning to appear on the side of my face, on my torso, and up and down my legs, and considered where I could possibly have left my electronic friends. Then I went to sleep. At least I think I did. I don't remember too much of the evening after that, anyhow.

The next morning was even a little bit worse. My head had blown up to the size of a muskmelon and I had developed a jitter in my legs that made it impossible for me to sit still without humming.

In my car for the one-hour commute to the office, I felt stripped of the armor I need to function while outdoors. I was in interstitial space, with no hope of connectivity. I didn't have my BlackBerry to give me my e-mail on the way to work and I didn't have my cell phone to check in, as I always do, with Brewster, Schuster, Kolnagie, and Martinson, and all the guys in Skokie and Harrisburg. What was I to do? As I swerved across the road, dodging an inexplicable number of tiny pink badgers that seemed to be everywhere at once, I listened to the radio without turning it on and tried to establish equilibrium, but I was feeling weird . . . cold and hot at the same time, with a freezing crown of perspiration ringing my fevered brow.

I parked my car on top of a fire hydrant and lurched spastically to the office. As I went, I was aware of the same kind of feelings that beset warriors who lose a leg in a battle. Years later, they still reach to scratch at an itch that is tormenting them in the limb they have long been parted from.

I kept reaching for my jacket pockets, first the left, then the right, only to find empty space, if you don't count the lint. There wasn't a lot of lint, don't get the wrong idea. But each time I faced those two voids, this terrible feeling of being at loose ends filled me from top to bottom. I don't like feelings that fill me from top to bottom. I'm generally over those.

When I got to my office, I found that neither my BlackBerry nor my cell phone was on my desk, in my desk, in my credenza, on my credenza, in the cushions of my couch, or even under the wall-to-wall carpet. Man, I can tell you that stuff was really difficult to rip off the floor, almost as if it had been bonded down by some kind of adhesive! Anyhow, they weren't there.

Of course, I was okay when I was in the saddle. I canceled my lunch and worked very hard to eliminate all phone messages and e-mails, knowing that later in the day I would once again be cut off from my electronic umbilicus. The thought of it made me feel kind of lightheaded, which may explain why I found myself dozing at several occasions during the day, my head lolling on my chest, a small bubble perched at the rim of one nostril.

The drive home was a nightmare. Uncontrollable drooling made it difficult for me to keep both hands on the wheel. I was incapable of thinking straight or even in a circular fashion, cogitating in little bursts that would splutter out like wet sparklers on the Fourth of July. At the end of each burst, I would think, "Gee, I'd better phone Bortz about that," or "I'd better pull over and e-mail Thomaschevsky immediately," and then I would realize I had no way of doing either! Then, whatever had been in my head, pfft! It was gone! And it came to me suddenly, as if in the middle of a dream: We have reached the point where any idea that is not immediately communicated electronically might as well not have happened at all.

I stumbled through the door to my home, shaking in every corner of my being. There was an ache deep inside me. I yearned for my Black-Berry. I hungered for my cell. I curled myself into a little ball in the corner of the kitchen and gave myself over to the craving.

"Hey," said my wife. "I found these in your gray suit." She handed over my two wireless toys. "You're lucky," she said. "I almost left them at the dry cleaner's."

I held my cool little friends to my cheeks and felt the burning there subside.

"Thanks," I said. "I didn't miss them a bit."

2001

Log Off, You Losers!

They say all good things must come to an end. Thankfully, the same is often true of bad things. Sometimes you have to give the evil that men do a little guidance in the direction of the door, however. So let's do that right now.

I want all of you within the sound of my voice to pause. Put your hands in your laps. Close your eyes and ask yourselves: Is the e-mail I'm about to send necessary? And if not, is it at least fun? If you cannot answer yes to either of those questions—don't hit that Send button. Electronic flatulence must cease!

I saw it clearly last week. Some guys wanted to set up a conference call with me. That's fine. I can sit on the end of a telephone line and look out the window as well as the next person, and some people need elaborate conference calls set up by professional conference-call setter-uppers to feel good. There were three individuals who needed to talk to one another, so why one of us couldn't just dial one of the others and then patch the third in I don't know. But a professional was designated to establish the important communication hookup, and off we went.

First we all exchanged e-mails about our schedules. That was okay. I thought it was interesting that Bob was going to be in Denver and Ted was going to be in Chicago, although it had nothing to do with the subject of our call. Then it developed that Thursday looked good until it was Tuesday because Bob was flying and Ted was driving, and then there was a mix-up between Thursday and Tuesday, and then there was some more effluvia that went back and forth about 3:00 vs. 3:30, and once the great event was established for Wednesday then everybody had to thank everybody, and a lot of jolly huzzahs went back and forth, and self-congratulations all the way around, and pretty soon there was a confirmation e-mail that got one thing wrong so a bunch of stuff had to then fly around clarifying the situation, and then there were observations about the amusing snafu and more thanks and high-fives for one and all, and by the time it was over I believe more than 100 e-mails of one form or another had crossed the electronic portal, popping up like cockroaches that keep pouring into a nighttime kitchen no matter how many efforts you make to kill them.

How many phone calls would it have taken one good assistant to set up this thing? Three? Come on!

During this time I noticed that several of the people who work for me were indulging in similar shenanigans. Supposedly entertaining e-mails were making their way around the system with trenchant observations like "See you there!" and "Will do!" I was copied on all of them, because people like to copy executives on things, for obvious reasons.

It got to the point where I had to fire off a message to all on the distribution list, saying "This is a relatively unimportant matter that has occupied us all for far too long. I will kill the individual who sends the next unessential e-mail on it." I have no idea whether it stopped the chain, but I was no longer copied on anything. That's something.

So here's what I'm suggesting:

1. Stop telling people you Will Do something. The best way of telling people you Will Do something is to Do It and then send a message saying the job is done. Until then, I assume you Will Do It. So Go Do It.
2. Stop thanking people so much. If I get one more message telling me "tks" for something, I'm going to crush the one who sends it like an anchovy. I'm also not interested in hearing that there's "No problem." Know what? There better not be.
3. Stop using e-mail when there's a damn phone on your desk. E-mail is for confirmation and simple discussion. Phones are for doing business. Here's how it goes: You think about the e-mail you are about to send. You realize that the distribution list is very long. You further see that if you simply talk to one person, you need not send the e-mail nor the 124 subsequent ones that it will generate. You call that one person. End of story.
4. Never hesitate to send an e-mail that has actual data in it. It's the follow-up that says "Way to Go!" that's got to be run through the karmic shredder.
5. Stop copying me on transitional crud. I want stuff that's fully baked, not half-baked!
6. And absotively posilutely no e-mail chains of more than ten individual communications! None! Once you reach that number, it's over! Have a meeting! Get a cup of coffee! Send a telegram! I don't care what you do! But if I see the same subject line in my in-box once too often—you're toast! Toast!

Look. I recognize that this is a big change for us. We're like junkies who started off with a little recreational pot in the '80s and are now mainlining a couple ounces of horse every day. Well, it's time to hit the e-hab! We'll be glad we did!

Okay? Will do? Tks!

2002

Love Me, Love My Spam

What does the daily onslaught of spam tell us about people who use the Internet? A perusal of my in-box might be instructive. But I'll tell you from the get-go, it's not pretty. If my spam is any indication, Internet users have some pretty serious problems, and not all of them are psychological.

First, they seem to be overly interested in establishing contact with their former high school classmates. Now, I don't know about you, but my high school classmates were a pretty motley bunch. The ones I actually remember I still talk to now and then—all two of them. The thing that's interesting about this spam is that when you click on the offer to see "7 of yr classmates for free!" you get a form on how to pay money to see them.

So I guess we have our first theme here. Internet marketers have determined that Internet users are stupid.

Further proof of this postulate comes from a spamster who offers me a good deal on the pot with the holes on top as seen on TV. It is a pot for people who don't know how to use a colander. It looks very convenient, and I'm going to be sure to click on that link really soon, as soon as I feel confident in giving my credit card information to an organization that sends me spam daily offering me a pot for people who don't know how to use a colander, one that you can order on TV every night and is also available at my local mall at a kiosk dedicated to products that one may obtain only on television.

And right after I give my credit card information to those people, I guess I'll also have my brain completely removed and give them my banking data so that I can secure the lowest mortgage rates in the world outside the former Yugoslavia, and give them my mailing information to collect that cool $1,000 in grocery coupons that I've been cleared for after, I am sure, a rigorous investigation of my qualifications for this perk.

In addition to being stupid, spam marketing pundits must have also ascertained, Internet users are insecure, possibly for good reasons. A good number would seem to have yellow teeth, because dozens of companies have been kind enough to suggest ways that I might whiten mine. Many, in addition, would appear to be bald, or at least balding, given the profusion of opportunities I am offered to enjoy painless hair replacement or simply thwart my genetic heritage and regrow thick, lustrous hair. I have some hair that is thick, but only in certain places. And as for lustrous, well, what is anymore?

Legions of online citizens are also fat, if you take the number of products aimed at such people to be any indication. I am not fat. But I do have big bones. I find it kind of insulting to be continually offered products that will help me drop ugly pounds of adipose tissue, usually pills with names like Meta-Muscle. There's no way of knowing what's in them, but I assume they've been thoroughly tested by the FDA before they are allowed to go out over the Internet to millions of people.

But most important, I suppose, is the information that Internet users are distressingly small in a number of key areas that can drastically affect social opportunities. I am at a loss to soft-pedal these inadequacies, so I must urge any queasy reader to stop here and go to the section of this magazine that deals with technology or hardware or something. Because we're talking about the softest software of all.

That's right, after months of studying the subject, I have come to the conclusion that Internet users have tiny penises. At least the men do. At least 50 percent of my spam on the subject deals with that condition. I'm starting to take it personally, but there's really no reason for that. I lived a long time before it occurred to me that I might want to be, you know, improved in that area, or even that such a thing was possible. Now I don't know. Why are they sending me this stuff? And in such profusion? Do they know something I don't?

I have literally hundreds of offers from various companies that make clear what's possible in this new and exciting arena of medical practice. I clicked on one of the links once, and it sent me to a page with a picture of a lovely young woman stretching in a bathing suit, but there wasn't a whole lot of medical discussion. So it's unclear to me how it works. It must, though, or why would dozens of companies be promising the benefits?

Right now I'm a little confused about what to do. I wish the spam would stop, you know, but I don't think it's going to. This morning I had sixty-one messages in my in-box, and most of them had to do with my software. I don't know what to think. I guess I'll respond either to the free African safari I've been offered or the two-week free stay in a condo in the Bahamas, and let it percolate.

You don't want to let the good things in life pass you by.

2003

What's Your Sign?

Aquarius (January 21 to February 19): With Uranus lumbering around and making everybody nuts, you may find yourself feeling like squeezing an associate in an inappropriate fashion. Don't. Watch out for Pisces, by the way. He's jealous of your position in the zodiac and wants to eat your lunch. The way things are going with serving portions these days—tiny stacks of vertical greens drizzled in bizarre vinegar on enormous plates—each lunch serves only one. Make sure that's you no matter who's paying for it.

Pisces (February 20 to March 20): There's an Aquarius out there who means trouble for you. For some reason he's suspicious, combative. So quick—stomp on him in public meetings and take over part of his job description. Keep in mind, however, that he's been warned about you and is probably armed. On the lighter side, Mercury isn't just rising, he's practically beaming up to the mother ship. You can't go wrong by playing on other people's emotions.

Aries (March 21 to April 20): You're a peace-loving soul with a tremendous ability to lose yourself in other people's agendas, make them better, then fade into the woodwork while they take the credit and the stock options. In other words—you're a chump. What's the matter with you, huh? But where there's life, there's hope, and this month there's opportunity. With Capricorn butting up against the side of your house like Charlie Sheen at a bachelor party, you've got power to burn. Don't waste it. Target your options. Engineer your solutions. Mount a campaign. You can do it, and you will. People like you. Good luck!

Taurus (April 21 to May 21): Aries is on a stupid positive-thinking kick. Now's the time to come up behind him and push him into the swamp, where the alligators will eat him. But he's not your worst adversary, pal. Your worst adversary is yourself. You know, people would like you if you weren't so darned aggressive. Still, there's aggressive and there's aggressive. With the moon in the eighth house and Saturn doing the macarena on six continents, it's time to kick back and take stock. Life isn't just about winning and losing. It's about money as well. And certainly sex too, although let's not talk about that now.

Gemini (May 22 to June 21): While Taurus is dealing with Aries, sneak around to the back of his house and break in. Once you're inside, find the computer on the desk in the small makeshift study at the top of the stairs. Quietly boot up the machine and copy all the diskettes marked "Binty." Then slip out the side window. Don't worry about getting caught. Pluto floats in the sixteenth house like a gas bubble, so you've got the chops to get the job done. Once you're safely clear, sell the information to Microsoft, which one day will control all intellectual property benignly and to our mutual benefit.

Cancer (June 22 to July 23): You're the idealist, the dreamer, the one who wants to think the best of people. Fortunately for you, Venus is ascendant, Jupiter is declining, and Neptune has water in his ears. Seize this moment to help those who can't help themselves by purchasing tickets to expensive black-tie banquets. Once there, you can have fun with industry chums and do well by doing good at the same time. Take as many people out to expensive lunches as you can get away with. This has nothing to do with your horoscope. It's just damn good advice.

Leo (July 24 to August 23): Corruption is everywhere. Thanks to your properties as the vigilant lion of the zodiac, however, you're aware of the weaknesses of friend and foe alike. Cancer, for instance, is into feathering his nest with prestigious hobnobbing and face sucking. Using your sidelong, scuttling style, slide into Virgo's office and inform him that Cancer's expense account could bear some looking into. He'll take it from there.

Virgo (August 24 to September 23): That Leo is a good guy, isn't he? Real straight shooter. You'll want to start that audit on Cancer right away. Wow. Look at that $300 dinner at the Hilton last week! Don't you wonder who that was with? Find out! You're a probing, investigative type with intellectual muscle to spare—that's why you went into accounting! Oh, one last thing: Make sure you get invited to the retreat at Sanibel Island in the fourth quarter. Anyone who isn't there will be dust.

Libra (September 24 to October 23): Incoming fire from human resources may enrage you to the point you're tempted to engage with the problem on an executive level. Scream at a subordinate instead. There's never a bad time for that, so why not give it a try? And don't forget, as you make up that invitation list for the upcoming Sanibel retreat, that bad vibrations from intrusive Virgos and Scorpios could wreck the ambience of the meeting. It should be small and tasty, with plenty of time for interchange. Keep that list lean and selective. It will pay off for you as the stars move into the next quadrant.

Scorpio (October 24 to November 22): That repulsive Libra with the small potbelly is trying to keep you out of the Sanibel thing. Focus on destabilizing him. Take him out with senior management. For that you'll need courage, because infighting can be scary. And with your stars in quizzical alignment you don't have a superfluity of guts right now. This means you should probably start drinking immediately. Nothing before noon, naturally, but at lunch any serious hitter should be able to handle a martini, a couple of glasses of wine. Don't forget the grappa!

Sagittarius (November 23 to December 21): Okay. Scorpio is drunk on her butt. Everyone else is fighting. Juno is in the last house on the left with Kukla, Fran, and Ollie. Get with the chairman and grab some face time. He's lonely, and he longs to just kick back with somebody thoughtful like you. Be bold. Even the King needs friends.

Capricorn (December 22 to January 20): Oh boy. What's this now? Who's that moron at your door with a beamish expression? Oh, no! He's coming in! He's sitting down! He's . . . talking! Close your eyes. Maybe this is all a dream, and you're actually on a golf course. In fact, with Venus rising and Juno on the nineteenth green, now is the time to sneak away. Go ahead! Get outta there before Taurus comes in and tears your ears off!

If today is your birthday: Today all planets are warm and toasty. The moon is rising. Why are you listening to all this stuff? Don't you have anything better to do? The future lies not in the stars, but in ourselves. So have some cake and give yourself a pat on the back. You're the one who got you here. Happy birthday, stargazer!

1996

6

ON THE ROAD AGAIN
(AND AGAIN)

You name a place, I've been there. Well, perhaps not everyplace. But certainly a lot of them. Many of them are the same. Some of them are different.

Vegas, for instance, is different. You have to watch yourself there pretty closely. In that way, it's like New Orleans, except of course that New Orleans is not essentially a theme park but an authentic city, like Boston, except that Boston has seasons, like Chicago, except Chicago has very extreme weather, unlike Los Angeles, which really does have a beautiful climate, particularly in the wintertime, when it's not too hot at all but very temperate, like San Francisco and, for that matter, Seattle, which is also a little wet, but not as wet as Paris in the springtime, which can really be a pain in the neck if you're there for thirty-six hours and just one meeting and have to stay inside the whole time because it's too wet to go out. A couple of years ago, some guys from an investment banking firm got fired because they ordered a $5000 bottle of wine at dinner in Paris and then tried to expense it. It was probably raining then, too. Business people do weird things on the road, particularly if they are forced to spend a lot of time with other business people in unstructured environments, indoors, and everyone has heavy plastic.

There are dangers in outer space. Some spin off into the universe where there is very bad gravity and never come back to earth. Others get space madness and blow up. But there are pleasures. It's better in First Class, where the nuts are hotter and the seats go all the way back, and there's nothing like kickin' it in a nice *suite in a city far from home. The windows are open and a breeze comes in. Your first meeting isn't until tomorrow. The room service pizza is good, and has chorizo. The world, for a moment, takes a breath. . . . Ah. That's nice.*

Thirty Seconds over Houston

Zero Hour, Minus 24: The night before is always the hardest. You try to push the black sludge from your mind, but still they come, the fears, lush and lurid. Flaming planes broken and toasting on open runways. Your skull screaming white in the moonlight of a faraway city, laid open by some geek who wanted your wallet. Lost luggage. Yet fear or no, the reality is there, hard and ineluctable as a hazelnut. Tonight you must pack. For tomorrow, you travel.

Minus 12 Hours: They tell you the city to which you've been called is hot as hell, except when it's meat-locker cold. It doesn't rain often, but when it does, folks get out the sandbags and ride their floating cars to safety. Bottom line, you're going to need duds to meet any terrain during your one and a half days at the front. The good soldier travels light.

- 12 pairs of socks, in all colors and weights
- 4 suits, 2 sports coats
- 5 pairs slacks (two worsted, two khaki, one in a bold lime that will serve on the nineteenth hole)
- Every white shirt you have clean
- 12 pairs of underwear (thanks to your lifelong fear you might get found dead in a pair not up to snuff)
- 12 T-shirts
- 1 pair new pajamas (packed on every trip since 1983 but never really used, since by the time you all fall into bed, usually drunk, you can't expunge pins from a new garment)

Your bag, built to hold two suits and a box of Chiclets, is obscenely engorged. It doesn't matter. Years ago, stranded at Mobile, Alabama airport in jeans and old Keds, you determined never again to check anything you aren't prepared to lose or give away.

Day One, 08:31 Hours: Guys in your outfit are expected to fly coach, whatever the size of their egos, legs, or paychecks. For the first time, as you nestle between two steer-fed sales guys from an IBM clone, your mind turns to the job ahead, then skitters away as you enjoy your mystery microwave meal and sixteen Diet Cokes and meditate over *USA Today, Sports Illustrated* (July 1986, no swimwear), *Business Week, The Wall Street Journal, Better Homes and Gardens, Black Enterprise,* and a précis of something by Tom Peters in the in-flight magazine. Thus enriched, you sink inexorably into the deepest sleep of all, the one that comes on moving vehicles, streaking toward a confrontation that will test your soul to its depths, if it has any.

15:42 Hours, At the Bivouac: As you pull into the general Hiltonesque, you wonder if the cab really should have cost $47.50 but decide that you don't care, since it's expensed. Your room is small, but what do you expect for $180 a night? As you unpack, you watch the final twenty-six minutes of *RoboCop* on Spectravision ($6.35) and get your shirts together.

16:08 Hours: Peering at the keypad, you finally figure out how to make a long-distance call, and touch base with your secretary. You are careful to return all calls while you're out of town. Last year, a division V.P. nearly went up in fumes when he failed to do so. On the road for ten days of back-breaking labor, he let his stock molder back at headquarters, where there be vipers. "If George intends to survive with the big boys, he's got to learn to keep his head in three places at once," one senior suit observed, "and that means being able to work the phones with a suitcase in your hand." So you do.

16:21 Hours: You realize you have forgotten to pack razor, shaving cream, deodorant, toothbrush, dental floss, and, yes, shoes. Purchase of same in hotel lobby sets you back more than 168 personal dollars.

18:00 Hours: You prepare for your dinner with associated vendors. Shower, shave, and watch the first thirty-one minutes of *RoboCop* ($6.35 more).

20:00 Hours: Planning dinner with working group in preparation for big dog and pony scheduled for 09:01 tomorrow. Gang of four from a variety of companies, all dedicated to selling and retaining the vast wash of clients now pouring in from fifty states and Japan, consumes eight cocktails, four steaks, five bottles of fine wine, and assorted after-dinner potables. Guys roll out of restaurant at 23:13 and proceed down the avenue to do further damage, mostly to themselves. You buy a T-shirt as a memento ($23.95). At 01:00 you find yourself in the elevator with the V.P., Marketing, of a friendly firm. "Now we got rid of the rest of 'em," he drools. "Let's go and seriously party." You decline. Tomorrow your ass is on the line, and you want it to be awake.

06:00 Hours, D-day: You bolt upright, anxiety and the time change kicking in with a vengeance. Although the confrontation is three hours away, you're ready to boogie. Suit up. Get your notes in order. Have a good breakfast from room service ($16.96 plus tax), watch the middle twenty-four minutes of *RoboCop* (final total cost of picture: $19.05, plus tax), and stare out the window.

08:57 Hours: Refreshed, in your most flamboyant gray suit, you enter the Millard Fillmore Room to face what, for the next sixty minutes, will be the only world you know. Or need to know.

Zero Hour: Your opening salvo, "I'll talk real slow this morning for those of you who were down on Main Street until dawn getting in touch with the marketplace." This mows them down, even the Japanese. The rest goes off without a hitch. Execution makes the world go round, especially on the road, where death is the only excuse for failure.

10:21 Hours: Your back hurts from the ferocious pounding it's recently endured, but that's all right. With a sheaf of business cards in your kit, the flush of post-presentation adrenaline endangering your heart, you step out onto the street, your plastic burning a hole in your pocket.

14:35 Hours: The pilot is a garrulous quipster with a Right Stuff drawl, but you don't care. You're going home. For the hell of it, you call HQ from the cellular phone. A couple of messages, but they can wait. You cop some z's. You've earned them, good buddy.

22:30 Hours: Your kids are happy to see you. Your dog is happy to see you. And your wife is real happy to see you. Likes that teeny pin you bought at the intensely quaint jewelers near the hotel, too. You pop a brew, kick off your brand new hotel Weejuns, and enjoy the spoils of the returning victorious. Things are good. And why not? Clean living has its benefits occasionally. Sometimes a man has to travel to find that out.

1988

Scenes from a Mall

On the way out: They don't serve meals on airplanes anymore. You have to be on a nine-hour flight to Sri Lanka to get one. But the snack is quite enough for me in my current festive mood—turkey bologna on a roll with jalapeño peppers, an apple, some crackers, a chunk of processed-cheese food, and an oatmeal cookie sandwich with marshmallow filling. To my right, a baby is screaming. His face is blue, contorted. Cute little guy. Why is he going to Vegas? Hey—why does anybody go to Vegas? To live free or die! Or go to a convention! Maybe both!

In the airport: This place is titanic. We walk and walk. There seems to be no end in sight. There are slot machines by the baggage claim. A few semicomatose party animals walk by them gingerly, get close, move in, circle thoughtfully, like dogs regarding a particularly fragrant stump. One, a dead-pale cowboy in a huge Stetson hat, tall and bone-thin, plops down on the comfy stool and begins to drop dollar coins down the slot. In less than two minutes, he's lost forty bucks. I feel my bankroll nesting in my right front pocket. A thousand dollars in twenties. I resist the urge to set it loose. Dropping a wad at the airport doesn't seem like an auspicious beginning.

At the hotel: Vegas sits in the middle of the flat, unarticulated desert like a jewel on flypaper. Mountains loom in the middle distance, a rented backdrop. Somewhere not far away, the land must be beautiful, pristine. Here, though, things are definitely man-made. Fabulous marquees tower over us. Siegfried and Roy! David Copperfield! Stephanie Powers and Robert Wagner in A. R. Gurney's *Love Letters?*

I step into the lobby of the Mirage. I feel my jaw clank wide open. This place is huge. The reception desk goes on forever. There is a gigantic fish tank behind the clerks, with all kinds of colorful specimens in it. In order to reach the elevators, you have to walk through the jungle area, with hanging ferns and other outsized greenery, then through the heart of the casino, which is beyond enormous and laid out for maximum confusion. Bells are dinging. Lights are flashing. Several apparently dead people are playing slots. I see an ancient Asian woman smoking a two-inch ash. In front of her, a machine is coughing out dollar coins in huge amounts. When it is done, she begins to put the money back into the machine. I drop a quarter into a slot as I pass by. Sixteen quarters pop out. I'm ahead already!

My room boasts a remarkable view. Down below, a colossal man-made volcano is belching fire and smoke. A group of Asian businessmen are videotaping the show. Massive temples of pleasure rear up close by, neon winking, dancing, flowing in waves over their displays. I look for a minibar for some nuts or crackers, perhaps a drink. There is none. No minibar? I call room service and ask how long it would take to get a sandwich. "Not long! About an hour!" the chirpy voice tells me. I've never been hungry before while residing in a large luxury hotel. It's a strange feeling.

First-night party: It is ten o'clock in the evening back where I come from. Still, I'm looking forward to this dinner of about fifty people. These are our business partners, with whom we share an uneven amity at this point in our relationship. So there is a great deal of jocularity, and a comedian who's been prepped about us makes pointed jokes at our expense. People are literally wiping away tears of mirth. Before the festive meal, there are great little fried nuggets of either chicken or fish, I can't tell which, and deviled eggs with lots of paprika on them, something I almost never get at home. The entrée is steak and chicken. Not either. Both. Each has been microwaved to a turn, so they're nicely hot. I eat them. The dinner breaks up at 10:00 on the dot. The room is cleared by 10:06. With my stash in my pocket and a song in my heart, I'm off to make some money. Look out! Somebody stop me!

In the casino: I sit at the ten-dollar blackjack table, a free drink by my elbow. My pal Rafferty had given me some sage tips. "Stick on 16 if the dealer is showing a 6 or above. Take a hit on 12, 13, and 14, unless he's got a 9 or a 14. Always split everything except 10's, although you can split those, too, if the dealer is showing less than 6," is the way I heard it. I play for three or four hours and win forty dollars.

On the floor of the convention: The next day, I go to the convention floor and hang around until my face hurts from smiling. Then we go to lunch.

At Spago: Even though we have a reservation and there is an enormous dining room in the back virtually devoid of human life, we are told there will be a fifteen-minute wait. Another group, steeped in L.A. shtick, appears and is immediately seated. The restaurant is in Caesars Palace's atrium, a faux-Roman street filled with statuary and designer stores, with an indoor backlit sky that runs through the day's light-show every hour or so. By the time we are seated, the dome above is streaked with red and pink. Night is falling. The place is filled with convention-eers, laughing, chewing with their mouths open, hoisting glasses at one another, and barking like dogs.

We get a bottle of wine for the table. Our lunches come about an hour later. The pasta is cold and stuck together. Our basket of compli-mentary rolls comes with the check. The sky has gone from dawn to night and back again three times during our meal. Why am I not having more fun? On the way out of the hotel, we pass by what looks like a large stone fountain with a Bacchanalian figure seated among nymphs. As we pass, the statues creak to life and bellow, "Welcome to Caesars Palace!" It scares the hell out of me.

Second-night dinner: This hotel is truly tattered, even if it is famous. The carpets smell of smoke from cigarettes no longer manufac-tured. Herbert Tareytons, maybe. The menu at the restaurant features hits of the 1950s: shrimp cocktail, Caesar salad with real raw egg (pre-pared at your table!), lobster thermidor, stuff like that. For some reason, the conversation is a bit forced, which is strange, since back home we are usually quite convivial. After dinner, we order glasses of port and bran-dish cigars. Then we pile into Town Cars and ramble from nightspot to nightspot, drinking more at each one.

Back at the hotel, I cash a twenty-dollar bill and begin to feed bucks into a machine that says, Spin Till You Win. On the third dollar, it hawks up twenty. Ten dollars later, the machine begins to spin wildly, looking for a match. I win sixty. A wizened Asian woman has come up tight upon my space and is eyeing my machine covetously. She hangs over me, smoking. My machine has begun to ring loudly. A hundred and eighty dollars belches out of it. The woman is now standing very close to me, emitting a huge cloud of blue smoke, her bucket of coins ready. I figure I've had enough luck for one night. On the way out of the area, I pop one last coin into a gargantuan machine that says, Big Winner! Sixty bucks clanks out. I turn my coins into cash and walk up to my room $345 ahead. I sit on the edge of my bed and count my money over and over. It feels good. At 4:15, I fall asleep. I awaken two hours later, still drunk.

Lost in Caesars Palace: I have a 9 A.M. meeting in the Cubic Zir-conia room of this hotel. I enter through the entrance closest to the Mirage, which is next door only about a quarter of a mile away. It is raining. In fact, it's been raining since we got here, a thin, putrescent drizzle that wets you through with surprising efficiency. I enter the atrium door at 8:25 and begin to walk. After a while, I pass Spago, where I had lunch for three hours yesterday, and enter the casino. I walk and walk. It is now 8:45. I ask a guy who is sweeping up how to find the conference rooms. "Yes!" he says. No English. Is there no front desk in this gaudy wasteland? I pass baccarat tables, crap tables, roulette wheels, and miles and miles of slot machines, but no meeting rooms.

It is now 9:05. I have been in the hotel, this one hotel, for forty minutes, walking all the time. Suddenly, there is a bank of elevators and then—yes! Four small meeting rooms. I go in the first one. I'm completely overheated. My guys are there, eating ham and eggs and cheese with translucent, glutinous sauce. Don't these people have arteries? I eat a whole plateful. It's good! I feel better! We're living large! Isn't that why people go to Vegas?

I've had it: All day, I sit around the booth. Dinner is another company party. The scallops are so huge and mealy you could play stickball with them.

Back in the casino at night, I play blackjack for two hours. I win ten dollars. On the way to the elevators, I decide to win more money at the slot machines and spend two and a half hours losing instead. Over and over, as if pulled by the currents of the moon, my money goes into the machine and elicits nothing but a couple of desultory dings, a click, then silence. Yanking myself free with a Herculean effort of will, I go back to my room. I now have $1,085 in my pocket, plus a couple of quarters. Counting the depletion of the cash in my wallet, I figure I have broken completely even for my three days here in Vegas. I fall asleep in front of a movie I have paid $8.95 to watch. I want to get out of this cruddy town.

On the way to the airport: The sun is rising, gleaming off the distant mountains in parabolas of red and purple and gold. The rain has stopped. The air feels warm. In my gut, I can feel the stirrings of a certain fragile pride aborning. I have gambled and not lost. I hit the nightspots, did the meetings. I did not throw up on myself. And, yes, goddamn it, I had fun. Fun? Hell! I had a blast, didn't I? Doesn't everybody? Isn't that why everybody goes to Vegas? I mean, why does anybody go to Vegas?

1988

Long Day's Journey into Pittsburgh

What are the common experiences that unify each form of human enterprise? If I am a farmer, be it in the outskirts of Istanbul or the inner heart of Iowa, I must glance upward on a parched August evening and look, with hopeful heart, for rain. If I am a lion tamer, no matter in which circus I make my home, I am destined to feel the hot breath of my partners on my neck, and fear the blood lust that pounds beneath their tame, obedient hides. And if I am a business person, old or young, fat or low-fat, smart or well informed, from the rough, sophisticated New York City canyons to the pulsing industrial Micronesia that stretches from Atlanta to Los Angeles, there is one experience I cannot shun. Before the final Wittnauer is placed like a hospital tag on my ancient, weathered wrist and my old eyes can no longer read the fine print on a joint venture agreement, I must, I say I must, eventually be . . . stuck in Pittsburgh.

I'm not talking metaphorically. In saying "Pittsburgh," I'm not talking about some symbolic Pittsburgh of the soul. I'm talking about Pittsburgh, broad-shouldered titan of the Allegheny. USAir's got a hub there, you see. All domestic roads go through it. Only a few are paved with good intentions. And once you're in, good luck getting out.

Last week I was stuck in Pittsburgh. It wasn't the first time. Several years ago, to cite just one occasion, on a summer day so hot the airplane virtually sank into the tarmac, I boarded a USAir jet at 5 P.M., and after a series of unexplained equipment breakdowns, found myself hours later flying on a TWA prop-jet that had trouble attaining a cruising speed over 200 miles per hour. We didn't arrive until midnight, and I've never been so happy to set foot on the soil of Long Island. Not being stuck in Pittsburgh can do that to you—make you appreciate all other places no matter how flat or ludicrous.

It's not that Pittsburgh is so bad. It's not. It's America's most livable city. If you stay there, they'll tell you that a lot. And they're right, I'm sure. On the main street, there are signs that say Park All Day—$1. Can you imagine? There are other great things in Pittsburgh too numerous to mention, really.

You just don't want to be stuck there.

Last Tuesday, then. It was supposed to be a quick hop in, quick hop out. I got to the airport early. The Pittsburgh airport is very large. Only O'Hare is more humbling. Beyond the mean heart of the hub that is the central terminal, spokes emanate outward: A, B, C . . . perhaps there is a D; I can't remember. Lots of stores and restaurants. Not long ago I was stuck here with DiBlasi, a vivacious reengineering maven. Just as they were finally calling our plane, DiBlasi got a burbly, intoxicated look in his eye and, grabbing me by the elbow, hauled me the length of two spokes, at least a mile. Finally we got what he was looking for: delicious, hot, soft pretzels coated with butter and cinnamon. They were good. Had to run like a gemsbok to make that plane, though.

Pittsburgh does that to you. Makes you want to grab every pleasure, no matter how tiny. Who knows how soon all joy may be wrenched away, leaving you deposited where you began? Seize the pretzel while you may!

It is a little-known fact that one end of the Pittsburgh airport is in Pennsylvania and the other is in Indiana. All planes to New York are at the rag end of the longest spoke, somewhere near Muncie. I walked. Fifteen minutes later, I was there. Winded but alive. I sat down and thought of my little children, of my wife waiting at home, my doggie sitting by the door and wagging his dopey tail. Hadn't seen them in two days. Couldn't wait to get out. But still. I could feel the magnetic pull of destiny drawing me back, dragging me inexorably groundward, and that destiny had a name and that name was Pittsburgh.

I saw fog outside. My stomach tightened. A certain terrible knowledge began to creep up my spine. I got on the cellular phone and dialed home. The connection was poor. My son was jabbering about a double date he was scheduled to have with his new girlfriend on Friday night. It was kind of tough to get off the phone, but I had to. I could hardly hear anything because there was an announcement blaring out of the PA system. I pressed End and went to the counter to see what was going on.

"What's going on?" I said.

"There was an announcement," said the USAir representative with a disapproving glare.

"I know," I said, and waited.

"You should have been listening," said the USAir representative, quite incredibly.

"Well, I wasn't!" I almost shouted. "I was on the phone, okay?"

"Your flight is canceled," she said, turning away to examine some sort of form.

"Can I get on the next flight?"

"It's full," said the USAir representative. And so it was. And so was the flight after that. And all flights to Newark, too. And half the flights for the following morning. There was fog all up and down the Eastern Seaboard. It was an act of God. It was God who had decided that I was once again to be stuck in Pittsburgh.

Ten years ago. A much smaller me. My best friend, Dworkin, is getting married in Boston while I stand in snowy Pittsburgh waiting for spring to free me. I stood on the phone, not yet a cellular one back then, and yelled into the receiver, trying to grasp a tiny shard of real life and suck it into my heart. It was useless. Pittsburgh is what happens to you while you are making other plans.

I can't say I remember much of what happened afterward. I thought for a while about staying at the airport like a leprous mendicant, leaning against the wall with my coat about my legs and my head tipped back against the cinder block, drooling. But I was with two associates, Kim and Elaine, who had never been stuck in Pittsburgh before. I thought it important that they see how a real executive handles being stuck in Pittsburgh.

So we checked into a hotel, put on the TV, watched the fog roll in on the weather channel, and started drinking tiny ponies of gin. Not long after, we all went out to the Ruth's Chris Steak House—a fine place, except if you don't stop them, they will put butter on your steak. Why not simply deliver a portable medevac unit to your table? But that's the way they do things in Pittsburgh. Pedal to the metal. Flat out. No prisoners taken. Except you.

Don't remember much after that. Remember trying to get a cab sometime after dinner. No cabs. Had to walk. After a night spent dreaming lonely wistful dreams, sometime the next morning, almost too easily, Pittsburgh loosed its hold on me and let me go to Newark. From there I went to the office. My desk felt so good. Later that night, I breathed the free air of home again.

Today I received an e-mail. In three weeks there's a facilities team meeting in Pittsburgh. If I'm not too busy, says my correspondent, it might be advisable for me to come. I stared at that damned e-mail for a long time. Then I blew it off the system.

I'm at a loss. What should I do? I could try to avoid Pittsburgh, but what kind of way is that to live? Jumping at my own shadow? Trembling every time I open my electronic mailbox? I don't think so. No. I'm going to suck it up and go. Then I'll suck it up and stay as long as I have to. Fate is fate. I embrace mine. Pass the butter, O Pittsburgh! I am yours!

1996

Terror at 35,000 Feet

The Los Angeles night had set in a couple of hours before, after one of the truly spectacular sunsets that filter the last glimmers of sunshine through the wheeze and exhaust of a million moving cars. The party in the canyon was in full swing. Clients and executives were mingling over beer and barbecue. The band was pounding out a country disco beat. Still, it was time for me to go. I had a redeye to catch.

The limo to LAX was long and cool, but that didn't help much. I knew what I had to do. I knew where I had to go to get that job done. And there was only one way to get where I had to go to get done what needed doing. A moving cigar tube suspended six miles in the air.

First thing, I stowed my carry-on luggage. One foldover suitcase. One big briefcase with several reams of paper and one six-pound laptop in it. Another, smaller, cloth bag, bursting with laundry. I was afraid to check my bags, this for two reasons. First, I wanted to see them again. Second, when my plane touched down on the other end . . . if it did . . . I wanted to get out of the loathsome, fetid dungeon that is Kennedy airport as fast as possible. So nearly one whole overhead compartment was dedicated to my stuff.

I could have hung it up, of course. They offered. It's one of the nice things they do for you. But I don't like my stuff to be out of sight, mixed in with other people's stuff. Something could happen. If, say, one of the engines came loose and tore into the main fuselage, like it did on that Delta MD-88 out of Pensacola a couple of months ago. People might go through my luggage afterward and find embarrassing material. If I'm going to be torn asunder by flying shreds of metal, I want my possessions macerated with me, safe from prying eyes. . . .

Gee, it wasn't a very good track my mind was taking. I had to chill. Flight attendants were offering complimentary champagne. I took some. Maybe it would help me sleep. And I had to sleep. Those who do not sleep on redeyes are condemned to two days of psychosis afterward. I thought of arriving in New York six hours later, unshaved, unrested, with no work done, having seen *The Truth about Cats and Dogs* for the third time in four weeks. I felt afraid. Suppose I was awake when a rocket launcher in militialand down below took out our checked-luggage compartment?

I nursed the champagne for a while. It was pretty good.

The plane's engines started up, and did not explode.

The seats were certainly big enough. Mine definitely could have accommodated a hippopotamus. It was wide enough, and sufficiently soft and yielding to soothe the average hippo hide over extended hours of uncomfortable constraint. The plane taxied down the runway, and I surreptitiously reclined. I was apprehensive that I would be caught doing so, but it seems business–class passengers are exempt from keeping their seat backs in an upright position. It was a good feeling. Everyone around me seemed to be reclining during takeoff and loving it. I passed out.

I awoke suddenly, after a dream in which I was falling from the sky, screaming, my entrails trailing behind me in the sky above my head like a parachute.

I took out my work and looked at it. I determined that the best thing to do was to go through the entire bag for crud I could throw away. Turns out there was quite a bit. Then I did the same to my hard drive. It's amazing how cluttered your directories get if you don't take care of them. That was all the work I could handle for a while. I closed my eyes, only to discover the ground rushing up to meet me at 300 miles an hour. I decided to look out the window, then decided against it.

Before long came the hot nuts. This is one of the big perks in business class, and is among the clear arguments for the price differential vs. coach. Hot nuts are real bad for you, and they terrified me, but I ate them anyhow. It was a generous portion, too, and I ate all but one filbert. Pistachios in particular were salty, fatty, and delicious. There were also cashews, pecans, macadamias, all forms of lovely, high-demographic nuts, warmed by microwave and presented in a small, white ceramic bowl.

The airline dinner was served at about two in the morning, New York time. The meat had attained a microwaved perfection. I believe it was intended to be taken for chateaubriand, and it looked the part nicely, the way those polystyrene portions of sushi approximate the real thing in Japanese restaurant windows. The sauce was kind of gummy, but I ate it; I guess that's the bottom line. There was also a cube of Gruyère, with crackers. Scalloped potatoes. Quite good, really. The roll was particularly satisfactory. There was white wine and then red, then after-dinner brandy . . . I had a little. On came some strawberries with chocolate. An oatmeal cookie afterward. I declined a second. I was on a diet.

A warm feeling of physical well-being stole over me, only slightly offset at one point by the sudden image of my body torn to pieces by a faulty piece of replacement equipment. This was a particular fear of mine. It had come to my attention that many spare parts are supplied to airlines by people who think it's okay to take an old slab of metal, paint it silver, and call it new. Sometimes these bogus pieces don't work. I figured that's probably what happened to ValuJet down in the Everglades. I wondered what it was like to hit the water while you're still alive.

Everybody around me was drinking brandy. The Japanese fellow to my right had so far taken in one Bloody Mary, a half-bottle of red wine, and a big snifter of Remy, and we weren't all that far into the flight.

Within thirty minutes I had three glasses of cranberry juice and one and a half bottles of Perrier. I was hydrating. After a while I closed my eyes, and was out about three and a half hours. One time, I woke up and watched Janeane Garofalo and Uma Thurman kidding around on the screen.

I woke once more, about 5 A.M. It was gray in the cabin, but a little shine peeked from behind the plastic curtains. Everyone was asleep but me, even a couple of flight attendants. The plane moved smoothly through the dawn. In about an hour, there would be small pastries and fruit, coffee and hot towels, and not too long after, sunshine. I leaned back in my recliner until I was just about prone, and closed my eyes. Things were going to be all right. If I made it through the landing.

And I did, too. This time.

1996

Twenty Things I Really Like about Japan

1. The Japan Air Lines lounge in New York. It's ten in the morning. People are drinking Scotch and beer and smoking up a storm. Dudes!

2. The flight over. *Men in Black* is screened in English, then in Japanese. Just as good both times, particularly the big roach. How often do you get a chance to eat, sleep, and watch TV for fourteen hours with no phones around and nobody to discuss the key implications of proactive activity?

3. Full employment. Off the train from the airport, there's a person in a uniform to take the first portion of my ticket, another several yards farther on to take the second portion, still another several paces beyond that to take the final portion. Then there's an elderly woman ushering us onto the waiting escalator with, I must say, a very nice flourish, and, at last, another to make sure we alight in safety and comfort.

4. The bullet train is very keen. Take the Green Car. Wowzers. Luxury and how. They come around and give you a hot towel and, somewhat later, bitter Chinese tea in a small paper can. It's not really paper, but it isn't cardboard or plastic either. What the heck is it?

5. Bogus English. It's everywhere. On that can of Chinese tea, for instance, it says Delicious Refreshing Beverage Drink. On a yo-yo I buy as a present, it says Fabulous Fun Spinning Toy. Getting off the train at my destination, I spot a very big business building in the central square. On top of this big business building is a large, neon, English message that says Big Business Building.

6. Vending machines. Toss a coin, and you'll hit one offering just about anything you could possibly want. My favorite items: (1) strong coffee in weeny little cans that comes out of the machine piping hot; (2) tasty shirt-and-tie combinations; (3) a sports drink called Pocari Sweat. It's "refreshment water" that is "quickly absorbed into the body tissues due to its fine osmolality." I drink some. It tastes like a combination of Gatorade and, yes, sweat.

7. Fish. Fish is what it's all about. Fish is where it's at. Fish, fish, and fish, with fish in fish sauce. Can I have some fish with my fish? If you don't like fish, you can go to McDonald's, or to KFC, if you have a reservation.

8. Squid on a stick. It's for sale at the 7-Eleven, in a little vat of water where the Slurpees ought to be. People buy them at breakfast time.

9. The whole business-card thing. The ritual is, offer the card with both hands with a slight inclination of your head, its information facing your colleague. He'll do likewise. Make sure to read the contents of his card and indicate approval with a certain amount of

bobbing and weaving. Under no circumstances produce a card from a wallet in your back pocket, by the way. I would tell you what message that conveys to a Japanese business person, but this is a family magazine. Isn't it?

10. Bowing. I'm with Donald Trump, who prefers it to handshaking. Of course, it can be taken to ridiculous lengths. Anyone who has seen a group of guys uncertain about their relative status trying to enter or exit an elevator knows what I mean. But then, we have backslapping.

11. Making change. When you buy even a package of Xylish chewing gum, you get your change back in a small tray, eliminating all hand-to-hand contact. It makes every sordid little transaction kind of elegant . . . and hygienic too!

12. Little surgical masks. Speaking of clean, fully 10 percent of the population seems to be walking around wearing them, either to protect others from their germs or vice versa. Both ways, I think that's nice.

13. Gum. After Xylish, I like Black Black, the "triple combination high-tech chewing gum," and Muscat, with a "fresh and fruity fragrance" and a taste that mingles floor wax, soap, furniture polish, and grape Fanta, with a soupçon of Ban Roll-On.

14. Other cool products. I also like Pocky, a cookie stick covered with chocolate. Inexplicably, Pocky comes in two varieties: Pocky for Men and Pocky for Women. After much discussion, colleagues are incapable of ascertaining a difference. I think that's very '90s, don't you?

15. No room service. Masks notwithstanding, I get the flu. In bed with a temperature of 103.5, I call down to the front desk and inquire if I might have some orange juice delivered to my room. "To your room?" says the bellman. He is absolutely mystified. After a while he says gently, "I suppose I could bring it to your room as a personal favor. . . ." I reply, "I would take it as a very great personal favor." Two minutes later the orange juice is there—two liters of it. The guy won't accept a tip, either.

16. No tipping. Yes, you heard me right—the nation seems not to understand the concept of additional money for services rendered. My new friend with the orange juice recoils at my proffered coins as if insulted. I feel bad. When you think about it, who pays a pal for a personal favor?

17. Karaoke. My friend Ko takes me out one night. We drink a lot of

beer and sing many tunes. Ko takes the drill very seriously, unlike my American friends, who try to make out the whole thing is a joke. Ko sings "My Way." It's a great performance, and reveals some lovely things about him. I sing "Foxy Lady" and do the same.

18. The food test. The next night, Ko takes us out for dinner and drinks. Somewhere near eighteen beers later, he comes up to me with an enormous grin and what looks like a gigantic fried sardine on a plate. "You eat this!" he commands. I have a choice. Head or tail. Without thinking, I put the head in my mouth and eat it. It has eyeballs. They are sour and crunchy. Ko's face explodes with good fellowship. We hug. I know guys who've been asked to eat raw horse and live shrimp. Both did as they were told. It's a great custom and really cements a friendship.

19. Japanese TV. There's CNN in Japanese, and a show where a man and a woman simply walk around a golf course, playing and talking. On channel 11, a man pours a fish-based brown sauce over a large, white, gelatinous cube. Another channel broadcasts nonstop action—people fishing. At 3 A.M. there is *Gunfight at the O.K. Corral,* with Burt Lancaster and Kirk Douglas, in English. I nearly weep when I realize it isn't dubbed.

20. Going home. I don't mean it the way it sounds. On the bullet train back to Tokyo, the sun is rising over the Japanese Alps . . . wood smoke wafting over tiny ancient homes . . . the Green Car filled with the sound of families laughing together, eating their breakfasts of, okay, fish . . . the feeling of having done business a world away, and done it well . . . the strangeness of the Japanese landscape, crammed with houses and churches and power stations and driving ranges and farms and gas stations, all in close proximity . . . the sensation of coming back into my office afterward and looking out the window at the same old thing . . . and seeing it for the first time . . .

And it is good.

1998

Twenty Things I Really Like about L.A.

1. The new Lincoln Town Car. I get to LAX and there it is, gleaming at the curb. A complete redesign of the basic box Dean Martin rode in. A rounded snout. Heavy duty grillwork. My driver isn't a talker. After the mandatory comment about the weather, which is excellent, by the way, we respect each other's space. There's a cellular phone I can dial without screwing with an access code, and mucho big-time air-conditioning. I get on the horn, and I can practically see my breath in the icy cold of that big backseat.

2. Did I mention the weather? Really terrific weather. Bright sunshine. A little heat, but dry, you know? Makes you glad to be alive. All in all? Great weather.

3. The freeways. They get you nowhere, real . . . slow. Why not? It's later in your head by three hours, and you don't need complete immersion in the L.A. thing just yet. You want to hang a little. So you get on the 405, and you just sit there, man. Chill.

4. Getting places. It's a very big deal. You arrive where you're going to, and you're . . . there, baby. But where? Are you south of where you were before? How close are you to that little tower that was on *Dragnet* and *Perry Mason?* Where is West L.A.? West of here?

5. It also rains very little, incidentally. The sunsets turn the canyons to bronze. People have pools where they can sit and enjoy all that weather.

6. Max's Jaguar. Out in L.A., people judge you by your car, and I respect that. At least you know where you stand. My friend Max has a black, twelve-cylinder Jaguar that he drives from place to place. It's a very cool car in a land of cool cars. Where I live, everyone has an off-road vehicle that combines the feel of a small, well-appointed truck with the power of a four-cylinder subcompact sedan. I like Max's car better.

7. Polo shirts. People wear them to business meetings all the time. And khakis. And comfortable shoes. I had a meeting the other day with a guy on reengineering. He was wearing moccasins. We didn't come to any conclusions. Good!

8. The roof of the Four Seasons Hotel. There's a pool up there. A few years ago I watched the L.A. riots get closer and closer from that vantage point. "Wow, lookit that!" says this guy next to me as we watch the smoke and fire moving up Doheny. You know who it was? Harvey Keitel!

9. Fruit. Everyplace you go, people have fruit. You can just go up in your polo shirt and unstructured sports coat and take, like, a plum. And when they give you coffee? It's espresso.

10. Pasadena. You have to travel by limo for a long time to get there, and after a while, there you are. There's a good Chinese restaurant there and several bookstores.

11. Venice Beach. You travel on one of the boulevards for a long time, and suddenly you're in this extremely quaint little beachside town that has real authenticity. Blue skies. A little breeze. We have dinner in a fabulous place where people are not allowed to smoke at the bar. Michael Keaton is talking to a guy at another table. We don't bother him, though. He looks like he's eating.

12. Downtown L.A. I stay at the Biltmore, a great old hotel very much like one you might find in any American city, except slightly more Chinatown, if you know what I'm talking about. At about 5 P.M. I figure I'll take a walk around, you know, outside? See what's going on. I get about fifty yards from the front door of the hotel before I realize I'm the only person on the street. I walk a couple of seconds more, listening to the sounds of my shoes on the empty pavement. It's weird, and beautiful, kind of like being in a great urban space that has recently been hit by a neutron bomb. Then I go back to the bar and have a very good martini.

13. Bungalows. Real little ones. They're all over the place. You'd think tiny mice live in them, but they don't. Agents live in them.

14. Earthquakes. They could have one at any time. A really big one. But they don't think about it. After a while, if you go there, you won't think about it either.

15. Malibu. I go to a party there. We take a big, long stretch limo and have fun fiddling with the climate control. After a very, very long time, somebody points out the Santa Monica pier, which looks nice from the road. The party's at a house some star rents to groups when he's out of town. I mean, I think he's out of town. I don't see him, at any rate, or if I do I don't recognize him, and that's what counts.

16. Century City. It seems to be very close to Beverly Hills, although maybe it's not. You are driven by what looks like a very quaint and

lengthy enclosed parking area that goes on for miles, and then you turn left onto a big boulevard and a gigantic forest of stone and glass emerges from the ground before you and looms over your head. Enormous Lincoln Town Cars in black and white purr by on the desolate, futuristic streets.

17. Red carpets. Outside the Hyatt in Century City, there is one rolling away from the front doors. A gaggle of photographers hovers behind a velvet rope. This is not for me. I walk past the cordon of paparazzi, and not one razzi pops. I am nobody. It's an interesting feeling, and not bad at all. In L.A., everybody is nobody eventually.

18. All of a sudden, it's happening! The Hyatt is host, it turns out, to the Festival of Fantasy and Science Fiction movies. A lot of fans show up. I watch for a while as I wait for the car that will take me someplace either north or south of Century City to some portion of Los Angeles that is not called Los Angeles to have food that is a combination of Texan, Mexican, and Basque. The electronic flashes are exploding. Limos pull up. In a pool of klieg light stands one of my all-time favorites, Martin Landau, talking very affably with the press. He looks happy. He has on black tie, big black-framed glasses, and a bodacious blonde on his left arm who appears to be some years his junior. I could be wrong. I don't get that close.

19. The redeye. On the plane back home I sit very near NBC star Al Roker. We have a little chat, but I don't want to bother him. After that, I sleep, and not one person talks to me for more than five hours.

20. When I get back to town, dawn is breaking, and it is raining, thank God.

1998

Terror on the Corporate Jet

I think, sometimes, of golfer Payne Stewart. It frightens me to talk about it, but I guess I must. In my waking dream, I see a little plane loaded with friends and formerly jolly associates, cruising at 50,000 feet, at the edge of what must be considered outer space. It's cold in the private aircraft because a window has cracked, depressurizing the cabin, and at this altitude there is no warmth, there is no oxygen, there is only sky—dark, tinged with blue and black, filled to the horizon in every direction with stars. There is the sound of the motor, but beyond that the little plane flies on in eerie and bottomless silence, because everyone inside it is dead. The tiny tube of steel and broken glass climbs upward into the void, awaiting the moment when it will run out of fuel at last and fall back to earth in a ball of fire and light and screaming metal.

The phone rings while I'm getting ready for the company dinner. This is one of my favorite moments on the road. It's late afternoon, and there are no more meetings that day, none at which I will be required to make sobriety a virtue, at any rate. I've been up on the roof at the outdoor gym, and a nimbus of righteous sweat hangs about me like glorious raiment. I am just about to step into the shower and have decided afterward to watch a Pay-Per-View movie in the two hours before I'm supposed to meet Dempster and Creeley for martinis downstairs. Best of all, tomorrow I will go home in a big, comfortable airbus. I will eat hot nuts. I will sleep, and not be required to converse, and forget that I am 35,000 feet above the hard crust of the planet.

"Hello," I tell the phone.

"Ken would like you to join him in the corporate jet tomorrow morning." It's Eleanor, Ken's assistant. I have successfully turned down this invitation before by simply telling the truth: that I am afraid to fly in a minuscule conveyance that hangs like a dust mote in the eye of God.

"Er . . ." is all I have time to get out. Then I hear Ken's voice in the background. "Tell Bing he's a wuss! And if he doesn't come with us I'll bash him!" He's kidding, of course. But then . . . if there's one thing you don't want to be, it's a wuss. And you know, I do want to be with the guys. And why should I be all phobic and immature about this thing? It isn't even the Jetstream, it's the big G3. If I turn it down now, I may never be asked again. And things happen on the jet. One time my pal Polito rode with the chairman, and by the time they landed, a whole new career path was mapped out for him, and he was the golden boy of the company for six months. I could use a new gig like that, particularly on Monday mornings.

"I'll go," I hear myself say. I am immediately filled with dread. I see myself burning merrily like a juicy gobbet of fat that has fallen into the barbecue.

"Great," says Eleanor.

In the morning my Town Car pulls up to the plane right there on the tarmac. The luggage dude takes my bag; I don't even have to touch it. I climb the gangway. The rented G3 seats twenty or so, and it's beautiful inside, all blond wood with quiet stainless-steel touches. The armchairs are ample. Ken arrives with Tolan and Gordon and Erlanger and Studtz and a few more of the gang, all of them tanned and good-lookin' in their casual duds, and nobody shuts up for a good long while. My, this is fun!

The moment arrives. We must fly.

Takeoff is by no means gradual. One minute we're rolling fast, the next we turn nose up and dart into the sky like a clay pigeon out of a trap. I see Markoff, normally a frosty adversary of evil responsible for the crunching of very tough walnuts, grab the arms of his comfy chair. "I don't like this part," he says. I am not the only one with an irrational fear of being ripped from the middle of my life and flung flaming into the sky like Icarus.

The little hollow cigar levels off, and we all immediately eat between 800 and 1,200 pounds of food. The flight attendant, unlike those in the commercial fleet, is blond, buff, and beautiful. There is no moment when we do not have beverages. The purpose of the libations could not be clearer if little rubber nipples were placed over our glasses.

There follow a good four hours of amiable musical chairs. I go from the best seats, a foursome in the middle of the craft, to the couch by the windows for a chat with Markoff and Studtz about the economics of back-end deals; then to the more private niches in the stern, where Erlanger and Gordon are strategizing over the launch of something or other; then back up to the front for some mindless video with Tolan and Kuhn; then finally into the seat opposite Ken, who is chatting, working a little, reading. The whole team thing is very strong up here. I love these guys, and we're in this together.

The moment arrives. We must . . . land.

The plane hitches a little and yaws to the right. Ken takes off his glasses and looks out the window. "We're starting our descent awful early," he says. He pushes a button, and the motorized shade descends, blotting out the view of the countryside that is rising up to meet us fast. A few minutes later Ken says, "I do this trip twice a month, and this isn't the way it's supposed to go." My tongue feels like a washcloth bunched up and jammed into the back of my throat. The plane is silent, all of us studiously rummaging through things, staring unseeing at magazines, or simply clutching fixed objects to steady ourselves. It's bumpy.

I grasp my armrests and close my eyes. Is it possible to sleep through one's own death? As the interminable banking and descending continues, I open my eyes a tad and glance at Ken, and find that I am looking at myself. His eyes are closed. He is breathing for control. His hands are on his knees. He is waiting to see whether we make it and, like everybody else in the sarcophagus, trying not to shriek. I see why he wanted me to come. I see why all those who must fly these things regularly want you with them. Facing the ultimate reality is lonely work.

We get down okay, of course. I'll go again if I'm asked. You don't get to go up against the infinite every day—and enjoy unlimited sandwiches and condiments while you're at it. I particularly like those tiny gherkins, and mean to get as many of them as I can the next time around.

2000

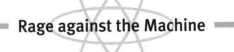

Rage against the Machine

I am standing at the baggage claim at Kennedy airport in New York City, consumed by rage. I haven't been so angry since the last time this happened. I feel the blood rushing to my face, a churning geyser of bile launching itself upward into my esophagus. My head is spinning, and I believe that if I were just a couple of years older I might have a stroke. Where is my goddamn limo?

In this low-ceilinged, mildewed, darkening antechamber between one form of pampering and the next, I have come face-to-face with the last area of executive life that consistently demonstrates how powerless and insignificant we are . . . how it doesn't matter what we earn, how big our reporting structure is, how meaty our bonus, how large a chunk of the chairman's ear is in our pocket. Where is my Town Car?

People bustle here and there, but I do not move. I am the calm in the middle of the maelstrom, staring with my inner eye into the pasty white face of truth. I see it clearly. I am nothing. Everyone in the concourse is larger than I, even the little guy in the brown suit and blue club tie who ordered the low-salt meal in coach. I control nothing. My Town Car has failed to arrive.

The man in the brown suit and the tie with salad dressing on it walks smugly by, a squat luggage handler in a dirty blue uniform trailing a little wheelie cart behind him, and stuffs into his jacket pocket a small card that says Mr. DeBakey in bad handwriting. So Mr. DeBakey's world has come together and mine has not. My Town Car is Not Here.

There are, certainly, different levels of Not Here. There is the Not Here that places my Town Car back in Connecticut, its driver drooling into his foam-rubber pillow. There is the Not Here in which my Town Car is stuck in a massive tie-up on the Van Wyck Expressway and might as well be in the asteroid belt between Mars and Jupiter. There is the Not Here where the foolish driver has simply misestimated his timing and is right now parking the car in one of the massive lots dedicated to our inconvenience. In that case, while he is Not Here, he will be, in the parlance of the industry, Right There.

My hand trembles with the force of my displeasure. My clamshell works. The signal goes through. Yes! I am an executive with a nice cell phone that works in difficult surroundings. I stand a little taller. "I'll get them on the other line," says Sally, who is used to such moments. There was the time I was standing in the pouring rain on the street outside my office, screaming into my little phone with such force that people crossed the street to avoid me. On that occasion, the car I had ordered three hours prior was not only Not Here, it wasn't even going to be Right There. It wasn't Right Up the Street or Just Turning the Corner. It was, in fact, There. "What do you mean it's there!" I screeched like a tern circling a herring in shallow water. "I'm standing here! There's nothing here!" Beyond the confines of executive control lies a land in which Newtonian laws of physics do not apply, and an object as big as a Town Car can be both There and Not There. What other rules are suspended in this vast, lunatic domain?

"He's just Crossing the Parking Lot," says Sally, adding a new category to the playbook. She does not believe it. Neither do I. It doesn't matter where he is on the physical plane anyway. He is not in my control, that's all.

I wait in the nonexecutive zone. I do not like it here. As I did not like grade school, with its teeming masses of people who could play basketball better than I could. I did not like the early years of my career much, where the guy who sold the newspaper downstairs could have told me what to do and I would have had to do it. I didn't like the years after the first merger—or was it the second?—when the power structure hadn't jelled and you never knew on which side your face should be buttered. But those days are over. I nestle in a carapace of executive function, controlling everything that surrounds me . . . except maybe for Mort and Dick and Ed and Fritz and Shelly and Ned and Ted and Morton and Jimmy-Boy, fellow executives all, and Rosenstern, of course, whom nobody in his right mind would try to control. And I guess you'd have to add to that list the guy who was supposed to deliver the snow blower last Tuesday but didn't because it Wasn't In Yet. And also I guess you'd have to include the macroeconomic system that seems to be moving toward wholesale consolidation, eliminating central corporate operations as it goes, and the weather, which has been lousy lately, so cold that it seeps right into your bones and reminds you that there will come a time for all of us, no matter how great, when the executive life that looks so permanent will spit you right back up on a hard and comfortless shore in which nobody flies first class and when it is asked where the heck you might have gone to, people just give a heavy look and say, "Not Here."

"What happened?" I ask the driver who materializes at my elbow a while later. He looks tired, and his hair flies away from his head, sparse and vertical. He is at least fifteen years older than I am.

"I got screwed up on the parkway," he says. He takes my bag, and I follow behind with renewed executive poise. "Sorry, sir."

Sir! Smart man. "Hey," I say, my anger flowing out of my cuffs and down the pavement as we walk. "It's under control."

2001

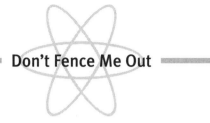

Don't Fence Me Out

I went to the Super Bowl and it was all right. The game itself was pretty terrible unless you came from Baltimore, which, sadly, I do not. But just being there made me feel like a very important person, and I had ample opportunity to enjoy that status for most of the four-day weekend. Except when I didn't. You'd think that being at the Super Bowl would make you a very important person ipso facto, a priori. But you'd be wrong. All it does is make you an important person. The "V" is up for grabs and as hard to get hold of as a greased pig.

There are people, and there are important people, and then there are very important people. The trick is to be as many of the three as possible—all at the same time. That's not easy, because the state of being very important is relative. That is, you may be a very important person only to find that there are very, very important people around, and even if you by some chance manage to ascend to very, very, there will most likely be others who are up to the job of out-verying you by one or two verys. I venture to say that there is always, in fact, someone more very than you are, unless you are, perhaps, the Pope, and he doesn't go to the Super Bowl, I don't think, or Frank Sinatra, and he is dead.

Plus, there is this consideration: that while you may be a genuinely very important person in one location, you may only be an entry-level important person in another one. Being just a run-of-the-mill important person after you have tasted veryhood is a comedown, creating tremendous feelings of inferiority and rage among those to whom it happens.

A drum roll, please. VIPs assemble! How noble they are, their aquiline noses flaring in the fumes from the steam tables! Yes, it's here that the contest is played out on a very public field of battle—the VIP room. There always is one, no matter where you are, and sometimes two or three, depending on the levels of caste that are being determined. There is the velvet rope! Here are we, and shall we enter? The blood runs hot—and cold too. For it is here that the entire pageant will be played out in all its infinitesimal glory.

At the commissioner's party in the Convention Center, there was a beautiful spread that took up acres of real estate, with fabulous decorations, very good food, and lots of bands. In the middle of the central ballroom was a very large space—cavernous, empty. Everyone who wanted to be in the VIP space was excluded. All those who were welcome were not interested in being there. It was a wonderful, pristine VIP room, expressing everything about all VIP rooms in its purity and emptiness. My friend Harold, an old friend of the commissioner's, approached him with a couple of friends. "Hi, Harold," said the commissioner. He and my friend hugged. "Have you seen the rest of the party?" the commissioner asked my friend Harold. We walked away from the VIP space, and it loomed huge in our imaginations, and there was nobody in it.

Later that night, or maybe it was the next, I went to a party thrown by *Maxim* magazine. It was way the hell out in the middle of nowhere, and you needed wheels to get there. A big screen projected images of the new arrivals as they pulled up to the front door in their forty-foot-long Lincoln Navigator stretches. We had a modest Town Car, and nobody looked at us. Inside it was a zoo. A huge, impatient line of people who had already proved they were On the List were being rudely siphoned through one little tiny door. Then, we were in! How very important! Except . . . the gigantic room was jammed, mostly with hungry, swarthy guys in open-collared shirts, circling a very small number of women in ornate lingerie. There were three very small bars at which you had to pay the bartender $20 just to get his attention. When I got to the front, they were out of beer. I didn't feel very important at all.

But good news. Outside the room, at the end of the lobby, there was a small door. In front of it was a rope, and on the rope it said VIP. That was for us, and we got in, too, because a pal of mine knew somebody who knew somebody. In the room were even more people per square inch than in the main room, and it was hotter. 'N Sync, I heard, had just left. The main VIPs in the room, other than myself and my friends, were Tom Arnold, Rob Schneider, and Gervase. If you don't know who any of those people are, I can't help you. You probably don't belong in the room anyhow.

The next night, or maybe it was the one before, I went to a Ricky Martin concert on an Air Force base. There was no VIP room per se—but there was a VIP seating area, where some genuinely important people crammed in rather than sit anywhere else. "Can you help me get in there?" said a fellow who would have been a legitimate VIP at Spago.

He was sitting right next to me, and I took this as an insult to our section, which was way better than the one to its left or right. "No," I said.

The following day I had lunch at Hattricks, which boasts one of the better cheeseburgers in Tampa, which means they don't put Cheez Whiz on it. The bar was very crowded with people celebrating the joy of Super Bowl, so when I was done, I left. To the right of Hattricks as you face it, in a parking lot next to the door to the kitchen, some rickety folding chairs nestled around three or four sad, saggy, little plastic tables. At one a guy sat with what remained of a beer, staring off into the middle distance. A hank of something like brown packing string was stretched across the front of the parking lot, so no cars could go in. On the string was a little sign on the kind of raw, brown paper they use to make garbage bags. I bet it once was a garbage bag. On the paper were three letters in what looked like magic marker. I don't have to tell you what they were.

Later that night I met a guy at the bar in the hotel who bent my ear awhile about how great things were in the VIP room of the strip club he had just come from.

I did finally go to one place in Tampa where there were no VIPs, or at least there was no room dedicated to them. It was my own company party. We had hot dogs and grilled-chicken sandwiches, and we all made a lot of noise. Maybe everybody knew who was a VIP in that group without the little roped-off room. Maybe after a few beers together it wasn't very important. But we all had dinner with the people we'd hung with a million times and were pretty thoroughly bored with, and we took in a bit of warmth on what turned out to be a chilly evening, and then we went out again to a waiting limo to see whether we could get into the Sports Illustrated party at Ybor City.

We couldn't, by the way. There were too many jerks in there. But it wasn't very important at all.

2001

LATTE BREAK

So, Are Ya Havin' Fun?

Hi, folks! How many times has this happened to you? You're sitting at your desk late in the day, with alligators happily snapping about your buttocks and a passel of Bosnian potentates waiting in your antechamber, when a pal you can't quite place appears with topcoat on and the whiff of a rather lengthy luncheon about him, and amusingly asks, "Are ya havin' fun?" And you don't know what to say.

Well, it's been happening a lot to me lately, so I figure it's way past time to roll out a little quiz designed to deliver a reliable answer to this time-honored and thoroughly inexplicable query. Two reasons: First, in these crazy, helter-skelter days, it's just possible you may be having fun and not even be aware of it! That would be tragic. Conversely, many of us who believe we are having fun may not actually be doing so—and it could get ugly should reality finally crash down on us without warning.

So without further ado, please complete the following statements.

1. I eat breakfast . . .
   (a) at home with the kids, spouse, and a newspaper, preparing myself for the day ahead with some quiet contemplation and a sense of perspective about the tasks that lie ahead;
   (b) on the train, with a buttered roll on my knee, a cup of coffee in my armpit, and a cellular phone making my ear feel like a baked stuffed clam;
   (c) What's breakfast?
2. Most of my meetings . . .
   (a) are very short in duration and focused around one or two specific action points. In fact, sometimes I go entire days without one formal meeting with more than one person other than myself;

(b) are very well organized, with quite structured agendas and large numbers of people in attendance. Recently I attended a six-hour session on positioning. It took me three days to catch up after that one! But if I didn't go, I wouldn't have been there, and people would have gotten the wrong idea;

(c) blow.

3. I have . . .

(a) one boss, but he's a big one;

(b) two bosses, but they respect each other and one of them is solid and the other is dotted line;

(c) three bosses, maybe four, and two of them are solid line but on different coasts, while the others are in a kind of matrix that relates to itself interstitially on alternate Tuesdays.

4. When my telephone rings . . .

(a) either I answer it or it's answered by Edna, who knows to whom I should be speaking better than I do;

(b) the cord gets all fouled up! Have you ever noticed that? Like, the more phone calls you get, the more twisted the cord gets until it kind of takes on a life of its own? The other day it was flipping around so bad it knocked over my third can of Diet Pepsi!

(c) I feel sick.

5. During a normal day, I see . . .

(a) between three and ten people;

(b) between eleven and twenty people;

(c) about a million people.

6. Most of the people in my company wear a beeper. I have decided . . .

(a) not to wear one, because I consider it a psychotic intrusion into my personal space. If I'm managing my affairs so badly that a crisis could come up at any time, bite me, and interrupt what sorry shards remain of my life, I shouldn't be in my position anyhow;

(b) to wear one, because if I don't, people might find out that I've been managing my affairs so badly that a crisis could come up at any time and bite me and I shouldn't be in my position anyhow;

(c) not to wear one but worry about the fact that I'm not wearing one so intensely that it ruins my life anyhow because I constantly check my voice mail by cellular phone every fifteen minutes.

7. The following statement best describes my feelings about my career:

(a) I'm satisfied about where I am right now, but in the next eighteen months I'll take a look at where I am and see if the cost/benefit ratio of my existence still makes sense;

(b) I'm doing okay, but I'm also kind of, you know, annoyed about the constant encroachment Krantz seems to be making on my territory all the time. In fact, the guy is junior to me. I don't really understand why he doesn't report to me, when you think about it. He should. And until he does, I'll never rest. It's burning through my soul like a hot rock. It's eating me alive!

(c) I hope they don't find out about me until I can sort of figure out what I'm doing.

8. For lunch, I would like to eat . . .

(a) a generous appetizer of selected vegetable and seafood antipasto, accompanied by a judicious martini with several olives for nutritional value, followed by a delicate paillard of chicken with roasted potatoes, a small dish of sorbets, a macaroon or two, and a couple of strong espressos. The fact that this repast is taken with an influential industry analyst makes it not only expensable but laudatory. Bravo!

(b) six pounds of raw fish and a brace of Kirin Light with Burbage, Morgenstern, and Shoendienst, the last five minutes of which is spent talking about future revenue trends, which makes it necessary for somebody to pick it up. This time, it turns out to be me;

(c) a ham sandwich and a bag of Lay's potato chips, which I pay for with my own cash and eat standing up while on the phone with the V.P. of human resources, trying to keep the crunching down because it's an important call and you don't want to offend the guy.

9. When I got that horrible flu last December . . .

(a) I stayed out of the office for the better part of four days. It was heaven. Of course, I spent a lot of time on the phone, but that was all right. And at least three or four hours of every day I napped. I guess I've got things pretty much the way I want them.

(b) I stayed out one day and went back still feeling pretty funky. Even so, I kind of like being sick at my desk. People are scared you're going to give them something, so they leave you alone. You get a lot of paperwork done and a lot of brownie points for being a good soldier. I liked it. Except for the fact that I didn't get completely well for more than two months, it was great, actually.

(c) I was forced to fly to Los Angeles for a marketing presentation. My eustachian tubes were so clogged up during the flight I punctured my eardrums. I had to be there, though, because it was my meeting. I called it. It was my agenda. Death would have been the only excuse, and a poor one at that.

10. At night, when I am sleeping, I dream . . .

(a) rarely, if at all;

(b) about Marcie Bruce, who developed an unbelievably mature figure in the seventh grade;

(c) that Ed Barzun, the assistant controller in charge of the zero-based time-management process, is chasing me with a meat cleaver screaming, "Cut head count!"

Okay! We're done. For every answer of (a), give yourself a 1, the lowest possible score. You're way too content, buster. You're cruisin' for a bruisin'. An answer of (b), on the other hand, earns you 2 points and a middling score that befits your middling status, spud. A response of (c), of course, is worth 10 points. You have no idea how happy you are. When you look back on it, you'll remember this as the happiest days of your life. Ironic, huh? I think so, too.

So, are ya havin' fun? Consider anything over 60 a very good score. If you scored under, say, 30, I'd just like to ask you one last question.

Are ya makin' any money?

1996

7

THE HUMAN ANIMAL

You are what you drink, and even at times what you eat. And then there's what you wear, and how close you shave, either your face or your armpits. How you manage what goes into and onto your body is of course of primary importance not only in business, but in life, which is also part of business. It's pretty clear that over the years the size of my body has been an issue for me, although today, after a lifetime of bacon, I still can fit into a pair of nonrelaxed jeans. That's because I view my body as a temple, and I always believe in going to temple once a year. Any more stringent observances, however, can get tedious, you know?

Drinking on the Job

It was well into the corporate Christmas shindig when the chairman and I found ourselves face-to-ruddy face at the bar. The noise swirled around us like a monsoon as waves of liveried servants passed by with indistinguishable blobs on plumed toothpicks and, yes, I was loaded.

"So! Stan!" roared the chairman, festive but sober. "I think we have every reason to be pleased with the fourth-quarter actuals, don't you?" In my foggy mind, I prepared a killer rejoinder. "Yes, sir!" I bellowed at close range. "They certainly are!" Then I laughed like an imbecile. The chairman gave me a quizzical smile and vaporized into the midst. Afterward, he never once mentioned my devastating attempt at conviviality. But I never let it happen again. In drinks, as in all other forms of corporate enterprise, loss of control is the ultimate display of bad form.

Drinking is one of the most venerated institutions in business life, the glue that bonds gray multinational droids to slick sharks in Hawaiian shirts. And most industries offer a wild variety of excuses for drinking together, from the random whim of two chummy executives to the official drunking of seven hundred middle managers at the annual picnic. Where the spirits flow there is, temporarily, no fear, no danger, and no agenda. And there's the rub. It's quite possible that, when drinking with the corporate pros—where the bourbon is free, the chicken wings are hot, and the female vice presidents have their ties off—you may say something stupid, play the macho fool, or simply barf upon your shoes. It is therefore best to be on your guard at liquid business functions, no matter how social they appear. And to drink with your head, not over it. It might help to follow some general rules arrived at after extensive consultation with fellow beverageurs:

When in Rome: Don't be odd man out, especially if it's the top banana who's doing the quaffing. My friend Les interviewed for the number-three job at a software firm managed with an iron fist by a free-wheeling entrepreneurial type. As Les entered the executive suite the big wheel greeted him with his feet up on the desk and a bottle of Stoly in his paw. "Have a blast?" the boss inquired. Les, taken aback, replied, "I don't think so, sir. I just had breakfast." The exec looked him over for a long moment, then politely asked, "What are you, some kind of pansy?" The fact that Les didn't get the job may have had nothing to do with his queasy stomach. But a moment of sodden camaraderie with an alien culture was definitely lost.

Know Thyself: If anything more than the odd highball makes you stupid, sloppy, or mean, take up nursing. Brian, a director in my corporation, would return from lunch every day with a bleary eye and an acid tongue. In one acute, gin-induced rage, he went so far as to dump an entire garbage can onto his weeping assistant's desk when she couldn't find a While You Were Out. For my part, I did my best to keep out of his way until he slipped from postprandial viciousness to late-afternoon lethargy. Brian, by the way, was fired not long ago, after barking up the corporate tree at a few people just as nasty as he.

Keep Your Eye on the Ball: Remember that where businesspeople gather, power is always on the agenda, no matter how subterranean the dance may be. So have fun, sure, but don't give folks an unrestricted shot at your underbelly. Phil, a consultant I know, was deep in the heart of the great and supposedly less cutthroat Northwest, at drinks with a large and hearty group he was consulting. At the height of the friendly do, the plant manager raised his brimming glass and said, "Say, Phil, I'll bet you can't down that drink in one pull. I'll race you." Assuming the contest to be a test of his New York jewels, Phil immediately poured six ounces of bar Scotch down his gullet. "An impressive display, Phil," said the local boss to the convulsed multitudes. "Of course, this here in my glass is water! And boy! Can you drink!" To this day, Phil hears of his legendary gullibility from vendors as far east as the Dakotas.

These maxims aside, certain recurring occasions do have firm protocols. The three questions you should ask yourself at such events are: Whether, When, and How Much.

DRINKS WITH BREAKFAST

Whether: Not alone. You don't want people to think you're a lush.

When: Not before the highest-ranking person. And only if you wish. Nobody blames a guy for not getting in the bag first thing in the morning.

How Much: One. And keep it to a discreet Bloody Mary or mimosa. A breakfast of dry toast with a belt of rye sends an unmistakable message about you.

DRINKS WITH LUNCH

Whether: Watch the ambience, but a white-wine spritzer is generally wimpy enough to be acceptable in all cases.

When: Don't be the first to order. It's no fun to call for a double vodka only to hear seven others order Perrier with lime.

How Much: One distilled spirit, one beer or wine with the meal, then maybe a brandy, if the other guy is amicable. But only drink what you can handle, unless lunching is your occupation. Strolling into a key meeting reeking of Velamints, rosy, jaunty, and jolly from good-fellowship and wassail, is suicidal. Control before 5:00 is the name of the game.

DRINKS WITH DINNER

Whether: Yes, indeed. You're on your own time now.

When: When the waiter arrives.

How Much: Break from the gate slowly and stay just a nose behind the pack. If you persist in retaining a tiny tad more couth than your fellows, you may find yourself graced with a reputation for moderation you do not deserve.

DRINKS AFTER DINNER

Whether: Sure!

When: Since you started three hours ago, what's the difference?

How Much: Don't do anything you can't live down. Remember, this isn't really the fun factory, no matter how much jocularity is zinging through the air. Taking a leak in the street while the chief financial officer looks on may be unwise, unless he's a remarkably fine man indeed.

Finally, as strange as it may seem, there are places where people are encouraged to drink less, light, or not at all. If you labor in such a gulag, you'll have to get bent on your own time. Never abandon your commitment to do so. Excess in the defense of liberty is no vice.

1985

The Bing Diet for Big Guys

Self-denial has never been one of my long suits. When I was just a little round fellow stuffed into my Husky chinos, my folks used to ring an imaginary bell to stop my progress through a third helping of Rice-A-Roni. "Boing," my dad would say, and my mom would whisk the plate from beneath my nose. Nothing much has changed since then. I love my food. Quantity, of course, has not been my only criterion; frequency concerns me, too. To this day, any disruption of my feeding schedule makes me feel like weeping. Yet up until recently, although I have been described by some as burly, stocky, and even beefy, I somehow managed to maintain a humanoid shape. Then I acquired a wife and a desk job, and the girth moved.

So there came a time last winter when I popped a button on an overcoat that once had fit me like a pup tent. I will always remember the *poit!* that button made when it hit the pavement. Horrified at last, I determined to go on a diet that would leave people gasping at my physical beauty. Three months later, I was done. It was easy. You can do it too, believe me, because this is a diet that doesn't require you to give up a single outstanding vice. It's a man's diet, built on rock-solid male assumptions that cannot be denied:

You've Got to Keep Up Your Strength. You want to get down to three substantial meals a day—anything less is likely to end in Twinkies. But here come all these other diets that tell you to practice all kinds of restraint for the rest of your life. Come on. Think how hard you had to work, year after year, to get as fat as you are. A diet that simply pulls you back to minor excess would do a whole hell of a lot, admit it.

You're Not Going to Exercise, Either. If you liked to work up a healthful sweat, you wouldn't be reading this. I, for one, have never even owned a jockstrap. A diet that relies on anything but the most sporadic, perfunctory exertion is out, and I mean it.

Gotta Keep Drinking, Too! Maturity comes with certain responsibilities. Sure, you can quit if, for some reason, you want to. But while you're cutting down on food as well? Be serious. The key is to drink enough of the right things to console you for the loss of French fries from your life.

Following, then, is the 1,200-calorie (or so) regimen in whose gentle embrace I divested more than twenty pounds in a merry three months, and which I still maintain, basically.

BREAKFAST

1/2 bran muffin, buttered lightly
6 cups of coffee
1 cigar

Breakfast is a negligible meal, but essential to forestall a gorge-out come noontime. See it as an opportunity to take in some fiber, which seems to have taken its place next to interferon as the wonder substance of the decade. You can alternate the muffin, if you wish, with a small bowl of designer cereal, or some of Arnold's marvelous Hi-Fiber bread, which they've actually gotten to taste Wonder-ous. The cigar is optional, by the way, but it works. After you smoke one, you won't be hungry for a long while, honest.

LUNCH

2 large martinis, with olives, which are food, you know
1 huge salad (don't worry, you won't eat much of it), or
1 Japanese lunch with all the fixin's
2 diet sodas
1 cigar (still optional)

It helps to have a drink in your hand when you order a mound of arugula with warm goat cheese, say, or that tender morsel of raw flesh from just inside the squid's armpit. It is my personal belief that clear liquors bust up fat globules that would otherwise stick to your ribs, thighs, and face. This makes a daily intake of alcohol mandatory, but don't forget to switch from brown drinks, which are fattening, to transparent ones, which, I contend, are not. A word about beer: don't. You might as well strap on a prosthetic gut. You can reintroduce the golden nectar when you've achieved something and want to backslide a bit.

DINNER

1 large gin (at least), forget the olives
2 Lean Cuisines
V-8 as needed
Raisins, for snacking (and that's all, big guy)

Here's where things get a little tough for boys who like to eat from the moment they get home (a couple crackers with cheese) to the instant they cease chewing and fall off to sleep (three Fig Newtons). Fortunately, modern science has come to our rescue by creating foodlike material that comes in 300-calorie portions. I don't know about you, but I sneeze at 300 calories. When I was in college, I used to eat one solid pound of linguine at night, with butter and ketchup. I can still inhale an entire large pizza, standing up. But two of these little mothers is all I can stomach.

More than any other single tool, what I will generically call the Lean Cuisine—be it by Celentano, Weight Watchers, Budget Gourmet, or the Great Lienmeisters themselves—gave me the control I needed to lose that third chin and some of the second. Boiled in their bag or roasted in the packaging, their guiding principle is the same: you know how much you're eating. This in itself is usually enough to engage a part of your brain somewhat higher in the cerebral cortex than the limbic region that serves your stomach, one that can order your mouth to stop chewing.

Also, while some are pretty good, all in all, they're not what you'd call a sensuous dining experience. A good number seem to employ an Italianate theme. The best of these is Celentano's Chicken Parmigiana, two of which will weigh on your midsection with pleasant authority. Worst, I believe, is Lean Cuisine's Meatball Stew, which, after emerging from its steaming pouch, excited a suspicious amount of interest in Frisky, my dog. But the range of dishes is eclectic enough to almost please any palate, so search to find your dream combo. The ability to eat two should give you the chance to mix and match with abandon.

Best of all, the teeny TV dinner is fast taking its place as the macho meal of choice. The other night around our smoke poker table, I was shocked to see a couple of hefty guys virtually coming to blows over the relative worth of Lean Cuisine's Mandarin Chicken versus Celentano's Chicken Primavera. And when all is said and done, there's nothing more masculine than sinew. Just ask my wife. I have to fight her off with a stick these days, especially when she tries to horn in on my Weight Watchers Baked Fish Divan.

1987

Gut Check

Ladies and gentlemen of the board: Good morning. That about wraps up the pleasantries. Let's get down to it. Things are dead. Those that aren't dead are kind of lying around on the carpet, twitching. Possibly we should throw some water on them. If it doesn't drown them, it could help. On the other hand, maybe nothing will help. We're recessing. And it's not just business anymore. It's personal.

You'll have to excuse me if I sound a little morose. I am morose. This corporation recently celebrated its fortieth anniversary of operations. Quite a few parties were held in its honor, and they succeeded in getting this speaker somewhat depressed in the way that only enforced merriment truly can. People were very nice. We ate large, steaming slabs of virtually raw beef and arugula with improbably soft and smelly cheese, and tuna pressed so thin you could see a credit card through it (not at the same meal, of course), and my good friends and business associates toasted me and roasted me, and in all, I figure the assorted multitudes spent in the low four figures in six separate locations before the week of festivities was, at long last, over. Fun was had. Gratitude was felt. Stock was taken and analyzed.

Today I report on the findings.

When a man turns nineteen, he can get pensive. When he arrives at thirty, he may be allowed the indulgence of some heavy contemplation, but unless he's Mozart or Bob Dylan, he still might expect to find his best years ahead of him. But when a man hits forty, he can fall to thinking, and from thinking into worrying, and from a worry to a fret, then to a sharp trembling, shortly descending into a pit of despond from which it is often impossible to escape without a shed of skin. Or perhaps a change of ownership.

Following is the state of Bing Corp. as we close off the second quarter of business and turn into the last, and final, two, which, I think, will tell the story. Are we positioned for success in the long term? Or are we headed downward into an inexorable spiral of flat growth, low margins, and diminished returns? Let's look at the ledger.

Age of corporate entity: like I said, forty years. Not exactly old, but not the embodiment of the raw, fresh entrepreneurial operation, either.

The physical plant has grown, but much of it is in disrepair. Fortunately, the basic equipment is all in good working order, internal services are somewhat aged but still functioning well. Externally, the facility has even kept most of its hair, and its nose has only grown 10 percent during most recent decade. The trend, however, is quite clearly not only to size, but also to bloat. Further, plant outfitting and appearance have slipped and do not add to the general marketing effort. Suits, narrow ties, and pointy shoes are aging and often appear to be out of keeping with the decade's zeitgeist, such as it is. The general impression created is of an establishment whose image was created in the '60s, allowed to run to seed in the '70s, and given a superficial facelift in the '80s. Obviously, this physical plant cannot be abandoned, but we can certainly make it look up to the job.

Hard assets: Corporation has accumulated a tremendous amount of property and just plain stuff in the last two decades, and is, even in this challenging time frame busily acquiring small objects that promote the superficial impression of comfort and forward momentum. But are these holdings producing value? I think not. Housing for the corporate officer and his family has depreciated at least 10 percent in the last two calendar years; and it's hard to figure out how state-of-the-art computer, electric shaver, stereo and video equipment, Barbies, Swamp things, Legos, and gardening tools are helping to produce good-sized out-year gains. In short, while sustenance has been achieved, dramatic growth being produced by current asset base is not in the cards.

Corporate staff forces the business to sustain a tremendous fixed-cost structure. Number of supporting players has grown 400 percent since 1978 (discounting pets), and now amounts to four full-time and eight part-time players, if you count deadbeat friends who must be kept in beer on selected nights out. Any conceivable staff reduction involves Pyrrhic human sacrifice, which renders any such action highly dubious. Additional staffing, of course, is out of the question, if present staff has any prospect of, say, going to college.

Debt, too, burgeoned radically during the '80s, and cannot now be sustained without the kind of growth this decade doesn't seem to generate. Worse, the actual price of money is growing exponentially in currency that is increasingly tough to fork over. That is, every dollar earned costs time, energy, and heaping amounts of aggravation. Is it possible to produce similar earnings at less egregious cost? Other corporate entities seem to do it. I know a guy, for instance, who's sold three screenplays in four years, none of which was been produced, and he has a swimming pool, for crying out loud!

Revenue, which grew in double digits during the '80s, has leveled off and is now one or two points below gross national product. A very real but ugly prospect rears its head at this time, one that cannot be ignored—that incoming cash flow has plateaued and that any serious upward hockey stick in this area is basically a fond dream . . . unless radical action is taken. But what? Huh?

The tax situation sucks, too.

My preliminary conclusion, ladies and gentlemen, is this: The current operating plan could be pursued for the rest of the decade, but will not lead to top quartile performance and eventual big payout on the back end. In short, we just might be sliding toward tight budgets and a crimped retirement apartment within walking distance of the nearest Winn Dixie. Like you, I find such a prospect unacceptable.

Clearly, a new strategic plan is necessary. And yet . . .

New ideas are not forthcoming. Certainly, this business is undertaking a wide variety of strategic actions to address the small tests that must be passed to keep the daily business profitable and moving in a generally positive direction. But where are the Sony-sized acquisitions, the Time Warner mergers, the Diet Coke-style product developments that will propel us into the next century? What are we doing to take charge of this situation?

Here are the major actions taken on a regular basis during the last five years by this corporation in its search for greatness or, lacking that, happiness. To that end, I:

• grow roses, badly, although this year I produced my largest crop to date. The Value (cost) of each flower produced now hovers in the high double digits.

• barbecue everything except chicken quite well, but as you know, chicken is all that counts.

• read tons of stupid stuff, including, recently, comic books. Mostly violent ones, with words like WHOOMMMPH and KA-BLOWWW in them. I buy them at the Pakistani newsstand, passing right by the shelf that contains the *Harvard Business Review*. Is this cause for concern?

• walk on a treadmill, all of a sudden, for two miles a day. And lift weights. Small weights, but weights nonetheless.

• find myself capable of getting excited about new software the way I used to over a new woman, hankering for it when I don't yet have a registered copy. Of the software, I mean.

• tinker with malfunctioning things until they are completely broken.

• sleep too well, too often.

• work like a dog in the traces whose food dish is on the other side of the tundra.

At the same time, this corporation no longer engages in certain past activities that once gave it pleasure:

• I no longer stay out until 3 A.M., nor do I drink as much as I should. In fact, I remain far too sober even when I have no intention of doing so.

• I no longer procrastinate as often or as well as I did in prior years, often completing projects hours before they are due.

• I can't eat a whole pizza anymore without exploding.

• I can't get a shave that lasts more than three hours.

• I don't wear sports coats. They seem jejune.

What do these actions add up to? I'm really asking.

The answer is unclear. For in the midst of all this doing and not doing, while focusing on the daily details quite adequately, I can feel everything large getting a little more vague, a little more distant, a little less important, including, believe it or not, the practice of business, which somehow suddenly doesn't seem like the thing a person should really be doing with all of his life. Unless he's running something.

Running something. That's it. The challenge is there to be met.

Somewhere men are sailing in a high wind. Somewhere men are singing, and getting paid for it. Somewhere men are walking across a high plain covered with tall grass ready for mowing, and cows are mooing. Am I mad? I think of huge mountain vistas, broad, empty sandpits on the edge of civilization, a rodeo in Cisco, Utah, I saw once. Mooses. Sometimes I think of mooses.

I eat more greens and try to cut fat and squeeze as much revenue from existing operations as I can, and take advantage of as many perks as are legitimately offered, eating and flying and drinking and riding bareback on the business of the company as is my due. And I wait for . . . something. Something good. And when it comes . . .

I'll seize it. Because I'm ready. I'm more than ready. In fact, I'm ripe. And ripeness is all. Okay, maybe not all, but something. Ripeness is something, that's it. Beyond ripeness, however, I'm not quite so sure, ladies and germs.

People start festering, I think.

1991

The Man in the Gray Flannel Sarong

I'm too sexy for my suit. This realization hit me recently while I was looking in the mirror before shaving. Why am I hiding the true depth of my casual self, I wondered, beneath what are basically undertakers' vestments? Underneath my bland exterior, I'm a man, coiled to spring. Suddenly I wanted people to know that. I wanted to be free, to be me, even while engaged in the smarmy process of making money. Until recently I have been forced to suffer inside the prevailing garb around here, looking like a cross between Louis Rukeyser and the young Raymond Burr, a deeply unappealing combination that doesn't play well in bars. I don't like it. You wouldn't, either.

What is the function of the traditional suit, anyway? To obscure your true character and keep you in line, that's all. And what of creativity? Eh? Bah!

Fortunately times have changed. According to a survey by the Marketing Research Corporation of America, between 1985 and 1991 there was a 34 percent drop in the number of business suits sold in the United States, which means (unless men are simply wearing their suits an extra year or two before sending them to the thrift shop) that men are wearing fewer suits, right? Also, nearly half the men surveyed reported that there were new "casual days" at work, when they were permitted to wear T-shirts and comfy sandals. Indeed, as we stand on the brink of the millennium, the entire loosey-goosey casual lifestyle look is down on us like sushi in the '80s, just as raw, ubiquitous, and refreshingly welcome.

We're into a relaxed, easy feeling with what we wear and who we are, and that's good news for fundamentally casual people like you and me who heretofore have been forced to present a bogus picture of themselves, folks who would be a lot happier in distressed denim instead of gray flannel, or even, on Fridays, a simple frock with large red polka dots. No, today, for whatever reason, a lot of us just prefer to be more and more ourselves instead of being other people all the time. We're out to establish a hipper, looser, more fabulous agenda, one in which a man can express himself no matter how formal the setting or structured the content.

From the start, I realized it wouldn't be easy. I've never been too good at casual. In 1987, for instance, I was invited to a management retreat in Williamsburg, Virginia, the kind at which people are expected to let down what hair they have left. Knowing I couldn't rely on my nice blue generic suit, I packed every article of clothing I had that was clean. Who knew what might pass for acceptable in those circumstances? Where there are no standards, it's possible that nothing, rather than everything, is permissible. I showed up on the first evening in a Lacoste shirt, blue jeans, and black running shoes. Unfortunately I had forgotten to pack white socks, so I had to wear thin black calf-length hose that did not show up well under the intense scrutiny of other executives, who looked equally weird but better put-together in their wide-wales and madras. "Lookit Bing's socks!" my friend Klein hollered as I walked through the door, my poplin bush jacket over my arm to hide my midsection, which has a tendency to declare itself. I was humiliated. Another time I came dressed in conservative business garb to a big dinner in Morgantown, West Virginia, that turned out to be all guys in khaki and cashmere golfing sweaters. I didn't have either. I had to make do with a big cable-knit monstrosity I borrowed, and its color was totally wrong for me.

To avoid this kind of mortification, I determined to keep my eye on genuine fashion trends and import them gradually—to do it right, in other words. I was also determined to stay away from the loser forms of utter nerdosity that, while masquerading as a relaxation of formal standards, are in truth an equally repulsive display of anal retention and, ultimately, servility. One time I went to my corporation's science and research complex. I was standing on the edge of a giant quadrangle. I heard a little bell ring, and suddenly at least eighty guys came bursting out of their buildings on the way to a tray lunch somewhere. Each had on an open neck, 80 percent polyester shirt with elbow-length sleeves and a big plastic pocket protector engorged with writing implements. That's not a form of casual we want to be getting into just yet.

Well, thanks to the looser, more casual times we live in, we don't have to. There are a lot of other choices for guys seeking to relax the envelope.

Naturally I started with ties. So many things are possible in that arena now that good taste and discretion have been abandoned in favor of whimsy. One morning I simply happened into our regular quarterly budget review (and when will those pesky numbers get better?) wearing my World Wildlife Fund "Save the Planet" tie, which sports a menacing yet jaunty orange-and-black jaguar crouching in some green underbrush, all on a field of navy blue. Several financial types immediately wanted to know "exactly what I thought I was doing," and Gerbert, our controller, was particularly grumpy about it, calling my entire look "jejune." "My tie is unmistakably playful and relaxed," I told him calmly as he attempted to hide the fact that we'd just been through six quarters without significant revenue growth. The next day, in a meeting with Chet, our chairman, I threw caution to the wind and wore a bright-red, maroon, and forest green tie that, when pressed at its tip, plays "Send in the Clowns," which I think sort of defines the left wing of the new world order.

"Nice tie, Bing," Chet said.

But wacky ties are old hat, a mere sop to the illusion of real social change. I wanted to go further, and I'm not talking about nutty socks with little tassels on them, either. Slowly, carefully, I moved into the new, casual White House look, in which men with big butts wear checked shirts and enormous Levi's, perhaps with some cowboy boots for additional credibility with organized labor. Of course, I buttoned my shirt all the way to the top like you're supposed to, making sure it was two sizes too big in the neck so that people would think me thinner than I once was, which could possibly be true in some parallel universe. I didn't pop into this radical new chic all at once. I began the theme by introducing a pair of stone-cool black-and-silver alligator boots with metal toe protectors, tucked under the cuffed leg of my classic Paul Stuart pinstripe. The next day, at a meeting about our credit rating with investment bankers, I added the jeans, shirt, and, for a touch of formality, a large tweedy blazer with elbow patches. I put a red bandanna in my breast pocket for éclat. I think I achieved it. If dangle of jaw is any indication, Chet was mightily impressed.

"Nice pocket rag, Bing" is what he said.

For some reason, I didn't have another major interface with senior management for a couple of weeks after that. Fortunately there was a perfect First Monday of the Month encounter that I was always expected at, and for that occasion I chose to move the entire look into deep Euro—a black shirt unbuttoned to reveal my splendid torso, light-green linen double-breasted jacket, skintight black jeans, and soft, pointy demi-booties from Italy that would melt in your mouth on a cold morning. I dyed my hair blond and wore it combed forward in a sort of modified ex-Green pragmatist Germanic thing. I also decided, as a part of my new informality, to start smoking in my office again, tiny acrid cigarettes that made people sit up and take notice. I really started to enjoy myself. Oddly, it was a very quiet meeting after everyone got over ribbing me about my new and less constrained look. Chet, for one, kept patting my cheek kind of aggressively with his big old red and sweaty palm and muttering, "Jesus Christ, look at you, boy!" They only do that kind of stuff if they care, you know.

A friend of mine had just come back from Seattle, bringing with him some old painters' pants, a ripped T-shirt he had used to clean his windshield in a rainstorm, a flat, wide belt studded with lots of pretty grommets, and a real nice pair of Doc Martens that he won in a poker game off an ex-nun living with former Weathermen in St. Louis. I wore the entire ensemble one morning in a casual review of West Coast business operations, along with the six new teeny-weeny earrings I had placed in a discreet row in my right earlobe.

"Bing," said Chet as the extraordinarily short meeting wound down. There was a lengthy pause. "Never mind." He got up and left. I thought about pursuing the matter but decided instead to take it, well, more . . . casually.

From that time on, I had nowhere to go but into the unknown. After all, I was the ne plus ultra in executive casualness—but I still didn't feel totally relaxed for some reason. Also, I knew that there were guys in other industries who were even more down-home and funky than I was, and that irked me. I couldn't go back to something mundane—slacks with a sports coat, a teal bathrobe over a silk nightgown, chaps. . . . It all seemed so done before. Then I saw what Donna Karan's dudes were into, and that cinched it. I knew that Friday we were having a meeting with a major industry player to discuss a potential acquisition. These gatherings can get so formal that nothing gets done, I thought.

I appeared that morning in perhaps the breeziest conceivable outfit for men today, when so many inconceivable things are possible. Over my completely naked upper body I draped an oversized, bright-yellow sports jacket with very broad lapels. On my head I wrapped a fetching red and white bandanna. The pièce de résistance was, of course, my new kilt, a hank of gorgeous plaid fabric buckled up into an audaciously brief skirt held up with a gutsy silver concha belt. I considered adding an Hermès scarf as a foulard, but rejected the idea as too flamboyant.

As the meeting was getting organized, I wandered by Chet's office to say hi. He's a boss, you know. But I also consider him something of a mentor and friend. He looked me over with that affectionate silent twinkle that has for so long been an integral part of our relationship. He rose from his chair, leaned over his enormous desk, and beckoned me close with one index finger. "Get into your fucking suit, goddamn it!" he screamed at the top of his lungs, his neck veins bulging. "We've got a meeting with grown-ups!"

I thought that was kind of a cheap shot, but I did what he said anyway. At the meeting, by the way, I sat in the corner looking very serious in a solid, dark blue, single-breasted, white shirt with radical collar stays, and red tie with gray baling hooks in the foreground. I said virtually nothing, although I thought a judicious nod at certain points was appropriate. At the end everybody shook hands and asked one another to lunch real soon. The acquisition probably will never come through, but at least we're talking, which is something in this day and age.

And I never could have played if I hadn't been wearing the suit.

What the hell. I'm casual inside. And that's what counts, don't you think?

1993

The Meaning of Lunch

Think back. Think all the way back. Go ahead. Do it.

You're running around in tiny little pajamas with a flap on the seat! You can hardly keep from sucking your finger! Whoa! Stop!

Okay, I guess that's too far back. Let's say . . . you're in grade school. You've suffered through the morning. Gym was pretty bad. Kirby Gaines picked you up by the waistband of your shorts again and gave you a wedgie. Mrs. Krinsky popped a quiz on photosynthesis in science. But in a few minutes there's going to be your very favorite period of the day. You know: lunch.

Morton called five minutes ago and blew a tsunami of steam up my butt about the Broder situation. Bob is mad about the amount of money being spent in Tucson. Harbert is fed up with Gewirtz and wants him transferred to someplace where nobody can see him. But I've got a 1 P.M. reservation at Michael's. It's not the only place to eat in New York. But it's the only place to eat in New York right now.

Close your eyes and take a deep breath, then say it quietly to yourself. "Lunch." What steamy images float up from the deep recesses of your brain stem? For me, it will always be baloney and cheese on white bread with a little mayo, and a thermos of Campbell's tomato soup on the side. Maybe a couple of Fig Newtons. On Wednesdays, it would be the special—meatball wedge made fresh, right on location. Everybody got the wedge, with two containers of very cold milk. And, oh, yes: an ice-cream sandwich.

Today I think I'll get the artichoke salad with goat cheese resting on prosciutto sliced so thin it would take an electron microscope to find it, followed by the chicken *frites*—half a bird resting on a bed of spinach, surrounded by a mountain of matchstick French fries. For dessert, a couple of bad cookies and a cup of decaf. Yesterday I had the same thing. Also the day before. If we skip the designer water and my partner decides not to have anything with lobster in it, I believe we could get out for under what it costs to buy a midrange Walkman.

It wasn't about the food, of course, in the lunchroom. It was about being there, about where you were positioned in the room, about who was placed next to whom that day, about the noise, the running around between courses, the occasional food fight. It was about the staff, too. There was Mrs. Ianello, who dished out the hot meals. You had to handle her very, very carefully, or she would ignore your order and give you something she thought you should have, like wax beans. There was Otto, who mopped, and Arturo and Lester, who were supposed to monitor our behavior but usually just ate our Fritos.

Steve handles the room now, since Peter went to Mesa Grill, and Lore'al generally takes care of the book. They know me. The waiters know me, too. They know everybody, along with our little weirdnesses. This one likes his Cobb salad mixed but not chopped. This one likes exactly three macaroons to be given to him free at the end of every meal. Every other week Michael himself comes in and nearly explodes with glee at each person he sees at his or her accustomed table. This is a group that bows to none in its tolerance for first-class sucking up. You know my name! I love this place! A couple of years ago the gorgeous coat-checker left us to become *Vanity Fair* cover girl and actress Gretchen Mol. This only made us feel better about ourselves and our lunchroom. If we play our cards right, one day we could possibly be as famous as the guy who's bringing us that $8 bottle of Evian!

My table was the third from the side door, six back from the front . . . me and Levine and Kaskowitz and six or seven other guys I didn't feel that strongly about. It was a good table, not a great table. All around me people were munching and slurping and yakking. We didn't all like one another very much—not by a long shot. In fact, a lot of us hated one another for the indignities and unkindnesses that mark human life at any age. But we had to eat together. We were, after all, in the same school.

Today Bryant Gumbel is with Joseph Abboud in the front window at the table where Tom Brokaw often holds court, and Susan Lyne (who has done such a fine job at Disney) is taking her place at the No. 1 slot along the wall next to the table recently vacated by William Weld, former governor of Massachusetts. Hard by the divider between the bar and the main dining room, agents from ICM and William Morris apply suction to their companions at adjoining tables, and Joanie Evans is doing something over there next to Walter Isaacson and his lucky lunch companions from Powerful Media. I see my pal Dworkin at a table often favored by Katie Couric. We pretend not to know each other, even though we will meet for drinks later this evening, because Michael's is not about friendship. It's about forging meaningful relationships that can endure for the term of at least one lunch. My table is No. 4, along the wall. It is a very good table, and I see people looking and wondering who I am. I'm the guy who eats here three times a week, that's who I am.

Thirty-eight minutes into the period, the bell rang, and the entire place cleared out as if it were an air-raid drill. It was time to move on to Mr. Trundle's social studies class, where the entire first semester consisted of memorizing the street addresses of every major building in New York City. Think I'm lying? Ask me what the address of the Woolworth Building is. Go ahead. Ask me.

Today we have to wait for the check for quite some time, as usual. And it's an outrageous sum, as always. We could linger for another cup of coffee (nobody drinks booze anymore, except perhaps for Liam Neeson, who had what looked to be a fine, robust Bordeaux the other day). But the bell has rung. In the '80s, it used to ring at 2 P.M. In recent years, 2:30 seems to be the moment when fear and ambition kick in, possibly in equal measure, and the lunchroom clears. This afternoon we have meetings with guys who want to know what our budgets are going to be in the year 2003. A more foolish exercise I can't imagine, but I'm prepared to give them what they want, down to the penny, and what I intend to do with that money three years from now. Think I'm lying? Go ahead. Ask me.

2000

How I Lost My Chins

The big news around my corporation these days is that just in time for the high vacation days of summer, I personally, myself, have lost not ten, not twenty, but a grand total of thirty-five pounds. This has been done while indulging in a full schedule of responsible business eating and drinking, I will have you know.

Modesty forbids me fully describing just how great I look without my carry-on baggage subcutaneously strapped to my torso, but suffice it to say that my transformation has left me with only one chin and a host of admirers yearning to know how it was done.

So as a public service and in response to all those who have asked, here is the diet secret that has enabled me to lose a bucketful of weight and feel just great. You can do it, too, even if you breakfast, lunch, and dine out at the poshest institutions with hungry, rapacious dudes—and drink as much as you want. That's right! Vodka! Gin! Rum! A frisky Cabernet with no little pretension! All can be yours, if . . .

Are you ready? Here it is, then, my secret, which actually works, I assure you:

Eat what you don't like. If you like it, don't eat it.

Simple? Sure. Let's see how it plays out during the typical business day.

I'm at breakfast with a starting forward from a company about to deconsolidate. He's upset since his options are so far underwater they have the bends, so he orders eggs, bacon, home fries, toast, and coffee. All of them look great to me, of course, but I hold my nose for a moment and then order some granola with skimmed milk and whole wheat toast.

A word about whole wheat. It works, for two reasons: First, it metabolizes some crustacea in your epiglottis or some nutritional bushwah like that, and two, nobody can finish anything that is made out of it.

And that's the key! Not finishing. By not finishing—now take this down slowly—you eat less. Know why? Because you want to.

Eating things you don't like makes dieting fun.

Sure enough, while the guy from the blasted Internet company is tucking into his 2,000th calorie, I'm pushing away a half-eaten bowl of brownish yak food and trying to choke down the second quarter of my toast. I have a lot of coffee and call it a morning. Mission accomplished!

At lunch I host a couple of guys who at some point I thought I should have lunch with. I forget why now. It's not important. It's lunchtime, and people eat, right?

Not me. While my guys order food that human beings would favor, I dig right into a tidy little plate of food that only a fish would find palatable, i.e., fish. Now the thing about fish is that it's both delicious and nutritious, but it is really no fun. Nobody in his right mind ever woke up drooling from a dream in which he dug into a plate of fish. Whereas me, I've been dreaming of a nice steak for several months now.

The thing is, I like steak and generally finish one once I've started. Not so with fish. Halfway through the lovely piece of fish, no matter how "nice" that fish might be, it generally becomes optional as a dietary target. And once food becomes optional, half the battle is won. I also skip anything that is not green on my plate, because I might like it. The green stuff I can take for one or two bites, then that's over, too. And if I have a cookie at the end of the meal, who cares? The whole experience added up to less than half one of those Cobb salads drenched with bacon, avocado, and fat masquerading as dressing.

Dinner is more of a challenge, because you have to break ranks with the high concept and drink alcohol. Many people believe that consumption of this foodstuff is inconsistent with weight loss. Nothing could be further from the truth, as long as you drink the right things. Several years ago I discovered the interesting fact that while any liquor of color is indeed detrimental to dietary constraints, all clear beverages are in fact fat-burning. Particularly effective in this way are martinis, which, when taken very cold with a twist, clear the veins and arteries of anything you don't want to be there. White wine is also good, but only after a couple of martinis.

While you're laying a good base in this regard, be careful to stay away from pretzels, nuts, and other salty stuff, because you like them. For dinner, having enjoyed yourself enough for one meal, you may proceed to order anything dry, leafy, and unappetizing. Skip dessert, of course, and order fruit. No matter how much people say they like fruit, nobody but a brown bear can finish a full plate of berries.

Those are the bare bones, and believe me, I'm almost down to mine. Try it, and let me know if you like it. If you like it too much, though, watch out. Something could be gaining on you.

2002

LATTE BREAK

Twenty Good Reasons to Cry

1. Your team has just lost the seventh game of the World Series.
2. Your stockbrocker is arrested for inside trading, and you realize the guy never did one single unethical thing for you.
3. Your wife has run off with James Brolin.
4. You decide to forgo your designer clip joint and have your hair cut by Rocco at the local barbershop. Six dollars and fifteen minutes later, you emerge with a kind of abrupt, vertical look currently sported only by military men and recently deinstitutionalized mental patients.
5. Indoor soccer
6. You shave off your mustache and remember that you hate your face.
7. You forget to preorder the vegetarian meal at TWA and, famished, eat two stuffed bell peppers in marinara sauce before you realize what you've done.
8. You spend $540 on a state-of-the-art compact-disc player, only to find out the next day, in the current issue of *Audiophile,* that digital tape has suddenly become the decreed format of choice.
9. Twenty-four-year-old M.B.A.s who earn in excess of a million dollars a year and complain their lives are empty
10. Two weeks with your parents at their geriatric enclave in Sun City, Arizona
11. You hear from your dermatologist that the only way to save your hair is to have injections of estrogen.
12. Your wife absolutely refuses to let you buy that personal helicopter you saw in the window at Hammacher Schlemmer.
13. In the course of a schmooze with a bright and frisky young woman you thought understood you, she inquires, "Woodstock? You mean Snoopy's little friend?"

14. Fatty corned beef
15. You find yourself actually paying attention to Fred Rogers.
16. You don your seersucker suit for the first time since last summer and find that, while you can still button the trousers by forcing every bit of air from your lungs, the fly flares so radically your zipper shows.
17. In New York City today, the only legal place to light your postdinner Monte Cruz is at home with your wife or in the middle of Central Park—and you don't feel all that safe in either location.
18. You enter a room filled with intelligent, dynamic, slender women, and realize that you will never know a single one except at exorbitant personal cost.
19. You are stuck on an elevator with Siegfried and Roy.
20. Your dog, Rags, with whom you shared every confidence and crisis for more than seventeen years, can no longer control his bodily functions. You make that last, inevitable trip to the vet. Afterward, you stand on the sidewalk in the bright sunshine, alone for the first time since your youth, wondering where life goes and, in your heart, knowing.

1987

8

THE MAN SHOW

T*he smaller pecker you are in the pecking order, the more difficult it is to be yourself. What distinguishes the big players is their willingness to indulge that inner beast. Take the stirring, mysterious, and ultimately inspiring case of Jack Welch. By all accounts a model of probity and professional sangfroid, Neutron Jack (so named because in his salad days he was capable of taking out the population of a business unit while leaving the buildings standing), obviously had a big swinging party animal inside his gray patina. The company coffers funded his personal lifestyle, which was as lusty as that of a medieval pope. And when the time came for him to shuffle off his executive function, that beast inside leapt out into public view, treating the public to a nice, tawdry sex scandal that entertained the business world for months. What a man! Even in his profligacies and foolishness, he was bigger than other people.*

The pieces that follow are all about this tension between the inner and outer selves created by the need to appear sentient eight to ten hours a day and have some fun at the same time. You will also notice some observations about relations as they may exist between men and women. These were written for a man's magazine and may appear, at this time, insufficiently evolved for the times in which we now are fortunate to live. Even back then, some people were annoyed with me. On the wall of my office is a framed copy of the third column in this section with the words, "YOU SUCK I'M CANCELLING MY SUBSCRIPTION!" scrawled on it in red lipstick. A couple of pieces later, you will see, I apologize. I don't think some people understood that it is always my intention to make fun of men, which is permissible.

Is That Rouge, Son?

I got a fright the other day. My son came out of his sister's room. He was, at that time, 2.6 years old, 2.6 feet tall. On his feet was an old pair of patent-leather pumps, size 8. On his bottom half, a diaper. Puffing around his neck, an ersatz ostrich boa, electric pink. His face was smeared with rouge, which he had carefully applied to his lips, cheeks, and chin. Crowning his head was my daughter's voile tutu, also pink, which flared out smartly and imparted a kind of Statue of Liberty effect that was not altogether unflattering. "I look booful," he said.

Frankly, I freaked out. Fully aware I was acting like a maniac, I insisted on eradicating most of the rouge with cold cream, explaining the customary relationship between boys and lipstick—that is, arm's length. I also politely removed the ballet headgear. He cried.

I want my son to be a Man. So I think it's only natural that I want him to play with toys that will prepare him for manhood: vehicles, swords, bulked-out action figures, sports gear. I don't believe I'm unusual in this. My pal Dworkin bought my son a bat and ball when the little guy was three days old. It wasn't a gift the kid could use; it was a message: "Hope he grows up to be more athletic than you. Perhaps if he starts early, he's got a chance." I appreciated it a lot.

Which is ironic. I never owned a jockstrap, not even for an hour. Running more than six hundred meters makes me puke, always has. To this day, the smell of a gym, any gym, leaves me feeling small and incompetent. Throughout my life, in fact, I have been forced to work out my own concept of what it means to be a man. Today that concept centers upon eating and drinking too much and too often, playing poker inconsistently, and going only to bad, violent movies. You can see why I would want better for my son. I know he's a normal little boy. I'm just worried. You'd be worried, too, if you knew me as well as I do.

I've made my feelings known. The other day my wife swung by Child World with the two kids to pick up a lunch box for my daughter. As always, she made the "one toy of your choice" deal with both. My daughter naturally gravitated to personal accessories, finding herself a shiny lavender purse with a pearl clasp. My son, tailing along, selected the same. "I knew how you would react if he came home with another pocketbook," my wife explained. So, totally against her nutritional philosophy, she found herself encouraging him to select an oversized chocolate bunny instead. I was pleased.

It's not just toys and fashion concepts I'm talking about, of course. It's all the decisive male issues I see rearing up to determine his character.

Take sports, for instance. I never could.

I remember weekends, or days at camp, or frankly just about any moment in my happy, nervous childhood; the morning is brisk and sunshiny, all the kids are laughing and bumping each other, and we're choosing up sides for a scratch game of baseball. One by one, all the kids are picked until the only ones left are me and Elliot Suber. Then Elliot, who is a real geek, goes. I'm trying not to cry, you know, to show I don't care. Why am I there? Because, now that I think about it, my father wanted me to be.

One team captain finally grumbles, "Okay. I guess we've got Bing." I bat tenth. I am assigned deep center field, a little-known position that involves standing some furlongs beyond the actual horizon of the game and chasing down balls that go into the parking lot of the Sunset Supermarket.

Like my own father, I want my son to be normal, and I am prepared to ruin his youth if that's what it takes. So the other Sunday I decided that the time was right to get off my back and introduce the kid to some no-pressure catch, just toss around a ball for a while and begin fielding the notion that physical activity is good and natural and something one's father occasionally does. It's a big ball, and soft, by the way, not a horsehide nugget or anything. So we went outside and I threw the ball to my son, and it hit him in the stomach. I could see he was making a decision whether to cry or not. He didn't. What he did do is take the ball and walk away with it. "Throw it here, son!" I called in an agreeable, coach-like manner. "No!" he hollered. "This my ballie! You get you own ballie!" After a while, my daughter came out into the backyard and we lobbed around a pigskin. My son had disappeared. I found him in the playroom, setting up a dormitory sleeping arrangement for a number of stuffed animals. "Don't you want to come out and play with a ballie or something?" I asked. "No tank," he said. At least he's stubborn, I thought.

But it bothered me. It was just a little too goddamned evocative for me personally. When I was thirteen, they made me play basketball. I was kind of round, and slow, and okay, I stunk. For the entire game, I ran up and down the court in confusion and profound mortification, clapping my hands together and shouting, "Hup! Hup!" and occasionally, "Over here, yadayada!" No one threw me the ball, of course. I don't blame them. Is this the legacy I want for my son?! No! I want him to play basketball, for chrissake, whether he's any good or not!

Things will be fine, I am sure. He swings a bat well, I'm happy to say. Not at a ball, it's true. But whenever I say "no" to him, he exits the room, ferrets around until he finds his big yellow whiffle bat, and bops me hard on the top of the head with it.

Being a man is more than sports, of course. There's also fighting.

My wife tells me there's this kid named Adam in his play group. Adam hits. It's mostly boys who do, not because girls don't want to hit, but because they are discouraged from doing so, as opposed to boys, who, after they hit someone, may have their hair severely tousled. My son, it seems, does not hit back, and under my wife's guidance is working on saying "I don't like that!" in a loud and angry voice when he is assaulted. The thing is, some guys need to be punched, not admonished.

When I was small, my enemies, for reasons only my mother found mysterious, called me "Fatso." I decided I wanted boxing lessons, possibly because there was somebody I wanted to beat up. For three happy months, I went to the community center, where a pair of father-and-son cops, Bunny and Mike, taught me the basics and called me "Champ." I made a friend there, too, Petey, about two years older, ten pounds lighter than I, a pal when pals who did not call me "Fatso" were precious.

The course culminated in a bout for the championship of each weight class. It turned out Petey was the only one who even came close to my weight. The gym was full. For forty-five seconds we danced around each other, filled with love and sorrow and the desire to win. Then I backed him into a corner and began punching him in the stomach pretty much at will. When he dropped his arms to protect his lanky gut, I punched him in the face. His eyes were wide, and yes! There was blood foaming out of his nose. I remember thinking, "Blood! Yahoo!"

Then I was crushed by a wave of pity, shame, and regret. They stopped the fight and I got a trophy, but I never hit anyone ever again, not even one of the morons who teased me and, unlike Petey, deserved it. So maybe I'd like my son to be able to flatten a foe without being overwhelmed by guilt. Maybe that would make his youth a little easier.

On the whole, though, things are getting better. I'm happy to report that when the boy plays with his sister's Barbie phalanx of fine characters, he now gravitates to Derek, with whom he shares hair color. He likes Ken too, and He-Man. For some reason, he seems to have torn off the right leg of all three. Better still, this morning he was working with Duplos to make some sort of projectile. "I makin' a gun here, to shoot," he said. "Pow." Dynamite. Best of all, later in the afternoon I saw him crouched over a Teenage Mutant Ninja Turtle, wrapping a string around its neck. "I a monster," he said, "and I choke you." This is exactly the kind of behavior I've been waiting for.

I have made sure his room is loaded with Food Fighters (vicious cheeseburgers, belligerent stacks of pancakes, hot dogs that transform themselves into nuclear missiles); dinosaurs with fangs bared; fire trucks. When asked his favorite toy, he responds, "Ghostbusters and a sandwich." That's fine by me. Truth is, the entire Ghostbusters line scares the hell out of him, especially the grandmother who opens her mouth to expose a gullet full of fangs. But he still plays with her. That's my little man.

I, too, am evolving. Last night I came home and walked into the kitchen to find my son and daughter dressed for dinner in matching nightgowns, tricolor sateen floor-length models in yellow, pink, and blue. I bit my lip, laughed with merry insouciance, and kissed them both hello without comment. Nobody can say I'm not trying.

See, I remember my first toy, the first toy worthy of remembering. It was a bunny rabbit. He was fuzzy, soft, and pink. I named him Pink, and when he fell apart in the washing machine from sheer old age, I cried a lot. My parents, in some foreshadowing of my present state of ambivalence, produced an identical bunny, in blue. I named him Blue. I lost him almost immediately. Some things can never be replaced.

1989

Everyday Wife Management

You'd better sit down. This is going to be a rather serious talk. A lot of you are married, have been married, or someday will be married. And a quick review of the prevailing institution indicates that many of you need help gaining control of this, your central power relationship outside the office.

People say marriage isn't easy, that you have to feed and water it, prune it, all that herbaceous stuff. Nonsense. I've been married for more than a decade, and I can tell you quite honestly that a successful marriage has little to do with work and even less to do with patience. It all comes down to whether or not you can manage your wife.

The man who can manage his wife while she is managing him may achieve happiness and marriage at the same time. The guy who can't is the miserable dink dribbling bar nuts onto his shirtfront between work and dinner every night. Do you want to be that guy? Of course you don't. Not every night.

Today I can report that after twelve years of aggressive management, I have my wife exactly where she wants me. You, too, can attain this happy state if you follow these simple precepts:

Just Say Yes. The überweltanschauung of successful wife management. The average wife makes 6.8 articulated demands per eight waking hours of married life, simply because, like Mount Everest, you are there.[2] The husband who seeks to act on each is doomed to a life of fruitless activity on the one hand and discord on the other. That leaves no hands free to horse around with.

Perhaps it's a task as simple as regrouting the bathroom. In my case, it's the continuous, onerous demand on the part of my wife to fill out and monitor a continuous stream of medical insurance forms generated by our family, an omnipresent pressure to deal with trivial paper that invades my life and torments my few precious moments of peace and

---

[2] *"Demand Vectors as a Function of Anxiety in American Wives of All Ages." Zorn & Bjorn, et al., 1988, viz.*

quiet, moments when I do not wish to be pestered with inconsequential stupidities! Be that as it may.

Employed with a general policy of affable forgetfulness, strategic false consensus places the wife in the difficult and exhausting position of pestering a man who is apparently agreeable to everything. Hold central in your mind the traditional Zen concept of rolling over and snoozing until rudely awakened. What is the sound of one voice fighting? Silence, especially if you're wearing headphones.

Celebrate the Moments of Her Craziness. Wives seldom feel more righteous than when they are being unreasonable. Husbands are the same, but less often. When we first met, the future Mrs. Bing favored a certain restaurant that dressed up blocks of disgusting, puffy tofu in any number of guises. For more than a year it was the only place she would patronize. After a while, just passing by it in a taxi prompted me to gag. Did I insist on an alternative venue—as was my due? Not at all. I want my wife to be happy.

Instead, when we planned to dine out, I simply led the woman on an interminable review of all other locations. Eventually, inexorably, the collective weight of my sheer ornery reasonableness tired her out. Often after such discussions it was too late to dine out at all, and we ended up eating a lot of weird junk at her place. Not long after, we were married.

Do Your Housework, Spud. Even slobby wives hate messy husbands who force them to live in disorganized surroundings. The key is to push cleanup into the vast chasm of later, and then, when the inevitable time arrives, do your part in a massive spasm of effective activity. Mrs. Bing is perfectly content to allow our house to appear progressively more psychotic over the course of a week, as Hot Wheels, Barbies, Dereks, Skippers, sociopathic RoboCop villains, Popples, parkas, gnarled suspenders, old nipples, floppy diskettes, and dispersed breakfast cereals invade and conquer all living spaces. Suddenly, my wife's tolerance reaches critical mass, usually on Thursday. That means me, as well it should.

For years, I fought and wheedled and tried to wriggle free. Now I roll up my sleeves and move through the house like the black plague through Sweden. Some tips:

• When forced to confine edibles to food-storage bags, abjure the use of the hated twist-tie, opting instead for the lightning 360-degree spin, which, while it may compromise the occasional carrot stick, saves entire seconds.
• When picking up errant clothing, stash everything in the hamper instead of hanging up those few articles that might be worn again.

• When called upon to cleanse obnoxious microwave dishes with food fused to their molecular structure, accomplish the task industriously, but at the same time so poorly that your wife must consider the wisdom of doing it herself next time.

• Copious, unexplored spaces exist under beds and couches, and above and behind bookshelves seemingly stuffed to priapism. Explore them!

The husband who works with speed and imagination can limit the time devoted to housework to less than twenty minutes per week—without one word exchanged in anger! Good luck!

Attempt Competence—and Fail! A veil of comprehensive male ineptitude will convince your wife that you are actually the last person she wants adjusting the frisky flue or pruning the priceless hedges.

My friend Bruce established lifetime proof of his deficiencies in one stroke last August. He and his wife had put a small swimming pool in the backyard of their modest summer house; an enclosure around the pool was needed to protect their two tiny children. Bruce invited me over one weekend to help him do it himself, thereby compounding his stupidity by a factor of two. Twelve beers later, the fencing made its meandering way like a drunken snake across his acreage. When the couple went to sell the property late last year, they found that its value had been diminished by $30,000, thanks—according to the real estate agent—to the profound ugliness of that barricade. Now when they have a job to do, no matter how minor, they hire somebody! Well done, Bruce!

Go Forth and Spend Together! Don't play the role of the frugal money manager. Instead, encourage your wife's ongoing addiction to purchasing. She's ill-behooved to criticize your purchase of a six-bit data card after she's snapped up six exercise unitards in a host of zany colors. Buying isn't all, of course. Even more crucial is the issue of having enough money in your pocket. With a tight wife—especially one who works for half the cash—this can involve courteous extortion, purse snatching, cash stashing, and, in extremis, the establishment of a hidden bank account. I can say no more, and I mean it.

Except to mention that under no circumstances should you simply draw huge amounts out of your joint checking account and blow it on evanescent stuff. This is tempting, especially with the current prevalence of electronic money machines. Some years ago, I embarked on a blithe program of biweekly card dipping of which Mrs. Bing knew nothing. This went on for some time. One day, looking over our balance sheet, she made a guttural noise and inquired, "Why is there a $6,000 discrepancy between what I think we have and what they say we have?" She was upset. From then on in, she insisted on doing the bank statement, a policy that has made things somewhat difficult ever since.

Let Her Eat What She Wants. Women eat too little of some items (meat) and too much of others (raw vegetables and chocolate). You, on the other hand, must continually protect your ability to ingest tasty organs, meats, and links, articulated fats, starches, and nitrites. The issue here is mutual respect and satisfactory decision making—leading to an occasional steak for you whether she wants one or not.[3] Do not, by the way, allow yourself to become embroiled in her diets. If your wife is like mine, she'll send you out for Oreos, and when you return with them, streaming with rain and bonhomie, she'll accuse you of "undermining her." You can't win that game. So don't play.

Don't Get Even—Get Mad! When all else fails, stand your ground. My friend Berk allowed his wife to go ahead and actually purchase a suburban house without his express consent. This was most retrograde to his desire. When I asked him why he'd allowed things to go so far, he replied, "She asked me if I agreed. I told her I'd have to think about it. Before I was done thinking about it, she did it." A couple of months before they were scheduled to move, but after closing, he had a full-scale tantrum in the car, pounding on the steering wheel and screaming out the window, which was closed at the time. This uncharacteristic behavior scared the hell out of his wife, who, amazingly, caved in and unloaded the house posthaste. Berk had won! They're now in the process of moving to a much closer location right down the street that he doesn't want to live in.

Isn't You Romantic? Did you hug your wife today? Making love is almost always preferable to fighting, although couples may like to do both in no particular order. And even when you can't make love, what the hell—have sex anyway.

Romance, however, is more than base physical expression of animal lust. Express your admiration for her in a variety of ways reminiscent of your life before matrimony. Take her on dates and use your plastic. Let her sleep late once a month. And when life with you isn't a walk in the park, let her take a walk in the park. You'll be glad you did the next time you want to take a weekend in Vegas.

Remember, Bud, that when all is said and done, you married the

---

[3] *See "Getting Her In-flight Meal When You're Still Hungry After Just Eating Yours," Ned Reamer, Ved Pinsky, and the staff of the Bing Food Management Center, 1987.*

woman because of all the things that you find annoying in her personality, not in spite of them. If you'd wanted someone more comprehensible, you'd have married yourself, not someone exactly the opposite.

My wife is almost everything I am not, and I appreciate that in her. And as much as I prize her management, I believe she values mine. At the end of the day, when she gets that misty, dopey teenage look in her eye, wraps her arms around me, and purrs, "You're a good man, Stanky," I wouldn't be single again, not if you paid me.

I think that's saying a lot in these tough economic times.

1990

The Twelve Virtues of the Perfect Wife

1. She's trustworthy. Can be depended upon never to humiliate you with all the teeny peccadilloes that, if they became common knowledge, would compel you to jump in front of a milk truck. Perhaps you suck your teeth while reading. Maybe you simply must have warm Jell-O with saltines before retiring. Then there's what happened last night, when you had what you later described to the waiter as "a tiny accident" at the Indian restaurant. Imagine if she couldn't be relied upon to keep that kind of thing to herself.

2. She's loyal. Blind to the shortcomings you intend to retain. Even when you reach the point where you need to wear your pants somewhere below your pubic bone simply to allow room for your girth, to her you are beautiful.

3. She's helpful. Happy to cook something when you come home from the office with a man-sized hunger. Doesn't mind washing a few dishes, or even a great many, while you regard the interesting news about gigantic fruit from Harry and David. Often, while you are dozing before the video fire, you wake to find her crouched in

her favorite chair, unable to sleep until she has sewn that errant button onto your favorite pinstripe power shirt. Every Saturday morning, she takes the children to gymnastics, picks up/drops off all dry cleaning-related objects (boxed, w/starch), shops for alcoholic beverages and personal-hygiene solutions, while you stay at home and drill holes in a board.

4. She's friendly. Willing to drop everything and have sex with you, even when you have just come in all fresh and sweaty from the garden, filled with lust and beans.

5. She's courteous. Wouldn't dream of casting aspersions on your male competency when the smoke detector goes off in the middle of the night and you rip it completely off the wall and throw it beeping out the window, when a simple change of batteries would have done the trick.

6. She's kind. Allows you to eat one last four-egg omelet after you get back that 270 cholesterol count; spends hours each and every day wrestling silently with the question, "How can I make my Stanley's life easier?"

7. She's obedient. Knows that when you're right you're right. Also knows that when you're wrong you're right; when she's wrong you're right; and when she's right it's most polite not to press the matter.

8. She's cheerful. Goes about her many duties whistling. Enthusiastic that you went ahead and rented *The Guns of Navarone* for the fifth time when you specifically indicated, before leaving home, that you would look for something you both could enjoy, like *An Unmarried Woman, Women on the Verge of a Nervous Breakdown, A Woman under the Influence, Women in Love, The Women, Two Women, 3 Women, Woman in the Dunes,* and *Diary of a Mad Housewife.* "I'll put popcorn in the microwave, hon," she says, giving your hand a little squeeze.

9. She's thrifty. Now that you are making better money, she's stopped hoarding lint, but she's still always looking to save that extra piece of string she just might need to darn her plain cloth coat, which she got at Loehmann's after a fierce struggle. And even though recently forced by the demands of good taste to spend $3,600 on a new area rug for the foyer, the woman knows how to turn out a light when she leaves a room.

10. She's brave. Doesn't care about nitrites in breakfast meat, or the fat and alcohol contents of anything but herself. Not that she doesn't give a damn about your physical well-being. Being brave means risking the big things, sometimes even things as big as you.

11. She's clean. Always ready to clean things, that's her. Floors, light fixtures, windows, walls, diaper pails, dishes, saucers, cups and creamers, pans encrusted with ossified cheese, couches impregnated with Silly Putty, carpets sporting bright-red blooms of cranberry juice, and, sometimes, yes, the back of your neck, the small of your back, your hair. You name it—if she sees it, she wants to leave it sparkling, proud, standing tall in the saddle.

12. She's reverent. When you come home in toxic inebria for the first time in eighteen months and fall asleep with your cheek against the cool bathroom tile, she will never kick you soundly about the legs and buttocks, screaming, "Get up and go to sleep!" With a certain awe and dread, and some compassion, she brings you a pillow and blanket to make sure you are comfortable with your head in the toilet. Then, humble in the sight of the wretchedness that you yourself have sought, she retires to leave you in worship of your jealous, thirsty God.

1990

Sorry as I Oughta Be

That's right, Al. I did the crime. I did my time. Tomorrow I'm getting out. It's nice of them to give me a roommate on this, my last night in the joint. Hope you don't mind if I go on a bit. It's been a long time since anyone would let me talk, let alone listen to what I have to say. I lost my credibility, see. A sentence in feminist prison will do that to a man.

Lord knows I don't ever want to get sent back here. It's cold, and a man could go crazy from the spiritual hunger, you know, the loneliness, the terrible sense of isolation from the rest of polite society. Maybe the worst part is the knowledge that while you're doing your time, there are millions of women and politically correct men out there who despise you more than they do international terrorists or something. At least they're more vociferous about it.

My crime was making fun of women. I admit it. And I'm sorry, no, really I am, hee hee . . . ach, hm . . .

What's that, Al? Oh, it's quite a story.

Back in June, I published a short list of what a typical husband might seek in "a perfect wife." I suggested that such a mythic woman would be happy to stay up late to sew a button on her husband's favorite shirt; leap to make torrid, passionate love right after he has come in from the garden, full of compost; offer a pillow for his head when he is drunkenly barfing in the toilet. I wouldn't call it a very flattering picture of the bourgeois male. But that's okay. Nobody's going to arrest you for that crime.

In the process, it seems I blithely wandered into the area where exquisitely vigilant and possibly stupid people of all sexes might have perceived that I was making fun of women. This they resented. Look, Al, face it! I was making fun of women! My only excuse is to say that, at the time, I thought it was possible to find women amusing. Now I know better. After years of effort, women have won the right to be taken more seriously than they deserve! Good work! Haha ha ha ha ha!!

Sorry, Al. Sorry, sorry, sorry. Anyhow, I knew I was in trouble right away. Friends called to say that their wives were nauseated with me. Things go worse. The writer Cyra McFadden, whose book I loved, made fun of me in the *San Francisco Examiner*. The female anchor on the *CBS Morning News* read a bit of it on the air, said: "incredible," and made a dismissive noise with her mouth. I'm not sure if it was Paula Zahn or Edye Tarbox, but either way I felt very bad.

The next morning, they came for me. I was making a cup of coffee and a bowl of Oat Bake for myself when there was a knock on the door. It was Charles Osgood. "Get up off your knees and come with me, please," he said, cleverly rhyming. I went. I was scared.

"What'd I do?" I bleated as they dragged me into the dark swamp of the holding pen with what seemed like millions of hollering fellow miscreants. Many were clutching old issues of *Esquire*. Others were waiting with a glazed expression to be served a snack.

"While making fun of yourself, you wandered into that gray area where some unsophisticated readers might believe you were making fun of women," said a neutral voice from a small communicator at my belt.

"Make fun of women?" I screamed. "Me?! Har har HARDY har har!!"

An alarm went off, and several men wearing Izod shirts and Bass Weejuns without socks rushed in, and everything went black. When I woke, I was facedown on a lumpy mattress, sniffing a duvet cover that had been allowed to sit half-damp in a dryer for an unconscionable amount of time. "A man must have laundered this," I muttered. They hit me again, and the lights went out.

The next thing I knew, I was bound to a chair, a halogen lamp shining in my face.

"Hi, Stan," said an impersonal voice from the other side of the light. "We're going to have a little chat, if that's okay."

"Oh yeah," I said eagerly. "You guys have me all wrong!"

"I doubt that. And if you were one bit sensitive to current thinking and writing on the subject, you'd know we don't like the word guys."

"Sorry."

"You realize that what you said was quite offensive to women?"

"Yes," I said, "but I don't see why! All I was doing was expressing just how moronic and sexist are the expectations most men have of their wives!"

"Uh-huh. It's plausible. Still. It doesn't sound one bit like an apology to me. And you're going to stay in here until you apologize, see? Sincerely. In a way that shows a moderation of attitude."

"Yeah. Okay, I apologize."

"No, Stan. We want a real apology. Not the kind you find so easy to offer to angry women. Take your time. We'll wait."

I feel silent for a long time. I could smell coffee brewing in the darkness beyond the light. After a while I requested something to drink. They let me have a glass of Kool Aid I had to mix myself. It was horrid.

"Start at the beginning," said the voice.

"When I was little, I depended a lot on my mother."

"Good, Stan. Good."

"She . . . cooked things, changed my clothes, and hugged me when things got rough. My father hugged me also, by the way."

"Impossible. There's no evidence that any man before our generation knew how to be nurturing."

"Gee."

"You thought your mother was there simply to make life easier for you."

"Yes!"

"You want every woman to be your mother! Confess!"

At this point, I broke down crying. I think this won me points. A female hand with its nails bitten down to the quick slipped me three chicken nuggets that had actually been baked in an oven, as opposed to being microwaved.

"Let's get on to your adolescence."

"When I was twelve, I dreamed I had opened the door to Mrs. Pernod's French class, and there was Sharon Stang standing in the middle of the room, and she had no shirt on. There was her chest, gleaming white in the fluorescent overheads, and I was smitten with one of the most powerful bolts of sheer lust I have ever felt in my life. The thing is, I never did take Sharon seriously as a person, because, around me at least, she talked about nothing but hair and school. So I guess Sharon was the first woman I was interested in primarily as a physical object."

"Don't you owe her an apology?"

So I did, heh heh.

"Now, don't you think you should also apologize to Karen Leamer, Betty Oronsky, Rosalie Grundig, Marguerite D'Onofrio, Nance Albrecht, and your high school English teacher, Mrs. Kaplan, at least for what you were thinking?"

"How did you know about them?!"

"And how about Doris?"

"Doris was unfaithful to me!"

"You behaved like a Neanderthal. She's still getting over the hurt you put on her."

"Hey!" I was losing it. "You people insist on making a political issue out of the stuff that just . . . isn't!" At this point the male cast of *Thirtysomething* came into the room and kicked me into a light doze.

"These attitudes of yours, Stan! Honestly!" the voice gently offered as I lay gibbering and twitching on the floor. "Don't you think they're evidence of a deep hostility toward women?"

"No! I love women."

"All women?"

"Certainly not. I don't like you, for instance."

"But most you . . . love?"

"Oh yes I do. Want you to love me, too. The idea that I've inadvertently alienated more than one of you at the same time is deeply disturbing to me, dear."

"All right, Stan. Oh. One last thing. We'd like you to have come away with some insight. Got any?"

Her voice was severe, and my heart constricted in my chest like a walnut in a deep fryer. "Well, sister," I said, "I think I do. It would have something to do with respect . . . how you gotta have it and . . . if you don't, you'd better not show it."

"Good, good. Now, if you're willing to sign something along those lines I think we can be free of each other . . . for the time being."

My interrogator stepped into the light. Her honest face was filled with resolve, her burlap jumper was freshly pressed, and she had a friendly glimmer in her eye. "I'm sure I'll see you back here real soon," she said. "Until then, I'm off to lose all my body fat, after which I'll undergo surgical augmentation. That whole thing is permissible now, especially in L.A. Any comments?"

So that's where we are, Al. I'm gonna sign that damn statement tomorrow morning and get the hell out of here. And from here on in, boy, I plan to stay clear of this place. I have no desire to join the recidivists at the end of the hall: Lenny, who quietly regards women in restaurants and bars with the kind of interest that is totally unrelated to whether he will ever know them as people; Arnold, who feels smug that, after six years of aerobics, his wife still needs his help to open a jar of mayonnaise; Max, who will still buy a third new tiara for his daughter's sixth Barbie simply because she, Barbie, needs one.

They're all here, condemned thrice weekly to speak to a feminist . . . therapist . . . Ha ha ha ha ha!!

Oh God, excuse me, Al, I didn't mean to crack up like that. I'm so close. But the idea of these guys going in there and having a feminist interpretation put on whatever it is they're thinking and doing and heeee heeee hawwwwww!

Aw, look, Al—just between us girls, isn't the idea of taking women all that seriously all the time . . . ridiculous? They're women! Love 'em! Hate 'em! Yearn for 'em! Admire 'em, even! But take them seriously all the time??? Come on, Al!! Haaaawwwwww! Haawwwwww! Honk! Wheee . . . hm . . . Phhhhhlawwwww!!!!

Why are you looking at me like that, Al?

[Here Mr. Alda sets off the remote alarm secreted in his fountain pen. The sound of scuffling ensues, then:]

Chiseler! Screw! He's wearing a wire!! We know what to do with guys like you, don't we, boys? Boys? Why are there no frigging boys around when you need them?

[A loud series of clangs. Footsteps.]

Get your hands off me! I'll be good! I'll say whatever you want! Think whatever I should! Just don't throw me in the hole again! I'm afraid of the dark! Noooooo! Heelllllpppp! MOTHERRRRR!!!!

[Silence. In the distance, laughter.]

1990

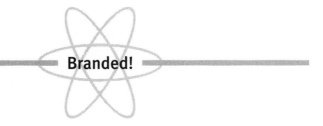

Recently, younger merchandise with bold claims but unproven track record and shelf life is now attempting to take over the marketplace with flashy niche concepts targeted to narrow demos. This should be of little concern to dominant products like you and me, having established our value over time. Still, now would seem as good a moment as any to take a look at yourself to see if your brand is in the kind of shape you need it to be in. Insufficient branding is the leading cause of personal obsolescence.

Your brand is you. It must at once reflect the genuine nature of the product or service you provide and also take the extra leap to offer something illusory, aspirational, emotional. A good brand promises not only what you can deliver but what you could deliver if the consumer dared to dream very simply in images even a child could understand. That should be easy for most of your customers, particularly if they are senior officers.

Branding isn't easy, and for cattle it can be quite painful. Even for those who accept the benefits of branding, it's sometimes far more natural simply to mosey along, grazing peaceably at the side of the road. But in an environment with so many choices, many of whom carry the inherent premiums of low cost, good attitude, and excellent hair, it's foolish not to take the time to set your brand up right. Since I did, I feel a whole lot better. Not that I wasn't feeling great before. Of course I was. Feeling terrific is part of my brand. Another brand characteristic is that I assume you're interested in my brand. And if you're not? Get out of here!

• **Overall brand concept:** I'm large and feisty. In a fragmented marketplace filled with small, ultrafocused products that are very immature and virtually indistinguishable, it helps to be a major brand with good recognition. Bing [trademark] is therefore a broad-based brand with great appeal to anybody who's willing to come even two steps out the front door to meet him.

• **Target audience:** Let the other guys aim low and to the right. Bing [trademark] is for everybody who has to work for a living and wants more than what he has: more fun, more parties, more food, more wine, more promotions, more clothes, more electronic equipment, more destruction to his enemies, more money, more power, more meat with less vegetables. True, some of his desires, problems, and concerns trend upscale, but the engine that drives him is just like yours and mine. You don't have to own a $50,000 car to want one. Bing [trademark] wants one. So do you. That's why you'll like Bing [trademark].

• **Product positioning:** One of the great aspects of American life is that in a real (if somewhat limited) sense we have succeeded where communism did not and are now heading toward a classless society. Sure, there are very poor and very rich people, quite a few of them. But in the middle there is an enormous horde of hardworking folks with access to Saks, Nordstrom, Costco, KFC, and designer water, cigars, and liquors. The guy who lives alone in a tiny apartment on $45,000 a year can reach for the same inflated, self-defining products as the family man who's squeaking by on $250,000. We all consume the same entertainment and media, and none of us, except perhaps for Michael Kinsley, has any established sense of moral or intellectual superiority. So there Bing [trademark] sits, right in the middle of that big middle class, as bourgeois as anybody. He's come a long way, and he's got a long way to go. Look in the mirror, pal. You're Bing [trademark].

• **Brand packaging:** Bing [trademark] tries to wrap himself tight but doesn't quite succeed. The brand tends toward dark blue, but once a week goes for brown and pulls it off handily. Doesn't do dress-down Fridays, because you never know when you're going to be called into a meeting and also because Bing [trademark] looks a little chunky in casuals. No pink or yellow power ties, nor any shoe that costs more than an hour of his time. Likes to surround himself with good quality objects, consumables, and accoutrements that offer Bing [trademark] as a brand a host of ancillary merchandising opportunities.

• **Possible tie-ins to the entire Bing [trademark] zeitgeist:** Macanudo cigars, Bombay Sapphire gin, Ketel One vodka, Laphroaig single-malt Scotch, Eddie Bauer, BMW, Kraft American singles (for the kids), any Brie as long as it's not too runny, Lincoln Mercury, Volvo, the Zagat restaurant guides, McDonald's, *Time* magazine, the New York Stock Exchange, Pellegrino/Evian/Ramlosa/Panne or any bottled water as long as it doesn't smell like eggs, Intel, KMD, Frito-Lay, the Metro North railroad, American Airlines, Zantac, Mylanta, Rogaine (but not Viagra), the Hyatt Hotel in Aruba, the city of New Orleans, Hebrew National salami, Pirelli (for tires), Peroni (for beer), Europe (the continent), and Kellogg, because Bing [trademark] gets going in the morning, and so should you. Merchandisers interested in approaching Bing [trademark] for a product tie-in are encouraged to do so, care of this magazine. See? Bing [trademark] isn't ashamed of selling himself! He's just like you, only he has this column to do it in! Isn't that great for Bing [trademark]?

• **Pricing:** Like all things that are good in this society, Bing [trademark] does not come cheap. In fact, Bing [trademark] is mercilessly expensive. This may leave some who don't have the scratch itching for more Bing [trademark] than their bucks can buy. But the Bing [trademark] brand is all about wanting just a little of what's outside your reach. So save your pennies for the day when you can belly up to the bar and say, "Gimme some more of that Bing [trademark]." Until then, you can let other people pay the freight and watch from outside the box. You've done that before, huh? Sure. We've all been there, perhaps Bing [trademark] most of all.

• **Logo:** I've got one. It's a guy with a cigar whose face you can't see. That's Bing [trademark]—only he's lost a couple of pounds since that picture was taken. That's part of the Bing [trademark] brand too! He's always just lost a couple of pounds.

• **Slogan:** I've tried out quite a few over the years, but here's the one I've finally settled on: "Bing. He's fictional. Just like you." I like it. It's punchy. And true.

Okay! Once you've got your brand, of course, you've only just begun. The next step is taking that brand, hitting the field, and leveraging it. What the heck does that mean? Your guess is as good as mine. But we'll be back with a coherent answer to that and other issues of self-marketing in a future installment of Bing [trademark]!

1999

But Enough about Me . . .

Dear Virginia:

Thanks for your e-mail! I'm gratified that your class has been assigned to read my column in each issue of this magazine. Here are my answers to your long list of excellent questions.

1. I work in a big office building in Manhattan. My office is in the corner, because I'm an executive vice president and a very important person!
2. I've been at my job, in one form or another, for almost twenty years. I started out in a small job with a small office and was promoted many times, getting more responsibility, money, and office space as I moved up, climbing over the bodies of people I used to work for.
3. I have no real daily routine, Virginia. I arrive at about 8:34 A.M., give or take, unless I have a breakfast out of the office, in which case I get in around 9:30. I eat a muffin or a banana at my desk, and drink a cup of very good decaf coffee. There was no really good decaf coffee until about five years ago, and now there's a lot. After that, whatever big monster has been hiding behind the phone leaps out and grabs me around the throat until about 6:14 P.M., when I start thinking about going home.
4. I like my job, except on days when I don't.
5. Well, I enjoy the power I've accumulated in business, and people listening to what I say, and getting meals and trips free because I have an expense account. I hope when you grow up you have an expense account, too. It's a good thing.
6. What I like least about my job is that no matter how big you are, there is somebody bigger than you are, and it's likely that at some point they're going to yell at you. Getting yelled at is exactly the same experience when you're 45 as when you're 4.5. If anything, it's worse, because here you are a grown-up person, and there's still somebody yelling at you.
7. Yes, I have to wear a suit. Unless you're in the Internet, you'll have to wear one, too.

8. I got my job in 1981, when I was looking for a position in which I could make money, as opposed to what I was doing then. My aunt knew someone who was looking for a person who could make stuff up and sound good while doing so, and I got the job. The company changed around me, but I never left.

9. I'm a little fatter.

10. My job is related to technology in that my business uses a lot of it to deliver its product to people, and also in that I use a lot of computers, e-mail, laptops, Palms, beepers, etc., to get things done. I like technology because it's the closest I can come, as an adult, to buying toys without having to explain it to people.

11. I graduated from college with a B.A. in English and theater arts. No graduate school. No business school. I was basically a clown before I put on a business suit, and many people think I haven't changed much since. I highly recommend doing what you love when you're young, or until you can't afford to do it anymore.

12. I can't tell you where I live, Virginia, because if I did I have no doubt that many well-wishers would visit me, including one or two who would boil one of my cocker spaniels in a pot. Suffice it to say that I live somewhere within hailing distance of both a beautiful lake and a McDonald's, in a house that is neither a dump nor a starter castle. We had a decorator, but we worked with her.

13. People in my field start at ridiculously low salaries ($18,000 a year is not uncommon) and at the height of the profession can make more than $500,000 per year. On average, a corporate professional makes about $50,000 to $75,000 a year. In addition to my work in business, I am a writer for this magazine. Writers make between nothing and a billion dollars a year. Working journalists make about $60,000 to $120,000 per year, and they earn it, believe me. Unfortunately, while they seldom have to pay for their meals, many drink up much of their salaries in cheap bars.

14. Room for a promotion? For me? Not really. I'm at the top of what I do now and I intend to stay here as long as I want to, and then get out and go hang-gliding.

15. Of course, Virginia. Who doesn't want to be promoted? What kind of question is that?

16. How can you learn more about a career in business? That's a good question. For starters, there are a lot of magazines about all kinds of jobs. Local colleges also teach courses in just about every field. If you want to do something financial, you'll have to go to business school and develop the ability to fake it on a much higher level.

17. Yes, sure. You didn't say what your grade was, but notwithstanding, here is my advice on what to do with your career:
    - Surround yourself with people who like you, not people who think you're a jerk. It's better to hang with people who make you feel good about yourself than to reach for people who are cooler than you.
    - Study, even the stuff you don't like. The practice you get doing things you don't like to do, and doing them well, is very valuable later in life.
    - Whatever you like to do, do a lot of it. If you sing, sing a lot. If you draw, draw a lot. If you like math, do that a lot. If you get very good at something, even if it looks like just fun, there's a chance somebody will pay you to do it when you grow up. Drooling, pimply computer hackers have turned into some of the richest and most fulfilled men on the planet. As have baseball players and people who study gorillas for a living. The happiest people are those who get paid for doing what they love. So love something.
    - Learn how to manage jerks. If you don't, they will manage you.
    - Life is good. Have fun. And don't do drugs, or drink and drive.
    - Work hard. Don't be discouraged for more than a couple of hours a month. You will get what you want if you work hard enough for it. And always stop to take time for the things you love to do and the people you love to be with. Don't be one of those numbskulls who are always on a cell phone either.
18. My specialty? It's writing stuff like this, very fast. This memo took me fifteen minutes, and I may turn it into a column!

2001

It's a !@#$% Man's World

Act 1: I go to my car the other night and it is a big, cool-looking doorstop. That is, the key goes into the ignition and then, quite dramatically, nothing happens. It has something to do with an antitheft chip that GM puts into its ignition keys. The car is deader than Napster. I take a train home and the next day bring in another key, which works just fine.

The idea of having only one key standing between me and a totally moribund Camaro gives me agita, however. A second key is clearly advisable. Like all great business executives, I delegate the problem to my chief operating officer in these matters, my wife—who is, as you may guess, a woman.

Act 2: My wife, who as you may imagine has other things to do and knows as little about automobile antitheft systems as I do, calls the local dealer, where we purchased the car. She reaches a guy in the service department.

The conversation goes like this:

"Good morning," says my wife. "My husband's ignition key won't start his 2000 Camaro. We think it has something to do with an antitheft chip in the key itself. The second key works fine, and we'd like to get a copy so that we have a backup. The car is on warranty still, so the new key should probably be free."

"I don't think I get what you mean, honey," says the service guy.

"Well, there's this chip that doesn't let the car start, right? Built into the key?"

"Chip?" says the guy. "You're gonna have to bring the car in and we'll see."

"You can't make a new key without the car?"

"Nah, you gotta leave the car here. Hold on a minute," says the guy and goes away for a while. Then he comes back.

"Then . . . can I make an appointment?" my wife inquires.

"You can come in any time after eight," says the guy brusquely. "Then it's first come, first served."

"Really?" says my wife. "You can't have a solid appointment?"

"Well, honey," says the guy, "it's not like everybody is just standing around the place waiting for your arrival."

My wife is no consumer cream puff. "You have some kind of a problem?" she says quietly.

"No," says the guy, immediately snapping to. "Is there some way I could be serving you that I'm not?"

"What's your name?" says my wife.

"Tom," says the service guy.

My wife then calls and tells me the whole story. I think I know what's going on. My wife is getting woman's treatment. I'm determined to handle this like a man.

Act 3: I call the dealer back. Tom is not in, having accomplished his goal for the morning, i.e., nothing. I get Barry.

"Barry," I say in my nastiest tone imaginable. "You have some !#$!@ named Tom who works there?"

"Yes, sir," says Barry. "Is there a problem?"

"Yeah," I say with maximum truculence. "You're damn right there's a !@#!$ problem. Your guy was rude to my wife and is wasting our @#$% time, that's the problem."

"I'm very sorry, sir," says Barry. "How can I be of assistance to you right now?"

"I need to have a key made for my Camaro. I need it today."

"We can do that."

"And you don't need the car to do it, right?"

"No, sir. We need your VIN number."

"You have the !#@$$ VIN number. You sold me the car, didn't you, Barry?"

"Yes, sir. Then we do have your VIN number, and there won't be any problem at all. When would you like the key? Later today?"

"I can pick it up tomorrow morning."

"It'll be here for you, sir," says Barry. "Say . . . about eight A.M.?"

"I'm very busy, Barry. Make sure it's there on time."

"Yes, sir. No problem, sir. See you then, sir."

"You know, Barry," I say, "it's been very nice to deal with you. But that guy Tom has some kind of problem dealing with women. You ought to do something about it."

"He's a relative of the owner," says Barry.

I go to the dealer at 7:45 A.M. the following day. The key is ready. Barry is waiting for me. As I arrive, dressed like a businessman in a suit and tie, the entire service department begins orbiting me as the moons orbit Jupiter. Barry offers me coffee. Another gentleman prepares the warranty work so I won't have to pay a dime. I scowl and prowl around as if I'm about to yell at someone.

I look around for anybody named Tom. No one fitting that description is there. I'm not surprised. Who would want to deal with a jerk like me?

I'm out of there in five minutes, tops, with my new key and an added appreciation of what it's like to live in a world where white, nasty men in business suits get all the breaks, particularly if they know how the !#@!$ game is played.

2002

LATTE BREAK

The Auditor

I

The wind was a torrent of darkness in every gusty tree
And the moon-faced pundits babbled, on Bloomberg and CNBC.
The carpet rolled, soft and plush, over the hardwood floor,
And the auditor came striding—
  Striding—striding—
The auditor came striding, up to the boardroom door.

II

He had a toupee on his forehead, a fat brown tie at his throat,
Tan slacks of polyester, set off by a blue sports coat;
A StarTAC in a holster, a BlackBerry on his thigh,
As he strode you could hear him beeping—
  Beeping—beeping—
With every pocket beeping, and a twinkle in his eye.

III

To the sideboard then he sidled, and had some fruit and cheese,
And he waited for several minutes, thinking about his fees;
Then he turned from the plate-glass window, and who should be waiting
  there
But the Enron senior officer,
  Ken, the senior officer,
Weaving some bogus partnerships into his sparse brown hair.

IV

"Farewell!" said the bold accountant. "For soon I may be dead,
I'm off to the Houston office, your records for to shred;
Yet if they press me sharply, or subject me to scrutiny
Then look for me by moonlight,
   I'll come to you by moonlight,
I'll meet you at Morton's by moonlight, and we'll have a drink or three."

V

He gathered his books and his papers and to the door did creep,
And a look suffused his features that would have made you weep.
Then they shook hands in the lobby, two grim and pasty men.
And he climbed into his Town Car
   —His bright and shining Town Car!—
How long would he rate a Town Car?—and returned to Andersen.

VI

He did not come in the morning, that brave and pudgy guy,
He did not come at noontime, while the stock was trading high,
But as shadows formed on the carpet, rolling over the dark wood floor
The pinstriped troops came marching—
   Marching—marching—
The scary Feds came marching up to the well-oiled door.

VII

Five hundred corporations are honored here within;
They fight for every dollar! Do what they must to win!
From value-driven Wal-Mart to Devon Energy
Each of them would rather—
   They'd really, really rather—
Be stabbed in the head by moonlight, than deal with the SEC.

VIII

They did not turn or falter, the men in the cheap blue suits.
They took one long perusal, then ordered more recruits.
They looked for documentation, and therein found they none
So the regulators wanted—
   They truly, truly wanted—
Oh, boy, how they really wanted . . . the auditor's head on a bun.

IX

Bam! came the explosion! Its noise boomed up to heaven!
The sound of a corporation declaring Chapter 11;
And somewhere out in the deepest deep, in the murky ethical waters
The auditor is spinning, And still you can hear him spinning—
  Just listen to him spinning—
"Hey! I was only following orders!"

X

Oh, somewhere the sun is shining, somewhere the stars are bright;
Somewhere there are investors who sleep like logs at night;
Consider these 500—how they grow! They burn! They strive!
And could someone please explain here—
  Exercise your brain here!
Can someone please explain here—Why is Enron still No. 5?

2002

9

THIS JUST IN:
STUFF THAT REALLY HAPPENED

The business of America is business, which is why we now have a bunch of businesspeople running America. Whether they're an improvement over the politicians who usually did the job is anybody's guess at this point. Right now, I'd say no, they're not. But history may prove me wrong, if we have a chance to enjoy any history after we get done with what the next couple of years have in store. But I don't mean to sound gloomy. I'm not. I have hope in my soul, always, and a firm conviction that no matter what happens in the world at large it's going to be good for some laughs, except when, as is increasingly likely, it's not.

The point is, the outside world very often intrudes on us when all we're trying to do is ignore it and put in our ten to twelve hours in the hamster wheel. Business does not exist in a vacuum, no matter how hard we try to make it do so. Anyone who doubts this real-world linkup is instructed to try making a joke about President Bush (either of them) on a golf course full of advertising executives.

Ross II: A New Beginning

I remember Carl. He was a boss here for a while. Carl had what it takes. Carl had vision. That means taking the long view. Seeing the forest while you cut down the trees. Guessing what the rest of the camel looks like when all you've got is the tip of his nose sticking through the flap of your tent. Torquing things up and watching their spin. Rolling things down the incline. Field-stripping the big concepts. Testing them in the trenches. The big picture is what I'm talking about. Kicking its tires. Buying it. Taking it for a turn around the block. That was Carl's great talent. Having balls, too, yeah, he had those aplenty, Carl did; although you'd never have known it, how soft the man talked, how creamy blue were the fabrics of his suits, how thoughtful he got in the face of stupid people. He also knew how to think big—real big, big with a b like in billions, that kind of big—and spend big too, when it looked like a big hit of raw dough was needed to get the corn off the field and into the silo. He never blinked. He never retched. And he could kick your dumb butt down the block when you deserved it, sometimes when you didn't. There wasn't a man here who wasn't dead afraid of Carl each and every day, and even some women, too. To know him was to fear him. That was one of his most attractive qualities. And when he left, it was boom—out of here. He saw the future and didn't like the cut of its jib, the hee of its haw, the warp of its weft. He opened the hood, flushed out its transmission, tried to make it work, couldn't, tried to fix it, wouldn't, decided to throw it away and start over again. He's elsewhere now, with a better balance sheet than the entire Third World, of which we in this nation are quickly becoming a part.

"Carl should run for office," we said when he rode off into the sunset on his big yellow Appaloosa. We thought we were joking. Carl in politics? Whew! What a gag! Business is business! Politics is politics! They don't mix! But you know what? We were wrong. Mr. Ross Perot has shown us that. Heck, Carl was thin, with just the right amount of marginal hair, thin on top and vertical in all the wrong places. He had eyes that could cut through a human heart like a laser cuts metal. He had no patience for process or unnecessary people. He would have made an excellent senator, or even president, and that's a fact.

So wake up, Mr. and/or Ms. America.

In spite of the fact that Mr. Perot saw fit to turn tail and run almost before the game had begun, it's obvious that the little jug-eared geek was on to something. The future of the world is big business, not big government. The old solutions don't work. They do not take out the trash. They do not clean up the barn. They do not get the winning run home from second base with two on and two out. They do not slam in the one-point margin of victory with no time left on the shot clock. It's only a matter of time before one of us busy hitters gets his rear in gear, jump-starts the dirt bike, and barrels it up the hill. Greases up the monkey and makes it bark. Get the picture? Sure you do. We're your business managers. And we've got strategies to make the old machine of this democracy hum and shimmy—so listen up or you're fired from your position as a member of the public!

I thought that would get your attention. We own the nation. Why shouldn't we run it?

Do I hear you laughing? You won't be laughing long. We run your industries. We motor your economy. We're the best this civilization has to offer. We've got brains. We've got teeth. We've got a big, wide agenda and the power, grit, and guts to make it happen. Here's the platform:

You get what you pay for. This publicly financed campaign business is for the birds. Who needs it? These check-kiting politicians have been on the public tit for too long—it's time to heat up the private one for a while. From now on let's get people elected who are willing to lay down the only currency that has any meaning—their own. This will mean that only the cream of the crop will be fit to run hard, run fast, put on that final kick when the last puff of wind has left their bodies. And the special interests? Golly, won't they be mad! Before, they had a pipeline into the heart of what made this country work. Now they won't be able to get arrested—unless we arrest them.

Kill the bureaucracy! We're against it. Got a job to do? Get the right people together, have a couple of meetings, allocate some resources against it, make the problem go away. When it goes away, the task force goes, too. Great! Worse comes to worst, maybe you can hang on to a couple of consultants for continuity, but no entrenched structures, that's the ticket. Got a problem? Have a meeting. Target the tasks. Delegate 'em. That's that. This means the minute we get in, big head-count reductions at corporate headquarters on the Potomac. That's job one. It works in business. It'll work in government. All you need is a tight cadre of loyal, determined, action-oriented henchmen working to influence right-minded people and clamping down on anybody—friend or foe— who doesn't get in line. Like Ross said when he announced that he'd broken his pick: We need one powerful party to get things changed around this candy store.

Lack of knowledge is power. It is possible, you know, to know too much. Get all balled up with studies and strategies and alternatives. Things are a lot more simple than they look when you first get under the hood and take a gander at all those bells, wires, and whistles. Ever been in a business meeting when folks are trying to justify an acquisition? It's a riot. Guys look over the profit projections. One of the numbers looks funky. "I don't like that number," says one guy. "Me neither," says another. What do they do? They change the number! That's business. It doesn't show disrespect for objective measurement. It shows creativity and a willingness to imagine different alternatives. We could do that on a national scale.

We believe in the people. Most of all, business is all about people. People who make our products and offer our services. People who buy our products or agree to be serviced. We love our people. All our people. They're some of the damn finest individuals ever trod God's green earth, except the ones who belong to unions, who will have to die. The rest are just . . . choke, sob . . . the greatest. I'm sorry. I get emotional.

If you can't fix it, divest it. Sometimes parts of your organization don't function the way they should. You can tinker with them for a while, but it's clear they're not growing, not even at GNP plus or minus a point or two. No future there. What to do? Get rid of them. Other people want them, you know they do. Right now, the business and residential populations of Japan, Korea, Eastern and Central Europe, a good portion of South America, and the Caribbean all want exclusive use of our cities. We don't know what to do with the darn cities any which way. Isn't there some potential synergy there? Entire regions of our great nation are no longer functioning on a good curve. We could divest them, take the cash, and invest it in high-growth regions that are right now building bright, spanking-new suburbs. The possibilities are limited only by our imaginations.

The world awaits. Imagine there's no countries. It's easy if you try. And if you can't, imagine that we're running all of them. It's possible. The president of Yugoslavia right now is an American. Did you know that? How about you? Want to run a foreign country? You can, if you've got the connections and the capital. Also, with alien nations buying up underperforming parts of our national portfolio of states and cities, we'll be looking for judicious opportunities to invest where the potential is high. Right now, I'm quite certain any relatively well-off individual could buy the entire republic of Bosnia-Herzegovina, with all its natural resources and, to a certain extent, people—as long as they were willing to position the property for subsequent Serbian acquisition. The entire non-American world is filled, may I remind you, with strong, beefy individuals who are willing to work for a nickel an hour! And believe you me, they're hungry.

This is not a democracy. The bottom line—the thing the established superstructure doesn't get—is the one big insight that business managements the world over were born to. The man at the top makes the decision. He takes advice. He hires consultants. He lets the people call in on their own very special 900-number (what a revenue engine that'll be!). He even lets the board reelect him every couple of years. But when it comes down to who's going to suck up the sticker price and order that new-options package, there's one guy making the call. And folks who don't like it can get out of the organization. Got something to say? Our door is always open. Just don't let it hit you in the ass on the way out, bud.

Say yes. The power of positive thinking is what made this nation great. That kind of outlook is basically gone from the world of public affairs. But it lives on in the business universe. It's strong as ever. Make friends. Influence people. Joint venture this. Cross-promote that. The squeaky wheel gets the worm. Hell, we'll eat the worm, too, if we have to! Because we're in business and we do what it takes!

Thanks must go to Mr. Ross Perot, of course, for being the first one on the block to go for his piece of the big machine. But he's just the beginning, boys and ladies. Next time around, we'll take a big dude, blond, with large, powerful shoulders, great teeth, and a Gardol smile. He'll be rich and smart and funny, and he'll know how to mix business with pleasure. And he'll market the stuffing out of that great gray mass that sits right smack in the middle of the American heartland, and we shall rule the earth! And lower taxes! And have some fun, too!

Well, neighbor? Do you stand with us? Call 1-900-CAPITOL, and let freedom ring!

1992

Information Underload

As a businessperson, I crave information. I can never get enough of it. I've always gotta get more of it. Ladle it up, chow it down, that's me. 'Cause information is good, ipso facto. Information is power. Information is money. Information is a fat slice of layer cake you've got to eat right now. Information is on the highway. Information is on the byway. Pile on the factoids! Bring on the proprietary data! Information—the lifeblood of the people! Keep it comin'!

So it pains me to tell you that I have in my possession a tiny little nuggetine of proto-information that I don't want you to have. It belongs to me. I don't have to disclose it. It would be bad for business if I did. It's not material in any legal sense, so I'm under no ethical or financial obligation to do so. Fortunately for me, the Constitution doesn't mandate your access to it. It's mine now, and if things go well, it'll stay mine until I choose to tell you about it.

You can console yourself with the thought that my precious nub of information is really nothing but a rumor of a suspicion of a hint of something that may someday, if sixteen other variables fall into place, turn into a fact. When and if that happens, the gob of potentialities will coalesce and boom! There will then be information. Get it early and you'll think you know something when in fact you won't. You'll know nothing. That's the information revolution in action.

Pardon me. I'm sitting at my desk on the thirty-seventh floor, staring out at the city steaming and belching vapor all around me. There's nothing much I can do right now. Just wait to see how Slag Week is going to deal with a grotesque sibling of the embryo of the information I'm trying to keep from you. It's not the thing itself; it seldom is with Slag Week.

It all started yesterday at 2:37 P.M. It was a day much like any other, which is to say, from hell. Then the phone rang. It was Larry Blatt, reporter. Now, Larry Blatt could be his real name or maybe not. If you know a Larry Blatt, perhaps it's he. Let's pretend it is, because it could be, and nobody's proved it's not.

"Hello," I say into the receiver. I like this as a response because it imparts no information whatsoever.

"Stanley Bing?" Blatt murmurs into the phone. "Larry Blatt. Got a minute?" I know immediately it's trouble. He's in his Bob Woodward-in-heat hat, chasing down an enormous scoop for *The Daily Planet*. "I have a very good source close to the negotiations who has told me you people are getting together with a consortium of players to buy Romania. I wonder if you'd like to get a comment in before we go to press."

I feel sick. It's false, completely without foundation. Romania's growth vectors are way south of any serious acquisition candidate on our roster. Still, the damn thing isn't so radically, dramatically way-out that it couldn't be slightly conceivable. These cruddly little psuedopods of data pop up all the time. Last week, rumor had it that my entire company was being sold to Ron Perelman. Before that, we were purchasing Ron Perelman. Neither was ever true. Of course, on the other hand, they weren't untrue per se, either, since they could be happening right now in an alternate universe.

"No, Larry," I tell the reporter. "Nothing of the sort is happening, let alone contemplated. You've got a bum steer. Sorry." As I'm saying this, I can feel his cynicism, professional disappointment, and raw ambition seeping through the phone and running down the inside of my ear. I switch the receiver to the other side of my head. That, too, is quickly moistened.

"I'm not asking you whether it's happening," says Blatt. "I know it's happening. I just want your comment on it. Should I put your denial on the record?"

"No, Larry," I tell him. "Nobody believes a denial. What I'm telling you is not a denial. Its an assertion that what you are about to report is not only not happening, its not going to happen. Not ever. You have bad information. Why report it?"

"I have to report it," says the reporter. "I have a source on it."

"Can we go off the record, Larry?"

"Off the record. Yeah, sure."

"God's honest truth, Larry, this is bogus. And if it appears in your paper, it will create enormous chaos and at least five follow-up stories that will gain in collective weight until it won't make any difference whether it's true or not. All that will matter is what has been reported."

"Uh-huh," says the reporter. He is typing. This makes me nervous. What's he typing? I haven't said anything! I can feel a bubble of bile float from the bottom of my stomach and into my esophagus. What can I do? I rack my brains.

"Tell you what, Larry," I said. "If I can find three totally reliable sources who will tell you the absolute truth, will you consider not reporting a completely erroneous thing as if it's news?"

"It's a big story," says Blatt.

"No, Larry," I tell him, "it's not a story. It's a leak planted with you to benefit the person who leaked it to you. Can't you see that?"

"Well," says Blatt, "you'd have to get me quite a lineup to make me believe that this isn't going down."

"Fine," I say. "We'll be back to you."

At 3:21, Blatt talks with Kline, a gigantic player who would indubitably be part of the crafting of any such deal. Kline asserts, on the record, that we're not buying Romania. "I can get all the pastrami I want right here in New York," says Kline. "He typed that," he tells me later. "It was a joke. I hope I don't come out looking like a jerk."

4:07: Blatt talks with a representative of our supreme executive structure in Houston. He is told that "the company does not comment on idle rumor and speculation." This, I later learn, he takes as confirmation of his rumor.

4:32: Blatt talks for three minutes with Walt, our chieftain. Walt tells him that we are not buying Romania but lets him know that we could if we wanted to. This, I later learn, Blatt takes as confirmation of his rumor.

5:12: Blatt talks with three of our operations V.P.s from around the nation, who tell him why it would be stupid and dilutive for us to buy Romania and that as far as they know, we are not doing so. This, I later learn, he takes as confirmation of his rumor, since none of the commenting parties are in a position to know what might be going on behind their backs.

5:55: I have a vodka and tonic on the train.

7:15: I am having a vodka without tonic at the kitchen table. My daughter is doing her math homework. My son is wrestling with our cocker spaniel. My wife is cooking something that smells good. The phone rings.

"I'm just about ready to put this thing to bed, Stan," says Larry Blatt. "My editors want me to pin down whether, even though you say it's not happening right now, you think it could happen. It's well known that Romania is in play. There are tremendous opportunities to reengineer it and make it profitable. You guys make perfect sense as a buyer. So . . . could it happen? What do you think?"

"Could it happen? Sheep could fly at some point, Larry. Anything is possible. What I'm telling you is that it is not happening. Doesn't that make any difference to you?"

"So what you're telling me is that it's not impossible for something like this to happen," says the reporter.

My daughter has begun to sing, "What's the frequency, Kenneth?" very loudly and dance around the room, bumping into things. There is a dish of spaghetti in front of me now. I want this to be over.

"Not impossible, Larry?" I say. "Are you in the business of reporting what is not impossible?"

"Honestly, Stan, I have this monster space to fill, and it's really late in the day."

A comment. On what? "We're in a growth mode," I say, wiping a rivulet of tomato sauce from my chin. "Any creative move within our industry is interesting to us, but we're not about to do anything in the near future. I hope you'll be careful to characterize anything that you write, Larry, as a rumor."

"I need a picture of your chairman . . . what's his name?" says the reporter.

"No picture, Larry. You don't need an illustration of something that's not happening."

"Maybe we have one in the file," he says and hangs up.

That was last night. This is now. The afternoon mail is placed on my desk. Ah, here it is. Slag Week. And, oh, look. Right there on the front page is our logo next to a screaming headline that reads: Romanian Rhapsody? Underneath that banner is a smaller headline that reads: "Anything Could Happen," Says Toledo Corp. Spokesman. There is a picture of Walt, my boss. The story itself is two hundred words, tops. It jumps to another page, where the runover takes up a quarter of an inch:

Industry sources today confirmed the imminent purchase of the entire nation of Romania by the Toledo Corporation. Romanian officials could not be reached for comment, although they have in the past expressed interest in any serious offer. The purchase of the economically challenged Eastern European nation, which was rumored for months and reported on recently in these pages, comes at a time of great global expansion for American corporations. Industry consolidation also continues apace. In the past months, the Furtz Company merged with Titus Products, Gretz Brothers was acquired by Merblin Manufacturing, and in the largest sale to date, Vizcor gobbled up Burtzheim, once a leader in the global-distribution side of business. This acquisition could put Toledo in the top ranks of those companies both domestically and abroad. "We're in a growth mode," said Stanley Bing, vice president of Toledo. "Any creative move within our industry is interesting to us." Bing went on to deny the reported transaction. Sources close to the negotiations indicated that a formal announcement would be forthcoming.

Not a bad story. I almost believe it myself. I wish I could tell you more, but I have to get going. There's a reporter on line one from *The Wall Street Journal* who is angry with me for not giving her the story first. There's another from the *Times* who wants to make sure they're spelling Walt's name right. And a camera crew from CNBC is waiting in the lobby. I told them not to come, but they're here anyway, and I don't blame them. The people have a right to know.

1995

Keep Your Mitts off My Options, Dear!

This ridiculous Wendt situation has me in a complete swivet. Corporate wife receives at least $20 million for thirty-two years of marriage, contending that the completion of her spousely duties for that time entitles her to fully 50 percent of not only the marriage's hard assets but also the value of her husband's business career, including a piece of his stock options. His stock options, mind you! This is a disturbing precedent, particularly for people who have stock-option money they want to spend on their second wives.

According to my calculations (I'm not very good at arithmetic; my wife does that kind of low-level stuff for me most of the time), that means Mrs. Wendt has earned . . . at least 700 grand a year for completing the duties of a corporate wife during the course of her marriage.

I don't know. That seems like a lot to me. Not that corporate wives aren't important; of course they are. But twenty million big ones? Honestly!

Think about the differences between what the corporate guy and his wife do every day. In the traditional marriage, the husband is first of all responsible for showering, shaving, dressing (in clothes provided by his wife), and conveying himself to work. This is often anything but pleasant. I sat on a train this morning with a fellow who had hair in his ears and kept saying "buh" in a soft voice while reading a brochure on dog paraphernalia. Is this what I wanted my life to be like? I leave that to you. For a corporate player whose career ends up being worth about $100 million over twenty-five years or so, the morning commute should probably be evaluated as at least 15 percent of that, or approximately what—$600,000 per year? That seems fair, if not overly generous.

At the same time, what is the corporate wife doing? While he's getting into the city, she's usually waking the children, who are always so cute and pliable in the morning. Then there's breakfast, making the bag lunches, getting the kids into various layers of clothing, rustling them into the car, and driving them to school. Big deal! Even throwing in a couple of cocker spaniels, total value of these kinds of morning duties over twenty-five years of marriage couldn't possibly come to more than twenty grand a year.

Somewhat later on, while the corporate husband is sitting in an overheated midtown restaurant eating a $40 breakfast with stultifying marketing types from Oswego or Bratislava, the wife is probably sitting at home with a cup of coffee and the newspaper. What wouldn't you give to be at home with the newspaper, even if there never is any decent breakfast meat in the house? Plus, a lot of big business is done over breakfast, and it's not relaxing in any way. So I guess that portion of the corporate day would be worth in the neighborhood of $187,500 per year. Give or take.

Mrs. Wendt also made a big deal about all the hard stuff that she did all day long. Look, I don't doubt she was tired when the 10 P.M. news hit the air. But come on. Some of the things she mentioned include the making and keeping of doctor's appointments, carpooling with the Pfitzers, writing sympathy notes, acquiring foodstuffs, and other effluvia of daily life. All good things, no question about it, and it isn't easy to create a viable daily life. But wouldn't she have a daily life even if she weren't married to a big-shot corporate executive? Admit it. She would. So let's give her a hundred grand for her effort. But not a penny more!

At the same time, as she putters around the bucolic suburban ecosystem, dropping off the dry cleaning and shopping for tidbits, the beleaguered corporate executive is at his desk, making phone calls that will shape the lives of millions. After those phone calls, he very often goes into a conference room and eats free Danish while making decisions that will shape the lives of millions. Then he goes to a free lunch and talks over very serious issues that will shape the lives of millions. Later in the afternoon, he may be back at his desk again, or even on the road somewhere, having meetings, taking part in conference calls, and eating snacks that will shape the lives of millions. Value of his time: millions! Most people start with one or two, but by the time you get to be really big, you can have more millions than you can shake a stick at. And it's all yours! Yours!

Corporate wives also seem to feel they need big compensation for activities in the social realm. Mrs. Wendt was asked to throw annual New Year's lobster dinners for her husband's department. She also contends that she was required to work the room at vapid social functions, be hypocritical when called to do so, and go on dream trips to China, Egypt, Greece, and other exotic places with bad plumbing so often that after a while it became annoying.

All this was undeniably an important part of the husband's career, and, in fairness, should confer rights to 50 percent of all monies earned while lobster dinners were hosted, boring people were entertained, rooms were worked, and business hypocrisy was practiced, be it at home or abroad. Value of said actions? I suggest $150,000 per year. I know a lot of people who do it for less.

While his wife was engaged in these important duties, however, the husband was doing things that had nothing to do with her. And was it not in those vineyards that the heavy lifting was done? These include:

- Moving vast sums of money around for no purpose except to generate more of it
- Firing enough people every year to satisfy the investment banking community
- Playing golf a real lot
- Not being afraid to speak when he had nothing to say
- Taking credit for the good stuff
- Assigning blame for the bad

All right. It's true. Except in the case of about twelve guys, those jobs could have been done just as well by any other fungible executive in a suit. But that's beside the point! He's the one who did them. Our guy. Her husband. He gave his life for the business! And what's one life worth? In the case of a successful executive, I believe we have an answer: a lot.

Naturally the spouse wants half at the end of the game, when the poor old fellow is doddering off into the sunset with an attractive young nurse on his arm. And all right, she was there at the beginning and deserves credit for term papers typed, shirts ironed, noses wiped. But 50 percent! It's fair. But is it just?

I'd say no, except I just asked my wife about it. She says it damn well is, and I always listen to her about stuff like this.

1998

Hail and Farewell, Chainsaw Al!

Good evening, ladies and gentlemen. I know you're as pleased as I am to be here tonight to honor Mr. Al Dunlap on the occasion of his, er, retirement from American senior management. Yes, the big boy is hanging up his chain saw, and I'm sure that all of you out there would rather give up a flight of stock options than miss his good-bye bash. So . . . let's bash! Hey, Al, just kidding, you big lug. Who luvs ya, dude?

You know, ladies and gentlemen, when you've been in business as long as I have, you've looked at a lot of rubber chicken. But I think I speak for everyone concerned when I say that never in my experience was an evening like this one more eagerly anticipated, or richly deserved.

Well now, enough sentiment, huh? Let's cut to the chase—and I do mean cut!

But seriously, ladies and gentlemen, we've invited a long, long list of folks Mr. D. has touched at some point in his long life and career, people who wanted to be there when he bade farewell to the executive suite. Let's get to 'em.

I hate to start off on a down note, but we were hoping that first up would be Mrs. Greta Lovish, our man's first-grade teacher. We called her just a few days ago, and she was chockablock with fantastic stories about our guy when he was just a little hacksaw. I've just been handed a note informing me that Mrs. Lovish will not be able to attend tonight. She has sent a message, though. Let me read it. Well, ha, ha. What a kidder. "I'm too scared to come," she writes. "Albert used to bite the other children, and he never really liked me, either."

Oh, well, the heck with her. We've also asked a number of the Almeister's good friends from high school and, of course, from West Point to come up here and regale us with stories of deeds done and battles won way back before our "Rambo in pinstripes" became what he was smart and bold enough to call himself—America's best CEO!

Hm. That's strange.

They were all supposed to be at table 2, but it's completely . . . empty. There's nobody at table 2. Not at table 3, either, where all the young turks with whom our honoree grew to business maturity were supposed to sit. Or at table 4, where suppliers and former partners were expected. Huh. It's odd, I have to tell you, ladies and gentlemen, because not long ago I attended an event at which Mr. Dunlap was the bragger—I mean the speaker—and it was very well attended. Afterward a whole bunch of people rushed the stage, practically climbing over one another to get a chance to touch the hem of his goddamned garment! Now, where are they all? Fickle fate! Oh, well. Screw 'em. Come to think of it, he probably did!

But seriously, ladies and gentlemen. It's now my pleasure to bring up the senior and middle management of Lily Tulip, one of Mr. Al's first big corporate assignments, where he forged some of the dynamic solutions that would stand him in such good stead throughout the years and make him the guy we're all honoring tonight. While he was there, he cut 50 percent of the corporate staff. Of this brilliant approach to growth he said later, "You've got to get the right management—and that doesn't mean tweaking it a little here or a little there. . . . The people who have created the problem are not all of a sudden going to improve, so I get rid of almost all the senior management and bring in people who have worked with me before." By the way, are any of those people who worked with him before here now?

No? Why not? It's weird!

Gee, none of the Lily Tulip people seem to be here. Okay, then let's call on the table purchased tonight by Crown-Zellerbach, where our man laid off 20 percent of the employees and mashed a bunch of tasty concessions out of the labor unions. What? Not here? Okay, well how about some words from the folks at Consolidated Press Holdings, where the Sawman sold off noncore businesses and revoked all kinds of lifestyle niceties. No? How about the guys over at Scott Paper, where he laid off about one out of every three workers, some 11,000 people. No again? Man, is anybody out there? Hey, maybe everybody he's ever known is too busy doing the jobs formerly held by three people!

But seriously, ladies and gentlemen, there must be somebody here from Sunbeam, where he laid off more than 6,000 workingmen and -women in very short order, driving the stock price up to $54 this past March. Doesn't anybody want to salute our man today, when the stock is at sixteen bucks? Why not?

I don't believe this! Aren't we talking about a hero, a big, bold hero of American business lore? Wasn't Mean Business an anthem of the decade, a best-seller touted by critics and senior managers worldwide? How about some of the bellhops, waiters, and soon-to-be-laid-off workers to whom Al generously gave autographed copies? Aren't they here? No?

Then surely there must be somebody from Wall Street, which rewarded him with glowing first calls and analyses for decades! Nobody here to sing his praises now? Just because of a couple of bad quarters? I guess that would also explain why the tables reserved for *Business Week, Forbes,* and *The Wall Street Journal* are empty too—all the reporters who used to require bibs in his presence are busy writing stinging condemnations of his vicious, inhuman style because this time it didn't produce sufficient profit.

Okay, Al. I give up. It's a big ballroom, and it seems there's just you and me in it. Come on up to the dais and say a few words.

What? Incredible. It seems that Mr. Dunlap cannot, at this time, be reached for comment. Well, that must be some kind of first.

I suppose there's nothing left to do but hand over this gift, one we always award upon retirement these days: a small quartz watch that will break by the time you get it home . . . and just for you, Al, because you taught us all what really made business work on Wall Street's terms, a gazillion-dollar severance from the shareholders of Sunbeam.

Now I'll just dig into my chicken leg. You get to work on your filet mignon with that chain saw. Sure it's a little tough, but don't despair. The first cut is the easiest.

1998

I Miss the Old Millennium

Something about Hastings . . . the French fighting the English for some reason . . . and then a couple of Italians figured out how to paint in three dimensions . . . and then there was some guy who discovered germs or something . . . and then, bang! TV.

Ah, the old millennium! I'm already starting to forget you, my dear. It happens. You think at the time all that stuff is making an impression on you, that it will never leave your mind, your heart. But things catch up with you, you get busy, and pretty soon you can't conjure up what was going on at that most important year of your life, what she looked like, why you wanted whatever it was so badly, why you cared. Can anybody remember what happened during the first thousand years of the current era? Beowulf. That's about it, huh?

And yet . . . it was a great millennium, this last one! I don't want to see it go. I want to hold it close for a moment before it slips away.

It began, like I said, in 1066, when Ralph Hastings hosted a big party on his field, which was huge. Only English guys were invited, with their wives, of course. That made the French angry, because they were right across the Channel and felt left out. This was before the invention of cheese, even, so the French were very different and warlike. They attacked and there was a big fight and that's why the French rule England today. Except they don't, because later on they kind of left or something, and the Anglo-Saxons moved in and took over everything, and that's the way it stayed until recently, when they all moved to Connecticut and left England to Eurotrash, supermodels, and former Socialists.

In 1200 or thereabouts, Pope John felt there wasn't enough freedom for people, so he tinkered around with several big policies, which he put on public signs people could post everyplace, which were called Cartas. He started out with a smaller one, which they called the Micro Carta, then moved on to the Midi Carta, and finally settled on this really big one that gave white men who owned things already an amazing amount of freedom, as if they didn't have it already. This, of course, was the famous Magna Carta, which was very long and extremely hard to read, because people spoke Middle English back then.

Before long the Middle Ages were ending, mostly because people were incredibly bored. Around 1400, anybody with four good limbs got on a horse and went to kill other people for what they believed in. This was called the Crusades, and they succeeded in pretty much blowing the world wide open. People who thought they had seen everything got to hack strangers to pieces and take their women as chattel. Things went nuts for a while and pretty soon it was the Renaissance, because once you let a little light into a musty room it's hard not to tear down the entire window treatment and start over with a new one.

Science was invented, and Copernicus realized that the world did not revolve around Poland. This impressed Galileo, who told Newton, who discovered gravity, and the race for nuclear weapons was on. We can't possibly go over all the scientific achievements of the last millennium here, but suffice it to say that as far as science goes, it was outstanding. In fact, it's quite possible that, with the current rise in spiritualism and decline in scholarship, we have seen the best and now must live with the rest. Already, inferior science is superseding the great work of the past 1,000 years, and odd, semipoetic conceits like string theory, warm-blooded dinosaurs, and creationism in Kansas are taking the place of the good, solid stuff we grew up with.

Lest we be accused of being Euro- or phallocentric, it should be mentioned that China, Africa, South America, and Asia all had a lot of history during the last 1,000 years, as did women. For the most part, all we know about these aspects of the millennium are Marco Polo, Vietnam, and Martha Stewart. Marco Polo, as you recall, went to China and found spaghetti. Europe took over Africa and ran it for a long time and almost wrecked it. Martha Stewart you already know. She will not be forgotten.

Not so with older, and just as crucial, events. In 1465, for instance, the first bourgeoisie was developed in Holland—a class of people more interested in shopping, housing, and family life than they were in world domination. This is an undervalued accomplishment of Western civilization, but one that I look back on fondly. No bourgeoisie, no you and me. Up with them!

More recently, two economic systems were invented that shaped the world as we know it today. In 1776, as the chimes of liberty were ringing from the teapot dome in Philadelphia, Adam Smith invented capitalism, a very, very good economic system that leads to happiness and freedom for everybody. Sometime later, Karl Marx formulated communism, a very, very bad economic philosophy that produced untold human misery. Today, communism has lost everywhere but Cuba and Seattle, and capitalism is now perched on the verge of total world domination, the economy of the entire planet being run by one gigantic multinational steering group that will make things much better for everybody.

This almost brings us to the twentieth century, and that's completely ignoring the Hundred Years' War, the Gutenberg Bible, Napoleon, a whole lot of things about Mexico, and the Industrial Revolution. And how about the last 100 years! It's almost as if we've had more history since the turn of the last century than in the 1900 years preceding it— or the six billion years before that! I can't even begin to get to it all. There were the usual wars, of course, but also the great technological milestones that brought us where we are today: the creation of the automobile, the airplane, the radio, the television, the computer, NutraSweet, the palmtop, the cellular phone, basic cable service, those teeny satellite dishes that can go just about anywhere. Burma turned into Myanmar but didn't stop torturing dissidents. Cambodia became Kampuchea, then went back to Cambodia again. Remember when these things were new and important? How they changed our lives?

No, you don't. And neither do I. That's because it's already a new millennium. And all these things, people, places, accomplishments . . . well, they're all fading, aren't they . . . all becoming as relevant to us as the Venerable Bede was to Ben Franklin. In a couple of years, we're not gong to care about either of them, either.

But the convergence of video and computers . . . now, that's interesting!
2000

I've Got Your Cheese, You Nitwit!

Hello. I'm elated to be able to bring you this little fable, which has transformed the lives of many both professionally and personally, rendering all human experience instantly manageable even when the situations that give rise to confusion and suffering remain completely unchanged and unacceptable. I'd get to the story right away, but I have a full page here and a whole column on the next page to fill. By offering this little introduction I am using up more than a hundred words even before I get started. That makes things easier for me, and that's what this story is all about.

A few more words before we end this little section of remarks that appear before we start. The story that you are about to read is a parable. For those of you who are moving your lips as you read this, I will tell you what that means. No, it doesn't mean two male cows! Ha ha ha! On the contrary. It means we will be writing mostly in words of one syllable to give the illusion that what we have to tell is a very, very simple story that even a child could understand. The fact that this is indeed the case makes my job even easier, and as I said, that's just fine, too.

So that you are not confused by the weighty matters in this tale, I will even tell you what the characters represent. There are two rats, Grab and Gimme, and two tinyfellows, Whoa and Whazzup, who are the size of rats both physically and emotionally but are actually humans in business suits. Grab takes things because he thinks they are coming to him. Gimme wants a lot but is afraid to take it, allowing Grab to do most of the work but in the end getting most of the Cheese himself because he has sharper teeth. Whoa, our little friend in the Armani blazer, is amazed at everything and likes to think things are going fine the way they are because he has a few stock options. And Whazzup just wants to hang around and drink beer. These are all parts of ourselves, get it?

Good. Now we can begin.

Once, long ago in a land far away, there lived four animate life-forms who ran around looking for things to fill up their miserable existences until the time that Providence saw fit to release them from this mortal plane. Sometime around 1986, all four creatures fell into a vat of Cheese that was very plentiful and tasty. They were very happy with their Cheese, but what they didn't realize is that it wasn't their Cheese at all. They were only borrowing it. The Cheese belonged to a global, trans-industrial corporation that had no knowledge of their existence and couldn't possibly have cared less about them.

This wasn't always the case. Early in their careers, both rats and men worked for a corporation that actually made Cheese. Those were happy, carefree days! They had company cars, and there were no faxes to make them move their Cheese around on a real-time basis, and e-mail had not yet been invented to make their Cheese all runny and hard to grab, and there was time to just sit with the Cheese now and then in an enjoyable and pretty unproductive fashion. Many times, the Cheesegiver would drop by and give them a little Cheese, just to watch how happy it made them.

In the late '80s, however, it became clear that the Cheese could no longer stand alone, that stand-alone Cheese, in fact, was unable to com-pete with Cheese that could achieve economies of scale and back-office efficiencies. So in the early '90s, their Cheese was moved to a cheaper part of the maze and at the same time lumped together with a lot of other Cheese to create one very large, smelly, and synergistic mound.

Grab and Gimme and the two tinyfellows were left with hardly any Cheese whatsoever, and what Cheese they did have was processed and almost completely without character. This was very disappointing, because they had given the best part of their lives for their original, beloved Cheese and believed they had a right to feel proprietary about it. In fact, in the previous decade they had been encouraged to take Ownership of that Cheese, and now it was gone!

Grab and Gimme, because they were, after all, rats, put on their itty-bitty Nikes and ran back into the maze, chewing through walls and other rats until they found a room full of Cheese they could glom onto for a while and sell books to.

Things were tougher on Whoa and Whazzup, however, because they had brains and not just limbic regions surrounding rudimentary ganglia. Whoa, for his part, carefully ventured back into the maze, leaving scrib-blings of crushing simplicity on the wall. "If the Cheese is bad, don't eat it," he wrote at one point after a disappointing meal at a restaurant that also featured very small portions. "Cheese is where you find it," he observed at another juncture while shoving a smaller tinyfellow off a cliff and snatching his stash. He left these messages, of course, for Whazzup, but his poor comrade never moved from his original Cheese location. He is, as far as I know, living there still, sleeping a great deal at his desk and subsisting on a diet of laser-printer toner and linoleum.

Finally, as summer turned to winter and then to spring, Whoa overcame his fear of the unknown, turned a corner in the gigantic maze of life, and found a room full of the most beautiful Cheese on the planet. Man, was that some cache of Cheese! Unfortunately, I was sitting in a very comfortable recliner in the center of the room keeping all that nice Cheese for myself. To this day, in short, anyone who wants any Cheese at all has to go through me or someone very much like me. Now and then I let the local tinyfellows have a scrap of Cheese, of course, but only when I feel like it, and when the Cheese hits a certain target price, I will move that Cheese again, believe you me.

And that's the end of the story. It's a great and inspirational one, I think you'll agree—so good, in fact, that I'm going to make everybody I know go out and buy it in bulk. Before long, millions of people will be reading it and wondering if they're the only ones who think it's simplistic, condescending, and infuriating. But by then it will be too late! Because the Cheese will be mine—forever and ever! And if you don't like it, you can lump it! There's only so much of it to go around! Get your own, you losers!

2000

A Critique of Pure Reason

I was seated with a group of fellow executives recently, immediately after breakfast, trying to listen to nonsense at that very early hour without falling asleep. This, of course, is our destiny, particularly for those of us who make our living producing little but decisions for others and money for our shareholders and ourselves.

It isn't the easiest part of the job, however, for those of us who suffer from meeting narcolepsy. A few years ago I had to attend, after a night of cordial socializing with my peers, a presentation on Quality by an individual from NASA. He had a stack of overheads eighteen inches high. He spoke in a military monotone. The room was dark. On that occasion I actually erupted into stentorian snoring, returning to consciousness, after a well-placed elbow in my ribs, with a honk that elicited unkind laughter from a room of more than 100 people. That was bad, career-wise. This time, however, I was not tempted to drop into the arms of Morpheus. Sleep and anger are incompatible.

There are some tired saws that personally offend me. "Love conquers all," for instance, is patently false, and people should shut up about it. Likewise, the other day I saw a book whose thesis is that compassionate, humane management is transforming the American workplace. I nearly lost my lunch on that one, which would have been a shame, seeing how that particular meal cost the corporation more than $80, plus tax and tip.

On the morning in question, the company brought in an individual to instruct us on the rationality of the stock market, the rules that govern it, and how we could manage our company with those rules in mind. I wish I could create for you the noise I would like to make in response. But you must imagine one for yourself. Make it now, if you like. Got the picture?

Perhaps I am being unfair. The circumstances of this little chat could have been better. That morning the Dow Jones industrial average had fallen into the chasm that lies immediately below the infrastructure of corporate capitalism and was spelunking down there in earnest. The Nasdaq, too, had dug a nice trench and was at that moment facedown in it.

The guy at the front of the room was showing slides demonstrating the relationship between cash-flow growth and share appreciation. It looked pretty simple. The charts he displayed had a lot of numbers on them. As you know, numbers are objective things and denote predictability and certainty. He was also using a lot of acronyms, which always make inexplicable things sound plausible.

The only problem for this fellow, who was very young for the enormous job he holds and pleasant-looking in a crew-necked-sweater sort of way, was that sometime in the past couple of years everybody had been issued a pager, cell phone, Palm, or other gizmo with which to keep in touch with the world, and that everybody's wireless friend was at that very moment buzzing, whirring, vibrating, chuckling, humming, or playing either Beethoven's Ninth or "La Cucaracha." And on each little screen was the same message. The world was ending. The market was in a swoon. And there wasn't a single respectable reason for it.

As our presenter played his merry tune of multiples and growth rates and quarterly consistency and fa-la-la and wang-dang-doodle, certain questions swept through the room as if by telepathy. These questions included: (1) Why was this happening? We were the same company we'd been yesterday! Our sector was growing in double digits! Nothing had changed! And here we were, being swept into the mung with everyone else! And (2) Why in the world was this happening?

And still the band played on. In his defense, I am sure he believed what he was saying, this minister of the macroeconomic state. He must, I suppose, in order to manage with equanimity the billions (and soon to be trillions) of other people's money in his control, and move the piles of lucre from here to there without fainting, without a sense that it is all a gigantic crapshoot.

Of course, people once had proof that the world was flat and supported at its edges by four giant tortoises. That didn't make it true. And the fact that there were no tortoises didn't stop them from sailing off westward to go eastward either.

Came the question and answer period, and we just sort of looked at the poor guy for a while, many of us stifling the urge to rip his face off. Much of what he'd said had been unintelligible, but perhaps that was because we were uninitiated. So we reached for clarity, since he was, after all, in the clarity business. Why, we inquired, was the market so insane, if rational laws were in place to keep the giant clock ticking with the regularity of a goose? Momentary vagaries and corrections that would smooth themselves out over time, we were told. The virtuous who produced results would ultimately be saved. What was one to do in the interim, before this righting of all wrongs took place? Buy more securities, we were told. All crashes such as the one we were now experiencing were great opportunities for those who had faith in the system. And there it was: In the end it was all about faith.

The friendly priest from the Church of Adam Smith departed to a nice round of golf applause. We took a break, marching off to the rest rooms like abashed cattle, mooing a little. There I found myself standing, staring into the middle distance, next to a senior officer of the corporation. One hand was occupied with personal tasks. The other held a cell phone to his ear. I cannot relate what was said into the phone, but it was highly scatological in nature and pertained to the drubbing the market was taking.

"Jack," I said to him after he bade a brisk farewell to the mashed turnip on the other end of the line, "do you think the market is rational?"

"Rational!" he said. "It's not @#$! rational! It's !#@$ insane!" To which, I believe, we must all say amen. And so, driven by fear, greed, and the stupidity of its least courageous members, the market goes on swinging up and down like a giant, malevolent pendulum. And we who live on its vagaries work, and watch our pagers and Palms for signs, and wait for the madness to subside. And in the meantime, we pray that things will be all right, that we will be all right.

In the end, you know, all we really have is our faith. Faith, as ever, would seem to be the most rational stance of all.

2000

God, Am I Angry!

Lord, it's me again. I know I don't talk to you very often, but that's not because I'm not thinking about you. It's just that most of the time I kind of go along without thinking too much, caught up in the daily tasks and duties that are put before me.

Then, once in a while, something like this Lizzie Grubman thing happens that makes us think about how close we all are to the boundary beyond which no soul ever returns, even with the help of a bunch of great PR people and attorneys. We look at the poor, tortured souls as they are shoveled by devils into the mouth of media hell, and we think, "Wow, I'm glad that's not me."

But it could be, Lord, it could be. Our sins are many. There is the sin of pride, which is annoying to others, and gluttony, which is more fun than pride. But the worst of all the sins, Lord, is the one that afflicts all executives—the sin of rage, rage that burbles and sputters just below the surface of our executive calm, rage that may explode with malevolent force when we least expect it, destroying us immediately and forever.

Keep us from it, Lord!

That's why I am on my knees before you today, thinking about Lizzie Grubman. You may not remember her, since you've been pretty busy trying to help Al Dunlap explain his résumé, so let me remind you.

A few weeks ago Lizzie Grubman had it all. A huge public relations business. The key to every hot club and tub in the city. The little world around her in Manhattan and the Hamptons lapping her shoes with their tongues. You notice I use the past tense, Lord, for she is now dead in show business. Whether her acts were intentional is unclear, Lord, but the papers tell us these things are not:

• Lizzie Grubman became enraged at a bouncer in front of a late-night club in the Hamptons for which she did some work. The employee had the temerity to ask her to move her car from a fire lane.

• The enraged woman said, "Get someone with a higher authority to move me." Later on she allegedly used a four-letter word to the bouncer and called him "white trash." The person to whom she so referred has since sued her, making allegations, carried on the front pages of both local tabloids but denied by Lizzie, that Lizzie Grubman was on drugs that night.

• When she was at last forced to move the Mercedes-Benz SUV, the enraged woman leaped into the vehicle, slammed it into reverse, and backed up into fifteen or sixteen people, breaking bones and damaging the front of the building. The car hit with such force that people inside the club were injured.

• The enraged woman then stumbled out of the car and in a few minutes took her angry self home without receiving a breath test. That may have been inadvertent, but many people do not think so, Lord, and it's hard to argue with them.

• The next morning, sober and with her public relations and legal team in tow, she surrendered to the police. She looked drained. The rage had passed. By then it was too late.

Since that night Lizzie Grubman has been on the front page every day. They never choose a very nice picture of her. The *New York Post,* which immediately convicted her, at first suggested that she might be required to serve more than 100 years in prison. It has since knocked that down to twenty or thirty.

The angry woman was the queen of the world just a month ago. Now she's the queen of the underworld. And there she will stay. Because she got too angry, Lord. And in the end her anger made her into a moron. Anger does that. It makes you stupid.

You fire people who should be retained, because they pissed you off. You kill deals that are better left made, because the other guy pulled a fast one. You make people cry, because the rage is overpowering and empowering. Lord, and makes you feel like no matter what you are doing, it must be right. How else do we explain the executive golfer who, in front of fellow sportsmen, killed a rare black swan with his driver, instantly becoming famous throughout the business world?

What of Judge Thomas Penfield Jackson, whose anger at the pride of Microsoft became so great that he could not keep his hatred of the company from poisoning the proceedings against it?

And what of the greatest example of them all, O Lord? What of Gerard Finneran, president of an investment company, who grew enraged on a flight from South America to New York a few years ago? He had been drinking, Lord, and was denied further service. At any rate, Gerard Finneran's rage exploded, and it made him do a terrible thing, inexcusable even for a chief executive. It is reported, and the facts are not disputed, that Gerard Finneran climbed upon the food service cart in first class, lowered his expensively tailored slacks and . . . no, I can't go on, Lord, not in this venue. There is no doubt in my mind that Gerard Finneran, as he was doing this inconceivable act, felt an executive entitlement to do so, an entitlement conferred by rage.

Let us pray.

Give me strength, O Lord, not to scream at Lenny, who was supposed to finish that spreadsheet by eight this morning but didn't because he's a complete numbnuts.

Give me strength to forgive the waiter when my tuna arrives undercooked yet again, because at every restaurant I eat in there are a bunch of tuna Nazis who want to make me eat it blue even though I've told them again and again that I like it cooked!

Give me strength to resist the urge to strangle the taxi driver who ignored my advice to avoid the Midtown Tunnel to the airport when even a slug in the bottom of a tequila bottle knows the tunnel's completely bollixed up at this hour!

And give me the strength to read the newspaper every morning without hurling it across the room, even though it's so filled with opinionated nonsense I can barely stand to read it without holding it at arm's length, with one hand clamped over my nose. You know, Lord, every day plus Sunday in the *New York Times* they have a different article with five economists saying how bad everything stinks when you know very well that if they took even a little bit of trouble they could find five equally intelligent economists prepared to say that things were improving! What's up with that? Every day! Gloom and doom! And then they run a front-page article saying it's people's paranoia and pessimism that are holding the recovery back! Well, come on! Why do they think people are ready to hang themselves, anyway? Because they read the *Times* every day, that's why!

Aw, what's the use? Being mad? It's what we do, right?

Thanks for listening, Lord, but I'll take it from here.

2001

Lessons from the Abyss

Looking at the whole horrible Enron mess, even a veteran cynic has to feel pretty good about the future. Look what we now know that we did not before! True, it was a wreck unlike any since the *Titanic,* a craft destroyed by the arrogance of its designers and the inattention and stupidity of those who ran it. Yet in spite of the lives lost and the hardship for those who had to attend the movie with a young girl not once but four or five times, even the great *Titanic* produced some worthwhile lessons.

Let's see, what were they? Oh, yes. Nothing is unsinkable! Hm. Perhaps we didn't learn that yet. Wait! How about: If you have a lot of people onboard, you want to set aside one seat in a lifeboat for each. Back then, you know, only the first-class passengers stood any chance of getting off the ship alive. . . . Uh-oh. Come to think of it, maybe we didn't learn that either.

Okay, maybe we didn't learn anything from the *Titanic*. But let's not make that same mistake with Enron! At least a dozen lessons may be garnered from what happened to the morons who ran that enterprise into the ground.

1. **Accountants are people, too.** We used to think they were wise, honest, and probing, necessary to keep gung-ho management straight. Now it's clear: They're not. Accountants are potentially a bunch of gonzo-maniacs—and greedy to boot! They also can be convinced, it seems, that anything is okay as long as they're following orders. That sounds familiar. So now you know that if something has been vetted by one accountant, that doesn't mean squat. You probably need two.

2. **Think before you shred.** The idiots who fed miles of documentation into their shredders certainly did so at the behest of senior management. What bureaucrat ever did anything important on his own? Sadly, shredding makes things easy on the investigators. If all the tons of paper were still around, the courts would have spent years trying to figure out what the heck Enron was doing and whether it was legal, semilegal, or felonious. Now the whole bunch of them are liable for obstruction of justice, a relatively easy rap to prove. Instead of causing a lot of confusion and trouble, they're going to the hoosegow! Except they won't get the real guys! They'll get the teeny-weenies! That's the lesson. Wait—we knew that already!

3. **Even big guys have problems just like you and me.** When the man George W. Bush calls Kenny-Boy—the infamous Kenneth Lay, the Enron mastermind (if such a word can be used in this context)—was asked why he needed to cash in hundreds of millions of dollars in options, he said he had . . . expenses. Well, we can certainly see the problem. But Kenny-Boy Mr. Lay, he has expenses that lesser mortals can only dream of. In addition to his lifestyle, which is very costly, he also has debts, which are even worse than expenses. Most of those debts came from—guess where?—bad investments! That's a problem any Enron shareholder or employee can sympathize with. So, no man is completely unworthy of our sympathy. That's an excellent lesson.

4. **Analysts are whores.** Yes, incredible as it may seem, people sometimes don't have the best judgment in the world if they're being paid both to analyze companies and to finance their deals. That

often happens when securities analysts advise management while at the same time evaluating their stocks. Hello!

5. **Don't worry about the Feds. They'll be along later.** As citizens of the United States, we pay taxes to fund government entities like Congress and the Securities and Exchange Commission. Why? To protect us from scoundrels who can't see the forest for the fees. Right about now, those guardians of the public weal are riding into battle, just in time to pick up the dead. There's a lesson in there somewhere. Let me know when you find it.

6. **It's better to be big and crooked than small and trusting.** Yes, it's the little people down in Texas and the small investors with their life savings tied up in rancid stock who are taking it hardest. The rampaging beasts will hire sleazy lawyers, and pretty soon they'll be laughing over their juleps at the nineteenth hole. It may be a while until such an opportunity for filthy lucre comes again, but when it does, it's probably better to be numbered among the despicable winners than the pathetic losers. Is that a good lesson?

7. **If you blow the whistle inside and nobody hears it, blow it outside, for goodness' sake!** Sherron Watkins let her senior management know what's what. She really had everybody's ear— six months later! Next time, call a frickin' reporter!

8. **Internal communications are important for hoodwinking employees.** When Kenny-Boy Mr. Lay wanted to keep the Hindenburg in the air for several more months, to whom did he go? His employees! He was open! He communicated! If he's out there on the message board, he must be a good guy, right? The lesson here is to distrust anything that you find on the Internet. It is an untrustworthy medium, good for a few giggles and nothing more. That is a truth that transcends this debacle. Ignore it at your peril, you credulous fools!

9. **Stonewalling is still the best defense.** Just because it brought down Richard Nixon doesn't mean it hasn't worked dozens of times since. It's working for David Duncan, the Andersen guy in charge of the Enron account, who has been taking the Fifth when need be. And Dick Cheney is fighting the General Accounting Office for possession of his documents. Says it's his right to maintain radio silence on considerations the administration used to determine energy policy. You go, girls!

10. **Your 401(k) ain't worth diddly.** I don't think we need to say any more. If you don't have Retirement Plan B in place, you haven't been listening.

11. **Nicer guys finish last.** Why is it that the one halfway decent guy in Enron senior management, Cliff Baxter, is found dead in his car with a gun by his side and a suicide note, and the rest of the bastards are walking around with hundreds of millions of dollars in their pockets? Help me out with that.

12. **Hope springs eternal.** On January 28 the *New York Times* stated, "Many think that Enron's business model for virtual trading remains sound despite the company's problems." Really? "Despite Enron's collapse," the paper wrote, "its goal of merging the best thinking in energy, finance, and information technology as an online commodity trader still garners respect."

Well, suppose they're right. Then the fellows who ran this, the greatest failure in the history of American mercantile capitalism, were simply bad guys with a good idea. They weren't the first. They won't be the last. Get rid of them, and we can all go on with business as usual, right?

Business as usual! What a concept! And my, how far we've come!

2002

The Shareholders Are Revolting!

Okay, I know about the whole corporate-governance thing and how it needs to be scrutinized every day and twice on Sunday, and also, of course, how an individual with $152.34 invested in our company owns the corporation.

But still. Isn't it about time we blew up the annual meeting? I just came from one. As a display of democracy in action, it was inspiring. That is, it inspired me to get out of there and go back to work.

It began as they all do—a gaggle of mostly elderly and truculent people filing into the auditorium complaining that there were no cookies. It seems that in the old days of corporate annual meetings there were not only cookies but also cake and sometimes even little sandwiches to accompany coffee, tea, and soft drinks, or so they tell me. Those were the days!

Then they get started. You know the drill. First the chairman gets up and shows the flag. The president comes on to lay out the company's strategy with pretty graphics. No matter how good the story, the crowd is edgy, fidgety. This is not what they came for. "We will now entertain questions about the board candidates," says the general counsel and bweeeeeeee—the puck is dropped, and we are off. It's gadfly time.

The first is the editor of an investor letter. Her question, actually an impassioned speech, is offered in a thick Transylvanian accent and winds like a vine around any number of topics until the audience is writhing and booing. She touches on the outrage she felt when "minimum-wage employees" asked to see her ID—"Why," she cries, "do we need so much security around here!"—and makes insulting comments about the general character of several ultrasenior managers, who attempt to smile benignly from the stage.

Next comes a gentleman of some seventy-five years of age, very careful, very neat, and intense. "I have been attending annual meetings," he says with great thoughtfulness, "since February 23 of 1958, which was on a Thursday, and since then I have come from my house at 212 Main Street, Tuckahoe, New York, and asked 543 questions at 198 separate annual meetings involving $1.6 trillion of assets . . ." and so forth. This fellow gets up several more times with additional numerical documentation. I'm sure he's an excellent driver.

Time is passing, and nothing of substance has been done. Except . . . could it be that . . . this is the substance?

Another investor rises creaking to his feet. "I have it from a very excellent source that this company is planning to divest its flute reamer division!" he cries, outraged. When asked what his excellent source was, he replies, "I can't remember," and sits down. The audience laughs. Things are getting out of hand.

A woman the size of R2-D2 goes up to the mike and begins to read newspaper articles about executive malfeasance in the American corporate scene at this point in history. This is interesting to some people but not to others, a fact made clear when a rowdy bunch of shareholders stand and begin screaming for her to sit down. They seem acquainted with her. Perhaps they have seen this act at other annual meetings?

"I don't have a proxy!" yells the woman from Transylvania, after which there is a rumpus from a number of people who feel they, too, have been neglected. There is an attempt by the general counsel to establish order. It fails.

A scattered group of gesticulating, yammering townsfolk are now heading for the mikes, brandishing pitchforks, clubs, and torches. What are they going to be talking about now? Corporate investment in totalitarian dictatorships? Nuclear power? Big tobacco? Acquisitions and divestitures? Sex? Drugs? Executive comp? All of the above? Something new? The noise level in the room is rising. Cheeks are turning pink, then red.

I guess I decided to get out of there when an entire roast turkey sailed past my ear on the way to the stage. The chairman and the president and the general counsel were up there trying to do their best, but there was nothing a guy in the audience could do. When a bunch of midgets on unicycles burst in from the lobby and began bouncing down the aisles asking whether corporate overhead was in line with historical norms, I quietly rose to my feet and squeezed myself down the row and out the door.

As I left, I saw the guys on the stage rising to their feet. The chairman was yelling, "Back! Back!" and threatening the audience with a laser pointer. The president was on his feet, arms akimbo, laughing like a swashbuckler. The general counsel was crouched behind the table muttering imprecations to himself, his logbook over his head. I don't blame him. The better part of valor is discretion, particularly in events mandated by law.

Next year . . . you know? I think they should serve cookies. Sometimes it's just nice to have a cookie. It certainly couldn't hurt, right?

2002

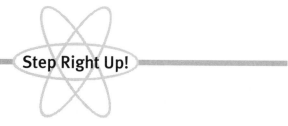

Step Right Up!

Exciting developments came from the world of marketing this month with the introduction of an intriguing new product designed to repair the reputation of American business. It's called Corporate Responsibility, and all indications are that it will be hot. Whether it has a long-term shelf life remains to be seen, but as a high-profile launch it's certainly off to a good start.

Corporate Responsibility was given a massive kickoff by the president of the United States himself, who rolled out not only the concept but also the simple, elegant, brand-identity treatment.

With his usual focus, passion, and preparation, the president stood in front of a curtain festooned with the words Corporate Responsibility. This method of making sure the public knows what the president is talking about is now state of the art at the White House, and marketing gurus agree that it's a lot more effective than a blank curtain.

There was some grumbling in fussy journalistic circles about the president's suitability as a spokesperson. It was pointed out by the professional party poopers that the president himself has not always been in tune with the product's selling proposition, having engaged in youthful activities that didn't necessarily embody the letter and spirit of Corporate Responsibility. Fortunately, the across-the-board media launch all but overpowered naysayers, most of them Democrats, who haven't stopped whining since the day before yesterday.

There was a lot of excitement on the front and editorial pages about Corporate Responsibility. All the papers were pleased to use the graphic featuring the bold legend behind the Chief Exec.

W., for his part, looked stern and enthusiastic and left little doubt that the product was going to receive continued support. This kind of commitment from the top will be necessary if Corporate Responsibility is going to get the job done and put the stock market back on its feet.

To be effective, a great product must have creative packaging, but there has to be something underneath, too. Corporate Responsibility seemed to have it all. First, there was a hard, crunchy shell of outrage, vague enough to at once threaten and entice those who didn't already have the thing and needed some. Inside that crust was a soft, gooey center that tasted pretty much like anything the consumer imagined it would. Best of all was the hint that purchase of the product would essentially be mandatory for all those in the business world, much as greed and a copy of Peters and Waterman were necessary for enjoyment of the '80s.

After the rollout, public demonstration of how Corporate Responsibility works was necessary almost at once, and for that a target was necessary. Several miscreants who were fat and bald were deemed too unattractive for wide-scale use. In short order, however, some handsome celebrities were found who suited the purpose well. They were immediately targeted for flogging, tarring, feathering, and front-page scrutiny by a variety of media outlets, which went to work with great energy to show what happened to people who didn't use Corporate Responsibility. The level of interest in these famous and sexy alleged criminals was equal to that given the abdication of King Edward the VIII of Great Britain in 1936. And the public cheered. Corporate Responsibility was back in town!

Apart from the good work done by the media, the federal government got busy passing laws that made the product even hotter. Work was begun with significant fanfare to strip middle management of the hope that stock options might lift them out of the ranks of the petite bourgeoisie. Other bold legislation was initiated to implement penalties for crimes that were already illegal.

Today, everywhere you look, everybody who is anybody is out there buying as much Corporate Responsibility as the production team can churn out. In small businesses and large, leaders of capitalism are embracing honesty in all their dealings, eschewing bad accountants who lie and shred and don't tell senior managers what's going on, and embracing all those good things that we, as a nation, have forgotten. At the same time, everybody is determined that people who do not have Corporate Responsibility should go to jail or media prison, whichever is more effective. Experts estimate that by the end of the decade, more than a dozen ugly white guys will be in minimum-security prisons.

As noted, research can't yet ascertain whether Corporate Responsibility will be a lasting addition to the grab bag of products that define our culture, like Tide or Pepsi. Whether it attains cultural longevity or not, however, one thing is clear. If this great new product is purchased and applied in a timely manner at this stage of the game, quick, permanent relief may be just around the corner.

And then look out, Wall Street! The bulls will be back!

2002

Dr. Jekyll and Mr. Investor

This is to relate the sad story of a certain Dr. Henry Jekyll, who has become notorious because of the depredations he has wrought upon the civilized economy. Perhaps in telling it I will find some peace and be able once again to sleep at night with confidence in my portfolio.

When I first knew Dr. Jekyll, he was a respected physician with an interest in the stock market. It was his contention that with proper research and study of the events of the day, profit could reliably be wrested from the arms of commerce. To this theory he dedicated his investigations.

Throughout the 1980s the scientist worked in his laboratory, studying the consolidation of industries and generally benefiting in a small way from the greed and brutality of the acquisition environment at that time. You should have seen him then! In his pinstriped suit and yellow polka-dot power tie, hair greased back to reveal a wicked widow's peak, he was the picture of rational avarice.

It was in the 1990s that his inquiries drew him into deeper waters. I recall visiting him one evening in his lair downtown. It was a dark and stormy night. There was lightning and everything. I found him in the midst of a pile of tatty prospecti, his hair disordered and a demented look in his eye. "I have found the secret of wealth beyond your wildest dreams!" he cackled, brandishing an offering from a company that promised to come to your house and wash the dog.

"Look at yourself, man!" I said to him then. "You are going beyond the bounds of nature!" He chuckled amiably and thrust me from his residence.

It was then, in the late portion of that tumultuous decade, that a vicious, cringing, drooling homunculus began frequenting the establishments that serve the capitalist classes. Dressed in ill-fitting, inappropriately casual garb and brandishing a laptop he plugged in at seedy Internet cafés, this troll inspired fear and disgust in all who saw him. Where others respected the stately nature of the market, he traded with no regard for rationality or research, buffeted by little but emotion and rumor. Where my friend Jekyll, even at his worst, was all Mind, this dark creature was all Gut, and he smelled like fear.

"Begone, foul creature!" I yelled at him one evening as I saw him hanging around the edges of a discussion of hedge funds at a local tavern.

"Grrrr," he said, scurrying off with a cell phone to his ear.

Something about the way he shuffled off, one leg shorter than the other, his brow beetled with determination and ignorance, reminded me of my distinguished friend. Perhaps it was the pinkie ring and complimentary ballpoint pen from eBay sticking out of his shirt front—I don't know. But heart in mouth, I followed this beast and indeed found myself at the doorway of my friend.

The portal was ajar. A foul odor came from the laboratory. I peered into the darkened enclosure and was somewhat relieved to see my old associate sitting in his Barcalounger, exhausted, trembling.

"Jekyll!" I ejaculated in sheer relief and good humor.

"Come no closer, Bing," he said. As I ignored his request and drew near, I could see his laptop, plugged into his online financial site. "Look," he said in a voice hollowed out by suffering and confusion. "Last Thursday . . . up 300 points! New housing starts are good. Inflation is not a consideration. Some corporate earnings appear to be swinging back."

Then he picked up a sheaf of newspapers, and something unutterably horrible happened. His voice, always a fine musical instrument, grew guttural, wild, and uncivilized. "But look!" he grunted in a mucous-filled baritone, brandishing the papers. "Planned cuts at United Airlines will mean layoffs! Massachusetts is suing First Boston! War with Iraq! Martha Stewart being investigated for fraud! General Electric caught up in accounting issues! Are these opportunities or liabilities? Who can say?!"

He rose to his feet, and the skies above cracked with a gigantic boom and suddenly what stood before me was no longer my old friend but a ravening, irrational beast with hair in its nose and a mind like creamed corn. The creature was laughing. "Ha! Ha! Ha!" it said. "My transformation is complete! I am Mr. Investor! I know nothing but what I heard five minutes ago! One minute I have confidence! The next I have none! I'm an idiot, and I'm going to drive the market to historic growth one day and down to unprecedented destruction of value the next! And I am in control! For the foreseeable future! Hahahahaha!!!!"

I stumbled into the night, completely grossed out. I have not seen him since. But given the way the market has been behaving recently, I have no doubt he is out there. And I have an equally chilling conviction.

He is not alone.

2002

Things Are Looking Up, America!

I was talking to my friend Tom the other day, and he was bumming me out pretty good. He always does. He's a downbeat guy, possibly because his options are so far underwater he'd get the bends trying to retrieve them. He also reads the newspaper far too much, I think.

Anyhow, he was in a good mood that morning because of what had just happened to his friend Andy. It seems that Andy was standing in the doorway to his office when one of the acoustic tiles that make up the ceiling fell straight down and hit him on the head. Only one tile fell, and it was the one directly above him, and it simply detached from its moorings as if designed to do so, and hit him smack on the noggin.

"You can make of that what you will," said Tom. "But I think it sort of shows where things are going for everybody these days."

It's that kind of attitude that produces negative vibrations, and I, for one, think it's time we shook ourselves out, stood up straight, and headed off in another direction. It's time, in short, to get positive.

Remember positive? It's what we were all about until sometime in 1999, when those crazy nimrods started trying to scare us about Y2K, with a side order of global warming. Well, the millennium has come and gone, and this is the coldest winter I can remember. All the bad stuff swirling around us is made up of things nobody prognosticated. In other words, the doom-and-gloom meisters haven't any more idea of what's going to happen than you or I do. So why not be optimistic? We have good, solid reasons to be.

First, the recession is over. I saw that on TV and in the newspapers. The economic picture is so good that a huge number of people have given up looking for jobs and aren't even being counted in the unemployment rolls. I have a mental image of all these people who don't even need to be engaging in the humiliating process of looking for work—sunning themselves on beaches, sleeping late every morning, rising at noon to enjoy a delicious brunch. More and more Americans are doing exactly that, and I think that's reason enough to put on a happy face.

Next, the stock market is in the toilet—and you know what that means: upside and nothing but. Take Microsoft. Please. But seriously, I bought it when it was around 90, and now it's in the 40s. It has to go up from there, and just the thought has me whistling a happy tune. I must say I also enjoyed the $8.47 I got from Microsoft as a dividend last month.

Third, we seem to be over the worst of the white-collar crime and creative accounting of the past few years. The really bad guys are going to jail, except for those who aren't, and the days of corporations overstating earnings and inflating the value of their securities are over, thank goodness. Do you think that's in some way related to how stale, flat, and unprofitable the market is these days? Banish that thought! I'm going to focus on the corporate responsibility busting out all over and on how nobody is getting rich quick on greasy stock options anymore, except for those who are, and maybe that could be you or me! Because if you got options this year, they were probably issued at a pathetically low price!

Also, did you know that you're doing better than you think? I saw a column that said that if you make more than $60,000 a year, you're in the top rank of the nation's earners. That means that if you're reading this, you're probably considered rich by somebody. Even more positive for readers of this magazine, tax cuts for the very rich, the moderately rich, and the modestly rich seem a pretty sure thing, since our president views them as a solution to everything but eczema.

And finally, I guess, there's this war.

And aside from that, we have a lot of entertaining reality stuff on television, and the Oscars are coming up pretty soon, and we're the last superpower on the planet, which makes things kind of toasty, and baseball is right around the corner, and if baseball is here, can spring be far behind?

And then there's this war.

That, and the fact that the jug-eared guy who runs Homeland Security keeps coming on the news to scare people. Why does he do that? He never has any solid advice. Be careful. Who's not careful at this point? What's the function of those news briefings, anyway? To show us that somebody is on the job color-coding our level of danger? That guy really harshes my mellow, and I don't appreciate it.

And then there's this war, you know? That would be a real acoustic tile on the head, wouldn't it? . . .

But what's the point of obsessing about that? There's so much good going on and a whole lot more to look forward to.

What, we worry? I think not! Life's too short!

2003

The Love Song of Alfred E. Neuman

April is the cruelest month.
But not this April! Let's do lunth!
Why not? It's spring! What fun! Hoorah!
Hey, nonny nonny! Cha-cha-cha!
God bless us all and everyoney.
Nobody's not making money!
Every office, desk, and bureau
Crammed with—what is that? A euro?
Ha-ha-ha! La-la-la! Nonny nonny! Rah! Rah! Rah!

Yes, friends, as newly sprouts the vine,
And Dow and Nasdaq fat as swine (And multiples at 99!),
With crispy green stuff all encumbered,
Here they come! Our fat 500!
From big GM to li'l Tribune, a
Crowd of achievers, each a kahuna.
Mergers up the big wazoo
Have transformed the neighborhoo.
Travelers! Chrysler! Buh-bye! Toodle-oo!
So many gone! So many gobbled!
To another firm they're cobbled.
Dance we to the discombobbled!
Hey, nonny nonny! Wow! Yahoo!
Oops! Since we're based on revenue,
Not speculative whoop-de-doo,
There's no Yahoo! Oh, no! Boo-hoo!

No Amazon? No schmooze.com?
For eBay we bay! They're the bomb!
How can there be no Internet?
No sweat. Don't fret. It's just not yet.
Next year there will be more, you bet.

Until that time of them we sing
Who make real cash flow bulge and ring.
Clorox! Gleaming at the rear!
Twenty percentiles up this year.
A Cheer! (No, Cheer is made by Procter & Gamble,
Which also of growth is a good example.)
And here's Fortune Brands!
They're no idjits,
Producing growth in triple digits
After acquiring something or other.
Tell your mother! Tell your brother!
Tell your Uncle Fritz's lover!
Strange how plans come to fruition
After you eat the competition.
Like No. 443, Suiza Foods of Dallas,
Which grew faster than a presidential phallus.
Who knows what they did to quicken our pulses?
All that counts is their resultses.
And United Stationers of Des Plaines, Illinois?
Step on out here! Don't be coy!
With profits up thousands and thousands percentages,
You not only broke records, you put 'em in bandages!

And those are just the guys at the bottom.
You want some from the middle?
We got 'em. At No. 327, Starwood. They lodge people
And generate gains that make others look feeble.
3Com! Dynergy! Cinergy!
Good folks a lot like you and me.
And Safeco! Tenneco! PPG!
Building shareholder equity!
AFLAC! CSX! SCI! Microsoft! Unicom! TCI! Top them! Try!
And now . . . Best Buy!
Here's 5,000 percent profit growth in your eye!

On the other hand, whoa: Owens Corning.
They must wish that last year died aborning.
Profits down—ouch—1600 percent?
Which way did it go, guys? Which way did it went?
Zooming now up to the toppety ranks!
A lot of brown water and several banks
Have cause to offer thanks.

So many companies, so little time, nonny nonny!
For the kind of rare dudes who made the most money!
Safeway! Costco! And Conagra!
And how 'bout those guys who gave us Viagra?
Upward! BankAmerica merged and splurged,
And more than $50B regurged!
That's gross! And we mean that nicely.
And Citigroup just did their revenue twicely.
So they're up ten points to No. 7 Good!
IBM holds fast at No. 6—they should!
GE and Exxon! La-di-da! Booga-booga!
Turn in performances as sweet as sugar!

So crack open those celebrity sodas!
For Wal-Mart! Ford! And General Motors!
The top three of all in the world's greatest marketses!
Let's plant big wet kisses all over their carcatses!
So nonny nonny! Hi-di-hey!
Let's make this year a big-biz one!
See you all in Y2K.
If there is one.

1999

10

WHAT, ME WORRY?

The answer, of course, is yes. I do. I worry all the time, don't you? If you don't, can I have a little of what your psychiatrist has been prescribing?

No, I worry first thing in the morning about what the day might hold, and during my commute in I worry about whatever is on the news and whether I forgot to set something up that could emerge to bite me in the butt, and during the morning I worry about phone calls that could come and spoil my equanimity and at lunch I worry that I'm missing something while I'm away from the office or whether the position of my table at the restaurant is indicative of my social standing, which of course it is, and during the afternoon I worry about why I am or am not at a meeting that is either important or isn't, or if people like me enough or whether I'm going to get some perk or other that I feel is owed to me, and if I hear a siren, this being New York, I worry about that siren, and if I don't hear a siren I sometimes worry about that, too, because when the bad things come there is very often no siren, not at first, and I worry when I fly and I worry when I drive and I worry when I walk through crowds of people on a busy city street, and I worry about what I eat and I worry about what I drink and with whom I drink and when I might be having my next one. That's just for starters. I believe, on the bright side, that if I didn't worry so much I wouldn't be doing half as well. Worry is a good strategy, although it obviously takes its toll on the worrier and those in his or her vicinity. I worry about that, too.

I used to think I was paranoid. I had all the symptoms. High anxiety.

Depression about the way the world was going. The feeling that unseen adversaries were out to get me. Now I realize I wasn't one bit paranoid. I was just paying attention and reacting to the world with good old-fashioned American common sense.

Even Paranoids Have Enemies

One recent night in the hours before an unwelcome dawn, as I lay awake formulating the worst-case scenarios, I amused myself by trying to recall the days before I was paranoid. Without much luck. I've been in business a long time.

Back in the green days when virgin wing tips still cramped my toes, I trembled in the shadow of multiform superiors, exquisitely aware that I was teetering over a void where no one is overpaid. As the proverbial last hired, I worked like a mule and was afraid. "Don't be irrational," I would chide myself as I bustled back from a gobbled lunch. "They like you. Why exterminate you?" And the answer came: "Because you're head count, schmuck."

Then, suddenly, the company was sold. As I waded through blood to a higher floor, I was gripped by a gelatinous new fear born of what I now had to protect. "Don't be nuts!" I once again admonished myself. "What more can they do?" The response came in a new round of mass executions that left me on a lonely, almost lunar terrain.

Today, after no fewer that two Pyrrhic divestitures and any number of gory reorganizations, I clutch a mature, full-blown paranoia to my bosom as proof of my abiding mental health. In a sane world, the paranoid is a man apart, torn by delusions. Where I work, he just might be the only guy in possession of the facts. "Even paranoids have enemies," mutters a friend in advertising. To which I say amen pretty much daily.

Some of us got it and some ain't—that duodenal barometer that forecasts imminent destruction. The fortunate, one or two of whom I've actually met, don't waste energy worrying over the basic unreliability of the cosmos. Maybe they believe in something higher, or even themselves. The rest, and our numbers are legion, must stagger, lurch, or careen forward under the weight of dank imaginings that go way beyond simple pessimism.

"No matter how much swaggering you do over drinks, when the lights are off and you're lying next to the loved one you're supposed to be insulating with your salary, the terror is biblical," says my buddy Weaver, a superb copywriter who lives with a gigantic case of nonspecific disquiet. "You know you have the vulnerability of a gnat and the boot heel of God is going to squash you flat."

Sure, its an extreme world view, but it's ours. And in the current era of membrane-thin corporate loyalty, it's a wise man who metabolizes his paranoia to best advantage. To which end:

Out of the closet, Jack! All great performers learn to channel their stage fright and get on with the show. "Whenever I have a hangover, I succumb to atrocious paranoia," admits the aforementioned Weaver. "I walk around saying 'I'm a charlatan: I have no discipline. I make lousy money—I'm a forking failure!' " Does this concert of bad vibes set Weaver whimpering behind closed doors? No way. "It gives me tremendous energy!" he crows. "I go right to work! It's like pure, NASA-grade rocket fuel! You'll never have more power in your life!" In short, irrational fear is one of the greatest motivators around. Why not use it? It's using you.

You have nothing to fear but everything itself. The successful paranoid knows it's more profitable to obsess over the dumb stuff he can control than to gnaw over big issues he can't. "When people are even ten minutes late for work, I always think they're outside the office at a conference I've been excluded from," my bean-counting pal Drabek reports. "When I find out they were just at the dentist's or something, you can imagine how much better I feel." Whatever quietus he might momentarily take, Drabek still does some lunatic preventive maintenance at day's end. "Before I split for the night, I always check out other people's in-boxes to see if there are any important memos I didn't receive," he reports. "I'm not the only one who does it, either, because I've seen them rooting around in mine, too. I guess you can't be too careful around a paranoid place like this." Sure, it sounds petty, but don't knock it. Anything you can do to chill your jets is worth its weight in Valium.

Reach for feedback. While solid information may aggravate, only the Unknown inspires bona fide hysteria. "I live with this crushing sense of doom," moans my friend Carl, a graphic artist trapped in a humongous style factory. "It's because I get absolutely no word—positive or negative—about what they think of me. So I imagine they're thinking terrible things, when in fact they're thinking nothing at all. It's fairly paralyzing. I have flashes that my level of management will be eliminated. I tell myself they won't do it, we're too valuable. But there are moments while I'm reading *The Wall Street Journal* reporting on cutbacks in some previously healthy industry when I get a terrible attack. I stare at a blank sheet on my drawing table and feel the breath of the guillotine on my neck."

Snuffling in the corner is less fruitful, however, than a grab for the straight poop. My pal Jeffrey was flipped into the ionosphere not long ago when he learned a new tort guy was coming onboard his law firm. "I went in and said to my boss, 'Look, if you're trying to tell me I'm doing a bad job, why not just come out and say so!'" he recounts. His boss was shocked and said, "Are you crazy? What we're trying to tell you, you big jerk, is that you're one great litigator and should be spending more time in court, okay?" This made Jeff feel better for almost an entire day.

Don't drip! On the other hand, nobody likes a guy who goes around oozing his uncontrolled fantasies all over the place. "I've had some amazing scenes with this obsessed subordinate," says my friend Stuart, a bond man. "He tells me he doesn't trust me, that he has dreams where I attack him with long knives, literally. And I say, 'Do I look like the kind of guy who would stab you in the back?' And he says, 'As a matter of fact, yeah, you do.' It's exhausting." Stu admits the miscreant is talented. But the moment the guy screws up . . .

He probably won't, of course. If he's smart, he'll remain on friendly terms with his own paranoia and thrive. "I'm constantly filled with rage and insecurity," my buddy Drabek moans, ever tormented. Then he brightens. "I consider them the twin towers of neurotic success."

Which is as good as any other kind. There are times, though, when I stare out my window and dream of a little farm someplace pastoral, where only the poultry need be edgy. That's way down the road, but I guess I'll get there. Unless, of course, the bastards get me first.

1987

High Plains Drifter

Somebody spoke and I went into a dream. More precisely, I remembered a dream of the night before with such awesome clarity, such tactile recall that I rose from the conference table and spun reeling to the coffee urn with the force of it. I might have even uttered an audible "Ach!" but that doesn't matter. Grunts over budget planning aren't usually noticed.

Here it is: I board the elevator and push 60, which is the toppermost of the poppermost in my building. I am whisked upward in silence. The doors open. I get out. But hey, I don't recognize the surroundings. "You just got off on the thirty-fourth floor," says a creepy voice inside my head, "and there won't be another elevator, not for a long, long time." It is lonely there, and gray, and very low-down. And I feel like crying.

It isn't hard to figure what the sump pump of my subconscious is telling me. After a flying, friction-free beginning, my career has gotten off about halfway to where I thought I was going. I have plateaued. So have a lot of folks I know. What with mergers and resulting cutbacks, the drive for ever-greater efficiency and exploitation, and the general decline of middle management as a life-form, these are plateau kinds of times. The signs are unmistakable:

1. You arrive at your desk one fine morning to find a new, five-thousand-sheet supply of personalized stationery—each bearing your current, puny title—mounting like rank accusation on your blotter.
2. You drop by a senior vice president's office for a friendly chat and notice a memo on his desk, the interim statement from the committee to oversee planning breakfasts, maybe. Your name is not on the distribution list. There's no reason it should be. Every other name there is a Heavy Hitter. And you're not, babe, that's pretty clear. Or maybe the memo does get to your desk, addressed to "S. Bung." That doesn't feel too good, either.
3. At the annual managers' retreat, to which virtually everyone at Headquarters but the secretaries is invited, you must hike miles to

your room, which seems to be an annex of the maintenance closet. There is no executive bar. Since only Big Dudes do not double up, you must share this space with the manager of Financial Reporting. You wake to find Winkler reading *Business Week* in his underwear, a sight that fills you with a crippling internal ache that does not abate until evening.

4. When you were hired, your assignment was to formulate employee-benefits programs and assist the vice president of Human Resources in every little way. Six years later, beyond the ability to leave early on inconsequential Fridays and drink at lunch, you're still doing the exact same thing. The future looms before you, a vast, unchanging lunar landscape.

5. So you go in and rage, to see what a little pique will deliver. Soon the good news comes down. They are indeed changing your title— it's one you never heard before, like Senior Manager of Something or Other. Your duties will be expanded. And your raise will be the absolute maximum allowed: 3 percent.

6. And how about that neat ergonomic chair, the gray leather one with the high back? Didn't get it, did you? And given the economic environment, you don't feel free to pursue it anymore, do you? You'll make do with what you have, won't you?

7. And that's not all. When you first arrived, you had two moderately respected desk droids and Edna, the dedicated administrative assistant ready to hop when you said boo. Now the wind whistles through the empty cubicles around your workspace, Edna must be shared with two other becalmed hotshots, and when it comes right down to it, you're doing a whole lot of stuff formerly assigned to teeny people.

8. Certain thoughts obsess you. Deep, circular musings on the nature of standing still. Perhaps there is no such thing. Perhaps those who do not go forward must slide inexorably backward. Perhaps you're allowed to drink at lunch because you need to.

9. Come to think of it, lunch is getting to be an increasingly substantial part of your day. Sometimes you're gone for three hours or so and when you return—nobody's noticed! Fact is, you've got the gig down so cold you're practically frozen.

10. Then on Friday you heard that the chairman hired Arnold Lassiter to be director of something really good. That post is about comparable with yours, no higher, and yet those are exactly the duties you were hoping to inherit after they recognized your talent and bril-

liance. Now Lassiter has them. And Lassiter, he's one of the guys who's never completely bought your act. . . .

Look around you. Your corporation has fired everyone below and above you. It has no intention of hiring until the Second Coming of Ivan Boesky. It doesn't have to. Not only is your business contracting, but the whole industry is basically in sheep-dip shape. Those who remain would basically roll on the floor and bark like seals if they were asked to. I know I would. Especially if they awarded a vice presidency to any man prepared to do so with excellence.

1989

Having a Nice Day

I've been a mole at the heart of corporate capitalism for several years now, and looking backward, it concerns me that readers might think I'm a negative kind of guy. It's understandable. Fear, paranoia, the limitations of loyalty, the power of deceit, insane managers who victimize the workplace, jerks of all shades and descriptions—these have been my meat since I fell off the freedom train and landed here. My gorge is usually up and rising, I admit it. Beyond that, however, I view myself as a captain of positivity.

I love the smell of coffee in the morning. It smells like victory.

I love the software I get, whether I need it or not. Last week I got a gonzo graphics package, an updated mouse, and an international data base. They're great!

I love my phone. Last week I got a call from a guy conducting a poll: "What kind of military hardware magazine would best suit your professional needs?" I hung up. It felt good.

Sometimes it's someone who has to clear something with me, me, before it gets implemented. Sure, it's just a tiny bit of obeisance, but it's mine! And I always reward it, ladies and gentlemen. I love that about myself.

Once a month I love to open my paycheck and, you know, stare at it for a while, and remember what this document might have looked like in 1980. Do the words four figures have any resonance for you?

I love those precious moments of situational intimacy. After a high-torque meeting, the job well done and over, and you find yourself hanging out in the boardroom for a no-agenda chat with the chairman and a couple of other senior guys. At the pineapple of power, and comfortable there, talking box scores. At such time, a man could convince himself that clean living does sometimes pay off with a visit to the center of the universe. It's nice there.

I also love the day when my bonus check arrives. Not that it's an overwhelming sum. It isn't. I still love to open it and, you know, stare at it for a while.

I love the unexpected intrusion of beauty. Last autumn I attended our strategic-planning confab in downstate Massachusetts. For some reason, I arrived early. Rented my Taurus. Drove to the plush retirement community masquerading as a conference center. The first event, drinks at 6 P.M., was hours away. This was unique. Nowhere to go. Nobody to see. I took a drive. The leaves were red and gold and orange; a rumbling torrent of Waylon and Willie pounded from my stereo, and no one knew where I was, not even me. I got out of my car and took a walk. Couldn't think of a thing to think. Just smelled nature stuff. Got back to my room to find an executive attaché case embossed with my name. On it was a note that read, "Welcome to Excellence." In all, one of the happiest days of my life.

Serenity isn't all, of course. That evening, after nine hours of Scotch and beer, singing myself hoarse with the good guys down at the sports bar. I reeled back to my room and spent the rest of the night down on my knees in my duplex bathroom, wondering if this is how Jimi felt on that final night. How many times in this life can a man achieve that level of craziness and get paid for it?

Once a month my expense check comes in from Accounting. Sure, it's cash I've already spent on stuff long forgotten. But given my level of food ingestion, car rental, and associated bushwah, it usually represents a tidy chunk. I love to open it and, you know, stare at it for a while.

I love the whole Christmas season, when you can go out for lunch and come back merry to the point of incoherence; and indolent summer Fridays, when the only guys who punish lack of productivity are heading to the beach in their company Acuras.

And the big days. One Friday: I complete a breakfast boardroom presentation on the cost of nonconformance to requirements, which generates inchoate murmurs and the call for a follow-up report (Yes!); at 11:00, the chairman has his meeting with security analysts, for which I helped prepare him, and not once is the word undervalued mentioned; lunch with Wineum, Shineum Blather, our ad agency, the content of which I cannot remember; an hour spent with the Acquisitions Task Force, where decisions are made that could engorge the size of our revenue base and cost thousands of innocent people their jobs; annual-report numbers reiterated on deadline during typical bogus conference call with national sales staff (good squawk box); at 5:00, crisis blasts in by fax from Solid Fuel Group needing data on why pollution is good; half hour of electronic paper shuffling, leading to one brief slam-and-run with the chairman and out.

And finally, yes, I love that last martini of the week, all sweaty and frosty. My train awaits crosstown, huffing in the station. Let it wait. The gin is cold. The olives are salty. Just outside the bar, my skyscraper rears up, a smattering of fluorescent lights glimmering in the workaholic twilight. I loosen my wing tips, take an unfettered breath, look out the window and, you know, stare at it for a while.

Now, that's what I call living. Or something very much like it.

1989

Running from the Wolves

Hey! No! Don't eat me!

. . . Wow. What time is it? Three in the morning—again. Be still, heart. No point in bursting a ventricle. It was only a dream. The same dream for two nights in a row, maybe more. Who knows, with dreams?

I am running, running. Something is pursuing me. I look around and realize I am at the zoo—a zoo a bit like the Central Park Zoo in New

York City, which is about half a mile from my office. Say, I wonder if that means anything. At this zoo, however, it seems none of the animals are in cages. That's fine when it comes to the zebras, tripping gaily by in the middle distance. And I don't mind the odd gibbon gamboling in the bushes near that fire hydrant, scratching him- or herself.

But right behind me are what I think are wolves. I can feel the moist heat of their breath wilting the back of my summer-weight, pinstriped suit jacket, smell the rotting meat of previous victims on their teeth. They are chasing me quite seriously. If I slow down for even a nonosecond, they will pounce on me and bite me very hard, and it won't be nice at all. I am terrified. My heart pounds and every extremity in my body is seized with a massive weakness. And yet I continue to run, run. Because I am not only running away from the wolves . . . I'm also running toward something, looking for someone . . . very important. I know, it's my kids! They're at the zoo, too! Animals are out that might eat them! Help! Help!

And then I woke up. And here we are. Enough of this foolishness! I have three meetings before lunch, and a really bad lunch, too . . . with Milton Lassiter. Why did I agree to this? Milton Lassiter is going to wear me out with his industry-nabob routine. I won't be able to drink, even, because there's a two o'clock with Don, Bob, Ed, Ned, and Toby. Bad lunch . . . what a horrible concept. It should be the ultimate oxymoron. Still, there is veal.

What am I yammering about? I've got to get back to sleep! Have to relax. Think relaxing thoughts.

I wonder if Grabowski likes me. Sometimes I think he might not. Why not? I'm a likable guy. I'm affable. But is affable a good thing? Of how many really successful guys do you say, "Boy, is he affable!"? You don't. You think other things: "Boy, is he brilliant!" Or "Boy, is he vain!" Or a host of other enormous, dynamic personal qualities that help to define the intransigent self that lies at the core of true business genius. So what does affable buy you? Nothing. I'm wasting my time with it. It's not impactful in the near term. What the hell am I talking about? I'm daydreaming, that's what, instead of . . . going to sleep!

Got to calm down. Almost without volition, my body gets up. I've got to break the grip of this obsessive night-brain munching. There is nothing worse than being awake in bed for more than five minutes in the middle of the night. So I'm not in bed anymore. I'm downstairs.

My, how dark the street is at this hour. There is nobody out there at all. Why should there be? Anyone sane is sleeping now. The house is very quiet. The children are asleep in their little beds. They look so peaceful and secure, their hands folded underneath their tiny cheeks, visions of material acquisitions dancing in their heads. I hate it when I don't get to spend enough time with them. I've only got a couple more years before they won't be caught dead in my company. That's why the next two months are going to be so hard. First Phoenix, for the Marketing meeting with Beiber and his crew, one complete Saturday shot to hell. Why does he always have these things on the weekend? Saves a couple bucks on the room rates and airfares. Suppose that's laudable. Phooey on it anyway. Then three separate major gatherings in Los Angeles, one right after the other. All the money saved in Phoenix spent on travel to someplace 95 percent of those attending have no desire to see ever again, and aren't anywhere near. One of these meetings is right on my son's birthday. That will go over really big with the little fellow. Maybe I don't have to go. I'll ask Bob. Bob's a nice guy. Bob will understand.

I wonder if Bob likes me.

Of course Bob likes me! What kind of thoughts are these? Three-in-the-morning kind of thoughts, that's what. I'm going to go upstairs and get back into bed . . . and just lie there. No. Not yet. Fred the cocker spaniel is sitting next to me while I stand by the window regarding the streetlamps. He is staring at me, his head slightly cocked to one side. He is hoping for a biscuit at this odd, alternative hour. Will he like me if I don't give him one? Man. How far gone am I? I'm wondering if my own dog likes me. I want everyone to like me, that's the thing. Sometimes money will do it. But you can't give a dog money. You have to give a dog love. People like love, too. But money is easier to give sometimes.

Except I can't give Kroger that raise she wants. She just had a review four months ago, and HR is beginning to think I spend money like a drunken sailor. I have to be restrained. What if I lose her? That would be terrible. I'd have to manage the entire Summer Bratwurst Festival myself! I can't do that. I don't know the first thing about it. Did I say bratwurst? It's not bratwurst . . . it's . . . something else . . . can't think what. Can't . . . think at all.

I'm on the couch now. That must mean I'm going to read for a little while. Here is my book. It's a good book. I wonder whodunit. Actually, who cares whodunit? I don't. As long as I didn't do it, I'm okay with whatever happens. Maybe that's why I like it. What happens if we acquire BXR in August, when my vacation is scheduled? That would be a disaster. My wife is really looking forward to that trip to Montana. I wonder if while we're there we'll be held hostage by neofascist militarists. At the very least, I wonder if we'll fit in. They don't necessarily take to corporate senior vice presidents in the Old West where the outdoors is as big as all outdoors. I hope we have fun. I hope it costs less than $10,000. Why is my office smaller than Mulroney's? I report to the big guy. He doesn't.

I notice I'm not reading. This is ridiculous. I should get off this couch and go upstairs to sleep. It's 4 A.M. What is that I hear? Birds? Shut up, birds!

Okay—I'm back in bed now. Tomorrow morning I'm going to be a blob of burbling protoplasm. Tricks I plan to implement to stay viable: Get up and rub my face to keep from nodding off; walk around the room, looking extraordinarily serious during meetings; draw portraits of Coogan, who has one of those faces. Faces. Many faces to see in the next forty-eight hours. Big faces. Little faces. Faces in between. Faces with huge skulls and no hair. Huge protuberances of bone where their foreheads used to be. Big, mean faces on all fours and massive racks of horns leveled at anyone who comes into their path. They're pawing the ground! They're putting down their heads! They're chasing me around the zoo!

Hey! No! Don't butt my butt!

Oh, well. I guess it beats being awake.

1996

Stress Busters for Busy Execs

Hi! Got stress? Bet you don't need it. Gives you a headache. Makes you cranky. Doesn't help you work at all. Fortunately, there are a host of highly effective solutions that top executives carry in their bulging pockets all the time. When they need 'em, they pull 'em out and whammo! You can do the same—if you've got the tools. Here are all you'll ever need:

Get a mantra. A totemic word, repeated until it blocks out all others, can be a one-way ticket to a mental institution. But in the right hands, a little mysticism applied directly to where it hurts ya just might open your personal doorway to focus and repose. First, find yourself a small enclosure where no one dares to enter. Every bathroom has one. Now . . . close your eyes . . . concentrate . . . breathe in, breathe out . . . and obsessively repeat your mantra to yourself. Say only that word. Channel your entire aura into it until it obliterates all reality but your internal one. Feels good, huh? Any word will do. You might start out like most of us did with that old clunker "Om." Personally, I've found the word "kill" to have incredible restorative power. A couple of minutes letting that baby drum into my skull and I'm ready to hit the ground hard, and do what needs to be done.

Visualization is the acid of the nineties. So tune in, even if you can't do the other two things. The human imagination is a wonderful tool. Use it for more than generating next month's theme for the controller's conference. Just take a second to project what you want the future to be in your own mind—see it—then go and live there. Maniac puce-headed hoopster Dennis Rodman, for instance, imagines himself guarding every member of the opposing team, then goes out on the floor and lets his vision unfold. And it does. Or at least that's what he tells us in his new, best-selling book. Do you think he imagined every person in America buying his book? I bet he did! And so they are! So can you, except instead of visualizing yourself as Dennis Rodman, see yourself as You—waiting for Leonard Brush the budget muncher to finish his presentation on internal synergies, then rising to your feet to puncture his specious argument and retain your cost structure. Imagine him hanging from his tasteless club tie in the freight elevator! The future is as big or small as your dream. Don't think tiny.

Work your body. If God had meant us to sit at desks all day, blabbing on the phone and cramming down inexpensive meat sandwiches, he would have made us huge invertebrates with dappled green skin and suction cups for mouths. All right, so maybe you are. But still, every day, no matter what's going on, take fifteen to twenty minutes to get your heart rate up to the point where it can be measured by an EKG from ten to twelve feet away. Getting a phone call from the chairman doesn't count; fright is not cardiac exercise. And no, you don't need to belong to some club that would have you—or, even worse, your management consultant, Lutz—as a member. Just find any old staircase and walk up and down on it until you feel your heart about to leap out of your chest and your temples straining to pop from your skull. Still concerned about the slight premonition you've been feeling about receivables in the near term? I bet not!

Drink a lot of wine. I was reading the other day about people in Assyria, back when the wheel was invented, basically, who discovered how to plant grapes and immediately started out imbibing wine in large quantities. Believe me, those people felt less tension at work than we do. That's why busy executives, at the end of a day, often drink quarts of the stuff to replenish their mental juices and get back that feeling of bonhomie that's so much a part of their personal powerbank. The good thing about wine is that, unlike hard liquor, it's not really a drink at all, actually. It's more of a food, sort of, with lots of frisky vitamins and minerals. Apply it liberally to your stress zones, and watch 'em melt away.

Get out of touch. Physically as well as mentally. The cellular world stinks. Did you know that one of the guys who died recently on Mount Everest had just called a couple of people on his cellular phone? Isn't that depressing? This thing has gotten way out of hand. Toss away your beepers! Let your batteries run down! Let the world know that there are times when you cannot be reached!

Scream at people, if you can. At the same time you're asserting your human rights, strip others of theirs. This is one of the big perks of truly stressed-out people. Wait until you're ready to molt out of your skin, then find somebody weaker than you and bark at him for a while. Sometimes a small "woof" may do the trick. But on Fridays at 4 P.M., when everybody decides it's time to pass along all remaining issues to you, nothing less than a full-scale "bow-wow-wow," complete with growls and occasional snapping noises, will do.

Obsess yourself. Ultimately, however, these lifestyle choices, while vitiating much low-level stress, cannot be nearly as effective as full-blown business fixation, which is possibly the most effective palliative of all. Nothing can help you arrive at your destination more efficiently than inappropriate grandiosity—a really enormous idea that replaces eating, drinking, exercise, mantras, the whole schmeer. Okay, if you're not Carl Icahn, you can't buy Tasmania. But every business person, no matter how small or crushed by anxiety, can dream. Keep in mind that this is true, narcissistic, overweening ambition you're reaching for, some object so huge and unattainable you'd have to be either out of your mind to want it, or a genius. Once you've settled on your acquisition target, let nothing stand in your way. Think only about It. Plan in detail for It. Torment your subordinates with preparations for It.

Surround yourself with people you trust who know what you need. Now that you're focused, it's essential to sweep all impedimenta aside. That means hiring staff who will anticipate your needs. Soften the edges on things a little. Take out your dry cleaning. Get you a soda when you're thirsty. Torch a rain forest if that's required, so you don't have to. Find those people. Then shut everyone else out. After a while your stress will be just a tiny little whisper behind the great façade of calm you have built around yourself.

Grow your fingernails and hair very long and don't come out of your office except maybe once a day, when it's dark out and nobody will get in your face. It doesn't hurt to line your office with cork either. Cork keeps out noise and dust. Dust is really bad, too. Dust has germs in it. There are billions of germs out there that can make you sick and cut down on your peace of mind and productivity. Doorknobs have germs on them. Spoons? Teeming with them. All those bacilli. Crawling over things. Causing . . . stress. Get rid of them. Now.

There. We've done it. Eliminated stress from our lives. And it hasn't been all that difficult, has it? In a world full of disorder, we've taken a few simple steps to put things in place, where they can be anticipated, handled, controlled. Yeah. Control is what it's all about. Control eradicates stress. Must maintain control. No surprises. So we can go about our business calmly, in a focused fashion, without, you know, going nuts. And we don't want to go nuts. Do we.

1996

Being and Nothingness

Usually, something's up. We are going somewhere. We are scheduled to arrive. The agenda is on. The train is waiting. The kids are in the car. The alarm has rung. The rooster has crowed. The day's a-wasting. Get a move on. Maximize.

That's the way we want it, of course. What would we be without the requirements that shape us? Who would we be? Quite often I lie abed for seconds at a time in the morning, waiting for the first sharp pang of obligation to set in. When it hits, I rise, knowing what I have to do. What would it be like to be without that? To not have to be somewhere? To sit in a hotel lobby over a cup of coffee and a newspaper with no watch on? To wander alone through the streets of an alien city, without anyone to meet, anything to do for the next several hours, free of the need to be clever, or incisive, or decisive?

I just got back from New Orleans. While I was there, I had an opportunity to come face-to-face with the nothingness, and it was sweet. I almost missed it, though. Nothingness is fragile. The smallest wind can blow it away. Who knows when, once rejected, it will come again?

My trip began well. I flew alone, in sneakers and jeans, and did not bring my briefcase. Yes, I had some papers in a legal folder, I think more out of guilt than anything else, but I dispatched those early. No, I did not bury my nose in *Vegetable Times* or *FiberOpticon* or *Extrude,* or any of the mandatory reading material of my traveling group. I just read a book for a while. Then I slept.

I awoke as the airplane descended, feeling strangely like myself. I realized what the difference was. I didn't have my face on. I often go about without my face on, but rarely in a public place where I might be seen without it, which can be dangerous. First, you might be forced to conduct an encounter without it, the other party free to plunge willy-nilly into your naked persona without any mediation. Just as bad is the possibility of another human being's having the opportunity to observe you putting your face on from scratch. That's ugly, too. Fortunately, there was nobody around to see me sitting there without my face on. So I left it off. After a while, I forgot I wasn't wearing it.

When I arrived in New Orleans, I realized that I had neglected to ask Sally to book a pompous limousine that reinforced my bogus executive image. I took a ratty cab instead. I opened the window and smelled the air, which was interesting, because it smelled like something . . . soft and wet and green. Little, low houses with grand porticos lined the highway. I wondered who lived there.

I leaned back and thought about what I had to do. There were several important meetings that had to be attended over the course of the next few days. No decisions would be required. I would preside. When I was not granting legitimacy to the proceedings simply by my presence, I would be off duty. I let the idea that I had nothing to be anxious about descend on me. I did not shake it off.

I was now ready, my spirit poised on the brink of the nothingness. I looked inside, but did not jump. Perhaps I wasn't small enough to get through to it yet.

The next day I took a walk with my pal Allenby. I caught up with him accessing e-mail like a dervish in the office we had set up in the hotel. "Let's get out of here and grab a bite," I said. "I'm coming," he said, bent over the keyboard of the laptop. It took me forty minutes to get him out of there. We strode down the street in great executive strides that ate up the pavement before us. "I've been working for seven days straight," Allenby said, his serious face bent to the pavement, his brow working at the job of getting away for a few minutes. "I have to tell myself, It's all right that we do this! This is fine! We owe ourselves! Right?"

I told him, "Right." I felt it then for the first time, walking with my buddy on a little expedition to nowhere. Me, very small, very free, in the big, wide world, with nothingness all around me. It was a strange, weightless feeling, not bad. I let it hang there. I didn't push it. I could sense something within me rising up to meet it, and I wanted to make it come faster, but that's a loser's game. You can't hurry nothingness.

That afternoon, after a meeting on the interface between marketing and product management in the field, I went back to my room and channel-surfed for a couple of hours. After that, my mind was completely empty. It was nice. I felt a little lonely, but called no one. I looked out the window at the city instead.

At dinner, and at the parties afterward, I had my face on, but not so tightly that I couldn't breathe. I drank, but not enough to hurt myself and kill the nothingness. A hangover is the apotheosis of something.

I finally got there on the last day out. I went to bed early the night before—about one. I left a wake-up call for eight the next morning and was out on the quiet streets a little after nine. I didn't do much. I walked into a real bookstore, the kind that smells like dust and old paper and has no eight-foot-tall, two-dimensional statue of John Grisham. Down the street I found a record store with nothing but vinyl. I poked through it. Didn't buy anything. Nobody noticed me. I felt tiny. It was good.

After that, I went to the airport. I had an hour or so to wait until plane time. I wasn't hungry. I had no messages to return. Most of my associates were on planes of their own, unreachable. I would see my family in a couple of hours. I stood there in the middle of all that nothing, and an enormous bolt of lightness smashed into me. I didn't know it was coming. I let it go through me. After a while it receded a bit, but I still felt like singing. So I did. Nobody heard me, I don't think, but it didn't matter. Nothing did.

Now I'm home, and the kids have a tennis lesson in a couple of minutes. My wife wants to look at a new floor lamp at the mall, since we've decided that halogen lamps aren't safe. I have a couple of calls to make to people who are sorry to bother me at home but are doing so anyway. What can I tell you? I'm back.

Still, a residue of nothingness continues to warm me like a tiny coal in the bottom of a grate. Whenever I can seek it out again, I will. Although I know you can't actually make it happen, I do believe it's possible to be receptive and to place yourself in locations that draw nothingness to themselves like a magnet. I've been thinking about Los Angeles sometime in March, just as the development season goes into full swing. I've got no good reason not to go.

1997

The Spirit Is Willing

A few weeks ago I was watching television, attempting to fill the aching spiritual void between dinner and the end of the millennium. I was watching the news, because nothing fills an aching void as well as news, except perhaps for game shows.

On the news I saw a large group of men hollering and hugging each other. There were tears in their eyes, and their hearts seemed to be full to bursting. Amazingly, it was not a group of NFL linebackers celebrating a touchdown as if they'd never got one before. That happens every Sunday. It was a group called the Promise Keepers, and they were giving support to each other in a very manly and spiritual way. Boy, I thought. No aching voids there.

As I wound my watch at bedtime, I lay back and felt the emptiness. I have nothing in my life that generates that kind of spiritual heat, I thought. And so many around me do. Why am I left out? And how can I get some?

I started with Buddhism. I've noticed many influential people are gravitating to it these days. Steven Seagal, the bad actor, was recently named a holy man by the Dalai Lama's people in Los Angeles, enabling him to channel the spirits of ancient departed masters and also raise money. Richard Gere, of course, was in on the whole thing way before anybody else, but now you rarely see an entertainer who isn't hugging some Lama or other at a chic benefit for Tibet hosted by Brad Pitt and his agent. I'd like to be with those people. So I tried to catch the Buddhist wave for a couple of days. It didn't really work. You have to sit for hours and hours and think about nothing. I normally get paid for that. And there are no guarantees such contemplation will pay off in anything more than a certain quiet satisfaction. Me, I'm looking for ecstasy. So I moved on.

For a while, I looked into Science, because there's a new series on PBS with Stephen Hawking that everybody is supposed to get into. I tried to read a book of his once about space and time, and ended up staring out a window, semiconscious, for more than an hour afterward. So I had high hopes. But that, too, failed, when I fell asleep during a discussion of quarks.

Next I tried to worship myself. I've always been a pretty fair hand at this, but I've never gone at it rigorously, the way you do with a genuine creed, with rituals and stuff. I began by eating all the right things, which I hated immediately. Then I started attempting to exercise on a daily basis, because I have heard that it is possible, in the high concentration achieved in the middle of a strenuous workout, to achieve moments of spiritual release, as opposed to a shooting pain in the side. I realized that given my busy schedule, the only time I would have to reach for the inner peace that comes with intense physical activity was at lunch. I thought about that.

I went to lunch instead. Perhaps there my soul would find peace and contentment and, dare I say it, release? It was possible. I went where I generally go, a place where all of the semi-important make themselves known to one another. At every table, a fatuous nabob preened. I sat myself amongst them, and was comfortable. I looked about me. At every table, a bottle bloomed. In each bottle was . . . fizzy water at $8 the quart. Nobody was drinking alcohol! An entire roomful of self-admiring people, all of them sober. Bah. None of us would leave here full of spirits, either figuratively or literally. I had the duck. It beat a sharp stick in the eye, but a numinous experience it wasn't.

I had another thought. Years ago there were those around me—in our sales and manufacturing divisions, primarily—who worshiped Quality. They read about Excellence, and studied the impact of Deming on the Japanese, and they held Quality Improvement Team meetings that looked very much like those of the Promise Keepers. Perhaps there were still some remaining embers of that once-bright fire, secluded ashrams of devotees practicing their arcana in private? I went looking, and I'll be darned. I found them. There were several dozen of them on the fifteenth floor. All of them were accountants. Each was engaged in zero-basing somebody else's department.

"What are you guys doing around here?" I asked.

"Cutting costs," said their leader. I got out of there fast.

I tried immersing myself in the company. There are people who do. They get a deep, warm glow whenever they enter the building, or use the letterhead, or brandish a business card: It is a mixture of pride and ambition for the common good. I must admit I did achieve a small buzz here, particularly on days the stock went up. But it didn't stay with me very well, possibly because worshiping the company doesn't take up much of the day. There's plenty of time left over to be spiritually bank-rupt. I hated that.

After that, I was in free fall. Money. Sex. Red wine. Ray-Bans. I tried them all. They were fun while they lasted. But as a spiritual path? Forget about it.

Then I found something. And of course, it was right at hand. I was riding up in the elevator one afternoon as the leaves were turning, and I ran into Zepp, the head of Management Information Systems.

"How ya doon?" I said to him.

"In the year 2000," he replied, "there will be a disaster like none the earth has ever seen. Computers will crash when they fail to recognize the turn of the clock at midnight! Elevators will tumble! The earth as we know it will grind to a halt!"

"We don't have much time, then," I said.

"We'll be all right if we all work together," he replied, and, grabbing my elbow, he forced me off the elevator at his floor. Down the corridor I found a group of wizened gnomes huddled over a computer monitor. "It is the end of days!" said one with hair in all the wrong places. "But if we all pull together and work very hard, we can make sure this com-pany is in Year 2000 compliance by the turn of the century."

So that's what I'm doing. It feels right. I've got myself a pair of glasses with tape on the bridge, and I'm digging right in. Did you know that all knowledge as we know it could be wiped out unless answers are found and implemented? We've got just two years until all hell breaks loose, and I don't want to be there if we're not in compliance. The alternative is too grim to think about.

1997

Does Your Job Make You Sick?

There are a lot of obnoxious people around. I'm sure you've noticed it. When you try to walk past them fast on the sidewalk, they go slow, to the point where you have to elbow them roughly into the gutter just to get ahead of them to the next Don't Walk sign. At gatherings, they fail to introduce you with alacrity, leading you to suspect that they might be having trouble remembering your name. When you ask them, before a critical presentation, whether your hair looks all right, they tell you, "No, it does not." What is wrong with such people? Today, startling news comes from the world of pseudoscience indicating that the instigators of such social atrocities are not, in fact, jerks. It turns out they suffer from a variety of diseases that afflict those of our class, ilk, and job description, and therefore are more to be pitied than censured. Cures for these conditions are doubtful, since research is in its pre-infancy. This is bad news for me, because I have most of them.

Party aphasia: This one is truly horrible. You are at a gathering of friends, or perhaps on the street with somebody whose name you should know. Your wife, say. Your boss. You come face-to-face with another human being who is well known to you. Your mother, perhaps. A split second before you are about to introduce the two, you find that you cannot for the life of you come up with either of their names. You look into the databank and . . . zzzp. This happened to me only last week. I was with my wife at a cocktail reception and we ran into a former associate of mine who is now more important than myself. I stood there like a fire hydrant. Was he Jack or Ralph? Perhaps he was Ned! What if I said the wrong name? Was that worse than saying no name? By the time I came up with the requisite information, he was across the room with another person more important than I. They were looking at me. "Thanks for introducing me," said my wife. She was not happy.

Post-dialing amnesia: This happened to me only yesterday. You dial the phone and it begins to ring. While it's ringing, you get involved in some requisition form or something. Before you know it, somebody answers . . . and you can't remember who you were calling. "Hello!"

you say into the phone. "Yes?" says the party on the other end of the line. If it's a friend, you can say, "Who are you?" and explain that you are not a nitwit, you are a victim of this new syndrome you read about in *Fortune*. If, however, it is Mr. Roover, who has no sense of humor, you simply have to hang up, muttering excuses. And if the recipient has caller ID, you're likely to be further humiliated when he or she calls back to humiliate you. At this time there is no cure short of retirement, when phone calls are made primarily to your druggist.

Bad positioning: This happened to me just last week. I was at a big meeting on the 175th floor. It was crowded, with so many gigantic egos in the room it was tough to find a pocket of oxygen to breathe. I found myself near the door, engaged in conversation with Bob Lazenby, who's the kind of guy who plants himself in a good spot and then commands it like a field marshal. I unfortunately found myself directly in front of the double doors that granted egress from the festivities. I didn't want to terminate the conversation because it was likely to be the most important one I had that day. Bob is big. But every time I tried to move to a more advantageous location in the room, Bob refused to follow, and showed signs of engaging Mortimer, who would love to ace me out of just such a conversation. Consequently, I was in everybody's way and felt like a doofus.

E-logorrhea: I have this one bad, and I'm sure you do, too. All day, every day, on the e-mail, yakkety yak, blah blah blah, wogga wogga wogga. Last night I missed my train when I got into a "thank you" and "don't mention it" orgy with Blaubert. Neither of us wanted to relinquish the final messaging rights and come back the next morning with a residual message that needed to be answered. So every time I'd put on my coat, my message indicator would pop up and I'd have to sit down and get off that last reply to Blaubert. What a loser!

Ugg: Now spreading among mid-level executives who have been on the circuit for more than a decade, this condition is best described as an excess of refined taste. It strikes at corporate gatherings where sociability is expected and a lusty good time is mandatory. Individuals have reported a sudden inability to eat even one more greasy, fatty, overly salted lump of something on a cracker. I'm happy to say I don't have this yet.

Scrutability: In this career-killing malady, the victim loses the ability to generate insincerity, revealing his true thoughts and feelings for all to see and comment upon. People say, "How're you doing?" and he tells them. They ask, "Do you like my new hairdo/marketing plan/husband?" And before an appropriately managed sub-truth can be filtered from the many possible answers, out blurts the unprocessed raw material. I hate this quality in other people, since I consider truth management to be what separates us from the lower apes. So I'm proud to say it's happened to me only once or twice, and then only with junior subordinates where no consequences were involved, and that's it.

F.O.: The initials are a polite designation standing for the unspeakable—Failure Odor. It's a simple but incurable condition that afflicts fully 10 percent of the executive population at any one time. It begins blandly enough, with a mild musty scent that hangs around the individual like bad aftershave. "What is that?" people ask. And then, after a while, the answer comes. "It's Dropkin." "Oh," people say. And they leave it alone. In stage two, the smell grows ranker, and unmistakable. People no longer ask; they just steer clear, because F.O. is quite communicable. I was seen talking to Dropkin last week, and a bit of his F.O. almost rubbed off on me! I won't be making that mistake again!

Disinclination: Boy, there's a lot of this going around. Patients report a general lack of willingness to do anything specific, and most everything in general. The good news is that for the most part there are no serious side effects over the short haul, and senior managers have reported cases that went on for years and resulted in nothing more than several promotions.

In fact, I've got it right now. And you know what? I'm done!

1999

The Mourning After

The commuter trains are running on schedule, and after two full days of looking at the carnage and at the courage of the people who live and work in this city, I am once again doing my extremely unimportant part of returning life to normal. But of course there is no normal. Not yet. Maybe not ever. At 8:46 we will arrive at Grand Central Station, one of the most beautiful public structures in the world, and suddenly infinitely more precious than it was a few days ago.

On Tuesday, September 11, just as I do every day, I reached street level at 8:48, the exact time that the first jet full of innocent people was slamming into the World Trade Center. It was quiet where I was, four miles uptown from the fire, the smoke, the screaming. A crowd of people stood at the monitors that fill the window of the Chase Bank on the corner of Forty-eighth. Nobody was talking. On the multiple screens, one of the two towers was burning. A plume of black smoke was billowing upward into a beautifully blue late-summer sky. A light breeze was blowing, and a hint of autumn crispness was in the air.

I walked into the middle of the avenue and stood in the street, looking south. From uptown and down, east and west, in the distance and nearer by, sirens faded in and out. An ambulance whizzed by. I turned north and started my short walk to the office. I'm supposed to be at my desk by a little after nine, and I owed the chairman a call at that time whose subject seems so unimportant now that I wonder why we generally care about what we do at all. I didn't want to be late, at any rate. I fished out my cell phone and speed-dialed my secretary. "Dialing," said my StarTAC, then nothing. My BlackBerry, too, was dead. It occurred to me that there were quite a few transponders on top of the World Trade Center.

About halfway to my building, which is about forty stories high, I noticed people crying in the street. At 9:05 a woman screamed, and I turned and saw a second mushroom of red and yellow flame belch from the side of the other tower. I watched it for a while and then kept walking. Walking seemed the thing to do.

A few years ago, after my dad died, I found myself seeing him in crowds, in shadows. I wanted him to be there, but he was not. And still I saw him in those random places. Until, one day, I didn't anymore, and then I knew he was well and truly gone.

Now I found myself wondering, as I walked through crowds of people standing inert on the sidewalks, if this World Trade Center thing was going to change the agenda for the day. We have a lot going on in our business right now. This is the start of our new season, and you don't want a lot of extraneous stuff to distract the public in the middle of that, you know.

I got to my office and noticed folks congregated in the hallway. They were crying and appeared to feel that they themselves might be in danger. I found that this idea surprised me, and a little worm of fright poked its head out of my consciousness. Danger? Here? I went to my office and called home.

I couldn't get a dial tone. It's one thing for cells to be down, but land lines? I turned on the television set in my office. On one side of the split screen, the left tower of the World Trade Center was collapsing into itself with thousands of people still inside. Could that be possible? On the other side of the screen the Pentagon was burning.

People began coming into my office uninvited. This is not an unusual thing—my door is always open—but it was not . . . normal. They didn't knock. A few young women were weeping. The guys were trying to look tough, but failing. I was aware that I suddenly didn't feel very managerial. I called my home again. "I'm sorry," said a recording, and I hung up.

People were jumping off the World Trade Center. A tiny body was falling, headfirst, from an unimaginable height. Then the right tower coughed up a puff of noxious smoke and ash and with a great groan disintegrated, live on TV. There were shots of terrified people running from the blast. "On any given day," the television said, "some 200,000 people work in or visit the World Trade Center complex."

We watched with that creepy sense of both observing and living in a part of history. "What's going to happen to Morgan Stanley?" said a friend of mine. "They have twenty-five floors in one of those towers."

I had to get out of the city. There is a car service that operates out of the space in front of our building. Five of us were going north, and although we heard that the bridges were closing, we got the last car out. On the way home we drove through the working-class neighborhood where my grandfather had a candy store and my mother grew up. Everything was still standing. In fact, the area looked a bit better than it had in the '70s and '80s, when a lot of it was gutted and burning and given up for lost.

It is now the day after the morning after. I am sitting in a train absolutely full of people headed back to work. They are reading, talking. The smoke and exploded sheetrock is still swirling above the common grave that was once the World Trade Center. New York has requested 6,000 body bags from the federal government.

The chairman of Morgan Stanley was shown on the news last night, addressing his employees over a teleconference. He did well, and spoke of going on, of how things aren't as bad as they first thought they might be. He seemed to be crying, but you can't really tell these things on video sometimes. Today they are reporting that that firm lost perhaps forty of its 3,700 people who worked in the building.

The newspaper is full of obituaries. On the radio three children were talking about their father, who was on the 102nd floor of one of the towers. They talked in high-pitched, wounded little voices until, choked with grief and the injustice of their loss, they could not go on. More than our skyline is changed forever.

Buildings can be rebuilt. Grief, as incredible as it may seem to those who have been hit hardest, will pass, even if it never entirely goes away. As time works its inevitable magic, life will poke its sturdy head up through the rubble.

But some things will not return to the way they were before. They say the ultimate goal of terror is to create not just fear in the enemy, but the same kind of atavistic hatred in the adversary that produced the act itself, the desire to abandon all pretense of humanity, to move forward blindly to destroy the object of one's animosity. If that is true, our assailants, who believe they act with the approval of their God, have succeeded far beyond their dreams.

This nation has an astonishing ability to transcend the unthinkable and move on. Whether that is good or bad I leave to you. But some things, I think, should never be transcended.

2001

I Lø(ea)ve New York

Last week I was walking down Sixth Avenue at lunchtime, and I saw about 700 people in the street. Everybody was looking up at one of the big office towers, necks craning, mouths open.

"What's up?" I asked a guy on a cell phone.

"Bomb scare," he said. He looked bored.

I don't want to live here anymore. I wish I felt differently. But I don't. So now I'm sort of thinking about alternatives.

Maybe a small town would make a good home for my family, a little village like the one that Ma and Pa Kent raised young Clark in. I grew up in one of those. It was nice. Movies were thirty-five cents at the Alceon Theater. The librarian knew all our names. It was flat there in Illinois, which meant that you could get on your bike and be at the other end of town in five minutes. In the fall we burned leaves in garbage cans, and the sweet, tangy smell filled the air from one corner of town to the other. Of course, this little burg was outside Chicago, where the Sears Tower looms over Lake Michigan, and only half an hour from O'Hare, the busiest airport in the world. That's not far enough away. Not by half.

I could find a really teeny-weeny village, I suppose, far from strip malls and the stench of the city. I'm sure they would like me there. I could be a pharmacist, if I learned that trade, or cut hair at the barbershop, or work for the local newspaper, and eventually people would come to accept me, the way I look, and talk, and dress somewhat differently from everybody else around, no matter how hard I try, and come to view me as a part of the community the way people do in small towns . . . after fifty or sixty years.

I should probably look at cities, right?

Los Angeles is the first one that comes to mind. I love Los Angeles when I am there. Of course, there's a possibility that I wouldn't be living in the Four Seasons Hotel on Doheny as I do when I visit now. I would probably have to buy a house of some sort. I saw a million-dollar home in Beverly Hills not long ago. It reminded me of a cottage my parents rented on the Jersey shore when I was a kid, only it was smaller. And then there's the fact that everybody in Los Angeles is sort of in show business in one way or another and the effect that has on their minds . . . and you sort of have to take into consideration that one day Los Angeles could be on a very large island just off the coast of Las Vegas. . . . All in all . . .

Miami is nice. It has a booming economy, I hear. There are many elderly people there, living out their days in ice-cold air-conditioning, mall-walking for exercise perhaps three times a week, but I wouldn't find much to do with them beyond that. Our mealtimes rarely coincide. Miami also boasts a large and flamboyant South Beach scene, but I was there once and felt out of place with no iguana on my shoulder.

Then there is Pittsburgh. I've spent quite a bit of time in Pittsburgh, because the headquarters of my dead corporation was there. I drank at Froggy's, which served an entire water glass full of Scotch as a matter of course. I've stayed at the Hilton and stared at the glowing red Westinghouse sign across the river, and treated six hungry businessmen to a steak dinner for $87. I've had meetings in conference rooms looking over the point where the Allegheny and the Ohio join to meet the mighty Monongahela. The green hills stretch out away from Pittsburgh over the fields of Pennsylvania where the Three Mile Island nuclear power plant sits, pregnant with uranium.

All right, then, what could be better than Boston? I enjoyed the ten years I spent there long ago. Met my wife and got married there. I was poor and drove a cab to make ends meet. I would get in at 5:30 A.M. in the garage near Fenway Park—the same garage frequented, it turns out, by several of the hijackers who lived in the city for years—and drive all day to places like Foxboro, Roxbury, Lincoln, and Medford. By the end of the shift, tired but happy, I would clear between forty and sixty bucks. Did you hear that bin Laden's brother lives in the Boston area? Or was it his sister? Whatever, right?

Seattle is very nice, although with the pop of the dot-com bubble perhaps not quite so prosperous and crammed with opportunity as one could hope. I could go there and live on one of those little islands you see in Meg Ryan movies, take a water shuttle to work at a funky little startup company where the biggest decision is what blend of coffee to send out for in the morning. It's a terrific city. I would love to go there. But I won't.

Why not Dallas? Or for that matter Monterey? Or wait—Atlanta! I haven't even considered Atlanta! Or Bridgeport or Rockport or Big Sky, Montana, or Fond du Lac, Wisconsin? What about them? People live there happily. Why shouldn't I?

Or . . . Canada! Yes. Let's get serious . . . in a tiny little cottage at the edge of the woods. A crystal river chuckles by against its banks. Birds twitter in the enormous pines that tower above our quiet home. On Sunday the wife and I get dressed up in our best outfits and head into town for the special dinner at the restaurant. They have pie for dessert, homemade pie. Afterward we take in a movie and then head back to crank up the satellite dish. The silence all around us stretches for miles. The air is as clean as God makes it. And aside from the odd French separatist here and there, there isn't an angry person within 1,000 miles.

Yeah. I might do that.

Last night I went to a cocktail party at the Century Club on Forty-third Street. As I walked down Sixth Avenue to get there, mountebanks were selling American flags and pins and World Trade Center T-shirts with America Fights Back! emblazoned below the Twin Towers. "Check it out, check it out!" they said, as if they were selling hot watches. People were smiling. They were also buying.

The Century Club is a nice old Victorian place, with elderly carpets, a lot of dark wood, and bad art donated by generous members. The room we were in was a large one, and drinks and canapés were being consumed in mass quantities. As always, people seemed to like the deep-fried stuff the best. There was nothing healthy on the menu, but for some reason that didn't seem a consideration all of a sudden. There were toasts for the honoree of the occasion, and a lot of hugging, and a fair amount of air kissing, and even a few tears, as one sees these days, and still more drinks, and then it was eight o'clock, suddenly, and a bunch of us went out to dinner. We stayed pretty late and talked about a lot of subjects, including a few unrelated to our present difficulties.

The restaurant was relatively empty, but nobody seemed too concerned. Time moves on. Things will change. It will come back.

2001

The Importance of Irrelevance

The days are getting shorter. I looked out the window at 5:30 today and realized that the sun had long since departed. I had to call Office Services and remind them to replace the fluorescents I'd allowed to burn out during the days when there was too much light all day long. Maybe I'll requisition a desk lamp and turn on that more humane source of illumination when dusk begins its shadow dance around the edges of my office. That would be nice. But when you come to think about it, dark . . . light . . .

It really doesn't matter. Does it? What do you think?

Becky came to see me. Becky is unhappy in her current position. She has every right to be. She's smart and ambitious and could do a lot more for the corporation if anybody would see it that way. "It's my résumé," she says, pushing an exquisitely processed sheet of paper across the desk at me. Becky watches me read. Her face is wrinkly around the edges of her mouth, and her eyes are huge and a little watery. "I'm sorry," she says. "I know my situation is, like, completely irrelevant in the vast scheme of things." She looks intently at me to see if I understand, which of course I do.

We're all feeling a little irrelevant, now that the scheme of things has suddenly gotten so vast. Across town, for instance, one of our people has come down with anthrax. Not the kind that kills you, but the stuff that gets onto your skin, which is far less serious. She's going to be all right, and we're all soldiering on, even those who work in the same office. Still, it's very creepy. I've been fighting the urge to scratch my cheek and monitoring a slight tickle in the back of my throat since I heard about it. Certainly nothing could be less important than Becky's résumé in light of these dire events. But when you think about it, in a world now obviously replete with crushing irrelevancies everywhere you look, is Becky's irrelevance more irrelevant than any other? Let's look at it.

Is Becky's future occupation more irrelevant, for instance, than next year's capital budget? Next year's capital budget feels very important now, or at least it did last month, but it isn't going to change the course of history in any way. The assumption is that it makes sense to build things, and that is certainly important, unless somebody is going to come along out of nowhere and knock it all down again, and of course the FBI has told us that could happen at any time. So spending an entire morning determining the level of investment in our infrastructure feels a little odd. We might as well do it, though. It is, after all, what we do.

Is Becky's desire to get a better job more irrelevant than the nonsense that takes place on Wall Street every day? One day it's up, based on the innate optimism of the jolly guys. The next day it takes a pounding, thanks to the gloomy, reflective ones who find solace betting against their own economy. What they do is important, of course, very rational and grave and essential, but when you watch CNBC it does sometimes look like a bunch of gerbils running around in a very messy cage, squeaking at each other. The whole exercise feels a little twentieth century, doesn't it? But I suppose they might as well do it. It is, after all, what they do.

Is Becky's résumé less important than what Jack Welch is doing? I saw him on television last week. He was in a bookstore talking with a bunch of fans. Jack, as any reader of this magazine knows, has a book out that recounts the events of his life as an American success story and provides insights about management, too. It was written at the turn of the millennium and is focused on the issues that seemed important then, many of which, of course, are eternal. Much of the planned promotional hoopla was derailed after September 11, but now Jack Welch is back. He's out there pumping and thumping, because . . . well, if you had a book, wouldn't you want it to be a success? I would. You have a book. You go out and sell it. It's what you do.

And how about football and tennis, and possibly even hockey? Or basketball, now that Air Jordan is back? He's back, right? Or baseball! Now that the World Series is on, isn't baseball somewhat less irrelevant than Becky's next step on the corporate ladder? Fifty-five thousand people who went to Yankee Stadium to see the Pinstripes whack Seattle seem to think so. I watched from home. In the back of my mind, I was still thinking quite a bit about whether the supply of smallpox vaccine would be ready in time to protect my sleeping moppet down the hall. But for a while there I lost myself. The big game was on. We watch. It's what we do.

Advertising? Is that irrelevant? Or the production of consumer goods? Packaged foods and eighteen kinds of Gatorade and blue jeans that cost $125 and sneakers that light up when you run and all the good things that the world seems to hate us for producing? Are those things less important than getting Becky behind a real leather blotter? I think not! They're every bit as unimportant and more so!

Well, perhaps the quality of the table to which we are assigned at lunch is still relevant. It feels that way. Two days ago I went to lunch, and they tried to give me half of the usual portion of chicken breast in my salad. Was that important, when you consider that the use of tactical nuclear weapons is now being openly discussed by some crazy people? How shallow am I? What happened to the sense of perspective we're supposed to all have now?

Ah, but I did care. I cared a lot. I gave them holy hell, and they brought me another piece of chicken that I didn't even want. My victory over the forces of small portions was complete. It was a stupid victory. But I fought for it and won. Because it's what I do.

My concerns are small and narrow. My occupation is ridiculous. My activities are, for the most part, mundane. That's my game. It has brought me this far, and I guess I'll stick with it.

The weather has been beautiful lately. The air is mellow for this time in October, to the point where the leaves have barely begun to turn. Some trees, of course, have erupted into a riot of red and gold and every conceivable shade of yellow. Behind the warmth of the sun there is a suspicion of the north country, a crispness that invigorates but does not chill. When the cold descends, I know it will come all at once, and the oaks and maples will simply go from high summer greenery to naked brown winter in a couple of days. Then there will be leaves upon leaves in the street, big crunchy piles of them that smell sweet and invite anyone with a child's heart to dive right in.

No, the leaves don't matter. They're destined for the compost heap almost immediately. In the meantime they look kind of beautiful, though.

Now, if you'll excuse me, I think I'll go get my car washed.

2001

The Broker: A Poem of Gothic Horror

Once upon a morning hairy, as I looked upon the scary
Ebitda projections for the business firms that I adore,
While I sat there, dread increasing, suddenly I heard a sneezing
And a babbling, not unpleasing, right outside my chamber door.
"Some consultant, then," I muttered, "out to earn his bucks galore.
Only this and nothing more."

Ah! I knew—and well I oughta—as we neared the second quarter
Profit growth in double digits lay beneath in smoky ruin.
And yet the Dow, in feats astounding, kept on mounting!
Mounting! Mounting!
Earnings? Cash flow? Hey, who's counting?
Something had to give, and soon.
"Come in, visitor," I hollered, "if to me you bring a boon!"
Quoth the broker: "How ya doin'?"

"Pal," he chirped, "you look befuddled, about your choices deeply muddled
As investment options mount, and you try to stay out of hock.
Actually, it's very easy. Come on, now! Let's don't be queasy.
There is nothing crass or sleazy 'bout the answer we'll concoct,
'Bout the wise and prudent answer we will build on solid rock."
Quoth the broker: "Buy more stock."

"But which?" I cried. "You fatuous boomer! Shall I buy on whim? On rumor?
How to choose among the thousands wanting of my pie a slice?"
Then I with passion unencumbered, picked up *Fortune*'s great 500
And across my space I lumbered forward, pleading for advice.

"Tell me now!" I screamed in anguish. "You won't have to tell me twice!"
Quoth the broker: "Roll them dice."

"Look!" said I, "today and ever, rolling like a huge green river
Comes the cash flow of the top four, towering, immutable!
GM, Ford, Exxon, Wal-Mart—they stand alone! A breed apart!
So little fat, and so much heart. A good investment? Irrefutable!
But will they keep on soaring daily? As a plan, is't executable?"
Quoth the broker: "Sounds indubitable."

"And what," I cried, "of Welch and Gerstner?
Procuring these, you could do worstner
At Nos. 5 and 6. Chrysler's at 7! And Mobil? Why, it's 8.
Philip Morris, doing fine, is up a notch, from 10 to 9,
And all wrapped up in optic twine, ATT rounds out the top-ten slate.
But will they all continue growing? Can you that substantiate?"
Quoth the broker: "They all look great."

"Monster!" said I. "Callous booster! Monster still if sage or rooster!
By that Greenspan high above us, by that pundit we adore!
Tell me now how things are going. And incidentally, what's with Boeing?
A twenty-five-slot improvement showing double grosses through the door!
Not to mention Morgan Stanley, four times what it did before!"
Quoth the broker: "They merged. Buy more."

"Monster!" said I. "Shallow jerk! Monster still, if . . . How 'bout Merck?
Travelers Group and Bell Atlantic; Microsoft and Dell, good gracious!
Each one's '97 posting, vastly better, cause for boasting!
Should we have a purchase roasting? Sate our appetite voracious?
A red-hot nugget socked away, as a shogun hides his geishas?"
Quoth the broker: "How bodacious!"

And so the broker, smoking, twitching, still is pitching, still is pitching,
Feet on my credenza perching, nibbling on some wine and cheese.
And, God help me, my portfolio? Well, every day it keeps on growlio;
Where it will end, nobody knowlio. Can someone out there help me, please?
Will he ever leave me, free me, from his greedy, needy squeeze?
Quoth the broker: "Pay my fees!"

1998

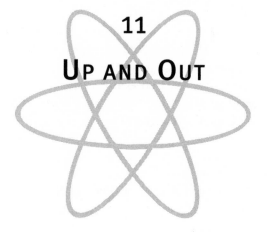

11
U P A N D O U T

F*rom the beginning, I've been trying to get out of the box. Keep in mind that I worked very hard to get into the box, and all the time I was trying to get out of the box I was doing my best to get ahead within the box. That didn't stop me from yearning for life outside the box: If this sounds confused, it is. But I don't think it's unusual.*

From the beginning, I knew it was all horse shit. The thing I didn't know is how many levels of horse shit there were in the world. Now I know. And I know that the quality of horse shit at the top is better than that which people at the bottom have to contend with. Even the middle is better.

The goal of any serious practitioner is to launch well, sustain a nice trajectory over a period of time, then boost into the ethosphere. Many people do it, each of them in a different way. At some point there comes a moment when one has to think of oneself, of one's own self-interest, which goes against the grain for a person who has worked in an organization for a number of years. But those who succeed are capable of doing it.

Where I'm at Right Now

And I saw them, rising over the hill like thunder, excessively young and strong, newly minted from the schools of the decadent East and the fruited Plains and the Great Northwest and even the beach-blanket nether regions of this great nation, and each did hanker to be in pinstripes, with collars that would torment their necks, and ties that bespoke nothing, and paisleyed braces that held up pants that were full unto bursting with salary plus bonus. And they were without form, and void, and darkness was on the face of the deep.

And while this vision was upon me, I figured that before these shiny disciples simply rolled lemminglike over my generation into the great gray world of their choice, they might like to hear the lowdown, for what it's worth. Read and consider, then, you of the target demographic who seek a business life.

You shall never know how weird you truly are. Oh, you shall feel plenty strange, stuffed into that monkey suit, concealing whole chunks of your original persona, but the full extent of your unadulterated self? Forget about it.

You shall have no job security, get used to that idea right away. If you work very hard and vault into a certain level of inured management somewhere, you may achieve a parachute, but management is not labor, Jack. You're too successful and smart to belong to a union. So you can be fired anytime.

You shall become cynical about people who work for a living, as opposed to those who manage people who work for a living, and come to believe in your right to pay them *bubkes,* sell their assets, and fire them.

You shall deal with jerks on a daily basis, and come to like jerks, and, if you are very lucky, become one of them. If you do not, you shall be forced to masquerade as a dynamic, precise, and driven young square until you are too old for that role, at which point you must masquerade as a thoughtful, responsible, and crusty old square.

You shall have no friends, only a really strange family made up of authoritarian parental units, annoying younger cousins, and a whole lot of stepsiblings. All your relationships shall be filtered through the issue of Rank. Think you have a true friend in senior management? Try getting under his skin at some point, the way you would with a real pal, you know? See what happens.

You shall never be satisfied with your money, your bonus, your perks, not even if they attain magnitudinous proportions. If they are too small, say, less than $250,000 a year at age forty-two, you shall feel you never really hit the big blintze and your life was a waste. If they're way up there, you're a slave to the industry who never gets to see a person he loves, other than himself. So if transcendent human bonds are likely to be important to you at some point in the future, think about farming. If they're not, you're in the right line of work, Fritz.

You shall have too many suits, all of them of the same color.

You shall shave 72 percent more often than a man should be forced to.

You shall use virtually none of your education, unless you have an M.B.A. There's a good chance that no matter how many Phi Beta Kappa keys you earned or stole, you'll report to a cultural illiterate who went to Wharton by way of the University of Bermuda Triangle.

You shall deal with a vast infestation of numbers, all of incalculable tedium, and you shall come to have contempt for them, and a snide disbelief in anything approaching certitude in this life, since you shall quickly learn that all situations, no matter how dire, can be manipulated to come out fine by the end of the quarter.

You shall laugh at jokes that are aggressively not funny, until one day you find them so, and are released from insincerity into stupidity.

You shall plumb the depths of existential being and nothingness, for most of the things you must write, meetings you must attend, and conversations you must have are meaningless, unless they are destructive.

For much of what you do, if you are successful in this, the latter part of the century, shall pertain to the buying and selling of assets and people, not the creation and sale of products and services. That's just the way it is, man. And you'd better like it.

And finally, brothers, my bet is that you shall always dream of what might have happened had you joined the circus—unless you become so magnificently huge that you have in effect become unrecognizable to your former self, the one that collected baseball cards, was too squeamish to hook a worm, and played the ocarina to pass Band because he had no talent in anything else.

Only one in a million reaches that deoxygenated zone. The rest of us, whatever deals we nail down, whatever bonzo vacation we can afford, whatever cars and women we drive, well, we're just in business, that's all.

Blessed is he that readeth, and he that hears the words of this screed, and keeps those things that are written herein. For the time is at hand. In fact, time is what it's really all about, guys.

Make it count.

1989

Doin' the Other Thing

Amazing news came from the education front the other day when it was announced that Benno Schmidt, formerly grand vizier of Yale University and possibly the coolest guy on the college scene, had resigned his august post to become chief executive officer of the Edison Project, Chris Whittle's $2.5 billion attempt to privatize public education much in the same way the Detroit Police Department was privatized in the motion picture *RoboCop*, hopefully to better end.

Why would Schmidt, I asked myself, relocate from New Haven to Knoxville, Tennessee, leaving a position with the highest respect per dollar in the industrial/education complex for a career move that could end in tears a hundred million dollars down the line? Of course, there was the enormous sum of money involved, but that couldn't be the only reason. . . . Then it hit me.

The guy was ready to do . . . the Other Thing.

My friend Morgenstern dreams of establishing his own crusading law firm while preparing briefs for the district attorney's office. My buddy Learner yearns to own a small stable of six or seven radio stations instead of munching on corporate spreadsheets all day long. Neary wants to write screenplays, six or seven of which he already has assembled in the bottom drawer of his desk. Borg wants to be a city selectman, a post that carries very little power and would earn him about eight grand a year. I have my dreams, too . . . dreams of freedom, fame, and incalculable wealth and the change of view that enormous money, meaningless in itself of course, can buy.

How about you? Are you ready to embrace It? Beyond Third World nuclear proliferation (which may relegate all other issues to minimal status), it's the big question as we home in on the coming century, in which we will die. What's it going to be? A trip to Tahiti like Gauguin? A run for the presidency like Perot? Life on the prairie with a cowboy hat and lasso like Yeltsin? Take the leap, I'll be in right along after you. Honest.

If we're going to be successful at this spiritual sea change, however, we can't just go thundering off into the underbrush, trumpeting and kicking up dust. Where should we begin?

Maybe we could join the circus. I did that once for two weeks back in 1977. A circus came to town, and at that time I sang for a living, at least part of the time. The Other Thing I did was drive a cab. I don't recommend that as a good Other Thing, though, or even a primary one. My first day on the highway, for example, my cab's hood kept flying up and obscuring my vision at sixty miles per hour. We had to pull over, and my fare missed a Patriot's game. He was mad, and I didn't get a tip. I barely got back to town in time to put on my tux and tails for the opening circus parade, which included one elephant, two tigers, eight clowns, some llamas, and a fire-eater who doubled as the tightrope walker. I was the ringmaster and sang "Be a Clown." It was in a place called the Boston Arena, an antediluvian, cavernous place that reeked with the unweary ghosts of failed show-business acts and sporting teams. At one show, we had eighty audience members. One of them had a cough, I remember. Most of the people I worked with were on leave from the big circus, which was on a break. This was their primary thing is what I'm saying, and they loved it. But I don't think it's my Other Thing, either.

Perhaps the specific job itself is not a great place to start. Let's go for location. Location location location, right? Right!

I'm living in the country, that goes without saying, because this city/suburb closed trapezoid has gotten old. It's time for air and sunshine and the noise of natural things emitting bleats and whinnies into the great beyond. I was in the country a lot when I was younger, and it was great. Gas stations. I remember gas stations. And many, many birds. People dress more informally than they do where I am required to labor. No one wears a tie. They wear rustic clothing and bear a tremendous sense of . . .

Fatigue. *Hmm*. I remember now. The look of people who don't get to eat lunch for the best part of the early afternoon and call it business, people who worry about things like whether it will rain or when the local factory will be shut down by people like me.

Our life will be different, though, and that's the point. I will rise in the morning and take a healthful shower while the last stars are winking out. I'll shamble downstairs to sit at the kitchen table for a few moments, wondering what my friends are doing back in the city. There are some chores to do around the house, so I do them. Right now, I'm just pointing out, I would rather have a fifteen-minute fight with my wife than do a thirty-second chore, but by then I'll be different because I'll have started doing the Other Thing. I'll have made a choice that completely alters the warp and woof of my persona . . . for the better! After my chores, I'll kind of walk around before I get to work. It will be very quiet, like, the only sound will be the electric clock and stuff. . . .

Brr.

But look at it this way: I'll be out of here and I'll be working too, of course . . . because I have to. I'm not looking for easy money like my friend Boschwitz, who went to L.A. to write for TV and is now apparently paid for not working much in the same way beet farmers were paid to keep their fields fallow in the 1950s. Come to think of it, why not? I can dream up any number of unproducible projects, and I love L.A.! I was there last May at the Four Seasons Hotel, where life was unbelievable! Phones by the pool! Great food! An incredibly amazing bar with marginally superb people marching through all day long! Did you know that there's a sign outside that hotel that tells you there are substances in the building that may cause birth defects? It's a courtesy extended to guests, that knowledge. When it was pretty clear the fires were coming closer, and the smoke made your eyes feel kind of weird, the telephones went out, and my friend Scheingold was called by the establishment to assure him that a cellular phone had been reserved for him! Isn't that something?

But . . . what would I be doing there, actually? There's lots of money in L.A. for anyone who can snare an assignment. But I don't want a "job." The Other Thing is not a "job." It's a "life."

Deals! How about deals? I could be doing deals in L.A.! That sounds good! Except nobody's doing any deals now who doesn't have $150 million in equity to play with, and I don't. I guess I could get a post that involved big and potent lunching behavior, that's not impossible, but I hear nobody who's a hitter is allowed to drink at lunch. *Pfui.* Here in this fine town, people are surreptitiously sneaking up the level of permissible cheer at noontime, and I've got the sensation that a roaring late '90s may still be possible before the financial devastation of the upcoming century slams in. Not in L.A. There's simply too much money around for people to tolerate any genuine loss of personal control. I don't like that. Also, I don't like bungalows. Forget it.

Besides, the issue shouldn't be where you do your Other Thing, but what Other Thing it is you do. You've got to feel absolutely right about it or it doesn't qualify. In that regard, I've got a very narrow portfolio.

I could get another job doing exactly the same thing I'm doing now in another corporation, perhaps in another city, one where people ride bicycles to work and go to company barbecues on the weekend, uprooting my entire family in order to earn less money in a venue totally off the beaten track. . . . Nah.

But wait. Maybe the slow track is where I belong. Why not chuck it all and get a job as a low-level word processor at a giant law firm for $85 an hour, write poetry and tend my garden, relax my ambition muscle until it loses all tone and substance and my vision of the future gets smaller, more clear, more translucent, and perfect in miniature? What a revolting development!

I could be a successful graphic artist. Except I can't draw.

I could open a restaurant, selling nothing but pancakes and noodles and frozen, no-fat, iced food product! Except it would fail.

I could open a quaint little bed-and-breakfast someplace in the boonies! Except for the fact that if I wanted to see strangers in the morning, I'd stay in business and let someone else pay me for the indignity.

I could run a small farm someplace like my friend Prager. He has a tractor and everything, but I think for some reason I would end up dead, frozen in a well or something, if I tried to do anything so utterly alien to my experience.

Let's get serious. I could be a battling consultant plying his or her trade in the open marketplace. Why not? It's basically what people like me do when they're fired, tired, or too wired to continue on the expected track. I ran into a former colleague, Kazan, the other day in the bistro of the moment, where somebody must have been buying her an individual pan pizza for $19.95. "Hi!" she said. "Are you guys outsourcing any PR work these days?" This before I even told her how I was doing, for goodness' sake. And then there's Milo, my friend.

Milo's gone now. It happened last week. We joined the corporation almost together, more time ago than I care to remember. He was busy rising from the plankton level on one part of our food chain while I was fattening up on another. He made V.P. first, but I didn't resent him for it. At one point, we even collaborated on our own time on that most fruitless of Other Things, a screenplay. Everyone who read it agreed it showed great promise, so we eventually dropped it. We were very close then. Sometime about 1989, Milo received by mail a bottle of Moët champagne in a mirrored bucket, the kind of Christmas present we used to get from importunate vendors on a pretty much monthly basis. "We'll open it when we have something to celebrate," I suggested. He agreed.

About three months ago, I heard a rumor that Milo was leaving to form his own company. I couldn't believe it. I dropped by his office to ask about it, and he seemed a little distant, cagey. I felt quite clearly that his spirit was elsewhere, in an imaginary office that was even then being set up in the central chambers of his soul. He had cut the delicate tendril that links all of us in this place whether we want it to or not, and was even then, as we spoke, drifting out to sea.

Last Thursday, we drank the champagne, and I wished him well. We'll see each other soon, I know. He'll only be in New Jersey. And yet . . . I felt so damned sad.

"You see that window?" he asked as we shared our last communal beverage together. He pointed at the eight-by-fourteen plate-glass pane that separated us from the ether, five hundred feet above the psychotic who was singing on the pavement below, a Bible in his hand. "I feel like I'm about to leap through that glass into the open world. And I can't wait."

For a nanomoment, the drink caught in my gullet. The image of my friend hurling himself through the window into the ether kind of caught me up short, I guess. On the one hand, it was kind of an appealing image. He was, after all, outside, flying with the eagles up there where the fumes and buzz of the city could not reach him. On the other hand, he was five hundred feet above the street, and the last time I looked, consultants did not have wings.

And I thought: *I'll see you, dude.* I wish I could say I'm coming with you soon, but I don't think that would be either truthful or accurate. One day, perhaps, I will find that Other Thing that's exactly right for me. Until then, I think I want your job, your title, and your salary.

More of the same thing may not be the best thing. But it's something.

1992

I Want to Be Paid to Go Away

I'm an ambitious fellow, like the rest of you. Each year, I set my sights higher. I expect to do better than my rivals and, more important, my friends, and when I don't, I'm disappointed with myself. I'm competitive, that's it. My internal clock is ticking.

This fighting spirit has paid off, I think, in improved personal operating performance on a pretty consistent basis. I still haven't got where I want to, though. No matter how high I climb or how much better I'm doing than my pals, there is still a distant beacon, a long way off, glimmering in the dusk that settles around the horizon. A tiny, beckoning, piping little voice speaks to me, just within the realm of my sixth sense, the heart of true desire.

Sometimes it says, "Your buddy Ted in Los Angeles just made a million dollars writing treatments for movies that were eventually handed off to other people who made less on their 120-page scripts than he did on his five-page memo!" Other times, it has faintly murmured, "Morty McDermott, who used to run Advertising Sales, is now a thriving industry consultant who works out of his house with his wife, cocker spaniel, and bottle of Glenfiddich."

Last week, while riding on the train and reading the paper, I clearly heard my little voice mutter in a disconsolate, husky tone, "Frank Biondi. You know what I'm talking about." I did indeed. Mr. Biondi, like some of my friends over the years, has achieved the pinnacle of achievement in American corporate life. After a luminous career building his company into a tower of power, his career at Viacom is over. He has been paid to go away.

Paid to go away! The mind swims and boggles. Think of it! You're a farmer sitting on the porch not growing tobacco. The sun is shining down. The check is in the mail. The future is nothing but upside, because it belongs to nobody but you. When the phone rings, you don't have to answer. You don't have to return your calls. When you do lunch, it sometimes involves peanut butter. No faxes you don't expressly requisition. No aggravation, as long as you don't read the paper. You are not in. You are not out. You are gone away. And you have been paid to get there.

Clearly, this is a lofty target. And realistic business professionals don't expect to arrive at this kind of place overnight. It takes a lifetime of work in the field of your choice, and most times, an enormous achievement that sets you on the launch pad. Even after a solid career filled with excellence, many of us don't make it. Still, the key is to keep the goal—and the requisite steps that just might take you there—ever before you.

It starts, I think, in your late twentysomethings, with a job that defines not only the present You, but the You you might be on your way to becoming. Being a receptionist or a guy who sells typewriter ribbons over the phone doesn't count, I'm sorry to say. I've done both, and I know, especially since nobody uses typewriters anymore. How was I supposed to sell ribbons? Anyway, it took me only one day to realize that $16 in revenue wasn't going to produce a great upside for me. After that, I did telephone direct sales for a manpower firm. I was instructed to say, "Hello! Do you have any temporary needs today?" I'll give you a few moments to come up with all the possible replies to that.

After a year or so of fruitless honking around, I landed a job in the corporation for which I now labor. That was fifteen years ago. I was light-years away from being paid to go away. I didn't even recognize the concept then. Ah, youth!

The next important step to be taken is a title with business cards attached to it. My first was Associate. What's that? It's something. But as you move forward, I figured, you want to add words to the thing as often as you can. When they delayed my promotion to Manager for a while, I asked to be Senior Associate. Okay, nobody knew what it was, but nobody knew what a Senior Executive Vice President was, either, and he was my boss. Titles and little brown-and-gold desk signs that have your name on them seem like horse hockey, I know, but they work at establishing a sense of place and identity, too. So I got some of those.

The point is to get into a position where a very little bit of work—one decision, one brief memo, one barked order passed in the hallway on the way to a meeting—can generate terrific value or at least the perception of it. When I realized I was finally making more decisions than paper, I knew I was getting closer to the point where someone would be willing to pay me to go away.

Those were happy times. To start with, I got my first door. Cubicles, as you certainly know, blow. Nobody who doesn't have a door he can take a nap behind will ever be paid to go away. So I got one, with an office around it. But my goal—a life of doing nothing for a great deal of something—seemed as distant as ever.

True, I was moving, albeit imperceptibly, forward. I had entered the enormous valley of enterprise where one is expected to produce big work for small money.

All people who are eventually paid to go away have been there. The drill is to work very hard for a long time and build the feeling that one is absolutely essential.

If you're not crucial in some way, you won't eventually be paid to go away; you'll simply be told to go away, and there's a big difference. No, to be paid to go away one must convey the message that, in some sense either definable or not, this couldn't have been done without you.

That's where I am today, trying to create that magic aura, and, I have to tell you, it's daunting. How many of us are truly crucial and essential to the point where people would feel awful if we left? I'm not there yet, I admit that. No matter how well I do my job, if I were forced to leave at this point, I'm not convinced there would be a bloodcurdling outcry, accompanied by a powerful feeling of collective organizational guilt toward me. But I'm striving. I'm sure you are, too.

The thing we need to establish here, those of us who are yearning to be paid to go away, is the message that we're individuals who never can, in some very basic sense, be adequately repaid for the waste of what, in other people, would be called a life. What amount of money, people should be forced to ask, could possibly reimburse us as human beings for the loss of the laughter of our little children, the pleasure of a warm bottle of Medoc taken at the riverbank on a lovely spring weekday next to one we love, the easy, mindless drone of the television on a long, lazy Sunday utterly uninterrupted by even one stupid phone call from a fellow vice president? Is there any amount of cash that could recompense us for all the blown dinners, school plays, model airplanes never built, lullabies never sung, drinks with friends never taken, anniversary dinners shot to hell?

What is the value of one business life?

A million dollars? Two million? Fifty?

Okay, only the greats collect that kind of change, but you get the idea of what I'm working for. And I think it's an admirable goal. To get there, I figure I have to work ten hours a day, eighteen days a week, 600 days a year. I have to live, eat, and breathe business. Only then will I be eligible to be paid to go away. Is it worth it? I don't know. But that's what I'm doing. Sometimes you have to put your head down and charge at the wall, if that's what it takes to get the job done.

The thing I'm not looking forward to is the last step. Right before they'll pay you to go away, you must grow ripe, and then rot. This isn't an easy step to take for the average superachiever, but you can't expect to collect that annuity on the beach without it.

Fortunately, the organization can often do most of the work for you, especially these days. Many people who have been paid to go away simply remain the same during a period of profound change and redirection.

As the company explodes around them, they stay calm. "What's he so calm about?" folks will ask. "He doesn't get it," others will respond. Or perhaps your entrepreneurial culture is settling down after its first decade of growth and becoming a nice, burbly bureaucracy. That's not your fault. You just go on doing your job same as always, inventing new products and stripping away the structures that mature organizations form to keep the business going at a higher plane of operations, but now you're out of touch with the new thing. People who are out of touch with the new thing must often go away.

The smart ones get paid to do so. And then what? The day comes. I see it now. I am paid to go away. I have what I have strived for all these years. And . . . it's weird. On the one hand, it hurts. On the other, there's a bright and shining patch of sand somewhere out there with my name on it. I've worked for this moment. I've put a career into making it happen. Why succumb to fear of success at this late date? I'm away! I've been paid to get there! Ain't life grand?

Now . . . where did I put the business card that headhunter gave me? . . .

1995

Yes, You Can Survive Career Death

Tales of life after death are common in the tabloids. Most responsible people pooh-pooh them. But new evidence has appeared that fortifies these incredible reports. Today, as inconceivable as it may seem, a growing number of business Americans walk among us who have had extensive tours of the world beyond success—and come back to tell their tales.

The moment of career death is very painful. Victims describe seeing a white light approaching them from very far off. Quite often they do not recognize this illumination as anything to fear. Once they view it up close, however, the horror sets in and they try to flee, but it is too late. Moments later they are sucked into a vortex that spins them down into a realm of surprising depth and scope, a world much like ours, except the restaurants aren't nearly as good.

"I'm very busy. Nose to the grindstone. Trying to get things done," said my friend Commander Zarcon, whose post-life experience was very fresh, given the fact that his career life ended just the other day. What was perhaps unusual about this case of career death was that I was actually privileged to watch it happen. It was grim. He was just walking along, minding his own business, when he was mashed into a small ball the consistency of anchovy paste between a 2,400-pound senior executive vice president and the four-ton chairman of a division, both of whom wanted to occupy the patch of ground he was standing on.

The experience is still so fresh that the Commander doesn't even know he's dead yet. This may actually not be a totally bad thing, since it obviously hasn't had a negative impact on his attitude, although he does seem a little disoriented. "Right now I'm working on developing fourth-quarter projections for the new interstitial fabrics group," he told me as he walked by, an enormous manila file under one arm, and I could see that although he was still in an expired state, he was already strolling around among the living and headed for his next career life.

Survivors claim that's the key, a quality that may simply be described as the desire to get back and, if possible, get even. Those who focus on these simple goals early in their career death are able to achieve excellent results. Others, who take longer to wake up and smell themselves burning, may have to languish in the nether region for quite some time. The amazing news that should bring hope to all business humanity is that it can indeed be done in virtually all cases! The only ones who don't seem capable of resurrection are people who have lost their companies a lot of money promising profitable services over the Internet.

Examples of hope abound. Ralph was the president of an important division of his company, having worked his way up through the ranks. He was highly thought of and recognized as a superb senior officer and people person. When the time came to select the new operating head of the company, everyone agreed he was a shoo-in. Except he wasn't. One Monday morning the company chairman, a small troll who lived under a bridge just outside of town, appointed an affable schmoozer to the position. "I was sort of crushed for a while," said Ralph, recalling his stint in purgatory with a compressed smile. "Then I went out and did what I had to do." What Ralph did was go outside the company and acquire the position to which he was entitled. A few years later he went back to his original firm with entirely new chops and the suits to match. Today he makes more money than God and has tons of fun doing it.

What fueled Ralph, and others who have died and come back to tell about it, was the dead's most important asset: rage against the machine. Martin, now a multinational Pooh-Bah of gargantuan proportions, was also passed over by his behemoth several years ago. Nobody needs to worry about him now. Wherever you are sitting, look out of your window. He owns it. What did he do to get back? He carefully sorted his options, waited for the right moment, told the dark side to stuff it, and went into consulting. When in 1992 the business world developed a healthy new regard for outsourced solutions and the people who create them, he was perfectly positioned to come back to real, functional life.

Beyond anger lies patience. My pal Dick was grossly underappreciated for years before a new regime swept him, quite deservedly, into power. He didn't do anything. He just stayed dead long enough so that the ground around his roots got turned. With new nutrients available, his natural hearty resilience allowed him to flower.

Yes, again and again the former dead pop up with tales of resistance, perseverance, and ultimate regeneration, marked only, perhaps, by a certain steely coldness around the corners of their eyes and a tendency to overuse their plastic. Not a few of the revitalized have been killed more than once—stomped, crunched, sliced, pureed, and left for career dead over and over—only to rise like one of those zombies in the movies to feast again on the blood of the living.

This reporter, in fact, can admit to being a member of the last category. Just last year, I suffered perhaps the most dramatic career death of my life when I drove myself into a large tree that had been set up by senior management in the middle of the road I was traveling on. It was pretty horrible. There was blood everywhere, and my fellows were strewn across the pavement. There was Ned, my companion on so many road trips, with his ankles broken, dragging himself along and asking anyone who passed by, "So . . . what's goin' on?" There was Murphy, sitting flat on his butt with his heart crushed, murmuring over and over again, "We're gonna come out of this thing fine!" And then there was me.

Many have asked what it was like to be beyond the vale of the living. It's hard to describe. First, there is the sense of dislocation. You drift, as in a dream, weeping for yourself. People don't talk much. Those who do speak natter on obsessively about matters of very little importance. Many are dressed in last decade's power clothing. Yellow ties and red-patterned suspenders prevail.

And yet today my friends and I are all, with some exceptions, basically all right. Best of all, I'm doing great. I don't fool myself, though. I know that just around the corner, inevitably, lies the next career death. Still, I'm not scared. No matter what happens, I know . . .

I'll be back.

1996

The Most Dangerous Game

I was browsing in the underbrush that morning when the phone rang. Not much was going on. The shrubs were tasty due to the thawing snow that had watered them recently. That always makes them plump and juicy. Maybe I wasn't paying attention, because suddenly a branch snapped behind me and there was this woman standing there kind of looking me over. She was wearing a pith helmet, which didn't go very well with her gray pinstripe suit.

"Hello," she said. She had one of those palm gizmos that you work with a little pen. I don't like those things.

"Hello," I said, swallowing a mouthful of twigs and branches, which suddenly seemed dry and tasteless. "I'm kind of busy reviewing substantial matters right now, so I'm wondering what it is you want."

"Oh, nothing much," she said, but I could see she was sizing me up something fierce. I saw her giving my haunches and shoulders a good once-over. Maybe I'm not what I used to be, but it's still pretty obvious when you look at me that I've got a couple of good years of hauling, plowing, and middle-managing left in me.

But she was talking. "I'm Nancy," she said. She gave me a last name, too. It sounded something like Glockenspiel, but I'm sure that wasn't it. For the first time, I could see she was armed with something strapped over her shoulder. I hoped she wasn't planning to hurt me. I'm effective at protecting myself against plant eaters, but carnivores still scare me.

"I'm working very closely with a company that I can't name right now," she said, coming right up to me and whispering in my ear, which felt sort of good, I won't lie to you. "This firm is looking for a person to take the top job in your area. It pays mid-six figures, options, reports to the chairman. Do you know anybody who might be interested in hearing more about a job like that?"

Every sense I possess went on full alert. My ears rose from the back of my scalp and tipped outward like saucers. My eyes flew full open and bulged from their sockets. My hair stood on end all over my body. I didn't know whether to fight or flee. I was being hunted!

They weren't going to take me alive, not if I could help it!

"Well," I heard myself say. "I might be willing to discuss something like that for a couple of minutes." What was I talking about? I had to get out of there before they bagged me! I turned . . . but by then it was too late. Instead of running, I had leaned in to feel that tiny whisper in my ear again, and in so doing had lost my physical advantage. "Aieee!" I thought.

"Don't move," she said. The thing on her shoulder swung around and I saw, too late, that it was a dart gun of some kind. "This won't hurt a bit." Then all I saw was black.

I awoke at a table in the Four Seasons Hotel, my mouth full of granola. It took me a moment to realize that I was bound to my chair by a small chain attached to my right fetlock. It was comfy, though. Nancy was across the table, giving me a look that made me very nervous. It appeared to be . . . hunger.

Making our table a threesome was a pudgy fellow in safari gear, a gigantic machete propped up at his setting. He was looking at me with an expression of admiration, and drooling ever so slightly. I realized he was telling me his life story, which was full of events that were both amusing and intensely tedious. Nancy chimed in with a long tale about her son's hockey team, but the conversation was a ruse. I could tell they were both mentally picturing me en croute.

"Now tell us a little about you," Nancy said after a time. It wasn't a question. I had to perform. So I did. First, I made the low, growling noises that often help me start off meetings. I moved over into guttural barking and mooing and closed with a fair amount of high-pitched yelping. This seemed to please them both. I could see lust for meat alight in their eyes.

"Let's get down to it," said the plump and jocular headhunter. Without losing eye contact, he picked up the machete. "The position is one of the largest in American industry, with a package of salary, bonus, options, hats, feathers, flying buttresses, hair plugs, plastic nose guards, and other perks that brings its value up into the low seven figures."

My jaw dropped, and before I had a chance to pick it up and run away, he and Nancy had leaped upon me, hoisted me to my knees, and dragged me over to a big scarred chopping block by the coat check.

"But . . . but . . . where is it? What is it? Tell me! I have the right to know!" I screamed. The specter of my life as I loved it—lost forever—dangled in the air before me.

"Well," said the headhunter, pausing for a moment over the block. "I suppose it doesn't hurt to bend our confidentiality requirements just this once." He looked down on me, panting in anticipation. I could smell the flesh of countless prior happy victims on his breath. "It's the Barfinger Corp. in Coeur d'Alene, Idaho!" he said triumphantly, and swung down on the space between my second and third cervical vertebrae.

"Nooooo!" I yelled. "I don't want to live far away from the Coast!" And with one massive lunge I rose up on two legs like a man and fled that place of career advancement and unlimited opportunity.

"After him!" I heard them both in full cry behind me, thundering down the marble steps of the hotel, down onto Fifty-seventh Street. I heard barking at my heels. Dogs! Would these people stop at nothing? My heart pounded. I knew if I could make it back to my office, I'd be safe.

"Please, God," I wheezed as I fled, "if you let me get out of this one, I'll never allow myself to get hunted again."

I hit my elevator bank with seconds to spare. As the doors closed I felt the force of the headhunters hitting them at top speed. "Which coast?" I heard Nancy say, and then the shouting grew fainter.

Now life has returned to some semblance of normalcy. Things around the office are pretty much as usual. I graze. I mosey. I run in large circles without getting nauseated. At times, I admit it, I do yearn for other fields, other forests, other streams to drink from.

So I guess I find it kind of funny. . . . Those stupid headhunters? After all they went through to get me? They won't even return my phone calls!

1999

Hail to Thee, Future Rich Person!

Parents, teachers, and graduates of the class of 1999 from Wharton, Harvard, Kellogg, and (your B-school here):

Good afternoon. It is my pleasure to address you on this fine and sweltering June day, as you stow for the last time your books and casual clothing and head off to a world where books are read only on beaches and casual clothing is as expensive and carefully considered as the finest formal wear.

I thought for just this once I would cast off my merry, ostensibly frivolous demeanor and offer some straight advice on how to get ahead and stay there. If what I tell you in this regard seems absurd, stupid, and brutal, good. The road to where you're going is littered with the bodies of those who believed that business was a rational occupation subject to normal human laws. Do not, young people, be one of those! Beyond that:

Eat a good breakfast. Follow that with an excellent lunch and dinner. It is often impossible to eat meat at every meal. But try to do so. Lacking that, try fish, particularly smoked fish, which is delicious.

Drinking should take place only after 6 P.M., this being a somewhat more sober decade than the eight that preceded it. If the rules change to permit drinking at lunch again, try to do so. The great booms took place in the eras in which people were basically bombed nonstop—the Roaring Twenties, the greedy eighties. Sobriety and big business do not mix.

Work out three or four times a week. You gotta be buff. If you can't be buff, achieve some level of sub-buffness but under no circumstances veer so far from buffity that you no longer look good in business attire.

Speaking of which, dear grads, dress better than you can afford, but not a whole lot better. The clothing we garb ourselves in is a costume. Observe your culture. Arrive each day dressed one discernible level above your status, not two or three. People will then perceive you as worthy of promotion to a status that is just conceivable for you. And men, keep your shirt tucked in!

Learn to fire people. It is, perhaps, the most difficult thing that you will have to do. The person comes in. They are always unsuspecting, no matter how many clues you have laid down. You cast the line. They are hooked. They thrash. They groan. They die. No matter how much they roll their eyes at you, you do not throw them back. For a while, you may consider yourself a terrible person. Then you realize: of course you are! You're a boss!

When you can, however, be kind. Be kind to yourself, when no one else will. Later, when others are kind to you because of your stature, be kind to your subordinates. In this way you may avoid becoming a jerk for, perhaps, decades, before turning into a loathsome approximation of your former self with nothing but the faintest echo of your true humanity left inside the crusted husk you present to the outside world.

Read a book now and then, stupid. Not big tomes of history, in which your fantasies about yourself and your greatness are played out on another person's stage. Not the third thriller from the same guy who brought you the 900-page techno-induced end of Saddam Hussein last time. And certainly not business books designed to scratch all the places you itch—except your brain. Read some fiction, why don't you? Dickens is good. He understood lawyers. Dostoyevsky had a real handle on the amoral psychopaths you'll be reporting to every day. Do yourself some good, for Christ's sake. You didn't get twenty years of schooling to watch your intelligence go swirling down the drain, loaded with nothing but the daily dreck from *The Wall Street Journal*.

If you have any desire to make the world a better place, nurture it within yourself, but do not speak of it. Others will try to dissuade you from it. But keep your flame alive, by all means. It would be a tragedy if you became powerful enough to do the right thing and then for the life of you couldn't remember what that was.

Don't be bad on the road. It won't be easy. Things you might never have considered become not only conceivable but seductive. This is true not only socially, where the mistakes can be terrible, but in business situations as well, where your status is unclear and your sense of daily accountability is gone. Be careful. And if you feel drawn to the dark side, get too drunk to do anything about it. Then go home, Sparky.

There isn't much time now. I can see those headhunters already knocking down your door, greedy to introduce you to hungry corporations that can get you for 20 percent of what they would pay a real executive. So I'll be brief.

Bend your plastic, but do not break it.

Employ as much high technology as you care to, but unless you are an engineer, do not become a geek. There are few geeks in senior management. Try to become a nerd instead. Nerds do better.

Love your company. Off that path lies nothing but boredom, a sense of superfluity, and ultimately a career in consulting. Love the people you work with, too. Love them with a fierce and sad love, because they'll be gone soon, or you will, and your memory of your friendship with them will fade as the remembrance of passion withers after romantic love has expired.

If you feel yourself losing your mind, do not worry. View it as a natural outcome of life in business and as an asset to be used. Night sweats. Inchoate rage. Fantasies of persecution and grandiosity. They're all to be expected as you enter the ranks of management. Used correctly, madness is your friend. The bigger the better, too.

Finally, young people, let me leave you with this: fear golf. Golf as a lifestyle is about as worthwhile as time spent with crack and a bong. I have seen the best minds of my generation, tanned and mumbling down the busy midtown streets, gibbering about lies and wedges and drives into a wind long gone, a wind that blows only for them. They are lost to us now, the golfers, in their fifties, at the height of their powers.

Instead, try work. Work hard. Work every day. And never, ever retire. Hold on to your life force until they come to your house in the middle of the night to wrest it from you. The business life is not the only one that has meaning. But it does have meaning. And it pays pretty well, too. Go out and do good and have fun for as long as you can, and when something bigger comes, always grab it. While at the same time staying the hell away from my job, by the way. If you get anywhere near me with that greedy, needy look in your eye, I'll rip out your ventricle.

Now get out of here! And good luck!

1999

Hello, I Must Be Quitting

So my friend Louis went and became an entrepreneur, but that's not what this story is about.

It begins two years ago. My friend Louis has been at his nice, tidy company for three years or so. The whole place suddenly clicks, revenue hits a geyser, and everybody starts having a good time. Pretty soon they're the number one growth company in the city.

Enter the consolidators—a venture capital firm with a lot of money and a vision of the future: to eat all companies in their industry and then extrude from that complex mess of nonsynergistic life-forms one great behemoth that eliminates the need for competitors. Huzzah!

"We were so good we got noticed," says Louis.

The goal of all consolidators is to bring disparate, puny things together to make a big organism that works better than the individual parts. Why? Because . . . well, just as it is in the nature of the physical universe to expand into the infinity of space, it is now the nature of the business universe to coalesce into ever greater agglutinations of operating entities.

The consolidators swung into action. They held what Louis calls "a series of wonderfully catered sales meetings." These were conducted by the new chief operating officer, who labored to whip the troops into a frenzy of ambition. Unfortunately, he also told the large audience that the ultimate strategy was to groom the company for divestiture. This had the effect of making middle managers nervous.

"They were working on an exit strategy before they finished the deal," says Louis.

God knows why the consolidator said such a thing. Perhaps consolidators, while they might have a lot of vision, aren't always so good on the management thing.

At any rate, the consolidators determined that it would now be fun to create an imperial headquarters that would function as the central brain stem of the new corporate body. Then they studied all the enterprises they had purchased, and planned, planned, planned. While they did, people operated as well as they could, except they were now a part of a big nation-state, and accountability and strategy were suddenly sort of squishy. Before long everybody was losing money, and suddenly the consolidation was not going very well at all.

"They created a central temple to control everything," says Louis. "The business went into the toilet quick."

The consolidators knew that this was not the fault of management. More control was clearly needed. So they tried to get Louis and senior management like him to move to corporate headquarters. Nobody wanted to.

"We needed to be close to our operations," says Louis.

So that's where Louis stayed, and after a while the consolidators at the imperial headquarters didn't talk to him all that much, except when the time came to cut his budget or force him to fire somebody, which they did with increasing frequency. When revenue stops growing, costs must be looked at.

And revenue had slowed, a lot. The consolidators needed money, because they had spent most of their money buying businesses and didn't have enough operating capital. Money was borrowed, and used, and then there was no money again. And then the lenders came in and fired a bunch of people, some of them consolidators, even, including all the big fellows who had built the imperial headquarters. They also got rid of a fair chunk of the workforce, and expenses went down nicely (along with revenues, since a lot of the people they fired were in sales and marketing).

So things were a mess now, and the company was kind of limping around dragging one foot behind it, drooling, and then there came some good news. Another big firm in their field wanted to buy them! And so they were consolidated. A lot of middle managers and line people were fired, and the CEO of the original company, who was Louis's boss, was moved upstairs.

"Sort of like Queen Elizabeth," says Louis.

But who was running the show now? Could it possibly be . . . nobody?

Then the day came when Louis decided to quit. And that is what this story, at long last, is about.

"I had nobody to quit to," says Louis. "We had this $300 million company, and no real lines of authority."

He had spent several months getting ready for this moment, establishing the groundwork of his future enterprise and tying up all loose ends in the old one. But he was stymied. To whom should he tender his resignation? "I didn't really report to anybody," he says.

Louis thought about the alternatives. He worked downtown, but there was nobody superior to him at that location. His paycheck came from Long Island, signed by somebody who had no sway over him. His sales manager was someplace in New Jersey, and Louis never had anything to do with him. The president and COO was in that splendid corporate center in midtown, and he almost never went there. And the CEO who had been stripped of power, who at least knew Louis, was someplace else entirely. He wondered if he should quit at all. Why not just quietly leave? "They wouldn't have known I was gone for, like, six months," says Louis. "They probably would have continued to pay me for that whole time."

But my friend Louis decided to do things the right way. "I came to the conclusion that I needed somebody to quit to," he says. So one Friday afternoon, five years after he had joined the company when it was much smaller and working fine, Louis dialed his cell phone and called the cell phone of a guy in New Jersey to whom he would have reported if there were any functioning lines of authority in the new, merged, reconstructed, and synergistically improved monolith.

"I quit," Louis said into the voice mail of this person to whom he did not report, but whom he had, at least, met in a professional context once. The next day he came into his office late. There was nobody there to see him. He cleaned out his desk, packed up his car, and drove off into the sunset. And now he's his own boss.

But that's another (and probably much better) story, isn't it?

2000

Phoning It In

Maybe it's the time of year. Or maybe it's the time of man, I don't know. But there's something going around, and it's worth evaluating.

I first noticed it in myself, since I'm around myself more than I'm with other people, which may be part of the problem. A certain . . . inability to take things seriously. Not that I'm taking them lightly. I'm just not taking them.

I called my friend Tom. "I think I'm phoning it in," I told him. It's an expression. He'd heard it before.

"Yeah!" he said, brightening the way you do when you hear that somebody else has something that afflicts you. "Are you having trouble focusing on things?"

"I don't know," I said, "but I appear to be having trouble focusing on things."

"Why do you think that is?" said Tom, but I had lost interest already since we weren't talking exclusively about me, although we were, sort of.

Later that day I called Mark out on the Coast. Mark is a killer. I mean, he doesn't actually kill people, but he would if he could. It's one of the corporation's most valuable assets. "What do you want to do about the Ehrlanger situation?" I didn't care about the Ehrlanger situation, but it was an issue on his watch, and I thought he might want to talk about it.

"I don't give a fig about the Ehrlanger situation," he said, although that was not the actual term that he utilized.

"You don't?" I said. "Well, if you don't, I don't, that's for sure." Then we talked about the stock price for a while, which is code for a whole bunch of stuff that has to do with freedom and release from servitude. Then we hung up.

I asked myself . . . so what? So what if this week it seemed that a bunch of guys were phoning it in from Planet Mambo? What's the big deal?

I sat there for a while and thought about Sandy Weill and Jack Grubman, suspected of manipulating the rating of AT&T, the first because he wanted to rule Citigroup alone and the second because he wanted to get his tot into some snotty nursery school. How much of what we do is like that? Stuff that looks like business but is really just a bunch of guys scratching an itch? Once you start to think that way, it's hard not to phone in the activities that feel inauthentic. And when you begin gauging the authenticity of the work you do, it's a short step to picking up that psychic receiver and phoning in the whole deal.

I put on my jacket and went outside for a walk. You know what I saw everywhere? Thousands of people quite literally phoning it in, walking down the street yakking into their little handheld receivers, nowhere near a place where people do any actual business.

The whole society, phoning it in from digital space. Who exactly, I inquired of myself, was not phoning it in? Anybody? I went back to my office and thought about that for a while, and as I was thinking, about six people came into my office with a bunch of stuff. I couldn't really tell you what it was, but it was very important and had to be adjudicated immediately. And all six had something in common. Can you guess what it was?

Then Landry called for maybe the fourth time that day. Landry is a good operator. She gives a big fig about everything, even stuff that isn't worth a fig. She gave me this long and involved story about a huge slight that was inflicted on her operation by some other entity someplace, and I was looking out the window and thinking, whoa, look at that BMW Z8.

"You know what, Landry?" I said at last, because I couldn't think what else to say. "Why don't you just handle it the way you want to? Your instincts are good. Go with 'em."

"Yeah?" said Landry. "Thanks! I will!" And she went away feeling good about herself, so I managed the situation all right, except that was by accident, because I was really just, you know, phoning it in.

So then I sat there thinking, what is it with Landry and the six other warriors who breached my ruminations and made me deal with stuff? Are they smarter? No. Faster? Maybe, but that's not it. How come they're the only ones who are not phoning it in? Then it came to me.

Let's put it this way. Jack Grubman remembers where he was when JFK was shot. So do Tom and Mark and I. These other guys rushing in with problems that need solving don't. Because they're too young. And we're not. We're young enough to smell the open road. But we're too old to care about stuff that doesn't seem worth caring about. At least not this week.

So the question is, Can we reclaim our lack of perspective and get back in harness? Or has the time come for us to hang up our phones and hit whatever portion of the highway remains to be seen? When I figure it out, I'll let you know. Until then, I'll have my people call your people.

2002

LATTE BREAK

Business Haiku

In honor of the Fortune 500

The Fortune 500

Mountains of crisp green
cash flowing in cool cascades
trickling down, right? Sure.

The Top Ten

Retail, cars and oil,
IBM and Sandy Weill.
So what else is new?

Wal-Mart Is #1

Hail to the Queen Bee
whose drones direct the rotund
to fairly-priced guns.

Microsoft Rules

Twelve percent sales growth,
wowsers. Thomas Penfield who?
Browse *this,* Your Honor!

Overheard at Viacom

Mel and Sumner and
Sumner and Mel and Sumner
and Mel and Sumner.

WorldCom Fell Off the List

Look! Up in the sky!
What a pretty parachute
for Mr. Ebbers!

AOL Time Warner

What is the sound of
one hundred billion dollars
gurgling down the tubes?

Tyson Moves from #177 to #72

Free trade or free range
there will always be chicken
to feather your nest.

Martha Stewart! What's Up with That?

Perfect bundt. Perfect
ham. Perfect inside trading
scam. And down goes Sam.

Upgrade from Smith Barney

See baby Grubman.
See one hand wash the other.
Look, Ma! New preschool!

Berkshire Hathaway Brings Home the Bacon

Warren is smarter
Warren knows the score, even
when there is no score.

Yum Brands Is #240

You gotta love 'em.
Up twenty-seven slots. Why?
'cause they so *YUMMY.*

And Congratulations to #501 Bed, Bath and Beyond. Coming Soon to the
*   List!*

How do they do it?
Today my wife will return
yet another towel.

LAST WORDS
(FOR THE TIME BEING)

I was walking around Staples the other Sunday when I ran into this guy who used to be a big wheel at my corporation. He looked good. He looked . . . rested. I realized I had seen him at Staples before, kind of cruising around. In fact, every time I've been at Staples recently, Potter has been there.

"How ya doon?" he says to me, elated to spot a friendly countenance. I wonder at this. There are very few people I would be this happy to see, and I would not be one of them.

"I'm okay, Fred," I tell him. Actually, I am not okay. For a number of reasons, I don't feel very good at this moment, but I need some toner for my laserprinter.

"What's up?" says Fred.

"Nothing," says I. This is not completely true. There's a lot up. I just don't want to go into it. Who needs to get involved in that kind of discussion, ever? Even on company time?

So Potter and I kind of grin at each other for a while.

"What's up with you, Potter?" I say at last. He seems to want to tell me.

"Lots of good things," says Potter. He does not extemporize, and for that I am grateful.

We part shortly thereafter. And therein yawns the chasm between the different worlds to which our jobs can take us.

I can't tell you how many people I've worked with and cared about. Hundreds, maybe. Each of us has had our own career fate. Some were meant to serve long and hard in the trenches of middle management, and still do. Some were destined to shoot to the top of the corporation and then be ejected into the air like steam. Others made the long march as Mao did across the great length of China, to be rewarded in the end with a lifetime of servitude to the regime. Others labored like Hercules and then were shafted most egregiously. Others became consultants. There are, in fact, as many fates as there are people at work. You have yours. I have mine. I think mine is going to turn out better than yours. But maybe not. Good luck.

The good news is this: There is no fate but what you make. And you can. The place in which you work is soft, spongy, and amenable to manipulation. In fact, you have many tools you can use in your daily effort to establish control over the organization and, not coincidentally, your view of yourself. But the best weapon of all is understanding of the organization itself.

So you keep looking, and trying to get it, and to get over on it. And I'll be there with you, as long as there's still a little fun left in it.

New York
April 26, 2003